Professional Examinatio

CW01624908

PART 2

Paper 2.6

Audit and Internal Review
(UK Stream)

ACCA Study Text

ACCA
Approved Publisher

ftc
FTC Foulks Lynch
A **Kaplan Professional** Company

British Library Cataloguing-in-Publication Data

A catalogue record for this book is available from the British Library.

Published by:

FTC Foulks Lynch
Swift House
Market Place
Wokingham
Berkshire
RG40 1AP

ISBN 1 84390 596 5

Printed and bound in Great Britain by William Clowes Ltd, Beccles, Suffolk

Acknowledgements

We are grateful to the Association of Chartered Certified Accountants and the Chartered Institute of Management Accountants for permission to reproduce past examination questions. The answers have been prepared by FTC Foulks Lynch.

Contents

Introduction

This is the FTC Foulks Lynch Study Text for Paper 2.6 *Audit and Internal Review*, and is part of the ACCA series produced for students taking the ACCA examinations.

This new edition has been produced with direct guidance from the examiner. It covers the syllabus and study guide in great detail, giving appropriate weighting to the various topics. Targeted very closely on the examination, this study text is written in a way that will help you assimilate the information easily. Numerous practice questions and exam–type questions at the end of each chapter reinforce your knowledge.

DEFINITION

- **Definitions.** The text defines key words and concepts, placing them in the margin, with a clear heading, as on the left. The purpose of including these definitions is to focus your attention on the point being covered.

KEY POINT

- **Key points.** In the margin you will see key points at regular intervals. The purpose of these is to summarise concisely the key material being covered.

ACTIVITY 1

- **Activities.** The text involves you in the learning process with a series of activities designed to catch your attention and make you concentrate and respond. The feedback to activities is at the end of each chapter.

SELF-TEST QUESTIONS

- **Self-test questions.** At the end of each chapter there is a series of self-test questions. The purpose of these is to help you revise some of the key elements of the chapter. All the answers to these questions can be found in the text.

EXAM-TYPE QUESTIONS

- **End of chapter questions**. At the end of each chapter we include examination-type questions. These will give you a very good idea of the sort of thing the examiner will ask and will test your understanding of what has been covered.

Syllabus and study guide

CONTENTS

- Objectives of the study guide
- Syllabus content
- Study guide
- Examinable documents

Objectives of the study guide

This study guide is designed to help plan your studies and to provide a more detailed interpretation of the syllabus for Paper 2.6 *Audit and Internal Review*. It contains both the syllabus and the study guide, which you can follow when preparing for the examination.

The syllabus outlines the content of the paper. The study guide takes the syllabus content and expands it into study sessions of similar length. These sessions indicate what the examiner expects of candidates for each part of the syllabus, and therefore gives you guidance in the skills you are expected to demonstrate in the examinations.

Syllabus content

1 AUDIT FRAMEWORK

a The development and changing nature of audit.

b Statutory audits, accountability, stewardship and agency.

c Professional ethics and codes of conduct, their application to external audit and internal audit, responsibility for fraud and error.

2 INTERNAL AUDIT AND INTERNAL REVIEW

a The role of internal audit and internal review and their relationship with:

- i corporate governance
- ii risk management
- iii organisational control
- iv corporate objectives.

b Scope and functions of internal audit, the nature and extent of internal audit assignments.

c Outsourced internal audit functions.

d The nature and extent of internal review assignments including operational, systems, value for money and financial reviews.

3 REGULATION

a Statements of Auditing Standards:

- i their development and role
- ii their relationship with International Standards on Auditing.

b Auditors:

- i regulation and supervision
- ii their relationship with Government
- iii the role of the Auditing Practices Board and other UK standard setting bodies.

4 PLANNING AND RISK

a Objectives of audit and review assignments, the relevance of stakeholder dialogue.

b Communicating the objectives of audit and review assignments.

c Analytical procedures.

d Risk assessment.

e Materiality, tolerable error, and sample sizes.

f Design and documentation of the plan and work program.

g Co-ordination of the work of others.

h Information technology in planning and risk assessment.

5 INTERNAL CONTROL

a Objectives of internal control systems.

b Inherent weaknesses in internal control systems.

c The use of internal control systems by auditors.

d Transaction cycles (revenue, purchases, payroll, stock, capital expenditure).

e The evaluation of internal control systems by auditors including internal control checklists and tests of control.

f Communication with management.

6 OTHER AUDIT AND INTERNAL REVIEW EVIDENCE

a Financial statement assertions: assets, liabilities, income and expenditure, including accounting estimates.

b Assertions reported on and opinions provided in review assignments.

c Analytical procedures as substantive evidence.

d Balance and transaction testing.

e Computer-assisted audit techniques, their uses and limitations.

f Management representations.

g Audit sampling and other selective testing procedures.

h Subsequent events reviews.

i Going concern reviews.

j The overall review of evidence obtained.

k Modifications to the plan and work program in the light of findings.

7 REPORTING

a Format and content of unqualified and qualified external audit reports on financial statements.

b Format and content of review reports and other reports on assignment objectives.

c Recommendations for the enhancement of business performance.

Excluded topics

The audit of groups is not examinable at this level. Candidates should be aware of the content, wording and meaning of external audit reports and they may be asked to prepare the explanatory paragraphs for inclusion in a qualified audit report. However, candidates are expected to draft full external audit reports.

Exposure Drafts (EDs) are not examinable for Paper 2.6.

Key areas of the syllabus

The key topic areas are as follows:

- professional ethics as they apply to accountants working in public practice and in business
- risk assessment and the response to assessed risks for external auditors
- the role of internal audit in risk management and corporate governance
- internal controls
- substantive audit evidence.

Additional information

This paper encompasses:

1 Internal review, which may be provided either by internal auditors or may be outsourced to external auditors.

2 External audit.

References to audit and auditors mean both internal and external audit and auditors, except where otherwise indicated.

Candidates need to be aware that questions involving knowledge of new examinable regulations will not be set until at least six months after the last day of the month in which the regulation was issued.

The study guide provides more detailed guidance on the syllabus. Examinable documents are listed in the Exam Notes section of *Student Accountant*.

Study guide

1 THE NATURE, PURPOSE AND SCOPE OF AUDIT AND REVIEW

Syllabus reference 1a, 1b, 2a, 4a

Explain the:

- nature and development of audit and review
- concepts of accountability, stewardship and agency
- concepts of materiality, true and fair presentation and reasonable assurance
- reporting as a means of communication to different stakeholders
- need for auditors to communicate with those charged with governance
- high level of assurance provided by audit assignments; the moderate level of assurance provided by review assignments; assignments in which no assurance is provided

NB: Students are expected to be aware of the nature and purpose of non-financial review services as described in Session 6. Internal review questions may deal with these subjects, as well as financial and systems reviews in the context of companies and small not-for-profit organisations.

2 STATUTORY AUDITS

Syllabus reference 1b, 3, 7a, 4a

Describe the:

- UK regulatory framework in which statutory audits take place
- development and status of the Auditing Practices Board Statements of Auditing Standards and their relationship with International Standards on Auditing
- reasons for, and mechanisms for, the regulation of auditors by Government and other regulatory agencies including other UK standard-setters
- types of opinion provided in statutory audit assignments
- explain the objectives and principal characteristics of statutory audit and discuss its value (e.g. in assisting management to reduce risk and improve performance)
- limitations of statutory audits

3 INTERNAL AUDIT AND INTERNAL REVIEW I

Syllabus reference 2a, 2c

Explain the:

- development and role of internal audit in achieving corporate objectives and as part of good corporate governance practice
- relative merits of out-sourcing internal audit and internal review services to external auditors and others, and the associated problems

- difference between the role of external audit and internal audit

4 REGULATORY ENVIRONMENT

Syllabus reference 2a, 2b

- corporate governance
  - explain the objective, relevance and importance of corporate governance
  - discuss the relative merits and disadvantages of voluntary codes and legislation
- Code of best practice
  - outline the provisions of the Code of Best Practice (based on the Cadbury Report) that are most relevant to auditors
  - outline the requirements of the Combined Code (of the Committee on Corporate Governance) relating to directors' responsibilities (e.g. for risk management and internal control) and the reporting responsibilities of auditors
- audit committees
  - explain the structure and roles of audit committees and discuss their benefits and drawbacks
  - discuss the relative merits and disadvantages of regulation by a voluntary code of practice rather than law
- internal financial control effectiveness
  - outline the importance of internal control and risk management
  - compare the responsibilities of management and auditors (internal and external) for the design and operation of systems and controls, and the reliability of management information (financial and non-financial)
  - describe the factors to be taken into account when assessing the need for an internal audit function

5 INTERNAL AUDIT AND REVIEW III

Syllabus reference 2b, 7b

Describe the:

- elements of best practice in the structure and operations of an internal audit function
- scope of internal audit work and the limitations of the internal audit function
- types of report provided in internal audit and internal review assignments

6 INTERNAL AUDIT AND REVIEW IV

Syllabus reference 2b, 4a

Describe and illustrate the:

- nature and purpose of internal review assignments including:
  - value for money
  - best value
  - IT
  - financial
- nature and purpose of operational internal review assignments including:
  - procurement
  - marketing
  - treasury
  - HR

7 PROFESSIONAL ETHICS AND PROFESSIONAL CODES OF CONDUCT I

Syllabus reference 1c

- describe the sources of, and enforcement mechanisms associated with, professional ethics and professional codes of conduct
- define the fundamental concepts of professional ethics
- define the detailed requirements of, and illustrate and analyse the application of, professional ethics in the context of independence, objectivity and integrity
- distinguish between the elements of professional ethics applicable to internal auditors and those applicable to external auditors
- describe the responsibilities of internal and external auditors for the prevention and detection of fraud and error and in relation to laws and regulations

8 PROFESSIONAL ETHICS AND PROFESSIONAL CODES OF CONDUCT II

Syllabus reference 1c, 4b

- describe the requirements of professional ethics and other requirements in relation to the acceptance of audit and review assignments, including situations in which there is an imposed limitation in audit scope
- define the detailed requirements of, and illustrate and analyse the application of, professional ethics in the context of confidentiality and conflicts of interest
- describe the importance of engagement letters and describe their contents

9 PRELIMINARY PLANNING PROCEDURES

Syllabus reference 4c, 4d, 4e, 4h

- distinguish between risk-based, procedural and other approaches to audit and review work
- describe the sources and nature of information gathered in planning audit and review assignments
- describe the knowledge of the business required by auditors
- describe the purpose of analytical procedures in planning and illustrate the application of such procedures
- describe the components of risk and the use of information technology in risk analysis
- illustrate and explain the importance of the application of risk analysis

- define and illustrate the concepts of materiality and tolerable error
- evaluate misstatements

10 THE WORK PLAN, THE WORK PROGRAM AND DOCUMENTATION

Syllabus reference 4f, 4h

- describe and illustrate the contents of work plans, work programs and working papers
- describe the nature of documentation required for different types of assignment
- explain the importance of documentation
- illustrate the use of information technology in the audit

11 THE WORK OF OTHERS

Syllabus reference 4g

Describe the:

- extent to which external auditors are able to rely on the work of:
  - internal audit
  - experts
  - service organisations and recognise where reliance is needed
- extent to which internal auditors are able to rely on the work of:
  - experts
  - service organisations
- conditions that must be met before reliance can be placed on the work of others and the planning considerations in co-ordinating the work of others
- division of responsibilities between auditors and others
- extent to which reference to the work of others can be made in audit and review reports

12 INTERNAL CONTROL I

Syllabus reference 5a, 5b, 5c, 6k

- describe the objectives of internal control systems and the responsibility for internal control systems in the context of organisational objectives
- describe the importance of internal control to auditors
- describe and illustrate the limitations of internal control systems in the context of fraud and error
- explain the need to modify the audit plan in the light of the results of tests of control
- distinguish between tests of controls and substantive tests

13 INTERNAL CONTROL II – SALES, PURCHASES AND STOCK

Syllabus reference 5d, 5e

- describe, illustrate and analyse how internal control systems over sales, purchases and stock cycles operate in both large and small entities
- describe and illustrate the use by auditors of internal control checklists for sales, purchases and stock cycles
- describe and tabulate tests of control of sales, purchases and stock for inclusion in a work program
- explain and illustrate how structural and operational weaknesses in sales, purchases and stock systems should be reported to management and how recommendations should be made

14 INTERNAL CONTROL III – REVENUE EXPENDITURE AND CAPITAL EXPENDITURE

Syllabus reference 5d, 5e

- describe, illustrate and analyse how internal control systems over revenue and capital expenditure transaction cycles operate in both large and small entities
- describe and illustrate the use by auditors of internal control checklists for revenue and capital expenditure transaction cycles
- describe and tabulate tests of control of revenue and capital expenditure for inclusion in a work program
- explain and illustrate how structural and operational weaknesses in revenue and capital expenditure systems should be reported to management and how recommendations should be made

15 INTERNAL CONTROL IV – PAYROLL

Syllabus reference 5d, 5e

- describe, illustrate and analyse how internal control systems over the payroll transaction cycle operate in both large and small entities
- describe and illustrate the use by auditors of internal control checklists for the payroll transaction cycle
- describe and tabulate tests of control of payroll for inclusion in a work program
- explain and illustrate how structural and operational weaknesses in payroll systems should be reported to management and how recommendations should be made

16 INTERNAL CONTROL V – BANK AND CASH

Syllabus reference 5d, 5e

- describe, illustrate and analyse how internal control systems over the bank and cash transaction cycle operate in both large and small entities
- describe and illustrate the use by auditors of internal control checklists for the bank and cash transaction cycle
- describe and tabulate tests of control of bank and cash for inclusion in a work program

- explain and illustrate how structural and operational weaknesses in bank and cash systems should be reported to management and how recommendations should be made

NB For items 13–16 an understanding of IT issues and computer controls is required.

17 OTHER AUDIT AND REVIEW EVIDENCE I

Syllabus reference 6a, 6c, 6d

- describe the sources and relative merits of different types of evidence available
- describe the financial statement assertions commonly reported on and the principles and objectives of balance and transaction testing
- distinguish between the interim and the final audit
- describe and illustrate how analytical procedures are used as substantive procedures
- explain the problems associated with the audit and review of accounting estimates
- describe the types of evidence available in smaller entities
- evaluate the quality of evidence collected

18 OTHER AUDIT AND REVIEW EVIDENCE II – DEBTORS AND PREPAYMENTS

Syllabus reference 6a

- describe and tabulate for inclusion in a work program the substantive procedures, including debtors circularisations, used in obtaining evidence in relation to debtors and prepayments, and the related income statement entries
- explain the purpose of substantive procedures in relation to financial statement assertions concerning debtors and prepayments

19 OTHER AUDIT AND REVIEW EVIDENCE III – STOCK

Syllabus reference 6a

- explain the importance of stock
- describe stock counting procedures
- explain cut-off
- describe and tabulate for inclusion in a work program the substantive procedures used in obtaining evidence in relation to stock, including the auditors' attendance at stocktaking
- explain the purpose of substantive procedures including direct confirmation of stock held by third parties, in relation to financial statement assertions concerning stock

20 OTHER AUDIT AND REVIEW EVIDENCE IV – CURRENT LIABILITIES AND ACCRUALS

Syllabus reference 6a

- describe and tabulate for inclusion in a work program the substantive procedures, including supplier statement reconciliations and creditor circularisations, used in obtaining evidence in relation to current liabilities and accruals, and the related income statement entries
- explain the purpose of substantive procedures, in relation to financial statement assertions concerning current liabilities and accruals

21 OTHER AUDIT AND REVIEW EVIDENCE V – BANK AND CASH

Syllabus reference 6a

- describe and tabulate for inclusion in a work program the substantive procedures including bank confirmation reports, used in obtaining evidence in relation to bank and cash, and the related income statement entries
- explain the purpose of substantive procedures in relation to financial statement assertions concerning bank and cash

22 OTHER AUDIT AND REVIEW EVIDENCE VI – FIXED ASSETS AND LONG-TERM LIABILITIES

Syllabus reference 6a

- describe and tabulate for inclusion in a work program the substantive procedures used in obtaining evidence in relation to fixed assets and long-term liabilities and the related income statement entries
- explain the purpose of substantive procedures in relation to financial statement assertions concerning fixed assets and long-term liabilities

23 OTHER AUDIT AND REVIEW EVIDENCE VII

Syllabus reference 6e, 6g

- explain the need for sampling
- distinguish between statistical and non-statistical sampling
- describe and illustrate the application of the basic principles of statistical sampling and other selective testing procedures
- describe and illustrate the use of computer assisted techniques in obtaining evidence

(Note: candidates will not be required to perform detailed sampling calculations.)

24 GOING CONCERN REVIEWS

Syllabus reference 6i

- explain the importance of going concern reviews
- describe the procedures to be applied in performing going concern reviews

- describe the disclosure requirements relating to going concern issues
- describe the reporting implications of the findings of going concern reviews

25 AUDIT FINALISATION AND THE FINAL REVIEW

Syllabus reference 6f, 6h, 6j

Describe and explain the:

- quality of management representations as audit evidence
- circumstances in which obtaining management representations is necessary and the matters on which representations are commonly obtained
- purpose of the subsequent events review
- procedures to be undertaken in performing a subsequent events review
- importance of the overall review of evidence obtained
- problems associated with the application of accounting treatments
- significance of unadjusted differences

26 REPORTING I

Syllabus reference 7a

- describe, illustrate and analyse the format and content of unqualified and qualified statutory audit reports
- identify and report systems weaknesses and their potential effects and make appropriate recommendations to management (e.g. accounting, procedures and financial controls)

27 REPORTING II

Syllabus reference 7b, 7c

Describe, illustrate and analyse the format and content of:

- internal review reports and other reports dealing with recommendations for the enhancement of business performance

28 NOT-FOR-PROFIT ORGANISATIONS

- apply audit and review techniques to small not-for-profit organisations
- explain how the audit and review of small not-for-profit organisations differs from the audit and review of for-profit organisations

Examinable documents

Prior to each sitting of the examination, the ACCA issues Exam Notes setting out which official documents are examinable.

The documents examinable for Paper 2.6 are set out below. We recommend that students read *Student Accountant* to keep up-to-date.

Introductory Statements

No	*Title*	*Issue date*
	Glossary of terms	Dec 2004
	Scope and authority of APB pronouncements	Dec 2004

Auditing Standards (ISAs (UK and Ireland) – issued by the APB)

No	*Title*	*Issue date*
200	Objective and general principles governing an audit of financial statements	Dec 2004
210	Terms of audit engagements	Dec 2004
230	Documentation	Dec 2004
240	The auditor's responsibility to consider fraud in an audit of financial statements	Dec 2004
250A	Consideration of laws and regulations in an audit of financial statements	Dec 2004
260	Communication of audit matters with those charged with governance	Dec 2004
300	Planning an audit of financial statements	Dec 2004
315	Obtaining an understanding of the entity and it environment and assessing the risks of material misstatement	Dec 2004
320	Audit materiality	Dec 2004
330	The auditor's procedures in response to assessed risks	Dec 2004

402	Audit considerations relating to entities using service organisations	Dec 2004
500	Audit evidence	Dec 2004
501	Audit evidence – additional considerations for specific items	Dec 2004
505	External confirmations	Dec 2004
510	Initial engagements – opening balances and continuing engagements – opening balances	Dec 2004
520	Analytical procedures	Dec 2004
530	Audit sampling and other means of testing	Dec 2004
540	Audit of accounting estimates	Dec 2004
560	Subsequent events	Dec 2004
570	Going concern	Dec 2004
580	Management representations	Dec 2004
610	Considering the work of internal audit	Dec 2004
620	Using the work of an expert	Dec 2004
700	The auditor's report on financial statements	Dec 2004
710	Comparatives	Dec 2004
720	Other information in documents containing audited financial statements	Dec 2004

Other documents

No	*Title*	*Issue date*
PN 13	The audit of small businesses	July 1997
PN 16	Bank reports for audit purposes	Aug 1998
Bulletin 2001/02	Revisions to the wording of auditors' reports on financial statements and the interim review report*	Jan 2001
Bulletin 2001/03	E-business: identifying financial statement risks	April 2001
Briefing Paper	Providing assurance on the effectiveness of internal control	July 2001
Briefing Paper	Effective communication between audit committees and external auditors	Sept 2002

* Students will not be examined on those sections of this document that deal with the review report, or Stock Exchange requirements.

Other guidance

ACCA's 'Rules of Professional conduct'.

Note: Documents under 'other guidance' are examinable only to the extent that they are relevant to topics specified in the syllabus and study guide.

The examination

CONTENTS

Format of the examination

	Number of marks
Section A: 3 compulsory scenario-based questions (no single question will exceed 25 marks)	60
Section B: Choice of 2 from 3 questions (20 marks each)	40
	100

Total time allowed: 3 hours

Examination tips

- Spend the first few minutes of the examination **through the questions.**
- Where you have a **choice of questions**, decide which ones you will do.
- **Divide the time** you spend on questions in proportion to the marks on offer. One suggestion is to allocate 1½ minutes to each mark available, so a 10-mark question should be completed in 15 minutes.
- Unless you know exactly how to answer the question, spend some time **planning** your answer. Stick to the question and **tailor your answer** to what you are asked.
- **Fully explain** all your points but be **concise**. Set out all workings **clearly and neatly**, and state briefly what you are doing. Don't write out the question.
- If you do not understand what a question is asking, **state your assumptions**. Even if you do not answer precisely in the way the examiner hoped, you should be given some credit, if your assumptions are reasonable.
- If you **get completely stuck** with a question, leave space in your answer book and **return to it later.**
- Towards the end of the examination spend the last **five minutes** reading through your answers and **making any additions or corrections**.
- Before you finish, you must fill in the required information on the front of your answer booklet.

Answering the questions

- **Essay questions**: Make a quick plan in your answer book and under each main point list all the relevant facts you can think of. Then write out your answer developing each point fully. Your essay should have a clear structure; it should contain a brief introduction, a main section and a conclusion. Be concise. It is better to write a little about a lot of different points than a great deal about one or two points.
- **Case studies**: To write a good case study, first identify the area in which there is a problem, outline the main principles/theories you are going to use to answer the question, and then apply the principles/theories to the case. Include relevant points only and then reach a conclusion and, if asked for, recommendations. If you can, compare the facts to real-life examples – this may gain you additional marks in the exam.

- **Computations**: It is essential to include all your workings in your answers. Many computational questions require the use of a standard format: company profit and loss account, balance sheet and cash flow statement for example. Be sure you know these formats thoroughly before the examination and use the layouts that you see in the answers given in this book and in model answers. If you are asked to comment or make recommendations on a computation, you must do so. There are important marks to be gained here. Even if your computation contains mistakes, you may still gain marks if your reasoning is correct.
- **Reports, memos and other documents**: Some questions ask you to present your answer in the form of a report or a memo or other document. Use the correct format – there could be easy marks to gain here.

Study skills and revision guidance

CONTENTS

This section aims to give guidance on how to study for your ACCA exams and to give ideas on how to improve your existing study techniques.

Preparing to study

Set your objectives

Before starting to study decide what you want to achieve – the type of pass you wish to obtain. This will decide the level of commitment and time you need to dedicate to your studies.

Devise a study plan

- Determine which times of the week you will study.
- Split these times into sessions of at least one hour for study of new material. Any shorter periods could be used for revision or practice.
- Put the times you plan to study onto a study plan for the weeks from now until the exam and set yourself targets for each period of study – in your sessions make sure you cover the course, course assignments and revision.
- If you are studying for more than one paper at a time, try to vary your subjects, this can help you to keep interested and see subjects as part of wider knowledge.
- When working through your course, compare your progress with your plan and, if necessary, re-plan your work (perhaps including extra sessions) or, if you are ahead, do some extra revision/practice questions.

Effective studying

Active reading

You are not expected to learn the text by rote, rather, you must understand what you are reading and be able to use it to pass the exam and develop good practice. A good technique to use is SQ3Rs – Survey, Question, Read, Recall, Review:

1. **Survey** the chapter – look at the headings and read the introduction, summary and objectives, so as to get an overview of what the chapter deals with.
2. **Question** – whilst undertaking the survey, ask yourself the questions that you hope the chapter will answer for you.
3. **Read** through the chapter thoroughly, answering the questions and making sure you can meet the objectives. Attempt the exercises and activities in the text, and work through all the examples.
4. **Recall** – at the end of each section and at the end of the chapter, try to recall the main ideas of the section/chapter without referring to the text. This is best done after a short break of a couple of minutes after the reading stage.
5. **Review** – check that your recall notes are correct.

You may also find it helpful to reread the chapter and try to see the topic(s) it deals with as a whole.

Note-taking

Taking notes is a useful way of learning, but do not simply copy out the text. The notes must:

- be in your own words
- be concise
- cover the key points
- be well-organised
- be modified as you study further chapters in this text or in related ones.

Trying to summarise a chapter without referring to the text can be a useful way of determining which areas you know and which you don't.

Three ways of taking notes:

- **summarise the key points** of a chapter.
- **make linear notes** – a list of headings, divided up with subheadings listing the key points. If you use linear notes, you can use different colours to highlight key points and keep topic areas together. Use plenty of space to make your notes easy to use.
- **try a diagrammatic form** – the most common of which is a mind-map. To make a mind-map, put the main heading in the centre of the paper and put a circle around it. Then draw short lines radiating from this to the main sub-headings, which again have circles around them. Then continue the process from the sub-headings to sub-sub-headings, advantages, disadvantages, etc.

Highlighting and underlining

You may find it useful to underline or highlight key points in your study text – but do be selective. You may also wish to make notes in the margins.

Revision

The best approach to revision is to revise the course as you work through it. Also try to leave four to six weeks before the exam for final revision. Make sure you cover the whole syllabus and pay special attention to those areas where your knowledge is weak. Here are some recommendations:

- **Read through the text and your notes again** and condense your notes into key phrases. It may help to put key revision points onto index cards to look at when you have a few minutes to spare.
- **Review any assignments** you have completed and look at where you lost marks – put more work into those areas where you were weak.
- **Practise exam standard questions** under timed conditions. If you are short of time, list the points that you would cover in your answer and then read the model answer, but do try and complete at least a few questions under exam conditions.
- Also **practise producing answer plans** and comparing them to the model answer.
- If you are stuck on a topic find somebody (a tutor or a colleague) to explain it to you.
- **Read good newspapers and professional journals**, especially ACCA's *Student Accountant* – this can give you an advantage in the exam.
- Ensure you **know the structure of the exam** – how many questions and of what type you will be expected to answer. During your revision attempt all the different styles of questions you may be asked.

Chapter 1

THE NATURE, PURPOSE AND SCOPE OF AUDIT AND REVIEW

CHAPTER CONTENTS

This chapter sets out why audits are performed, what audits are, and how auditing in the UK has developed. This, together with a number of the early chapters, sets the scene for the detailed work involved in an audit. It also introduces the reasons for performing other types of engagements.

Objectives

By the time you have finished this chapter you should be able to:

- describe what an audit is and how it has developed
- outline the differences between internal and external audit
- explain the concepts of accountability, stewardship and agency
- describe the nature of audit reporting and stakeholders
- describe the types of opinion provided in statutory audit assignments
- explain the high level of assurance provided by audit assignments compared to lower levels of assurance provided by other types of engagement
- understand the benefits and limitations of statutory audit.

1 The nature of audit and other assurance engagements

1.1 What is an audit?

DEFINITION

An **audit** is the independent examination of the evidence from which the financial statements of an enterprise are derived, in order to give the reader of those statements confidence as to the 'truth and fairness' of the state of affairs which they disclose.

An **audit** is the independent examination of the evidence from which the financial statements of an enterprise are derived, in order to give the reader of those statements confidence as to the 'truth and fairness' of the state of affairs which they disclose. The Auditing Practices Board (APB) describes the objective of an audit as being '... to enable auditors to express an opinion whether the financial statements give a true and fair view ... and have been properly prepared in accordance with the applicable reporting framework'.

This description encompasses the audit of *any* enterprise, not just that of a limited company. Unless specified in this text, the term **audit** is used where it refers to an independent examination of the financial statements of an enterprise, conducted with a view to expressing an opinion as to whether those statements give a true and fair view.

KEY POINT

The Companies Act 1985 requires auditors to state whether in their opinion the balance sheet and profit and loss account show a **true and fair view.**

The term **true and fair** is a standard one used by auditors and is derived from legislation. Section 236, Companies Act 1985 requires auditors to state whether in their opinion the balance sheet and profit and loss account show a true and fair view without at any point defining what is meant by true and fair view.

As will be seen later, the accountancy profession has derived its own interpretation. Note for the moment that auditors do not *certify* that the financial statements are totally correct, but report whether in their *opinion* the financial statements give a true and fair view.

1.2 Historical background

The role of the auditor goes back many hundreds of years. There are records from ancient Egypt and Rome, showing that people were employed to review work done by tax collectors and estate managers. In medieval Britain, an independent auditor was employed by the feudal Barons to ensure that returns from tenant farmers accurately reflected revenues received from the estates. The emphasis was very much on the detection of fraud and other irregularities. Thus, although the emphasis has changed and the role of the auditor become much more sophisticated, the concept of auditing is by no means a modern one.

1.3 Need for auditing

KEY POINT

A **fiduciary** relationship is a relationship of 'good faith', such as that between a trustee and a beneficiary, or between directors and shareholders.

It was recognised many years ago that whenever a **fiduciary relationship** with financial implications existed there was a need for an outsider with sufficient independence and objectivity to review the **accounts of stewardship** and to express an opinion as to their honesty or otherwise. A 'fiduciary' relationship is a relationship of 'good faith' such as that between a trustee and a beneficiary, between insurers and the insured and between directors and shareholders. This latter application is the one with most direct relevance to your examination, which is based on company audits. Remember that shareholders are the owners who finance the company; directors are appointed to run the company on the shareholders' behalf.

The financial statements of a company show how the directors have dealt with the funds of the company on behalf of the shareholders.

Modern auditing has developed since the concept of a **company** as a **separate legal entity** came into existence in the late nineteenth century. This led to the separation of ownership (shareholders) from control (directors) and a consequent need to safeguard the interests of the owners, who in all but the smallest of businesses (where shareholders and directors were one and the same) were not involved in the day-to-day decisions made by the management. The position can be summarised as follows:

Relationship between Directors and Shareholders

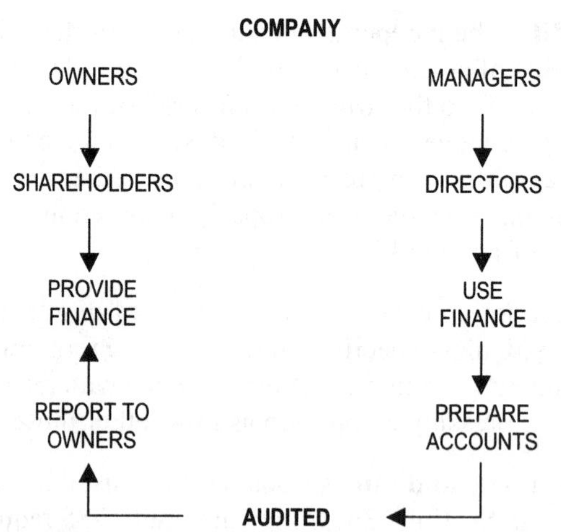

1.4 Development of auditing

Increasingly, the services of professional accountants were being sought and employed in the latter part of the nineteenth century and it was then that several professional accountancy bodies were formed. The **Companies Act 1900** re-introduced the compulsory audit requirement, although the auditor was only expected to express an opinion on the balance sheet. However, in the years preceding the Companies Act 1948, there were a number of cases which indicated the importance of the profit and loss account.

KEY POINT

The **Companies Act 1948** required auditors to **express an opinion on the truth and fairness of the profit and loss account and the balance sheet**. The Act also required auditors to have a recognised professional qualification, as well as laying down minimum disclosure levels.

The **Companies Act 1948** represented a major stepping-stone in the development of the modern audit. For the first time, the auditor was required to express an opinion on the truth and fairness of the profit and loss account and the balance sheet, both of which should be prepared by directors and presented to the shareholders at the annual general meeting. In addition, the Act required that auditors should possess a recognised professional qualification and detailed provisions were laid down regarding their duties, powers and responsibilities. Minimum disclosure levels were also laid down, together with the main objectives of the audit report.

The Companies Act 1948 together with subsequent Acts have been consolidated into the **Companies Act 1985**. This latter Act itself has been amended by the **Companies Act 1989**. The provisions of these Acts will be dealt with later in this text in so far as they affect this syllabus.

1.5 The detection of fraud and error

Following a judgement in 1859, stating that it was part of the appointed auditor's duties to discover fraudulent misrepresentations, the **detection of fraud and error** became the major objective of company audits. However, during the latter part of the nineteenth century, there was a growing school of thought that the **prevention** of fraud and error (as opposed to its detection) should be the major objective of the auditor (both external and internal), and that the management of a company should play a greater part and accept a larger degree of responsibility in this respect.

KEY POINT

The **Kingston Cotton Mill** case of 1896 established the fact that auditors should not be responsible for finding every fraud or error.

The leading case, which established the fact that the auditor should not be responsible for finding every fraud or error, is the **Kingston Cotton Mill** case of 1896. Here, the judgement pronounced that the auditor's role should be likened to that of a watchdog rather than a bloodhound, and that what was required of auditors was that they should act with such reasonable care and skill as was appropriate in the circumstances. Later cases confirmed this view of the auditor.

Obviously, with the growth of professionalism, the degree of care and skill expected of auditors increased in the eyes of the public. The various accountancy bodies recognised this fact and sought by various means to improve the standard of auditing, as will be seen later.

KEY POINT

There is no **statutory** duty on the part of auditors to seek out fraud.

There is no **statutory** duty for the auditor to seek out fraud. The auditor's duty under statute is confined to expressing an opinion as to whether the financial statements under review show a true and fair view of the company's results and position, and whether they comply with the Companies Acts. To discharge this duty, auditors must carry out such audit procedures as they think necessary in the light of the company's circumstances and of current auditing standards. Material discrepancies should be discovered as a result of normal audit procedures and, of course, the very existence of an audit may itself act as a deterrent. The detection of error or fraud is not the main objective of the audit.

It is interesting to note that one of the current challenges facing the auditing profession is 'the expectations gap' – the phenomenon that the public expectations placed on auditors exceed the **actual** role of the auditor.

1.6 Assurance engagements

DEFINITION

An **assurance engagement** is one whereby a professional accountant evaluates subject matter against certain criteria and provides a level of assurance about the subject(s).

According to the APB Glossary of terms, an assurance engagement is an assignment whereby a professional accountant is required to evaluate or measure a subject matter that is the responsibility of another party against identified suitable criteria, and to express a conclusion that provides the intended user with a level of assurance about that subject matter. An audit is therefore one example of assurance engagement. The auditor evaluates the financial statements, as prepared by the management and reports whether they give a true and fair view. It is important to distinguish between the levels of assurance given by an *audit* (which gives a high level of assurance) as compared to that given by other *assurance engagements* which, depending on the nature of the engagement, may give a lower level of assurance.

There is a broad range of assurance engagements, including any combination of the following:

- engagements to report on a broad range of subject matters covering financial and non-financial information
- engagements intended to provide high or moderate levels of assurance
- engagements to report internally and externally
- engagements in the private and public sector.

1.7 Engagements to review financial statements

KEY POINT

Reviews of financial statements enable auditors to state whether anything has come to their attention to cause them to believe that the statements have *not* been prepared in accordance with an identified reporting framework (**negative assurance**).

The APB Glossary of terms states that the objective of a **review of financial statements** is to enable an auditor to state whether, on the basis of procedures which do not provide all the evidence that would be required in an audit, anything has come to the auditor's attention that causes the auditor to believe that the financial statements are not prepared, in all material respects, in accordance with an identified financial reporting framework. In a review engagement, therefore, the auditor gives **negative assurance**, reporting that he is not aware that anything is materially wrong. Compare this with the **positive assurance** given in an audit engagement, where the auditor reports whether (or not) the accounts do give a true and fair view.

In carrying out his work the auditor should adopt an attitude of professional scepticism, recognising that circumstances may exist which cause the financial statements to be materially misstated.

2 The purpose of external audit

2.1 Users of financial statements

KEY POINT

The purpose of the external audit is to ensure that the financial statements are **objective**, **free from bias** and **manipulation** and **relevant** to the needs of users.

The users of the financial statements are known as 'stakeholders' of which the shareholders form one group; the need for an audit centres on their requirements. The financial statements specifically account annually to the shareholders for the stewardship of the directors and the management. There are also many other outside parties who form part of the stakeholders and use the financial statements as a basis for making decisions about a company. Bankers, the government, tax authorities, trade and loan creditors as well as potential investors and employees all have an interest in the state of the company's financial affairs. The requirement for an external audit to be carried out annually by an independent accountant fulfils the need to ensure that those financial statements are objective, free from bias and manipulation and relevant to the needs of the users.

Since the late 1940s, the emphasis in approaching an audit has shifted from the detailed checking of individual items towards an overall review of the systems in operation; followed by an examination of the records and the financial statements prepared from them. Amongst the reasons for this major shift of emphasis are the following:

- the increasing size and complexity of modern enterprises
- the development of more accurate and sophisticated computerised systems
- the requirement that the auditor should also report on the profit and loss account, which entails a review of all transactions during the period, not simply of year-end balances as before.

KEY POINT

There are inherent **advantages** in having financial statements audited:

- in settling disputes between management
- to facilitate major changes in ownership
- to enhance applications to third parties for finance
- to allow the auditor to give constructive advice to management.

2.2 Advantages of an audit

The need for an external audit arises primarily when the ownership and management of an enterprise are separated. There are, however, certain inherent advantages in having financial statements audited even where no statutory requirement exists for such an audit.

- Disputes between management may be more easily settled. For instance, a partnership which has complicated profit-sharing arrangements may require an independent examination of those accounts to ensure as far as possible an accurate assessment and division of those profits.
- Major changes in ownership may be facilitated if past accounts contain an unqualified audit report, for instance, where two sole traders merge their business to form a new partnership.
- Applications to third parties for finance may be enhanced by audited accounts. However, do remember that a bank, for instance, is likely to be far more concerned about the future of the business and available security than the past historical cost accounts, audited or otherwise.
- The audit is likely to involve an in-depth examination of the business and so may enable the auditor to give more constructive advice to management on improving the efficiency of the business.

KEY POINT

The **disadvantages** to having an audit:

- cost
- disruption to the client's staff and management.

2.3 Disadvantages of an audit

The disadvantages are basically twofold:

- The audit fee! Clearly the services of an auditor must be paid for. It is for this reason that few partnerships and even fewer sole traders are likely to have their accounts audited. The accountant's role as the preparer of financial statements, as a tax adviser and general financial adviser, becomes much more important to such concerns.
- The audit involves the client's staff and management in giving time to providing information to the auditor. Professional auditors should therefore plan their audit carefully to minimise the disruption which their work will cause.

2.4 Balancing the advantages and disadvantages of audit

An annual audit of the financial statements becomes more important as a company grows bigger: ownership and management of the company are separated, and larger amounts of money are involved. For smaller companies, the argument for mandatory audit is less compelling, though still arguable. The current statutory position is that large companies (defined as those with annual turnover greater than £5.6m) are required by law to have their annual financial statements subjected to external audit. Smaller companies (with turnover up to £5.6m) are not required to have their financial statements audited, but of course they may choose voluntarily to appoint auditors, to secure the advantages listed above.

KEY POINT

Internal audit shares a common history with external audit and has grown out of the increasing focus on the need to have effective internal controls within an organisation.

3 Differences between internal and external audit

It is important to understand and recognise the differences and commonalities between **internal** and **external audit** – your examination syllabus covers both. Internal audit shares a common history with external audit and has grown out of the increasing focus on the need to have effective internal controls within an organisation.

The internal and external auditor should work closely together, in particular to co-ordinate activity and maximise effectiveness and where appropriate external audit may rely on the work of internal audit. However, there are a number of fundamental differences in their objectives, scope and responsibility.

Internal auditors are usually employees of the organisation being audited; they work on projects as required by management. External auditors are employed by an independent external firm of accountants; their role is prescribed by statute, and they report on whether the financial statements give a true and fair view.

Differences between internal and external audit

	Internal auditing	*External auditing*
Objectives	To advise management on whether the organisation has sound systems of internal controls to protect the organisation against loss.	To provide an opinion on whether the financial statements provide a true and fair view.
Legal basis	Generally not a legal requirement. However the latest corporate governance advice recommends that if a listed company does not have an internal audit department, it should regularly assess the need for one.	Legal requirement for large limited companies and most public bodies.
Scope	All areas of the organisation, operational as well as financial.	Financial focus.
Approach	Increasingly risk-based. Assess risks. Evaluate system of controls. Test operations of systems. Make recommendations for improvements.	Increasingly risk-based. Test underlying transactions that form the basis of the financial statements.
Responsibility	To advise and make recommendations on internal control and corporate governance.	To form an opinion on whether the financial statements provide a true and fair view.

ACTIVITY 1

Outline the main differences in the roles of internal and external audit.

Feedback to this activity is at the end of the chapter.

The two sections which follow give a more detailed summary of the two 'types' of audit.

4 Introduction to internal audit and review

4.1 Role of internal audit

DEFINITION

Internal audit is an independent activity established by management to examine and evaluate the organisation's risk management processes and systems of control, and to make recommendations for the achievement of company objectives.

Internal audit is an independent activity established by management to examine and evaluate the organisation's risk management processes and systems of control, and to make recommendations for the achievement of company objectives.

Internal audit staff may also engage in a number of other activities:

- examination and evaluation of financial and operating information within the organisation – in certain organisations this can form a type of continuous auditing and may involve sophisticated information systems that capture monitoring of risks and evidencing of controls
- review of the economy, efficiency and effectiveness of operations
- review of compliance with external laws and regulations and internal policy and procedures
- review and advice on the development of key organisational systems and on the implementation of major change.

KEY POINT

The current focus of internal audit is on **adding value** to an organisation through risk control and reviewing all types of risk and recommending relevant controls.

Internal audit is a relatively new profession and its role has been subject to significant change as organisations have changed. Initially, it was an offshoot of the accounting profession, with a primary focus on financial controls and compliance. The focus of internal audit now is on adding value to an organisation through improvements in controlling risk and looking at all types of risk and control.

Developments in the approach of internal audit have emerged as organisational problems have become apparent. For example, in the early 1980s there was an upsurge in internal audit within the public sector arising from increased focus on the level of internal control.

More recently, well-publicised control problems such as those that led to the collapse of the Barings bank have resulted in increased focus on controlling risk and managing controls. Whenever problems occur such as with Enron, questions are asked about how risks have been managed and the role and scope of internal audit.

To look at the current role of internal audit, it is worth looking at the definitions of internal audit by the Auditing Practices Board and the Institute of Internal Auditors.

Auditing Practices Board definition of internal audit

'Internal audit is an independent appraisal function established by management for the review of the internal control system as a service to the organisation. It objectively examines, evaluates and reports on the adequacy of internal control as a contribution to the proper economic, efficient and effective use of resources.'

4.2 Institute of Internal Auditors definition

KEY POINT

The Institute of Internal Auditors' 1999 definition of internal auditing changed the focus of internal audit towards a more risk-based, consultancy type activity.

The Institute of Internal Auditors came up with a new definition of internal auditing in 1999, changing the focus of internal audit towards a more risk-based, consultancy type activity and recognising that internal audit is not always within the organisation, but can be an outsourced activity. The following are key elements of the Institute's definition:

- independent, objective assurance and consulting activity
- designed to add value and improve an organisation's operations
- helps an organisation accomplish its objectives
- brings a systematic, disciplined approach to evaluate and improve the effectiveness of risk management, control and governance processes.

4.3 Changing nature of internal audit

It is clear that the role of internal audit is significantly changing as a response to company and organisational needs, as well as increasing focus on the organisational risk. However, the role of internal audit can depend on the culture and approach of the organisation. Whilst the trend is towards greater consultancy and risk-based approach, certain organisations are still looking for a more traditional, inspection-based approach that they feel more comfortable with.

There is increasingly a demand for added value internal auditing, because of the environment of change. Organisations are looking to minimise costs and maximise efficiency. The internal audit is not immune to these trends and faces the same pressures as all other departments.

However, the fact remains that the modern view of the role of internal audit is based on a 'risk assessment' concept. The internal audit function is seen to have at its core the assessment of the existence of risks which may prevent an entity from achieving its objectives.

5 The scope of external audit

5.1 Stages of the audit

Auditing is essentially a practical task and no audit will be identical to any other. It is, however, possible to identify a number of stages. These are represented diagrammatically below. The auditing process can be similar between external and internal auditors, however the audit objectives are often very different. Internal auditing is considered in detail in chapters 4 and 5.

Throughout this text each of these stages will be considered in detail.

Stages of the audit

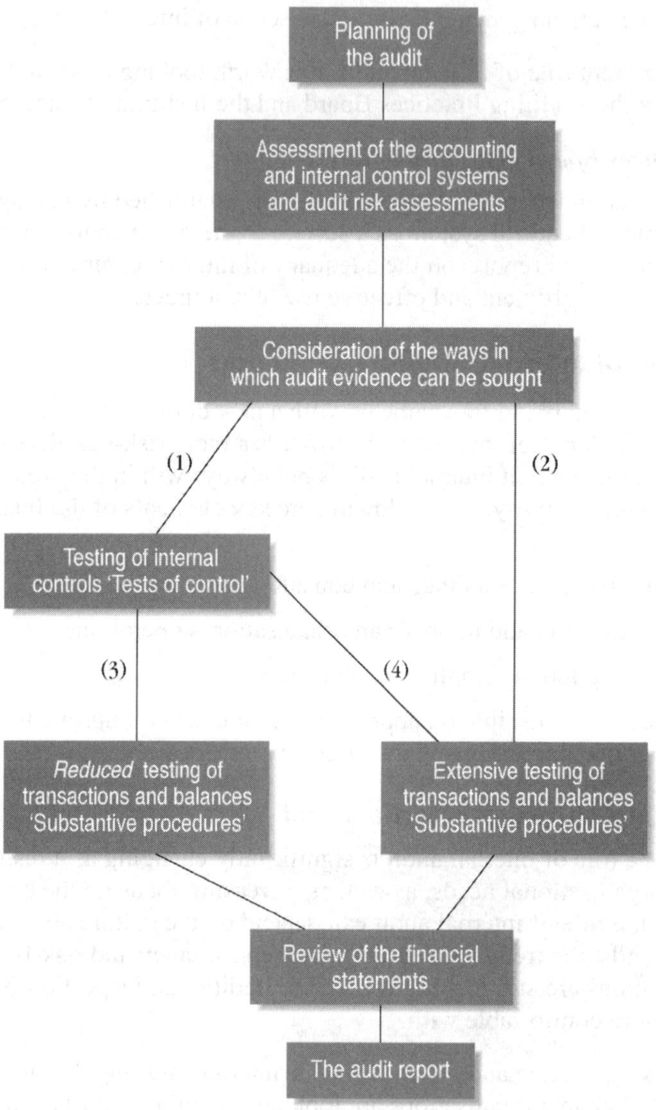

Notes

At this stage the auditor will make a preliminary evaluation of the enterprise's internal controls.

(1) If the controls are likely to lead to a 'true and fair' set of financial statements the auditor will test those controls.

(2) If they appear weak the auditor will not 'rely' on the internal controls but carry out extensive testing of the transactions and balances which appear in the financial statements.

(3) If the controls are operating correctly the auditor can reduce the extensive testing described above and adopt a 'reliance approach'.

(4) If not the auditor will be forced into a 'substantive approach'.

Finally the auditor will review the financial statements as a whole and formulate the audit opinion.

KEY POINT

The timing of audit work must be planned to suit the nature of the business being audited. Auditing may be:

- done **at** or **after the year end**
- divided into **interim** and **final** audits
- **continuous**.

5.2 The timing of audit work

The timing of audit work must be planned to suit the nature of the business being audited. There are three main possibilities:

- All the audit work is done **at or after the year end**. This is likely to be the case when the business being audited is small.
- The work is divided into **interim** and **final audits**, planning and tests of controls taking place at the interim stage and the substantive balance sheet audit taking place at the final stage.
- The third possibility is **continuous audits**, where the client is so large that the auditor is present at the client's premises throughout the year.

6 Directors' responsibilities

KEY POINT

Directors have specific legal responsibilities concerning the company's accounting system.

As discussed earlier, directors are accountable to the shareholders but they also have specific responsibilities.

- To safeguard the company's assets and to prevent fraud and errors in the company.
- To ensure that the company keeps proper accounting records as defined in the Companies Act 1985.
- To prepare annual financial statements to show the results of the company for the year and the state of affairs of the company at the balance sheet date.
- To deliver to the Registrar of Companies a copy of the company's audited financial statements within (for a plc) seven months of the end of the accounting year.
- To set up an internal control system in the company to ensure that all of the above are carried out. The directors cannot run the company by themselves; they must employ staff to carry out many of the accounting and other duties in the company. The system of internal control tries to ensure that the directors' other responsibilities above are met.

Identifying the directors' responsibilities can be seen as part of the wider topic of **corporate governance**, meaning the way in which a company is directed and controlled. While smaller companies may operate satisfactorily using the corporate governance arrangements contained in the Companies Acts, larger companies (particularly listed companies) are believed to require further regulation.

The Stock Exchange therefore requires listed companies to follow the Combined Code on Corporate Governance, which is explained later in this text. The Combined Code identifies further responsibilities that directors of listed companies must follow, for example:

- provide entrepreneurial leadership of the company within a framework of effective controls which enables risk to be assessed and managed
- include a balance of executive and non-executive directors such that no individual or small group of individuals can dominate the board.

See later in this text for a full discussion of the recent improvements in corporate governance arrangements, particularly with the issue of the Combined Code for listed companies.

7 The relationship between auditing and accounting

KEY POINT

Auditing and accounting are closely connected but **separate** activities.

Auditors should be **independent** from the accounting function.

Auditing and accounting are closely connected but separate activities. The directors of a company are responsible for establishing records which will accurately record transactions and which are used for preparing the annual financial statements. It is similarly the responsibility of the directors to adopt consistent and appropriate accounting policies in order to prepare the financial statements. The financial statements have to comply with legislative requirements and accounting standards.

Auditors are primarily concerned with the end result of this work, i.e. do the financial statements show a 'true and fair' view? In order to arrive at their conclusion, the auditors must have a deep knowledge and understanding of accounting and, in practice, the directors will consult with the auditors as to appropriate accounting policies to follow. Nevertheless, the auditor must ultimately stand back from the accounting function and consider the acceptability of the view shown by the financial statements to (primarily) the shareholders of the company.

Regulation of audits, and the influence of the accountancy profession, are considered in detail later in this text.

8 The social concept of an audit

Research has been undertaken over many years on the role that auditing plays within society. The narrower view of the social role of auditing concentrates purely on the role of financial auditing, noting that audited financial statements are more reliable than unaudited statements, so auditing adds value to society by adding to the efficiency of markets and encouraging investment funds to be rationally allocated amongst the available possible investments.

The wider view is that auditors should report on an organisation's overall performance. What, in social terms, does an organisation give to and take from the community, and how does an organisation justify its actions to its stakeholders and to the community? It has been argued that a social report should be issued, perhaps with the financial statements, and that a social audit can be carried out to assess the way that the organisation is fulfilling its duties; not just to shareholders, but to all the other stakeholders such as employees, customers and the general public.

KEY POINT

The **social audit process** can address the public's increasing desire for greater openness, by defining and measuring an organisation's social, ethical and environmental conduct.

Academics such as Professor Rob Gray of the Centre for Social and Environmental Accounting Research (CSEAR) have been at the forefront of formalising the **social audit process**. With the public demanding higher standards of corporate responsibility, accountability and transparency, a social audit can address this desire for greater openness, by defining and measuring an organisation's social, ethical and environmental conduct. The social audit should help ensure that, in an ever more competitive corporate environment, management do not sacrifice their social values in the constant quest for higher profitability.

9 Agency theory and auditing

9.1 Agents and principals

KEY POINT

Agency relationships occur when the **principal** employs an **agent** to perform a task on their behalf.

Modern organisational theory views an organisation as being comprised of various interest groups. The relationships between the various interested parties in the firm are often described in terms of **agency theory**. Agency relationships occur when one party, the **principal**, employs another party, the **agent**, to perform a task on their behalf.

For example, directors can be seen as the agents of shareholders, employees as the agents of directors and auditors as agents of shareholders.

Each principal needs to recognise that although he is employing the agent, the agent will have interests of his own to protect and thus may not fully carry out the requirements of the principal – a conflict of interests may arise. Note the debate on the level of directors pay and compensation for loss of office.

9.2 Examples of agency relationship conflicts

KEY POINT

Conflict can exist within agency relationships. For example, auditors report their opinion to the shareholders, but also need to remain on good terms with the directors who make the decision whether or not to reappoint them.

The directors have a duty of stewardship of the company's assets. However, they are also interested in their level of remuneration and if this increases, the assets of the company go down. The decision to award directors pay increases is effectively in the hands of the directors themselves.

The auditors report their opinion to the shareholders. However, auditors know the decision to reappoint them is effectively in the hands of the directors. They therefore have a potential conflict of interest in carrying out their function and also remaining on good terms with the directors.

These agency relationships need to be recognised so that, perhaps, steps can be taken by a principal to ensure that an agent works closer to the interests of the principal.

9.3 The application of agency theory to auditing

Despite having recognised the conflicts of interest that may arise, agency theory predicts that matters can be organised so that, by behaving rationally, the agent will not act against the interests of the principal.

For example, the theory assumes that shareholders will only buy shares if safeguards are in place to protect their interests. The legal requirement for audited accounts is one example of a necessary precondition. In addition, management will recognise the desirability of an audit. If shareholders are suspicious of the quality of an audit, they will not be prepared to invest. Management will therefore arrange for a proper audit as it is in their interest to do so.

KEY POINT

The practical effect of agency theory on auditing is to conclude that statutory regulation is unnecessary. The management of large companies have an interest in ensuring extensive audits (for informing shareholders), whereas small companies do not necessarily have the same need.

If this is true, then the practical effect of agency theory on auditing is to conclude that statutory regulation is unnecessary. The management of large companies will pay high fees for extensive and sophisticated audits as they have the greatest need to convince shareholders of the management's honesty.

In contrast, a small company where the management and shareholders are largely the same group will not pay high fees for an audit. It can be argued that in the latter situation this is a reasonable result, as the shareholders have no great need for an audit. However, this conclusion does not necessarily satisfy other users of the accounting information such as lenders (who may lend on the basis of the accounts) and the tax authorities (who assess liability to tax based on the profit reported in the accounts). The audit requirements for small companies have been substantially relaxed in the last few years such that far fewer companies are now legally required to have an audit. It is possible that there will be further relaxation in the future.

10 Audit reporting as a communication medium

10.1 The audit report

KEY POINT

The audit report is the primary means of communication between the auditor and the shareholders of the company.

The audit report is usually the only channel of communication between the auditor and the shareholders of the company whose financial statements have been subject to audit. As such the report acts as a bridge taking the large volume of information possessed by the auditors and conveying it to the shareholders in a much abbreviated form.

10.2 Categories of audit report

In order to convey information in a succinct form, the audit report has become an extremely formalised group of phrases, each of which has special significance. These are similar to legal phrases known as '**terms of art**'. Such phrases do not mean merely what they appear to mean on the face of it, and have a significance much greater than they first appear to. Any deviation from the standard format is regarded by accountants as being significant and may provide important extra information.

DEFINITIONS

An **unqualified report** is one which provides an opinion that the accounts are in order ie that they give a true and fair view

A **qualified report** is less common and is where an auditor disagrees with the view presented in the accounts, or if he has not been able to form an opinion because of inadequate evidence.

It is therefore important for the auditor to know the following details:

- the form of an **unqualified audit report** and the meaning of the phrases used
- the situations where a **qualified audit report** is needed and how such a report should be phrased
- the situations where, although the opinion is unqualified, it may be relevant to include additional detail emphasising one particular aspect of the accounts.

An unqualified report is the usual report issued by an auditor. In essence, it states an opinion that the accounts are 'in order' i.e. that they give a true and fair view. A qualified report is necessary in the less common cases where an auditor disagrees with the view presented in the accounts, or has not been able to form an opinion because of inadequate evidence.

The standard unqualified report is reproduced below. This wording is prescribed by an auditing standard (ISA 700) issued by the accountancy profession as supplemented by APB Bulletin 2001/2 – *Revisions to the Wording of Auditors' Reports* which requires audit reports to include an expanded statement of auditors' responsibilities and the title of the report to include the word 'independent'.

Note that students are not expected to reproduce the audit report in full in the examination.

A brief commentary on the main elements of the report is given below. The audit report is dealt with in detail in a later chapter.

Example of Standard Unqualified Report

Independent auditors' report to the shareholders of XYZ Limited

(Note that the heading refers to:

- *the independence of the auditor*
- *the fact that the report is addressed to the shareholders*
- *the name of the company.)*

We have audited the financial statements of (name of entity) for the year ended ... which comprise [state the primary financial statements such as the Profit and Loss Account, the Balance Sheet, the Cash Flow Statement, the Statement of total Recognised Gains and Losses] and the related notes.* These financial statements have been prepared under the historical cost convention [as modified by the revaluation of certain fixed assets] and the accounting policies set out therein.

(This paragraph is often referred to as the 'scope paragraph'. It emphasises that an ***audit*** *has been performed and identifies clearly the information which has been subject to the audit process.)*

Respective responsibilities of directors and auditors

(This section helps to address a further aspect of the 'expectations gap' – the respective responsibilities of the directors on the one hand and the auditors on the other. There is also an outline explanation of the way the audit has been conducted and gives further information on the 'scope' of the audit.)

The directors' responsibilities for preparing the Annual Report and the financial statements in accordance with applicable law and United Kingdom Accounting Standards are set out in the Statement of Directors' Responsibilities.

Our responsibility is to audit the financial statements in accordance with relevant legal and regulatory requirements and United Kingdom Auditing Standards.

We report to you our opinion as to whether the financial statements give a true and fair view and are properly prepared in accordance with the [Companies Act 1985] [Companies (Northern Ireland) Order 1986]. We also report to you if, in our opinion, the Directors' Report is not consistent with the financial statements, if the company has not kept proper accounting records, if we have not received all the information and explanations we require for our audit, or if information specified by law regarding directors' remuneration and transactions with the company is not disclosed.

We read other information contained in the Annual Report, and consider whether it is consistent with the audited financial statements. This other information comprises only [the Directors' Report, the Chairman's Statement and the Operating and Financial Review].** We consider the implications for our report if we become aware of any apparent misstatements or material inconsistencies with the financial statements. Our responsibilities do not extend to any other information.

Basis of opinion

(Here the auditor is confirming that the audit has been performed in accordance with appropriate standards of professional practice. Note the references to 'sufficient evidence' and 'reasonable assurance' – this should reinforce your appreciation of the fact that audit reports are frequently based on professional judgement.)

We conducted our audit in accordance with United Kingdom Auditing Standards issued by the Auditing Practices Board. An audit includes examination, on a test basis, of evidence relevant to the amounts and disclosures in the financial statements. It also includes an assessment of the significant estimates and judgements made by the directors in the preparation of the financial statements, and of whether the accounting policies are appropriate to the company's circumstances, consistently applied and adequately disclosed.

We planned and performed our audit so as to obtain all the information and explanations which we considered necessary in order to provide us with sufficient evidence to give reasonable assurance that the financial statements are free from material misstatement, whether caused by fraud or other irregularity or error. In forming our opinion we also evaluated the overall adequacy of the presentation of information in the financial statements.

Opinion

(This section gives the auditor's 'unqualified' opinion on the truth and fairness of the information contained in the financial statements.)

In our opinion the financial statements give a true and fair view of the state of the company's affairs as at … and of its profit [loss] for the year then ended and have been properly prepared in accordance with the Companies Act 1985 [Companies (Northern Ireland) Order 1986].

Registered auditors

Address

Date

---

* *Auditors' reports of entities that do not publish their financial statements on a web site or publish them using 'pdf' format, may continue to refer to the financial statements by reference to a page number.*

** *The other information that is 'read' is the content of the Annual Report other than the financial statements. The description of the information that has been read is tailored to reflect the terms used in the Annual Report.*

Two key features of the above report are examined in the paragraphs that follow: **truth and fairness,** and **materiality** (see sections 11 and 12).

10.3 Electronic communications

An increasing trend is for audit reports to be issued and be available electronically. Both financial statements and audit reports are now readily available on the internet. Until recently this would not have been the case, but the rapid growth of technology in general, and the internet in particular, has resulted in a vast range of data being accessible. The internet is a useful tool for the auditor but it also provides more challenges and will impact the future development of auditing. Where information is readily available, then there is a chance that the auditor will be more open to question on the quality of reporting provided.

An increasing number of companies are posting financial statements, including the auditor's report onto their web sites or allowing shareholders to receive the annual report electronically in place of a hard copy version (Companies Act 1985 [Electronic Communications] Order 2000). In these circumstances the APB Bulletin 2001/2 encourages auditors to check that the electronic version of the financial statements is identical in content to the manually signed accounts.

11 The evolution and meaning of 'true and fair'

11.1 History

KEY POINT

No statutory definition of the meaning of the term 'true and fair' has ever been provided.

The term **true and fair** was first used in the CA 1948. However, a number of preceding Acts had used similar phrases.

At no stage has any statutory definition of the meaning of these terms been provided.

11.2 Meaning of true and fair

'Truth' in accounting terms is quite different from scientific truth. Accounting does not deal with that type of truth which has a fixed and unchanging quality.

KEY POINT

Auditors should ensure that information is impartially presented and is clearly understandable to achieve the statutory true and fair view.

The word *fair* can have the following meanings: on the one hand *clear, distinct* and *plain,* and on the other *impartial, just* and *equitable.* All can be considered relevant when *fair* is used in an accounting context.

Auditors should attempt to ensure that the accounts which are the subject of the audit present clearly and equitably the financial state of affairs of the enterprise. This suggests that in order to achieve the statutory true and fair view, it is necessary not only to present certain information impartially, but also that this data is shown in such a way that it is clearly understood by the user.

11.3 Attempts at definition of the true and fair view

The following quotation from a standard auditing text represents an authoritative view on the meaning of true and fair view.

> '... true and fair has become a term of art. It is generally understood to mean a presentation of accounts drawn up according to accepted accounting principles using accurate figures as far as possible and reasonable estimates otherwise, and arranging them so as to show within the limits of current accounting practice as objective a picture as possible free from wilful bias, distortion, manipulation or concealment of material facts.' (Lee)

Note that the reference to 'accepted accounting principles' here means that auditors will often be guided by the requirements of Accounting Standards.

It must be concluded that there is little point in attempting precisely to define *true and fair*. What attempts have been made have not been very successful. J.G. Chastney in his report for the Research Committee of the ICAEW (*True and fair view – history, meaning and the impact of the 4th Directive*) found similar difficulties and concluded the term is almost impossible to define.

ACTIVITY 2

Summarise the points made above as to the meaning of true and fair.

Feedback to this activity is at the end of the chapter.

12 Materiality

The concept of materiality is fundamental to the presentation and classification of data in accounts. The following sections are based on ISA 320 *Audit materiality* and a November 1996 statement *The interpretation of materiality in financial reporting,* published by the Institute of Chartered Accountants in England and Wales (ICAEW).

12.1 Purpose of ISA 320

Auditors hope that their audit procedures will uncover any large errors in the financial statements that they are auditing. The larger (i.e. the more material) an error, the more likely it should be that the auditors should detect it in their audit testing.

ISA 320 was issued to provide guidance to auditors when considering materiality and its relationship with the risk that they might give an inappropriate opinion on the financial statements. (Such a risk is called '**audit risk**' and is discussed later in this text.)

12.2 Definition of materiality

DEFINITION

A matter is **material** if its omission or misstatement would reasonably influence the decisions of users of the financial statements.

'Materiality' is defined in ISA 320 to be an expression of the relative significance or importance of a particular matter in the context of financial statements as a whole. **A matter is material if its omission or misstatement would reasonably influence the decisions of users taken on the basis of the financial statements**. Materiality is not capable of general mathematical definition as it has both qualitative and quantitative aspects.

12.3 Auditing principle

'The auditor should consider materiality and its relationship with audit risk when conducting an audit.'

Explanation

KEY POINTS

Anything that would distort the view given by accounts must lead to a qualification, but only if it is material (SAS 220.1).

The key problem in practice is that of how 'large' an item has to be for it to be considered material.

The auditors' responsibility is to plan and perform their audit to provide reasonable assurance that the financial statements are free of material misstatement and give a true and fair view. From the audit point of view, anything that would distort the view given by accounts must lead to a qualification, but only if it is material.

Here are some examples that might fit the above definition:

- inclusion of deferred revenue expenditure, such as advertising costs, in debtors and prepayments
- a loan which could not quickly be recalled shown under money at call at short notice
- omission of an item of stock.

The key problem in practice is that of how 'large' an item has to be for it to be considered material.

12.4 Auditing principle

KEY POINT

Auditors should consider materiality when determining the nature, timing and extent of audit procedures.

'Materiality should be considered by the auditor when:

(a) determining the nature, timing and extent of audit procedures; and

(b) evaluating the effect of misstatements.'

Explanation

The initial assessment of materiality during audit planning assists in the determination of an efficient and effective audit approach. This preliminary materiality assessment helps auditors decide such factors as what items to examine and whether to use sampling techniques and which ones. This enables them to select audit procedures that will reduce audit risk to an acceptable level.

The application of the materiality concept in the planning and conducting of an audit is dealt with more fully later in this text.

12.5 Materiality and judgement

KEY POINT

Auditors must use their professional judgement in deciding whether or not an item is material. They must consider:

- qualitative aspects
- the cumulative effect of small amounts
- the relative nature of materiality
- the degree of latitude that is allowable.

Auditors must use their professional judgement in coming to a decision as to whether an item is, or is not, material. Important points to take into consideration are as follows:

- What qualitative aspects are involved, such as the inaccurate or inadequate description of an accounting policy.
- Relatively small amounts, such as a small error in a month end procedure, can cumulatively have a material effect, if repeated.
- Materiality is a relative factor and should be considered in relative terms. £1,000 may be absolutely immaterial in the accounts of a large company, whereas in a small organisation the reverse would probably be true. Further, under this heading an amount must be considered in relation to:
  - items at the overall financial statement level
  - items at the individual account balance or transaction level
  - statutory and other disclosure requirements which may require disclosure regardless of value, such as those relating to directors' emoluments
  - the corresponding amount in previous years.
- What degree of latitude is allowable in deciding on the amount attributable to a particular item. Some items, such as directors' fees, are capable of exact definition; others, such as depreciation and provisions for obsolete or damaged stock, are at best an intelligent estimate. The overriding consideration must be whether the accounts disclose a true and fair view. It is also clearly important that such items are consistently treated from year to year.

12.6 Auditing principle

KEY POINT

Auditors should assess the materiality of the aggregate of uncorrected misstatements.

'In evaluating whether the financial statements are prepared, in all material respects, in accordance with an applicable financial reporting framework, the auditor should assess whether the aggregate of uncorrected misstatements that have been identified during the audit is material.'

Explanation

This indicates that the **overall effect** of misstatements should be evaluated.

If the auditor believes that the aggregate of uncorrected misstatements may be material, they may wish to extend their audit testing to obtain more audit evidence in the relevant area, or request the directors to adjust the financial statements. In practice, once the directors have been informed of the misstatements in the draft accounts, they are likely to be happy for the accounts to be adjusted. If the directors refuse any adjustments, the auditor should consider the implications for the audit report.

12.7 Audit tests to determine whether an item is material

The ICAEW statement lists the following as being items likely to affect the auditor's decision as to the material importance or otherwise of an item, and states that materiality guidelines can be derived from answering the following questions:

- Who are the relevant users?
- What are their decision-making needs?
- For a given item, what is the appropriate context for assessing its materiality?
- In what range of values do items become critical in terms of materiality?
- How should particular items in these critical ranges be decided and reported?

The statement also notes that in the US, the Securities and Exchange Commission (the main regulator of US securities laws, normally referred to by its initials as the SEC) takes as a rule of thumb the following:

- errors over 10% – material

- errors between 5% and 10% – may be material
- errors under 5% – not material.

Please note that these figures are guidelines only – not firm rules. Judgement is required!

Conclusion

This chapter should have given you a historical perspective on the nature of the audit. The objectives of an audit have also been outlined and need to be borne in mind at all times.

Other engagements, such as engagements to review financial statements give a lower level of assurance to that provided by an audit.

Agency theory can be applied in the context of directors acting as agents of shareholders and auditors acting as agents of shareholders.

Using agency theory to help explain the nature of the connections between the parties involved in an audit is an example of using an imported theory, i.e. a theory developed outside the world of auditing is applied and found to be useful in the auditing context.

'True and fair' is the central underlying concept relating to the audit. The audit opinion relates to the material amounts in the financial statements. By definition, immaterial amounts do not distort the picture given by the financial statements.

SELF-TEST QUESTIONS

The nature of audit and other assurance engagements

1 What is an audit? (1.1)

2 Does true and fair mean the auditor is certifying the financial statements? (1.1)

3 Who are accountable to shareholders for their actions? (1.3)

4 What is an assurance engagement? (1.6)

Differences between internal and external audit

5 What are the main differences between internal and external audit? (3)

Agency theory and auditing

6 Does agency theory conclude that directors will encourage or discourage auditing? (9.3)

The evolution and meaning of 'true and fair'

7 What meanings could be attached to the words 'true and fair'? (11.2)

Materiality

8 What is meant by 'materiality'? (12.2)

EXAM-TYPE QUESTIONS

Question 1: New client

You have been approached by a director of a small company who has asked for clarification about the range of services your firm can offer. In particular he has asked for details about the following:

- Accountancy services
- Audit
- Review engagements

Write an appropriate letter, in language that a layman can understand, describing what an audit is, with particular emphasis on its nature and purposes and ensure you provide details of the other services.

(Use fictitious names and addresses. Marks will be awarded specifically for style as well as for content.) **(20 marks)**

Question 2: Introduction to audit

Give a definition of an audit, and explain the significance of the terms therein. **(10 marks)**

Question 3: Concept of materiality

What do you understand by the concept of materiality in relation to an audit? **(10 marks)**

For answers to these questions, see the 'Answers' section at the end of the book.

FEEDBACK TO ACTIVITY **1**

Internal audit departments are directly employed by the organisation and report within the organisation. Their responsibilities are set by management.

External auditors produce an audit report addressed to the shareholders and specifically report on the truth and fairness of the financial statements.

FEEDBACK TO ACTIVITY **2**

There is no statutory or professional definition of true and fair.

True and fair is a technical term and the phrase must be looked at as an entirety.

To show a true and fair view accounts must be prepared:

(a) in accordance with generally accepted accounting principles

(b) on a consistent basis

(c) so as not to be misleading

(d) on an impartial basis

(e) such that they do not contain any material misstatements.

Chapter 2
STATUTORY AUDITS

CHAPTER CONTENTS

This chapter summarises the regulatory framework in which statutory audits take place, as well as outlining the duties and powers of the auditor under the Companies Acts. The regulatory framework provides increasing focus of attention on the duties both of internal and external auditors, and corporate governance is covered in this chapter which is increasingly being given more prominence. Auditors are given certain rights under the Companies Acts to ensure that they can satisfactorily fulfil their duties and responsibilities, and enable them to maintain their independence. Auditors are also given some rights regarding their removal from office.

Objectives

By the time you have finished this chapter you should be able to:

- outline the regulatory framework in which statutory audits are undertaken
- describe the reasons for, and mechanisms for, the regulation of auditors by Government and other regulatory agencies including other UK standard setters
- state the powers and duties of auditors
- describe how an auditor is appointed
- describe how an auditor can be removed from office and how he may resign
- explain how changing legal requirements could impact internal and external auditors.

1 The statutory framework of auditing

KEY POINT

Auditors need to be aware of their own national regulations and those of other countries covered by audit.

It is important for all auditors, internal and external, to be aware of the regulatory framework for auditing and to keep up to date with any changes that occur. Changes in regulations could affect the audit role, how it is performed and the status of auditing.

This chapter deals with the statutory regulation of auditing. Regulation by financial institutions is also significant. One key aspect of this is corporate governance, dealt with later in this text.

There is a trend towards globalisation within companies and there is a similar trend in auditing. This means that auditors need to be aware not only of UK regulations but also of those of other countries covered by audit. There is also a greater focus on international standards for internal auditing, particularly in Europe. This could result in a change of approach certainly in internal auditing and could lead to more clearly defined roles and rules for auditors.

There are different types of regulatory impact affecting the operation of a company and of auditing. These include:

- Companies Acts
- common regulations affecting all organisations, e.g. Health and Safety at Work Act
- specific types of legislation affecting specific activities of a company, e.g. Compulsory Competitive Tendering Act
- industry specific regulations, e.g. Financial Services and Markets Act, Local Government Acts
- international regulations.

Auditors should be aware of the regulatory framework applicable to the industry, because a key objective of any organisation will be to comply with appropriate regulations.

KEY POINT

The statutory framework for external auditing involves **Companies Act requirements** and **public sector requirements** (where relevant).

However, the prime focus of this chapter is on the statutory framework for auditing, which involves these key areas:

- Companies Act requirements (the main focus for your examination)
- public sector requirements, where relevant. It should be noted that Company Law in the UK delegates much of the detailed regulation of auditing to professional accountancy bodies.

ACTIVITY **1**

Why is it important to keep up-to-date with trends in the regulatory framework?

Feedback to this activity is at the end of the chapter.

2 Auditing – regulation by the Companies Acts

2.1 Function of the Companies Acts

Most audit work involves companies incorporated under the Companies Act 1985 (CA85). This legislation sets out:

- the requirement for companies to have their financial statements audited
- rules covering the appointment, removal, resignation and retirement of auditors, in order to ensure independence
- auditors' rights, duties and necessary qualifications.

2.2 The changing role of the auditor under the Companies Acts

KEY POINT

The role of the auditor has changed over the years in particular where detection and reporting of fraud is concerned.

Successive Companies Acts have redefined the role of auditors. In the 19th century, auditors were expected to prevent or detect fraud and error. In the early 20th century, attention shifted to the certifying of accuracy in accounts; by the CA 1948, the 'true and fair' requirement was introduced.

Currently, there is pressure for the auditor to return to the prevention/detection role as the public still expects auditors to act as financial 'policemen', even though in law, this is not their function at all. The profession as a whole has resisted pressure to widen the scope of its responsibilities to include the detection and reporting role, especially in the face of ever increasing negligence claims against firms. Nevertheless, the legal requirements to report fraud, where it is detected or suspected, have been widened, particularly since the collapse of BCCI. This issue is generally known as the 'expectations gap': the difference between what auditors are expected to do by the public, and what they are required to do by law.

2.3 Delegation of standard setting

As we noted earlier, the competence of auditors is promoted by the CA85, as it requires appropriate professional qualifications for auditors.

The legislation delegates the setting of appropriate auditing standards to the auditing profession on the grounds that practitioners are best able to devise standards and change those standards in response to the changing environment. In other parts of the world, auditing standards sometimes don't exist at all; sometimes they are incorporated into legislation, and sometimes international standards on auditing are used verbatim, without being amended to reflect particular national circumstances.

2.4 The audit requirement – The Companies Act 1985

KEY POINT

Some limited companies are exempt from the requirement to have an audit.

Not all limited companies are required to have their financial statements audited. Nor are all companies required to produce financial statements in the same formats, as many exemptions apply to small and medium-sized companies under the CA 1985.

Broadly speaking, small private companies (those with turnover less than £5.6m) are totally exempt from the audit requirement; small and medium-sized private companies may file abbreviated accounts with the registrar of companies; and small private companies may prepare accounts with reduced disclosures for their members. This whole area of audit requirement is currently being considered and current requirements together with the issues surrounding this debate will be dealt with in a later chapter.

3 Appointment of auditors

3.1 First auditors

KEY POINT

Under S384 CA 85, the **first auditors** of a new company are usually appointed by the directors.

Under S384 CA 85, the first auditors of a new company are usually appointed by the directors to hold office until the next AGM. If the directors fail to do this, the company in general meeting may appoint the first auditors.

3.2 Subsequent appointments

KEY POINT

Auditors must then be appointed annually and **subsequent appointments** are usually made by the members at each AGM.

Auditors must then be appointed annually unless the company is a private company which has elected to dispense with annual reappointment. In this case, the auditors are automatically reappointed until there is a resolution to end the appointment.

Under S384 CA 85 subsequent appointments are usually made by the members at each AGM to hold office from the conclusion of that meeting until the conclusion of the next AGM. If no auditors are appointed or reappointed by the members at an AGM, the company must, within seven days, inform the Secretary of State who has the power to appoint an auditor.

3.3 Casual vacancy

KEY POINT

The directors of the company have the power to appoint an auditor to fill a casual vacancy.

The directors of the company have the power to appoint an auditor to fill a casual vacancy, i.e. a vacancy occurring between AGMs as a result, for example, of the death, removal or resignation of the current auditor. The surviving auditor, if any, may continue to act during such vacancy.

3.4 Remuneration

Whoever appoints the auditor has the power to fix the remuneration for a period of appointment. However, if the auditors are appointed by the members in general meeting, it is usual for the members to delegate this power to the directors.

3.5 Independence of auditors

Under S27 CA 89 a person may not be an auditor of a company (or of another company within the same group) if that person is:

- an officer or servant of the company (as such a person would not be impartial and could be influenced by the directors)
- a partner of, or is in the employment of, either of the above (again because of the necessity for impartiality and independence).

The auditor is not considered to be an officer of the company for the purpose of determining whether they may act as auditor, but they would be considered as such in the context of disclosure of transactions with officers. These are the only *legal* requirements relating to auditor independence. There are many more professional requirements under the ACCA's Rules of Professional Conduct; which are dealt with in a later chapter.

ACTIVITY 2

Who is qualified to act as an auditor under the CA85?

Feedback to this activity is at the end of the chapter.

4 Removal of auditors

4.1 Statutory provisions

KEY POINT

The Companies Act prevents directors from removing auditors simply because they disagree with them.

The provisions of the Companies Act were drafted to ensure that auditors cannot be removed simply because they have had a disagreement with directors. Again, it is the members who are empowered to remove an auditor or to reject a proposal by the directors that the auditor should be removed where they (the members) believe that the auditor has carried out their duties conscientiously.

4.2 Removal procedures

KEY POINT

A company may remove an auditor before the expiration of their term of office by ordinary resolution, but **special notice** is required.

A company may remove an auditor before the expiration of their term of office by ordinary resolution (i.e. a majority of those attending and voting), but **special notice** is required.

Special notice means that at least 28 days before the date of the relevant meeting notice of the motion must be given to the company by the proposer. The company must give the members notice of the resolution together with the notice of the meeting.

Special notice is required for a resolution at a general meeting of the company:

- appointing as auditor a person other than a retiring auditor; or
- filling a casual vacancy in the office of auditor; or
- reappointing as auditor a retiring auditor who was appointed by the directors to fill a casual vacancy; or
- removing an auditor before the expiration of his term of office.

KEY POINT

All resolutions concerning auditors (and directors) are **ordinary** resolutions.

Note: *All* resolutions concerning auditors (and directors) are **ordinary** resolutions. They require special notice in any situation in which the existing auditor is not reappointed in normal circumstances.

KEY POINT

The existing auditor can make written **representations** to all members concerning facts which they consider should be brought to the members' attention.

The existing auditor has the right to make written representations to the company concerning facts which they consider should be brought to the members' attention. The company must (unless these representations are received too late for it to do so):

- state the fact that representations have been made in any notice of the resolution given to members
- send a copy of the representations to every member of the company to whom notice of the meeting is or has been sent.

KEY POINT

Representations may **be read out** at the meeting, or the auditor may **speak** at the meeting in person if representations are received too late to send out.

4.3 The auditor's right to speak

If a copy of such representations is received too late to be sent out, the existing auditor has the right to demand that they be read out at the meeting. In addition to or instead of the representations being read out, auditors have the right to speak at the meeting on any matters which they feel should be brought to the attention of the members. They may also speak at the meeting at which their office would have expired.

KEY POINT

On ceasing to hold office for any reason, the auditor must deposit a **statement of circumstances** at the company's registered office.

4.4 Statements of circumstances

If an auditor ceases to hold office for any reason he **must** deposit a **statement of circumstances** at the company's registered office. This statement gives details of the reasons for the cessation, to the members. If there are no particular reasons then they must state that.

5 Resignation and retirement of auditors

KEY POINT

The auditor may **resign** at any time by depositing a written notice of resignation at the company's registered office.

5.1 Resignation procedures

The Companies Act provides that the auditor may resign prior to the completion of their term of office. The auditor may do so by depositing a written notice of resignation at the company's registered office. The notice must contain:

- either a statement that there are no circumstances connected with the resignation which the auditor considers should be brought to members' or creditors' attention, or
- a statement of any such circumstances.

This is the same as the statement required on removal noted above.

5.2 Action by company

The company must, within 14 days of receipt of the notice, send a copy of the statement to the Registrar of Companies. If the notice contained a statement of any circumstances which the auditor considers should be brought to members' or creditors' attention, the company must also send a copy to every person entitled to receive copies of the accounts.

KEY POINT

The auditor may require the directors to convene an **EGM** for the purpose of receiving and considering any explanation of circumstances which the auditor may wish to make.

5.3 The auditor's right to an Extraordinary General Meeting (EGM)

Where the auditor's notice of resignation includes a statement of circumstances connected with the resignation which the auditor considers should be brought to members' or creditors' attention, the auditor may require the directors to convene an **EGM** for the purpose of receiving and considering any explanation of these circumstances which the auditor may wish to make.

Copies need not be sent out nor read out at the general meeting if, on the application of the company or any aggrieved person, the court is satisfied that the auditor is abusing their rights to secure needless publicity for defamatory matter.

5.4 Retirement of auditors

It is very rare for auditors either to resign or to be removed. Usually, where the auditor and client decide to part company, the auditor will simply not offer themselves for re-election at the next AGM. In those circumstances, a statement of circumstances is still required.

KEY POINT

The Companies Act ensures that the **members and creditors** of a company can be made fully aware of the **reasons** for the auditor's resignation.

5.5 Factors affecting the termination of professional engagements

These provisions of the Companies Act are designed to ensure that the members and creditors of a company can be made fully aware of the reasons for the auditor's resignation. Moreover, they afford a measure of protection to auditors and to their independence, by making it impossible to resign where they are and have been subjected to undue and unacceptable influences and pressures from the directors without such facts being made public.

5.6 Summary of appointment and removal of auditors

Appointment

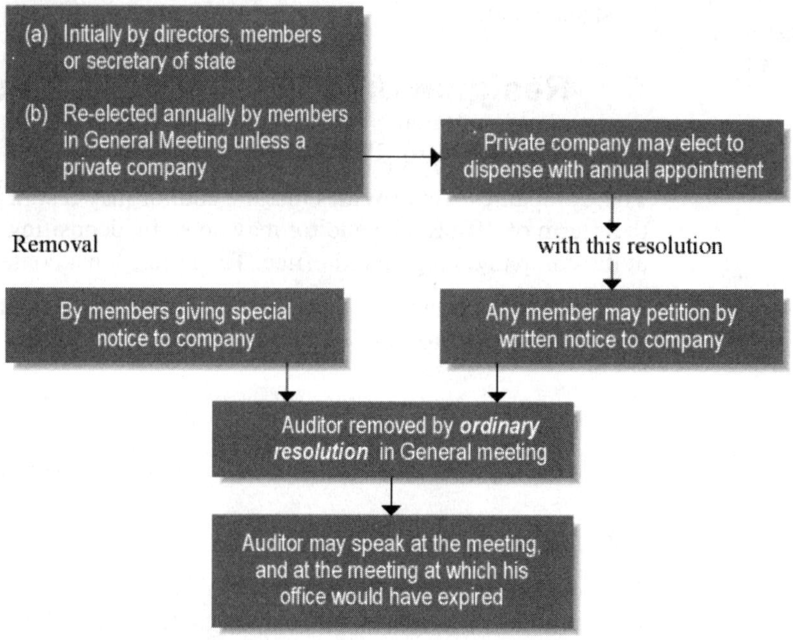

- Removal, resignation and retirement

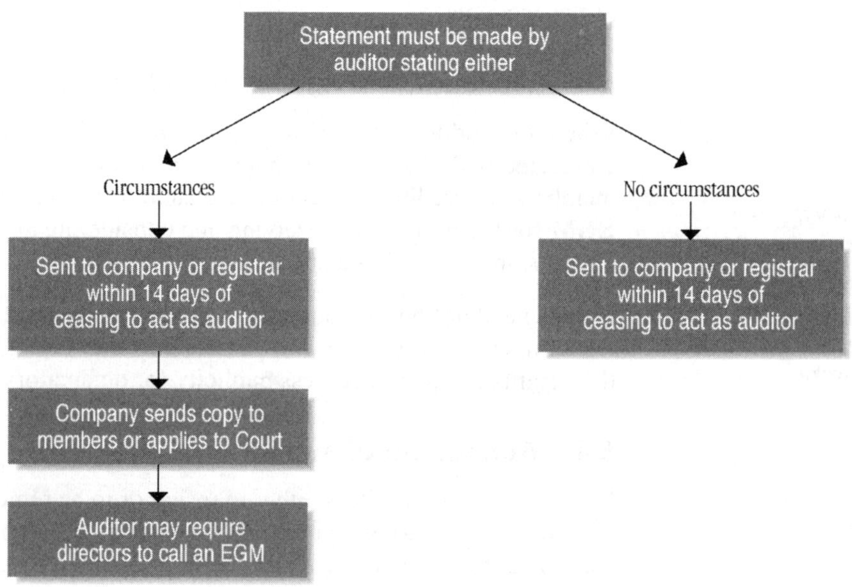

6 Auditors' rights and duties

The auditor has various detailed duties to perform in order to achieve the overall duty to report on the true and fair view. In order to fulfil these duties, various rights are given to the auditor.

6.1 Duties of the auditor

KEY POINT

The auditor's **duties** are detailed in the Companies Acts; the key one being that of reporting whether the financial statements show a 'true and fair view'.

The duties of auditors under the Companies Act are as follows:

- To report to the members on whether the financial statements of the company (or group of companies) show a true and fair view and have been properly prepared in accordance with the Act.
- To consider whether the information in the Directors' Report is consistent with the financial statements and, if not, to state the fact in the audit report.
- To give the following details required by statute in the audit report, if not given in the financial statements themselves:
  - particulars of directors' emoluments, pensions and compensation for loss of office
  - details of loans to officers
  - particulars of any directors' emoluments waived
  - disclosure of transactions involving directors and other connected persons.
- To form an opinion as to whether:
  - proper accounting records have been kept by the company
  - proper returns adequate for their audit have been received from branches not visited by them (where applicable)
  - the company's balance sheet and its profit and loss account are in agreement with the accounting records and returns
  - such information and explanations as the auditor thinks necessary for the performance of their duties have been received from the company's officers.

  No mention of the above is to be made if the auditor is satisfied in all respects. They are reported on by exception only.

  You will see how all the above provisions come into force later in the text when we cover audit reports.
- To make other special reports in various circumstances.
- To make a 'statement of circumstances' when they cease to hold the office of auditor for any reason.

6.2 Rights of the auditor

KEY POINT

Auditors have certain rights as defined by the Companies Acts to enable them to fulfil their duties and responsibilities.

The rights given to auditors under the Companies Act are designed to ensure that they are able to fulfil their duties and responsibilities to the members. These rights are fundamental to their independence. It is important that these rights are not confused with the auditor's duties outlined above. The auditor has a duty to make a report to the members, and this duty can be discharged with the help of the rights granted by statute.

These statutory rights are as follows:

KEY POINT

Legally, auditors have a right:

- to access the books of the company
- to require information from the officers
- to be involved in any general meeting of the company
- to make a representation at meetings considering their removal or resignation
- to require the directors to requisition an EGM on resignation.

- The right of access at all times to the books, records, documents and accounts of the company. The auditor must obviously exercise this right with discretion so as not to disrupt unnecessarily the company's operations. Equally, if the client refuses access to the records, auditors would never seek access to them forcibly, or even through the courts. They would instead consider either resigning or qualifying their audit report.
- The right to require from the officers of the company such information and explanations as they think necessary for the performance of their duties.

  An officer wilfully making a false statement to an auditor, knowing it to be false, commits a criminal offence. Moreover under S389A CA 1985, a criminal offence is committed if a knowing or *reckless* false statement is made.
- The right to:
  - receive all notices relating to any general meeting of the company
  - attend any general meeting
  - be heard at any general meeting on any part of the business which concerns them as auditor.

  It is obviously important for the proper discharge of their duties that auditors should be aware at first hand of what happens at meetings. Their right to speak at a meeting does *not*, if exercised, relieve them of the duty to make a comprehensive audit report to the members. If the auditor's competence is attacked, they will stand or fall entirely on what they have put, or failed to put, in their report attached to the balance sheet.
- The right to be sent by the company a copy of a notice of intention to propose their removal or replacement and the right to make *written representations*. This is in addition to their *duty* to make a statement of circumstances.

  These rights ensure that the auditor cannot be removed from office without having the opportunity of placing all the facts before members. In this connection, it is stressed that the fact that *directors* have lost confidence in the auditor is not of itself a valid reason for seeking the auditor's removal – what counts is the confidence of the members.
- The right to require the directors to requisition an extraordinary general meeting on resignation, and to attend and be heard at that and any other meeting which concerns them.

6.3 Rights of private companies under the elective regime

KEY POINT

Private companies may take advantage of the '**elective regime'** not to reappoint auditors annually. Auditors have certain rights under this regime.

Private companies may take advantage of the so-called **elective regime**. This means that a private company may elect by a **unanimously** agreed resolution:

- not to have *annual* reappointment of auditors if it so elects, then the auditors, once appointed, remain in office, and are deemed to be reappointed, whilst the election remains in force
- not to lay accounts before the members in general meeting – the accounts must instead be circulated to members.

In connection with this elective regime, the auditor has the following rights:

- to receive copies of background papers and written resolutions proposed to be agreed under the elective regime
- to be given notice that a resolution concerns them as auditor and should be considered in general meeting – the auditor has the power to attend and be heard at such a meeting
- to demand that a company which has taken advantage of the regime should hold a general meeting at which the accounts are laid.

7 Audit reports of listed companies

UK listed companies must comply with the rules of the Stock Exchange, as well as the general requirements of the Companies Acts.

The Combined Code on Corporate Governance of the Stock Exchange requires that directors of listed companies must report to shareholders on the effectiveness of the system of internal controls. The auditor must review this report. The auditor's additional responsibilities in the audit of a listed company are reflected in an additional paragraph in the audit report describing the responsibilities of directors and auditors. This is not examinable in this paper.

8 Regulation by the UK accounting and auditing profession

8.1 The structure of the UK accounting and auditing profession

KEY POINT

Professional accountancy bodies in the UK include: ACCA, ICAEW, ICAS, ICAI, CIPFA and CIMA.

In the UK there are a number of professional accountancy bodies.

- The **Association of Chartered Certified Accountants** (ACCA) – Members qualify in industry, commerce or the public sector, or in a practising firm. Once a practising certificate is gained they can audit limited companies.
- The **Institute of Chartered Accountants in England and Wales** (ICAEW)
- The **Institute of Chartered Accountants of Scotland** (ICAS)
- The **Institute of Chartered Accountants in Ireland** (ICAI) – Members of these three bodies qualify mainly in a practising firm, though some train outside public practice. Once a practising certificate is gained they can audit limited companies.
- The **Chartered Institute of Public Finance and Accountancy** (CIPFA) – Members qualify by working in the public sector (local government, etc.). They do not audit limited companies, but do audit other enterprises, mainly public sector bodies.
- The **Chartered Institute of Management Accountants** (CIMA) – Training does not involve external auditing, and members are not allowed to act as external auditors.

Between them, these six bodies comprise the **Consultative Committee of Accountancy Bodies** (CCAB). The CCAB co-ordinates UK accounting and auditing activities, and liaises with international accounting bodies.

The same professional bodies are relevant to internal auditing. However, in addition there is a specialist professional body: the **Institute of Internal Auditors – UK and Ireland**. Internal auditors can qualify in either the public or the private sector.

Initially, internal audit was part of the accounting profession but increasingly this is changing. For internal audit and review, there is a more diverse range of qualifications and experience required by organisations. Whilst external auditors must be accountants, there is no similar requirement for internal auditors. Internal auditors are not required to be accountants or qualified internal auditors but can be specialists in the type of activity undertaken by the business.

8.2 Eligibility to conduct company audits

KEY POINT

To conduct company audits an auditor must be:

- a member of a recognised supervisory body (RSB)
- eligible under the rules of the RSB.

In order to be eligible to conduct company audits an auditor must be:

- a member of a recognised supervisory body (RSB)
- eligible under the rules of the RSB.

The idea of RSBs was introduced by the Companies Act 1989. The current RSBs are:

- the Association of Chartered Certified Accountants (ACCA)
- the Institute of Chartered Accountants in England and Wales (ICAEW)
- the Institute of Chartered Accountants of Scotland (ICAS)
- the Institute of Chartered Accountants in Ireland (ICAI)
- the Association of Authorised Public Accountants (a small body) (AAPA).

Not all members of RSBs are eligible to conduct company audits. Broadly speaking, it is necessary to obtain a practising certificate from an RSB which involves 2 to 3 years' post-qualification experience in a practising office.

8.3 Rules of Recognised Supervisory Bodies

The rules of the RSBs must ensure that the following persons only are eligible for appointment as company auditor:

- individuals who hold appropriate qualifications
- firms controlled by qualified persons.

An auditor may be an individual, a firm or a body corporate (i.e. a company). You should be aware that large practising firms have traditionally operated as partnerships, but that some of them are now plcs.

The CA 1989 specifies that a firm is 'controlled by' qualified persons if 51% of the ownership and control is in the hands of qualified persons.

The rules and practices of the RSBs must be such as to ensure that only 'fit and proper' persons can be appointed as company auditors. This takes into account their professional conduct.

An RSB's rule book must therefore cover the monitoring and enforcement of compliance, admission, expulsion and disciplinary procedures, complaints investigation and the adequacy of professional indemnity insurance cover.

The Association's 'Qualification and Audit Regulations' came into force in 1991, and are effectively the ACCA's rule book as an RSB.

8.4 Recognised qualifying bodies

KEY POINT

Membership of an RSB requires a qualification obtained from a **recognised qualifying body** (RQB).

Membership of an RSB requires a qualification obtained from a recognised qualifying body (RQB). All of the RSBs noted above with the exception of the AAPA are also RQBs.

In applying for authorisation as an RQB the organisation must comply with the defined entry, examination and practical training requirements.

8.5 Regulation of the accounting and auditing professions

KEY POINT

The FRC is an independent regulator of the accountancy profession in the UK.

Following the failures of WorldCom and Enron, a 'Review of the Regulatory Regime of the Accountancy Profession' was published in 2002. The report's main purpose was to look at the way the accountancy and audit professions are currently regulated, and to consider improvements.

The key recommendations in the report were:

- establish a 'new' FRC taking on the functions of the Accountancy Foundation and thus creating an independent regulator
- the APB to have responsibility for setting standards for independence, objectivity and integrity for all auditors
- a new Audit Inspection Unit to be created
- the Professional Oversight Board to be granted additional responsibilities
- the planned Investigation and Discipline Board to be established as soon as possible.

The Financial Reporting Council

The Financial Reporting Council (FRC) is a unified, independent regulator responsible for:

- setting accounting and auditing standards
- enforcing and monitoring these standards
- overseeing the self regulatory professional bodies.

It is structured as follows:

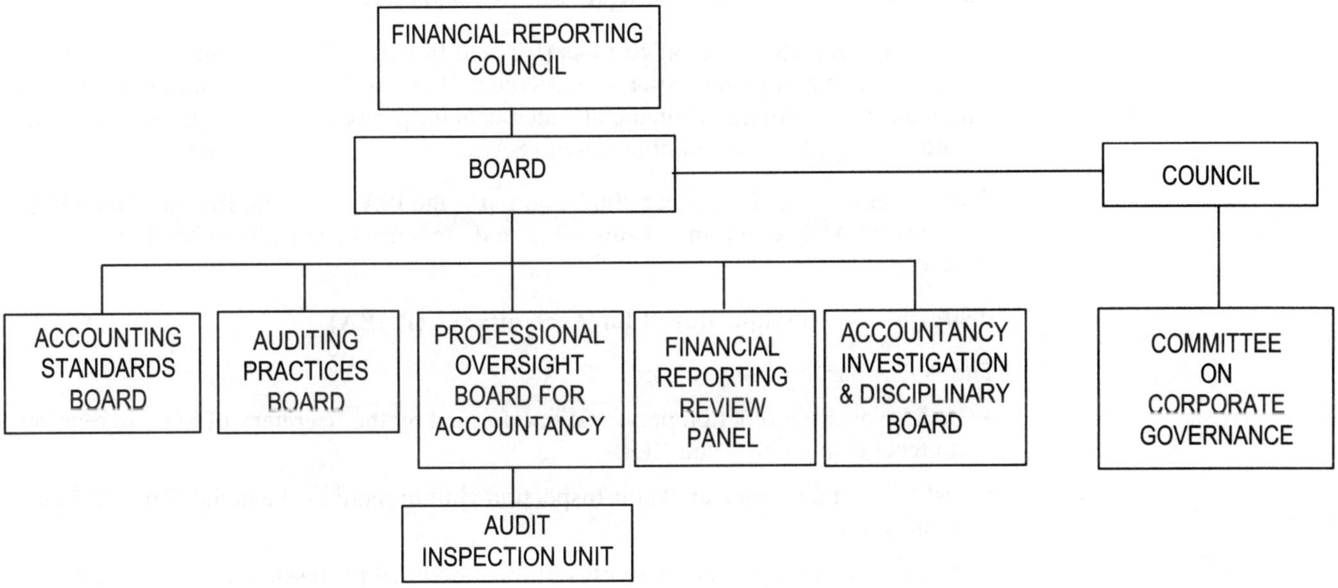

Accounting Standards Board (ASB)

The ASB makes, amends and withdraws accounting standards (FRSs). There are four committees supporting their work i.e. Urgent Issues Task Force, the Financial Sector and Other Special Industries Committee, the Public Sector and Not-for-Profit Committee and the Committee on Accounting for Smaller Entities.

With effect from 1 January 2005, all listed companies must prepare their consolidated financial statements in compliance with International Accounting Standards (IASs) issued by the IASB. UK accounting standards, as issued by the ASB, continue to be used by unlisted companies, although they too can choose to adopt IASs.

The ASB believe that it is unsatisfactory to have a choice between two widely different sets of accounting standards, so will be working over the next few years to eliminate the differences between UK standards and international standards.

Auditing Practices Board (APB)

The APB is responsible for developing and publishing UK auditing standards, and ensuring their application to enhance confidence in the auditing process. It is also responsible for the development of ethical standards relating to the independence, objectivity and integrity of auditors.

Until 2004, the APB issued Statements of Auditing Standards (SASs) which had to be used in all audits carried out in the UK and Ireland. However, as with the ASB, the APB has become increasingly influenced by international developments.

The International Auditing and Assurance Standards Board (IAASB), based in New York, has issued a comprehensive suite of high quality auditing standards which, in some areas, were seen as stronger than SASs. The APB therefore had a choice:

- it could try to ignore the fact that International Standards on Auditing (ISAs) existed
- it could amend the existing SASs for the improvements necessary to bring them up to the quality of ISAs
- it could adopt the ISAs wholesale, adding any additional material into the standards believed necessary to maintain the quality of UK auditing standards.

In 2004 the APB decided on the third of these options. It is likely that the EU will require the use of ISAs by member states in the future, so it is most efficient to adopt ISAs now, and hopefully reduce the amount of supplementary material added to the standards over time as the IAASB revises its standards.

The supplements ISAs are called ISAs (UK and Ireland). All audits of UK companies for periods beginning on or after 15 December 2004 must be carried out in compliance with these ISAs. Audits of financial statements for periods beginning before that date should be carried out in compliance with SASs.

With effect from the December 2005 exam, it is the ISAs (UK and Ireland) that will be examined in ACCA auditing exams. This study text has been fully updated to reflect these ISAs.

Professional Oversight Board for Accountancy (POBA)

The POBA has three key roles:

- to take over the function previously performed by the Secretary of State in relation to recognising RSBs and RQBs
- establish and oversee an Audit Inspection Unit to monitor the audit of major listed companies
- to oversee the regulatory activities of the individual professional accountancy bodies.

Financial Reporting Review Panel (FRRP)

The FRRP investigates any apparent departures from the Companies Act 1985 accounting requirements in large companies' accounts. If necessary it can apply to the courts to obtain corrective action.

Accountancy Investigation and Discipline Board (AIDB)

The AIDB manages an investigation and disciplinary scheme to handle public interest cases. The Government has clearly stated that this scheme should be one of the new FRC's priorities.

These new responsibilities that the FRC now has were previously undertaken by the Accountancy Foundation which was a self regulatory body established by the Accountancy Bodies. Although the FRC is the parent of the subsidiary boards, they are independent in their operation and are all companies limited by guarantee.

The FRC and its subsidiaries are currently supported and funded jointly by the accountancy profession, business and the Government.

Committee on Corporate Governance

The final FRC responsibility is to monitor standards of corporate governance and issue necessary changes to the Combined Code. This is covered later in this text.

8.6 APB Guidance

APB guidance on auditing now falls into **three** categories which are described as follows:

1 ISAs (UK and Ireland)

KEY POINT

International Standards on Auditing contain the basic principles and essential procedures with which auditors are expected to comply, along with explanatory material.

International Standards on Auditing contain the basic principles and essential procedures with which auditors are expected to comply (which are presented in bold type) along with explanatory material (in plain type). Failure to comply with standards may lead to regulatory action by the relevant accountancy body which might ultimately lead to the loss of audit registration (the right to conduct company audits). Standards are also taken into account in legal proceedings.

It is the IAASB that will develop new ISAs in the future; the APB will review the new ISA and supplement it where necessary, before issuing it as a new ISA (UK and Ireland).

2 Practice Notes (PNs)

PNs give guidance to assist auditors in applying auditing standards in particular circumstances and industries.

3 Bulletins

Bulletins provide auditors with timely guidance on new or emerging issues.

PNs and Bulletins have the same status as explanatory material in ISAs i.e. that they are persuasive rather than prescriptive. However, they do indicate what is considered to be good practice. They may be issued without the full consultation and exposure process that is used for ISAs.

Other categories of statement

It many be helpful to consider the range of APB pronouncements in the diagram below.

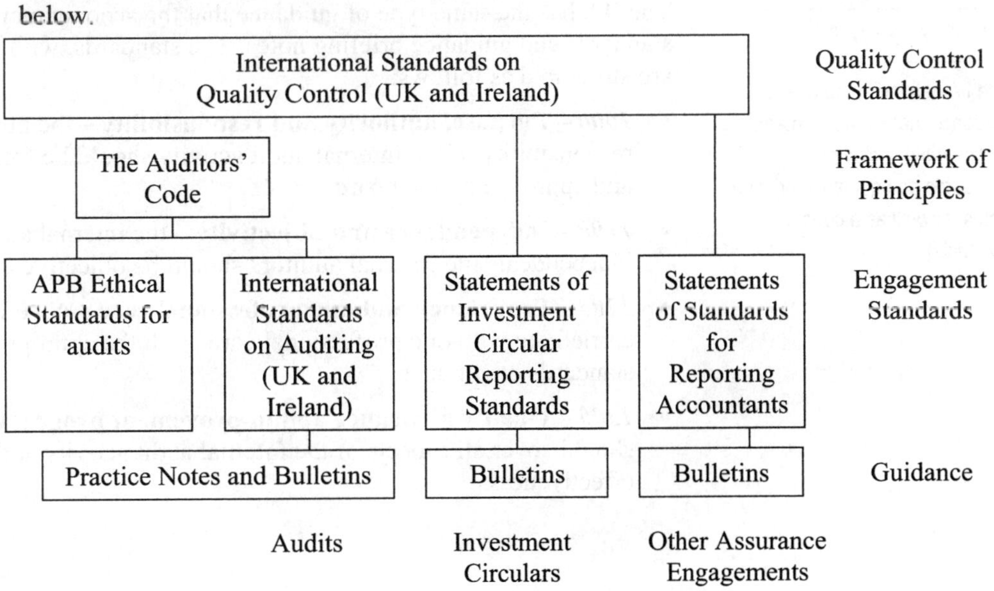

International Standards on Quality Control (ISQCs) aim to ensure quality control standards in assurance engagements and other related services.

The Auditors' Code provides a framework of fundamental principles governing the conduct of audits.

APB Ethical Standards for audits ensure that independence, objectivity and integrity of external auditors.

ISAs (UK and Ireland) establish the principles and procedures that auditors must follow in the conduct of their audit.

Statements of Investment Circular Reporting Standards (SIRs) establish the principles that reporting accountants must follow in their work on documents issued in connection with an investment opportunity, e.g. on the issue of shares offered to the public on the flotation of a company.

Statements of Standards for Reporting Accountants (SSRAs) establish the principles that reporting accountants must follow in connection with work other than audit on reporting on investment circulars.

Practice Notes and Bulletins offer non-mandatory guidance.

The APB documents that are currently examinable are listed at the start of this text.

8.7 Institute of Internal Auditors (IIA)

KEY POINT

The **Institute of Internal Auditors**, a worldwide body for internal auditing, has its own standards and guidelines for internal auditors.

The Institute of Internal Auditors is a worldwide body for internal auditing, with national bodies for the Institute established in many different countries. In this country, the national institute is the Institute of Internal Auditors – UK and Ireland.

The IIA has its own standards and guidelines for internal auditors. These are not mandatory for all internal auditors but are relevant and applicable to those internal auditors who are members of the IIA.

There is an international qualification in internal auditing, which has its origins in the US and North America, but is the recognised qualification in many other countries. This is the CIA (Certified Internal Auditor), which has reciprocity with the UK qualification.

The IIA published a new definition of internal auditing recently and are currently updating their other standards. This definition (see Chapter 4) places greater emphasis on the consultancy nature of internal auditing and on risk, recognising some of the key trends in internal audit. The Institute also recognise that not all internal auditors will belong to in-house departments but could be provided through an outsourced service.

KEY POINT

The IIA has the same type of guidance that the accountancy bodies have, including standards and guidance briefing notes, as well as a code of conduct.

The IIA has the same type of guidance that the accountancy bodies have, including standards and guidance briefing notes. The standards, with accompanying guidance, are structured as follows:

- ***1000* – Purpose, authority and responsibility** – the purpose, authority and responsibility of the internal audit activity should be formally defined in a charter, and approved by the board.
- ***1100* – Independence and objectivity** – the internal audit activity should be independent, and internal auditors should be objective in performing their work.
- ***1200* – Proficiency and due professional care** – covering the need for audit to be carried out with due professional care, with the appropriate skills and training, and standards of conduct.
- ***1300* – Quality assurance and improvement programme** – such a programme should cover all aspects of the internal audit activity and continuously monitor its effectiveness.

- ***2000* – Managing the internal audit activity** – the chief internal auditor should effectively manage the internal audit activity to ensure that it adds value to the organisation.
- ***2100* – Nature of work** – internal audit should evaluate and contribute to the improvement of risk management, control and governance processes using a disciplined approach.
- ***2200* – Engagement planning** – each engagement should be planned, and the plan recorded.
- ***2300* – Performing the engagement** – sufficient information should be identified and recorded to achieve the engagement's objectives.
- ***2400* – Communicating results** – internal auditors should communicate the engagement results.
- ***2500* – Monitoring progress** – results communicated to management should be monitored.
- ***2600* – Management's acceptance of risks** – the chief internal auditor should discuss with senior management the level of residual risk in the organisation.

The IIA has a code of ethics, setting out how all internal auditors should operate including the need for integrity, objectivity, confidentiality and competency.

8.8 Other influences

The role of the government in overseeing the auditing and accounting profession

Auditors carry out their task because of the legal obligations imposed upon companies to have an audit. As a consequence of this, it is reasonable for the government to frame statutes and regulations within which auditors must work.

It is the government which decides to what extent the audit function and the auditing profession are regulated. Auditors have always argued for self-regulation, and the government has sanctioned this approach in the RSB and RQB system which we examined earlier.

This does not mean however that the government is not monitoring the profession. A government representative observes at APB meetings, the Department of Trade and Industry issues continuing requirements for additional reports (especially in the financial services sector), and it has abolished the requirement for the audit of small companies.

DTI

KEY POINT

The detailed monitoring of the auditing profession is largely carried out by the **Department of Trade and Industry** (DTI).

The detailed monitoring of the auditing profession is largely carried out by a government department, the Department of Trade and Industry (DTI). The government minister responsible for the DTI is the Secretary of State for Trade and Industry.

EU and European Directives

KEY POINT

The **European Union** (EU) issues Directives, some of which (such as those on company law) have an impact on audit practice.

The European Union (EU) issues Directives, some of which (such as those on company law) have an impact on audit practice. For example, the 8th Company Law Directive was the Directive which resulted in the RSB system being introduced in the UK by the CA89.

More recently, the EU has proposed a voluntary community environmental auditing scheme. This aims to improve the impact that a company has on the environment. Environmental auditing is covered later in the text.

International auditing bodies

KEY POINT

International auditing bodies include the International Federation of Accountants (IFAC) and, in the EU, the FEE (Fédération des Experts Comptables Européens).

The IAASB is a committee of IFAC, the International Federation of Accountants.

The APB works closely with the IAASB to help develop new ISAs. The APB's hope is that future ISAs will include the best points of previous SASs, so that convergence of UK and international auditing standards will include the best of both sources.

In the EU, the FEE (Fédération des Experts Comptables Européens) attempts to co-ordinate the activities of European accountancy bodies, but does not publish standards.

9 Changing regulatory framework

9.1 Company Law Review

KEY POINT

The DTI's fundamental review of core company law offers a major simplification and re-structuring for small private companies and important changes for larger companies

The DTI launched a fundamental review of core company law in March 1998, with the aim of developing a simple, modern, efficient and cost-effective framework for carrying out business activity in the 21st century. An independent steering group was formed and has published a number of consultation documents, including a wide range of proposals on corporate governance and technical issues.

A final report was presented to the Secretary of State in July 2001. The Government then published its response and detailed its key proposals for reform in July 2002.

The Company Law Review made a number of recommendations specifically related to small companies:

- simplification of the statutory decision making requirements
- simplification of other legal issues (including constitution, directors' duties, shareholder disputes and purchase of own shares)
- reduction in accounting and auditing requirements (including increasing the audit threshold)
- simplifying private company legislation.

To date the government has legislated to increase the audit threshold for small companies to £5.6m, and to require large companies to publish a statutory operating and financial review each year. Further legislative changes may be made by the incoming government following the General Election in May 2005.

The proposals will clearly be important for both internal and external auditors. Internal auditors will need to be aware of the impact on corporate governance requirements, whilst external auditors will need to understand the requirements for scope of audit and liability, as well as the new accounting framework and reporting requirements.

9.2 European requirements

KEY POINT

The **European Union** has been reviewing the requirements for auditing and accounting as an important contribution to the establishing and functioning of the Single Market.

The European Union has been reviewing the requirements for auditing as an important contribution to the establishing and functioning of the Single Market, whereby accounts prepared by European companies are audited by an independent and qualified professional in accordance with auditing standards that are accepted world-wide.

A committee on auditing has been established by the European Commission. They have been reviewing the existing International Standards on Auditing developed by the IAASB and discussing audit independence, quality control, professional competence, the position of the statutory auditor within the company, and the role of internal audit. It is expected that in future the EU will insist on ISAs being applied to audits throughout Europe.

This would mirror the earlier EU decision that all European listed companies must prepare their consolidated accounts in accordance with IASs with effect from 1 January 2005.

10 Public sector auditing

10.1 Statutory arrangements

KEY POINT

Public sector auditing is the responsibility of the National Audit Office, Audit Commission and relevant Minister (Secretary of State). Private firms of accountants may also be appointed to audit public sector organisations.

Firms of accountants who spend most of their time carrying out external audits may also be employed in the audit of public sector organisations. If so, they will carry out their functions within the framework laid down by statute other than the Companies Act.

The statutory arrangements for auditing each of the elements of the public sector is shown below.

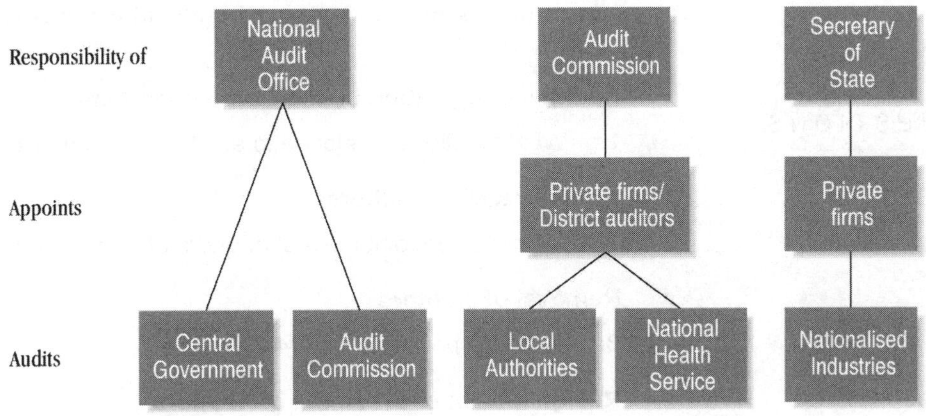

10.2 The National Audit Office

The Comptroller and Auditor General (C&AG) is head of the National Audit Office. As head of that office, the C&AG has three main responsibilities:

- control of issues and receipts of government funds
- regulatory audits of government departments
- discretionary reviews (including value for money reviews).

In carrying out these responsibilities, the C&AG will examine, certify and report upon the appropriation accounts (these are the main accounts of government departments).

10.3 The Audit Commission

The Audit Commission was set up under the Local Government Finance Act 1982 and its main responsibilities are noted below:

- appointment of auditors (after consultation with local authorities)
- preparation and review of a code of audit practice
- direction of extraordinary audits
- undertaking comparative and other studies of economy, efficiency and effectiveness
- publication of an annual report on the discharge of its functions.

10.4 The Secretary of State

One of the many duties of the relevant Minister (Secretary of State) is to appoint private firms of accountants to undertake the audit of nationalised industries. The audit is carried out in a similar fashion to that of large public limited companies (plcs) in the private sector, the similarity being that both nationalised industries and plcs are large organisations run on commercial lines.

Conclusion

The auditor must keep up-to-date with the regulatory framework for auditing, both internal and external. There are increasing demands on auditors, for example to provide support to comply with the corporate governance requirements arising from a Stock Exchange listing. The auditor has duties and a long list of rights under the Companies Act.

An essential feature of the protection of the powers of the auditor is the requirement for a company to appoint an auditor in the first place and secondly the auditor must be given some rights regarding his removal from office. The company law review and new auditing standards will significantly affect internal and external auditors.

SELF-TEST QUESTIONS

Auditing – regulation by the Companies Acts

1 What functions in relation to auditing are achieved by the Companies Acts? (2.1)

Appointment of auditors

2 Who may appoint the first auditors of a company? (3.1)

Removal of auditors

3 What is special notice? (4.2)

Resignation and retirement of auditors

4 What action should a company take if the auditor resigns prior to completion of his term of office? (5.2)

Auditors' rights and duties

5 What are the duties of the auditor under the Companies Acts? (6.1)

6 What is the elective regime for private companies? (6.3)

Regulation by the UK accounting and auditing profession

7 What are the five operating subsidiaries of the FRC board? (8.5)

8 What is the role of the FRC? (8.5)

9 Who originally issues ISAs? (8.5)

10 What is the role of the POBA? (8.5)

11 What does IIA stand for and what is its position in relation to internal auditors? (8.7)

Changing regulatory framework

12 What is the Company Law Review and how will it affect internal and external auditors? (9.1)

Public sector auditing

13 What is the responsibility of the NAO? (10.2)

14 What is the responsibility of the Audit Commission? (10.3)

EXAM-TYPE QUESTION

Growfast plc

Growfast plc was formed on 1 August in order to manufacture personal computers. The directors are unsure as to their responsibilities, and the nature of their relationship with the external auditors. The audit partner has asked you to visit the client and explain to the directors the more fundamental aspects of the accountability.

You are required to explain to the directors of Growfast plc:

(a) why there is a need for an audit **(5 marks)**

(b) how the auditor of a public company may be appointed under CA85 **(5 marks)**

(c) what the auditor's rights are under the CA85 **(6 marks)**

(d) the responsibilities of the directors in relation to the accounting function of the company. **(4 marks)**

(ACCA Level 2 Auditing, December 1990) **(Total: 20 marks)**

For the answer to this question, see the 'Answers' section at the end of the book.

FEEDBACK TO ACTIVITY **1**

Compliance with regulations is a key risk area for auditors, whether internal or external. Changes in regulations therefore could present additional risk to the auditor.

However, regulations could impact on the role of the auditor, particularly in the area of corporate governance. The auditor therefore needs to keep up-to-date because:

- the impact on the audit role must be anticipated at an early stage so that auditors can be geared up to meet any new or changing demands
- it may impact on the status of auditing (for example if internal auditing was to be made a mandatory function by the EU, with clearly defined roles and responsibilities)
- it may impact on the amount of work undertaken - for example where additional corporate governance demands are in place, the role of audit tends to be more prominent, resulting in additional work.

FEEDBACK TO ACTIVITY **2**

A person is qualified to act as an auditor of a company if that person:

- is a member of a recognised supervisory body (RSB); and
- is eligible for the appointment under the rules of that body.

Membership via qualification with a recognised qualifying body (RQB) is a prerequisite of membership of an RSB.

The RQB must comply with Government regulations as to entry, examinations and training.

Chapter 3

PROFESSIONAL ETHICS AND CODES OF CONDUCT

CHAPTER CONTENTS

This chapter covers some fundamental principles and concepts that affect auditing, namely ethical matters that auditors need to bear in mind in carrying out their duties. You may find some of the issues quite difficult to appreciate at this relatively early stage in your study of auditing; it will be worth revisiting this chapter when you have covered the entire audit process.

Ethical issues will continually be tested throughout the accounting and auditing examinations.

Objectives

By the time you have finished this chapter you should be able to:

- describe the sources of, and enforcement mechanisms associated with, professional ethics and professional codes of conduct
- define the fundamental concepts of professional ethics
- define the detailed requirements of, and illustrate and analyse the application of, professional ethics in the context of independence, objectivity and integrity
- describe the requirements of professional ethics and other requirements in relation to the acceptance of audit and review assignments
- define the detailed requirements of, and illustrate and analyse the application of, professional ethics in the context of confidentiality and conflicts of interest
- describe the importance of engagement letters and describe their contents.

1 The ethical base of auditing

There are two sources of basic ethical principles that ACCA-qualified auditors must follow:

(i) the ACCA Rules of Professional Conduct, comprising a Code of Ethics and Professional Conduct Regulations

(ii) the Auditors' Code issued by the APB.

More detailed guidance is given in the APB's Ethical Standards for audits, issued in December 2004.

1.1 Code of Ethics – fundamental principles

There are five fundamental principles within the code of ethics which ALL members are obliged to follow whether or not they are in public practice, these are:

KEY POINT

The fundamental principles cover the following matters:

- integrity
- objectivity
- competence
- skill, care, diligence and expedition, following technical and professional standards
- courtesy and consideration.

- Members should behave with **integrity** in all professional, business and personal financial relationships. Integrity implies not merely honesty but fair dealing and truthfulness.
- Members should strive for **objectivity** in all professional and business judgements. Objectivity is the state of mind which has regard to all considerations relevant to the task in hand but no other. It presupposes intellectual honesty.
- Members should not accept or perform work which they are not **competent** to undertake, unless they obtain such advice and assistance as will enable them competently to carry out the work.
- Members should carry out their professional work with due **skill, care, diligence** and **expedition**, and with proper regard for the technical and professional **standards** expected of them as members.
- Members should conduct themselves with **courtesy** and **consideration** towards all with whom they come into contact during the course of performing their work.

1.2 Code of Ethics – key areas

The key areas covered by the Code of Ethics are:

- integrity, objectivity and independence
- duty of confidentiality
- conflicts of interest.

1.3 Professional conduct regulations

These regulations include the following key areas:

- money laundering
- whistle-blowing
- advertising, publicity and obtaining professional work
- changes in professional appointment
- professional liability of accountants and auditors
- ownership of documents and papers
- fees
- client monies
- Financial Services and Markets Act 2000.

1.4 The Auditors' Code

The APB has issued a framework of fundamental principles which it expects to guide the conduct of auditors. These principles are:

- accountability
- integrity
- objectivity and independence
- competence
- rigour
- judgement

- clear, complete and effective communication
- association – allowing their reports only to be included in documents if the report is consistent with the whole document
- providing value.

1.5 Ethical standards for audits

In December 2004 the APB issued the following standards:

- ES 1 – Integrity, objectivity and independence
- ES 2 – Financial, business, employment and personal relationships
- ES 3 – Long association with the audit engagement
- ES 4 – Fees, remuneration and evaluation policies, litigation, gifts and hospitality
- ES 5 – Non-audit services provided to audit clients
- ES – Provisions available to small entities

You can see that several of the above topics are covered in more than one document. The remainder of this chapter covers the topics in the depth that you need for your exam.

1.6 Application to internal auditors

KEY POINT

The code of the **Institute of Internal Auditors** (IIA) places obligations on internal auditors to uphold four key principles:

- integrity
- objectivity
- confidentiality
- competency.

Internal auditors have the same obligations to comply with relevant codes of conduct. In particular, the **Institute of Internal Auditors** (IIA) has its own code, which has a number of similar ethical requirements to those of the ACCA. The IIA issued a new code of ethics and international standards for the professional practice of internal auditing with effect from January 2004, replacing earlier codes of ethics from 2000 and 1994. The most recent code of ethics continues to require auditors to apply and uphold four key principles:

- integrity
- objectivity
- confidentiality
- competency.

The code applies to both individuals and entities that provide internal auditing services. Breaches by members are evaluated according to IIA disciplinary procedures. The fact that a particular conduct is not specifically mentioned does not prevent it from being unacceptable or discreditable and therefore the member is liable to disciplinary action. Supporting the key principles are rules of conduct that describe the behaviour norms expected of internal auditors described in the table below.

Key principle	*Rules of conduct*
Integrity	• Perform their work with honesty, diligence and responsibility. • Observe the law and make disclosures expected by the law and the profession. • Not knowingly be a party to any illegal activity, or engage in acts that are discreditable to the profession of internal auditing or the organisation. • Respect and contribute to the legitimate and ethical objectives of the organisation.

Objectivity	•	Not participate in any activity or relationship that may impair or be presumed to impair their unbiased assessment. This includes those activities or relationships that may be in conflict with the interests of the organisation.
	•	Not accept anything that may impair or be presumed to impair their professional judgement.
	•	Disclose all material facts known to them that, if not disclosed, may distort the reporting of activities under review.
Confidentiality	•	Be prudent in the use and protection of information acquired in the course of their duties.
	•	Not use information for any personal gain or in a way that would be contrary to the law or detrimental to the legitimate and ethical objectives of the organisation.
Competency	•	Engage only in those services for which they have the necessary knowledge, skills and experience.
	•	Perform internal auditing services in accordance with the Standards for the Professional Practice of internal auditing.
	•	Continually improve their proficiency and the effectiveness and quality of their services.

2 Integrity, objectivity and independence

This section of the ACCA Rules deals with independence in an audit and non-audit context. We are primarily concerned with the former.

KEY POINT

The basic principle of **independence** states that a member's objectivity must be beyond question if they are to report as auditor.

The basic principle states that a member's objectivity must be beyond question if they are to report as auditor. That objectivity can only be assured if the member *is*, and *is seen to be,* independent.

2.1 Ethics and the Auditing Practices Board

The APB has issued its suite of Ethical Standards for audits, including ES 1 on integrity, objectivity and independence. The Professional Oversight Board for Accountancy will monitor wider ethical matters.

By giving the responsibility for Ethical Standards of audit to the APB and granting powers to the POBA this should help to strengthen auditor independence by having common standards across the profession. This is a particularly important area as, following the failure of Enron, it has been widely agreed that stronger mechanisms are required to ensure auditor independence.

In general, the ACCA rules from the Rules of Professional Conduct are more specific than the Auditors' Code or the APB Ethical Standards, so below we study the detail of the ACCA rules.

2.2 Integrity, objectivity and independence – areas of risk: members in practice

KEY POINT

Dependence on income from a particular client or group of clients may impair objectivity. Recurring fees paid by one client or group of connected clients should not exceed 15% (or 10% for listed companies) of the gross practice income.

Undue dependence on an audit client

It is recognised that a dependence on income from a particular client or group of clients may impair objectivity. A firm which derives most of its income from one client, for instance, may find it difficult to make a stand on a particular issue, as the loss of that client (either through the auditor's removal or resignation) would have a disastrous effect on the firm's financial position.

It is therefore recommended that recurring fees paid by one client or group of connected clients should not exceed 15% of the gross practice income (this requirement is relaxed for those years when a practice is being established or wound down).

However, where the public interest is involved (for example, in the case of listed and other public interest companies), the appropriate figure should be 10% of the gross practice income.

Where one particular office within a practice derives income over these limits, but the practice as a whole is not affected, the final reporting responsibility for the audit should be transferred to another office.

If clients are retained above these limits, special safeguards should be set up. Where fee income from one client exceeds 10% (5% in the case of public interest companies), review procedures should be triggered.

Family and other personal relationships

Problems may arise where:

- a practice or anyone closely connected with it has a mutual business interest with a client, or with an officer or employee of a client
- an officer or employee is closely connected with a partner or member of staff.

The following persons would normally be regarded as being closely connected with a *person:*

- spouse
- minor children (including stepchildren)
- a company in which the person has a ≥ 20% interest.

The following persons should normally be regarded as being closely connected with a *practice:*

- a partner, or in the case of a corporate practice, a director or shareholder
- a person closely connected with a partner, director or shareholder
- an employee of the practice.

KEY POINT

A **family** or other **close relationship** may pose a threat to independence, and safeguards should be in place to preserve independence.

These categories are not exhaustive. For example, persons not related in any way by blood or marriage, may nevertheless enjoy a friendship closer than any blood relationship. The auditor must always bear in mind the need to maintain not merely independence, but also the manifest appearance of independence.

The threat to independence may be less where a partner or senior member of staff is not personally engaged on the audit in question, where their office is distant from the reporting office and where effective safeguards are in place in the internal procedures of the practice. Such safeguards might include rotation of the engagement partner and/or of senior members of staff. Similarly, a connection with a junior member of staff of the practice is less likely to be a threat than a connection with a senior member of staff or partner.

A member should not personally take part in the conduct of the audit of a company if they have, during the period upon which the report is to be made, or at any time in the two years prior to the first day thereof, been an officer (other than auditor) or employee of that company.

KEY POINT

A practice should ensure that it does not have as an audit client a company in which any partner or anyone closely connected with a partner **holds shares** (or has a beneficial interest in shares).

Beneficial interests in shares and other investments

A practice should ensure that it does not have as an audit client a company in which any partner or anyone closely connected with a partner holds shares (or has a beneficial interest in shares). The practice should not employ on the audit a member of staff if that member of staff, or a person closely connected with them, holds shares (or has a beneficial interest in shares) in the client.

Shares inherited or acquired by marriage should be disposed of at the earliest practicable opportunity, being a date at which the transaction would not amount to insider dealing. Similar rules apply where a company becomes a new audit client.

There are further rules covering situations in which partners and employees are either trustees of trusts holding shares in client companies, or beneficiaries of such trusts, or both.

Loans

KEY POINT

A practice or anyone closely connected with it should not make or accept **loans** to or **guarantees** from an audit client.

Again, independence may be threatened.

A practice or anyone closely connected with it should not, either directly or indirectly:

- make a loan to or guarantee borrowings by an audit client
- accept a loan from such a client
- have borrowings or other obligations guaranteed by such a client.

This does not normally preclude:

- an account in credit with a client clearing bank or similar financial institution
- a loan, overdraft or home mortgage being accepted from a client provided it is in the normal course of business and on normal commercial terms – the loan must not be applied as subscription to the firm's capital and if the recipient is a partner, they must not be the engagement partner.

Goods and services: hospitality

KEY POINT

Goods or services should not be accepted by a practice or by anyone closely connected with it unless the value of any benefit is modest.

Objectivity may be threatened or appear to be threatened by acceptance of goods, services or hospitality from an audit client.

Goods or services should not be accepted by a practice or by anyone closely connected with it unless the value of any benefit is modest.

Acceptance of undue hospitality poses a similar threat.

Provision of other services to audit clients

KEY POINT

There is no objection in principle to the **provision of other services** to audit clients, but care must be taken not to perform management functions or to make management decisions.

There is no objection in principle to this, but care must be taken not to perform management functions or to make management decisions. Essentially, the key factor is that there is no conflict of interest between the audit and the other services provided.

Accountancy work, however, should not be performed for a public company except in relation to assistance of a routine clerical nature or in emergency situations. Such assistance might include, for example, work on the finalisation of statutory accounts, including consolidations and tax provisions. The scale and nature of such work should be regularly reviewed.

In all cases in which a practice is concerned in the preparation of accounting records for an audit client, the following safeguards should be observed:

- The client should accept responsibility for the records as its own.
- The practice should not assume the role of management conducting the operations of an enterprise.
- The practice should make appropriate audit tests even where it has processed or maintained certain records.

In general, a member should be careful not to go beyond an advisory role and drift into the management sphere.

KEY POINT

The existence of significant **overdue fees** can be a threat to objectivity.

Overdue fees

The existence of significant overdue fees can be a threat to objectivity (or appear to be). Before work is started on an audit, the situation should be reviewed to ascertain whether the overdue fees, taken together with the fees for the current assignment, could be regarded as a significant loan, in which case the area of risk described above comes into play.

KEY POINT

Objectivity may be threatened (or appear to be) where there is actual or threatened **litigation** between auditor and client.

Actual or threatened litigation

Objectivity may be threatened (or appear to be) where there is actual or threatened litigation between auditor and client. The adversarial position would call into question the auditor's ability to report fairly and impartially on the company's accounts. In an action, under the circumstances, management may be unwilling to disclose relevant information to the auditor.

The rules do not specify precisely the point at which it would become improper for a firm to continue as auditor, as it would be impossible to do so. However, if a writ has been issued for negligence, this would generally impair independence. A writ in respect of unpaid fees would not generally do so, unless the amounts involved were significant.

Associated firms: influences outside the practice

Pressures may arise from outside the practice from associated practices or organisations, or from other external sources such as bankers, solicitors, government or those introducing business. The firm's review machinery should be designed to deal with this.

KEY POINT

Where a partner or member of staff **holds shares** in an audit client company, they should not vote at any general meeting on audit appointments.

Voting on audit appointments

Where a partner or member of staff holds shares in any capacity in an audit client company, they should not vote at any general meeting of the company in relation to the appointment, removal or remuneration of auditors. It is occasionally necessary for auditors to hold such shares under the articles of association of older companies.

Employment of partners by an audit client

A key audit partner should not accept a key management position with a client unless at least two years have elapsed since the conclusion of the audit.

Rotation of audit partners for audits of listed companies

The engagement partner (the partner responsible for the audit) should be replaced within five years and not return for a further five years. Key audit partners should be replaced within seven years and not return until two years have elapsed.

2.3 Integrity, objectivity and independence – review procedures

KEY POINT

Every firm should establish **review procedures** (including an annual review) in order to guard against loss of independence.

Every firm should establish review procedures (including an annual review) in order to guard against loss of independence. These procedures should enable a firm to satisfy itself that each engagement may be properly accepted or be continued, and to identify situations where independence may be at risk and where appropriate safeguards should be applied.

Such safeguards might include (dependent on the size and circumstances of the practice/clients):

- the inclusion of a manager or other qualified employee in the audit team
- rotation of the engagement partner
- rotation of senior members of staff.

Rotation of key personnel is now required within ACCA rules as discussed for listed companies, however, the firm may apply this to all audits as an additional safeguard.

ACTIVITY **1**

You are an audit partner in a firm of Chartered Certified Accountants. A client has invited you and your spouse to a social function for Christmas. What should you do?

Feedback to this activity is at the end of the chapter.

2.4 Conflicts of interest

KEY POINT

Members should take steps to avoid **conflicts of interest** between themselves and clients, and between competing clients.

Members should place their clients' interests before their own and should not accept or continue engagements which threaten to give rise to a conflict of interest between the firm and their client. Any fees or commissions received which arise from the engagement or advice given should be fully disclosed. The advice itself should always be in the best interests of the client.

Conflicts between competing clients

Where clients' interests conflict (for example, clients in the same line of business), the firm's work should be managed to avoid the interests of one being adversely affected by those of another. Where this cannot be achieved (for example, unavoidable leakage of information), the member must disengage from one of the clients as speedily as is compatible with the interests of the clients concerned.

Safeguards to manage such conflicts of interest include:

- using different partners and audit teams for each client
- ensuring comprehensive instructions exist to instruct staff to prevent information leakage
- an independent review by a partner not involved with either client
- advising both clients to seek additional independent advice.

2.5 Ethical responsibilities: members in business

Members (and students) of ACCA who are employed by organisations as accountants, internal auditors or in any other position are bound by the same Fundamental Principles, the same standards of behaviour and competence as applied to all other members of the ACCA.

Although 'employed members' cannot be independent they should strive to be objective and act with integrity. They should decline to engage in any unlawful or dishonest transactions. This has been brought into sharper focus recently in the USA in the context of such matters as the collapse of Enron and WorldCom.

Employed members should therefore prepare reports and financial statements with objectivity and integrity in mind and not be persuaded, for example, to present a biased view regardless of whether it is for internal or external use.

Other matters which may threaten the objectivity or integrity of an employed member are receiving gifts and hospitality and financial and other involvements. The employed member should consider the situation as discussed earlier for ACCA members generally.

Employed members should ensure that they carry out their work with due regard for the technical and professional standards expected of them as members.

When faced with a conflict on ethical matters employed members should follow the established policies of the employing organisation. If the matter cannot be resolved in this way the employee should obtain legal advice, discuss the matter with the Members' Advisory Service and may need to consider resignation.

2.6 Internal auditors and integrity, objectivity and independence

Internal auditors are also required to demonstrate honesty, objectivity and diligence. Whilst their relationship to the 'client' is different from that of the external auditor, some of the same principles apply. Internal auditors should be seen to be objective and independent and avoid any activity that may be seen to compromise this.

KEY POINT

The internal auditor's independence is achieved through:

- the organisational status of internal audit
- the objectivity and professionalism of the internal auditor.

Independence itself has become a debating point for internal auditors. This arises from the changing nature of internal audit and, in particular, the move to a more consulting style and involvement in activities that could be said to compromise independence. However, in the latest definition of internal auditing published by the IIA, independence remains an important tenet. It is achieved through two key factors:

- The organisational status of internal audit – to ensure that they do not have their independence compromised by reporting to an area that they will provide audit reports on. The standard requires the chief audit executive to report to a level within the organisation that allows the internal audit activity to fulfil its responsibilities and that internal audit activity should be free from interference in determining scope, performing work and communicating results.
- The objectivity and professionalism of the internal auditor – internal auditors should have an impartial, unbiased attitude and avoid conflicts of interest to ensure that the appropriate independence of mind is maintained. The internal audit department would usually have guidelines/rules in place to ensure that conflicts of interest within the organisation are prevented. For example if an employee has worked in another department in the organisation such as financial accounting, and then transfers to work in the Internal Audit Department he would usually be precluded from auditing that department for a period of say one year.

A further requirement is that an assurance engagement for functions over which the chief audit executive has responsibility should be overseen by a party outside the internal audit activity, which means that if the department includes risk, compliance or other operational areas, there should be an independent oversight to protect the integrity and objectivity of the service.

To meet the requirements of honesty and integrity, internal auditors must comply with other areas of the code, for example avoiding conflicts of interest and not accepting anything that may impair professional judgement.

3 Confidentiality

3.1 The ACCA Rules

KEY POINT

Information **confidential** to a client acquired in the course of professional work should not be disclosed, except where consent has been obtained, or where there is a public duty, or a legal or professional right or duty, to disclose.

Information confidential to a client or employer acquired in the course of professional work should not be disclosed, except where consent has been obtained from the client, employer or other proper source, or where there is a public duty to disclose, or where there is a legal or professional right or duty to disclose.

A member acquiring information in the course of professional work should neither use nor appear to use that information for their personal advantage or for the advantage of a third party.

Where a member is in any doubt, the matter, if appropriate, should initially be discussed fully within their firm or organisation. If this is not appropriate, or if it fails to resolve the problem, the member should consider taking legal advice and/or consult the Association.

3.2 Confidentiality in practice

KEY POINT

An accountant should only act for a client on the understanding that the client will make **full disclosure** to them.

An accountant should only act for a client on the understanding that the client will make full disclosure to them. In the absence of such an understanding, the accountant should decline the appointment.

If, during the course of an engagement, the client fails to furnish all the information considered necessary, the accountant should disclose this in the audit report. The accountant should also consider whether they can continue to act.

Sometimes in the course of their work, an accountant may obtain information from a client that has a bearing on information supplied by another client.

In such circumstances, it would be a breach of confidence to reveal the information to the second client without the permission of the first client. (And in all probability any attempt to obtain that permission would result in a breach of the duty of confidence owed to the second client.)

The accountant should instead endeavour to substantiate the information with evidence obtained directly from the books and records of the second client. This may necessitate direct confirmation. Ultimately, the accountant may have to qualify the audit report or resign.

3.3 Disclosure of defaults or unlawful acts

KEY POINT

There are circumstances in which the auditor is **free** to disclose information regardless of the client's wishes, and circumstances in which the auditor has an **obligation** to do so.

Confidentiality is an implied term of the auditor's contract and members should not disclose information about a client's affairs acquired during the course of professional work. The auditor has neither a general right nor a duty to make unauthorised disclosures to the tax authorities, the police, or any other body. There are, however, circumstances in which the auditor is **free** to disclose information regardless of the client's wishes, and circumstances in which the auditor has an **obligation** to do so.

Members have an **obligation** to disclose to various authorities:

- where the courts order them to do so
- where they suspect their client of offences of terrorism
- where they suspect their client to be a drug trafficker or to be laundering the proceeds of drug trafficking
- under the banking, insurance, insolvency and financial services legislation, to the appropriate regulators where, broadly speaking, they consider that their client is either acting recklessly, or is not a fit and proper person to be managing such a business.

Even if members are wrong in their suspicions, they are protected against defamation claims under the general legal principle of 'qualified privilege'.

Members may **voluntarily** report in order to defend themselves in legal proceedings, to sue for fees and when they consider it appropriate to report 'in the public interest'. This is a well-known, but little used, legal principle that allows members to report without fear of defamation claims where:

- they report to an appropriate authority
- members of the public are likely to be affected
- the matter is serious, and
- the matter is likely to be repeated.

If a member is approached by any authority, where the prosecution of a client is concerned, they should act with caution. The member should establish what statutory authority they have for requiring the information and should always seek legal advice before acting.

3.4 Whistle-blowing responsibilities

KEY POINT

Where auditors become aware of a **suspected** or **actual non-compliance** with law and regulations, they should report this to the proper authority immediately.

Where auditors become aware of a suspected or actual non-compliance with law and regulations which gives a statutory right to report, they should report this to the proper authority immediately. Where the auditors conclude that the matter is of public interest, they should notify the directors of their view. If the directors do not disclose the matter, the auditors should themselves report it to the proper authority. Matters which cast doubt on the integrity or competence of management should be reported to the proper authority without delay.

Auditors should therefore obtain a general understanding of the laws and regulations that are central to the entity's ability to carry out its business. Examples of business activities which are subject to specific regulations include property development, waste disposal, investment business, and pension schemes.

Auditors are protected from the risk of liability for breach of confidence provided that it is made:

- in the public interest
- to the proper authority
- without malice.

For some types of client (e.g. in the UK, investment businesses), specific legislation and the regulatory environment have introduced the function of **whistle-blowing**. This has resulted in a fundamental change to the auditors' duty of confidentiality to their client in that they must report matters which are significant in determining whether:

- a person is a fit and proper person to carry on the regulated work
- disciplinary action should be taken.

Auditors should take legal advice before making any decision to disclose suspected or actual defaults, unlawful acts or non-compliance.

3.5 Money laundering regulations

Money laundering is the process by which criminals attempt to conceal the true origin and ownership of the proceeds of their criminal activity. The ACCA regulations were prepared on the basis of the Money Laundering Regulations 2003.

Clearly, members need to be fully aware of what the regulations are and if they suspect that the client is undertaking money laundering activities then they must report it.

Members will not be in breach of their duty of confidentiality if they report any money laundering in **good faith**. This protection applies even if their suspicions prove to be unfounded as long as the reports were made in good faith.

For the 2.6 exam, only a knowledge of the existence of the Money Laundering Regulations is required. A detailed knowledge is only required for the 3.1 exam.

KEY POINT

Accountants' working papers are their own property and any request for their production should normally be refused.

If the request comes from an Inspector of Taxes or the Enquiry Branch of the HM Revenue and Customs, accountants should ensure their response is in the best possible interests of the client.

3.6 Accountants' working papers

Accountants' working papers are their own property and any request for their production should normally be refused.

However, if an Inspector of Taxes or the Enquiry Branch of the HM Revenue and Customs requests the production of working papers relating to a particular client whose affairs are under investigation, accountants should ensure their response is in the best possible interests of the client.

If, in the accountant's opinion, the client would be best served by producing the documents, then provided the client has no objections, the accountant may do so.

Ultimately, the HM Revenue and Customs may be empowered under S20A of the Taxes Management Act 1970 to obtain documents from an accountant. Accountants should always take positive steps to dispel any suspicions by cooperating to the extent that it is in both their and the client's interests.

An accountant could suggest to the HM Revenue and Customs that an independent accountant should be appointed to report on them to the Revenue.

3.7 Internal auditors and confidentiality

KEY POINT

Internal auditors are also required to maintain confidentiality in matters relating to their work.

Internal auditors are also required to maintain confidentiality in matters relating to their work. Therefore, they should not use confidential information for any personal gain nor in any manner which would be contrary to law or detrimental to the organisation.

Internal auditors should have full access to all information necessary to carry out their role and this provides an obligation to be confidential. If such confidentiality is breached, the trust within the organisation is lost and internal audit could not then adequately perform its role.

DEFINITION

Whistle-blowing: the unauthorised disclosure by internal auditors, in good faith, of serious information relating to questionable practices, whose disclosure is perceived to be in the public interest. The information may comprise audit results, findings, opinions or information acquired in the course of performing their duties.

However, there are certain circumstances where internal auditors may want to release information to an outside body against the wishes of the organisation. This is **whistle-blowing**.

The IIA has issued a position statement on whistle-blowing: this requires that, in a potential whistle-blowing scenario, the auditor looks at whether the department is complying with IIA standards and whether the head of internal audit has direct access to the audit committee where the facts have been fully reported. This is the balance between confidentiality and integrity, and the key factor is whether there are robust procedures within the organisation to prevent such a dilemma arising. If the audit department has sufficient organisational status, independence and access to the board and audit committee, this will minimise any areas of risk because internal reporting should address any concerns. Where internal auditors work in circumstances that do not meet the IIA standards and code, the auditor still has a professional obligation to use their best endeavours to rectify the situation, although this may take time.

Internal auditors may also be faced with a situation where they are approached by other employees wishing to carry out whistle-blowing. Again, this will need to be handled carefully and the auditor will need to look at how internal reporting mechanisms can be used to address the concerns.

KEY POINT

Because of the potential serious consequences, whistle-blowing must be a last resort after all other methods of reporting have been taken – the key for the internal auditor is to apply the highest standards of professional conduct.

If whistle-blowing is inevitable, it must be carried out in accordance with the UK Public Interest Disclosure Act 1998.

Where internal auditors find that best endeavours have not resolved concerns, any whistle-blowing must be carried out in accordance with the UK Public Interest Disclosure Act 1998. The Act defines a qualifying disclosure, which is a circumstance in which the Act provides protection. This would include the reasonable belief that circumstances have or are likely to occur including criminal offence, failure to comply with legal obligations, miscarriage of justice, endangering the health or safety of an individual or damage to the environment.

Clearly, a decision to disclose information in this way is serious and the trust on which the internal auditor depends will be completely undermined. Usually in cases where whistle-blowing has occurred, the employee's position becomes untenable. Therefore, whistle-blowing must be a last resort after all other methods of reporting have been tried – the key for the internal auditor is to apply the highest standards of professional conduct.

Alan Lovell and Charles Robertson, in *Charles Robertson: in the eye of the storm*, wrote about the case of Charles Robertson, who was a chartered accountant working for Guardian Royal Exchange. He became aware of financial irregularities concerning taxes payable and raised the issue with other managers and the chairman. He was expected to cover up the problems he had found and, when he refused, he was suspended from his duties. He appealed to GRE's grievance committee, lost, and was dismissed. He went to the industrial tribunal on the grounds of unfair dismissal, representing himself because local law firms declined to take his case – four out of five of them because they did business with GRE. The tribunal ruled unanimously that he had been unfairly dismissed and should be reinstated in his job. However, GRE continued to appeal and, even when they withdrew from the appeal, they refused to reinstate Robertson and instead paid a relatively low fine for their refusal. Robertson then was faced with great difficulty in getting another job, which took some three years, and when he was employed, it was at a significantly lower salary. This case demonstrates the difficulties associated with whistle-blowing, even where the legal case apparently goes in the direction of the whistle-blower.

In the US, there is a website entitled 'Blowing the Whistle' set up by a father and son who have both carried out whistle-blowing, inviting others to log on with cases of whistle-blowing.

All auditors must be aware of the ethical issues surrounding whistle-blowing and the organisational cultures that may result in cases. If the right culture and governance are not there, then this increases the risk of cases of whistle-blowing.

4 Areas of controversy

KEY POINT

The main areas of controversy relating to professional ethics are independence and objectivity.

The main areas of controversy relating to the professional ethics covered in this chapter concern the issue of independence and objectivity. This applies to both internal and external audit.

Despite the comprehensive rules on independence referred to previously a number of practices persist which have a detrimental effect on the perceived independence of auditors.

4.1 Negotiation of the audit fee

Legislation in most countries provides that shareholders have the right to appoint auditors and agree their remuneration. In practice companies often pass a resolution at the AGM which empowers the directors of 'fix the auditors' remuneration'. Although there are obvious practical reasons for this it is hardly compatible with the goal of audit independence. However, in the case of listed companies this situation has been remedied by the existence of audit committees that have been required in the USA for many years and in the UK since the Cadbury Report (see chapter 4).

4.2 Provision of non-audit services

External auditors in the UK and the USA particularly are often seen as insufficiently independent because of the provision of non-audit services. The auditor is accused of being afraid of qualifying the audit report for fear of losing fees. This issue has been addressed by a number of discussion documents in the past, in particular *The Audit Agenda – Next Steps* issued by the Auditing Practices Board in the UK in 1996, and more recently Ethical Standard ES 5 *Non-audit services provided to audit clients*. There is no general prohibition on auditors providing non-audit services, however the audit engagement partner must be sure that carrying out the non-audit services is consistent with the objectives of the audit.

In the USA pressure from the Securities and Exchange Commission has led Ernst & Young and PricewaterhouseCoopers to devolve their consultancy arms.

4.3 Internal audit independence

For internal auditors, there is no longer the option of hiding behind the concept of independence to avoid making clear recommendations and taking an active role in addressing findings encountered during audits. As the move to be involved in major change initiatives, and in consultancy type work, increases, then so does the potential impact on independence. Again it is the auditor's objectivity and the department's organisational status that become important. One overall requirement remains, however: if the internal auditor has been involved in operating a function or operating the controls, then that auditor should not then be put into the position of auditing the function.

5 The auditor's responsibility in relation to detection of fraud and error

Both internal and external auditors have a role to play in the detection of fraud and error. Note that 'fraud' refers to an intentional act involving deception, while 'error' refers to an unintentional misstatement in the financial statements.

KEY POINT

Professional standards require **external auditors** to review the adequacy of systems to minimise the **risk of fraud**.

Professional standards require external auditors to review the adequacy of systems to minimise the risk of fraud. In Chapter 1 and above, the role of the external auditor is discussed, confirming that detecting fraud is not the primary objective of external auditors. Research in the US by IOMA in 1999 revealed that only 11% of external auditors were seen as valuable in the detection of fraud, while 42% were seen as cavalier, with fraud not seen as part of their job.

KEY POINT

Internal auditors should examine and review the risks within an organisation and evaluate whether adequate controls exist to guard against, and detect the risk of, fraud and error.

Internal auditors should examine and review the risks within an organisation and evaluate whether adequate controls exist to guard against, and detect the risk of, fraud and error. The IIA standards require that auditors should consider the probability of significant errors, irregularities, non-compliance, and other exposures when developing the engagement objectives.

A study commissioned by The Committee of Sponsoring Organisations of the Treadway Commission (COSO) reviewed instances of alleged fraudulent activity over a 10-year period (1987 to 1997) to review key characteristics and identify ways of improving the financial reporting environment (*Fraudulent Financial Reporting: 1987-1997 An Analysis of U.S. Public Companies, issued in 1999*). 200 cases were examined, with COSO finding that the frauds went to the very top of the organisation. In 72% of the cases, the CEO appeared to be associated with the fraud. The report raised some important issues including:

- Some companies may not be able to justify the cost of effective internal controls because of their size. Other companies may be unwilling to invest necessary resources to implement strong controls.
- Boards of directors, audit committee members and auditors need to consider the potential for pressures on management resulting from compensation plans and expectations from the investment community.
- Auditors need to look beyond the financial statements to understand risks associated with the client's industry, management's financial reporting incentives, and internal control, with particular emphasis on the strength of board and audit committee governance.

The UK's APB has also considered the matter in its publication 'Fraud and Audit: Choices for Society'.

What the report calls for is 'tone at the top' – an effective control and ethics environment fostered by an experienced, independent board of directors.

Both internal and external auditors should be aware of these issues and consider the corporate governance framework and ethical environment in conducting their reviews.

Current guidance for the auditor is provided by ISA 240 *The auditor's responsibility to consider fraud in an audit of financial statements*. The following principles are set out:

- in planning and performing the audit to reduce audit risk to an acceptably low level, the auditor should consider the risks of material misstatements in the financial statements due to fraud. The primary responsibility for the prevention and detection of fraud rests with management
- when the auditor confirms that, or is unable to conclude whether, the financial statements are materially misstated as a result of fraud, the auditor should consider the implications for the audit.

6 Client screening

6.1 The potential client

KEY POINT

When a potential client approaches an auditor asking them to conduct an audit, the auditor must decide **whether to accept the potential client** as a client – this is known as 'client screening'.

When a potential client approaches an auditor asking them to conduct an audit, the auditor will need to consider legal requirements (as discussed in a previous chapter) and ethical considerations (where the potential client has previously had an auditor). Ethical considerations are further covered later in the chapter.

However, from the auditor's point of view, there is the equally important process involved in deciding whether to accept the potential client as a client. This section is concerned with this decision.

6.2 Purpose of ISA 315

ISA 315 *Understanding the entity and its environment and assessing the risks of material misstatement* was issued to provide guidance to auditors on obtaining knowledge of the client's business and how to use that knowledge. Without such knowledge, auditors would be unable to decide whether to take on a prospective new client because they would not be able to weigh up the true risks and rewards of the appointment.

6.3 Auditing principle

KEY POINT

In order to accept an appointment, auditors should have or obtain a **knowledge of the business** of the entity to be audited.

'The auditor should obtain an understanding of the entity and its environment, including its internal control, sufficient to identify and assess the risks of material misstatement of the financial statements whether due to fraud or error, and sufficient to design and perform further audit procedures'.

Explanation

The necessary knowledge is obtained both before accepting the client and after. It should cover the following areas:

- general economic factors
- industry conditions affecting the client's business
- the entity itself
- the entity's products, market, suppliers, expenses and operations
- the entity's financial performance and condition
- the reporting environment.

This knowledge will be obtained from the previous auditors, where it is a new client, industry statistics, press reports, bankers and other advisers, prior year financial statements, and of course, from the client themselves.

The knowledge is used primarily in:

- assessing risks and identifying problems
- planning and performing the audit effectively
- evaluating audit evidence.

Risk is a key issue here, particularly in making the decision as to whether to take on the client in the first place.

6.4 Risk

KEY POINT

Client-screening procedures are designed to screen out potentially **risky audit clients**. A risky client is one which may result in costs exceeding the audit fees.

Client-screening procedures are designed to screen out potentially risky audit clients. A risky client is one which may result in costs exceeding the audit fees. Costs need to be viewed in their widest context; for example, if the client ends up suing the auditor for negligence, the auditor will incur costs in defending the action. Even if the auditor knows that they have not been negligent, their reputation may be damaged, particularly if a number of clients are pursuing negligence claims.

The considerations which are relevant in deciding whether a client is high risk include the following:

- evidence of client involvement in fraudulent or illegal activities
- the state of the economic sector in which the client operates (a depressed sector may indicate risk)
- the nature of the industry and the client's product lines or services
- the client's previous audit history (frequent changes of auditors, and/or qualified reports, are obviously bad news)
- the general abilities of the client management
- understanding, by the directors, of their own role and that of the auditor
- management permission or refusal to examine significant documents, such as the minutes of directors' meetings
- evidence of management intentionally failing to record a material transaction.

The review procedure is best carried out by means of a standard checklist. A client may exhibit some of the above risk factors and yet still be accepted due to the relatively high level of the proposed audit fee. It is very much a commercial decision to be made by the audit firm.

An area which the auditor has to be more aware of now is that of **money laundering**. Practice Note 12 was issued in August 2004 giving interim guidance to reflect the requirements of the new anti-money laundering legislation and significantly extends the auditors' responsibility to report. Auditors are required to adopt more rigorous client identification procedures. Also auditors are now required to report any knowledge/suspicion (or reasonable grounds for suspicion) of crimes that may not have any material impact on the financial statements. Failure to report is a criminal offence.

6.5 Non-risk factors

KEY POINT

Other reasons for not accepting an audit appointment include:

- strategic decision regarding type or size of clients
- clients' need for specialised staff
- limited opportunities to provide non-audit services.

There may be other reasons why an audit appointment is not accepted:

- The audit firm may have made a strategic decision to concentrate on certain types of client based on size or expected growth rates of the client. Some large audit firms would not take on 'small' clients.
- Clients in certain business sectors (e.g. insurance and banking) have audit requirements needing specialised audit staff and the firm does not wish to obtain such expertise unless it plans to obtain more audit clients in that business sector.
- There may be limited opportunities to provide non-audit services to the potential client and there is severe pressure from other audit firms on the level of audit fees.

6.6 Auditing principle

The audit engagement partner should ensure that the audit team obtains such knowledge of the business of the entity being audited as may reasonably be expected to be sufficient to enable it to carry out the audit work effectively.

Explanation

Following acceptance of an audit engagement, the audit team must be properly briefed about an audit client before starting the audit work. This knowledge could be communicated at an audit briefing meeting before the audit, and should be updated subsequently during the course of the audit. The channels of communication in the audit team should be two-way, so that members of the audit team are alerted to the need to share additional information learned during the audit which may have relevance to whether or not the auditors should continue to act.

7 Other ethical considerations

7.1 The ethical considerations concerning the auditor's appointment

KEY POINT

A member of the profession who is asked to accept nomination as auditor should, where applicable, request the prospective client's permission to communicate with the **present auditor**.

A member of the profession who is asked to accept nomination as auditor should, where applicable, request the prospective client's permission to communicate with the present auditor. This is covered by the ACCA's Rules of Professional Conduct 'Changes in professional appointments'. If permission is refused, or if the existing auditor is refused permission to respond to the request, the prospective auditor should decline the appointment.

The purposes of the **professional etiquette** letter are as follows:

- to inform the present auditor of the nomination as a matter of professional courtesy
- to ascertain whether there are any circumstances concerning the change of auditor which might affect the proposed auditor's decision on whether to accept nomination.

An example of a situation which might lead the proposed auditor to reject nomination would be where the present auditor reveals that they have tried to act in the best interests of the shareholders, but have had serious disagreements with directors over, for instance, the accounting policies adopted.

In general, the question of what constitutes a reason for not accepting nomination is one for the professional conscience of the person approached to act as new auditor.

It may be appropriate in certain circumstances to communicate orally rather than in writing.

The outgoing auditor would normally be expected to provide, free of charge, 'reasonable handover information', which would include a trial balance, reconciled to the last set of financial statements.

7.2 Ethical statement on fees

KEY POINT

Members should also be aware of the **ethical statement on fees** contained in the Rules of Professional Conduct.

This is also dealt with in the Rules of Professional Conduct.

The following points should be noted:

- Members are entitled to charge such fees as they consider appropriate. It is recommended that fees are referred to in the engagement letter.
- Where the fee is not agreed with the client beforehand, the auditor should charge a fee based on the amount of time worked, the seniority of the persons involved, the firm's cost structure and so on.
- A member may undercut another member's fees provided the client is not misled:
  - as to the precise range of services that the quoted fee covers
  - as to the likely level of future fees.

- Where a member is subjected to an investigation into allegations of unsatisfactory work, a suspiciously low fee would be taken into account.
- Fees should not be charged on a percentage or contingency basis except where allowed by statute or custom. Such work includes insolvency work and work relating to management buyouts.

7.3 Ownership of books and records

KEY POINT

When an auditor hands a client over to a new auditor, they are under an obligation to return to the client all of the **books and papers** belonging to the client which they possess, unless there are unpaid fees.

When an auditor hands a client over to a new auditor, they are under an obligation to return to the client all of the books and papers belonging to the client which they possess.

Reasonable transfer information should be provided free of charge.

Where fees are unpaid, however, the auditor may wish to exercise a **lien** over those books and papers. A lien is a right of a person to retain possession of the owner's property until the owner pays what is owed. A garage, for example, is perfectly entitled to refuse to let an owner drive away until the bill is paid, unless of course credit terms have been agreed. Similarly, auditors have a **particular** lien over books and records, i.e. can retain those on which they have performed work (and not those on which they have performed no work). The books and records must have come into the auditor's possession lawfully, a fee note must have been rendered and there must be no fee dispute. Unfortunately, legal precedent suggests that a lien cannot be exercised over books that the company is required to keep by law, and this includes most of them!

ACTIVITY **2**

The Chairman of Foley International plc, a large trading company with extensive overseas interests, has asked you to accept the nomination to replace the present auditor at the next annual general meeting of the company.

Before acceptance of any new audit assignment, there are a number of reasons for non-acceptance that have to be considered. List the circumstances in which acceptance of the nomination would be inappropriate under the following headings:

(a) legal

(b) ethical

(c) practical.

Feedback to this activity is at the end of the chapter.

8 The engagement letter

KEY POINT

The **letter of engagement** sent by the auditor sets out the terms of the engagement and forms the basis of the contract.

The letter of engagement is a letter sent by the auditor (or accountant) to the client at the beginning of any new audit (or accountancy work). It sets out the terms of the engagement and forms the basis of the contract. It should avoid any misunderstandings between the client and the auditor as to what the audit (or accountancy work) involves. ISA 210 *Terms of audit engagements* deals with this area.

It is now compulsory to provide a letter of engagement to all clients regardless of the type of work undertaken. The letter should contain details of services to be performed and the terms of the engagement.

8.1 Auditing principles

'The auditor and the client should agree on the terms of the engagement. The terms of the engagement should be recorded in writing.'

Explanation

In practice, the 'client' will be represented by the board of directors or the audit committee, and the client's acceptance of the terms will be evidenced by the signature of someone of appropriate authority, e.g. the finance director.

8.2 Auditing principle

Auditors should agree the terms of their engagement with new clients in writing. Thereafter auditors should regularly review the terms of engagement and if appropriate agree any updating in writing.

Explanation

KEY POINT

The contents of the engagement letter should ideally be **agreed prior to** the audit appointment, and the letter should be **reviewed** every year.

The contents of the engagement letter should ideally be agreed prior to the audit appointment and the letter sent soon after. Certainly, the contents should be agreed before the first audit begins.

The letter should be reissued each year with the details of the work to be performed.

The letter is in the interests of both auditor and client and constitutes part of the contract between them. It does *not* normally include the fee payable, but does refer to the basis of charging, which is usually on a time basis.

The letter sets out the responsibilities of directors and auditors, the scope of the audit and a description of audit procedures. It refers to other services but does not deal in detail with them, and it deals with fees, applicable law and agreement of terms.

8.3 New engagement

When invited to become auditor, the stages should be as follows:

- Obtain client's permission to write to the retiring auditors enquiring if there is any professional reason why the appointment should not be accepted.
- Meet with client to agree the scope of the audit, so far as not prescribed by statute.
- Send a letter of engagement to the client defining the scope of the audit.
- Ask the client to acknowledge receipt of this letter and to state whether it is in accordance with their understanding of the agreement.

8.4 Auditing principle

KEY POINT

If auditors are requested to **change the engagement** to one which provides a lower level of assurance, they should consider the appropriateness of doing so.

'An auditor who, before the completion of the engagement, is requested to change the engagement to one which provides a lower level of assurance, should consider the appropriateness of doing so. Where the terms of the engagement are changed the auditor and the client should agree on the new terms.'

Explanation

Examples of changes in the nature of an audit engagement include the following:

- a change in circumstances, e.g. falling within the audit exemption limits for a small company for the first time
- a misunderstanding as to the nature of an audit
- a restriction on the scope of the engagement, whether imposed by management or force of circumstances.

If auditors are unwilling to act under the revised terms of engagement, they must withdraw from the audit and comply with the procedures for resignation already described earlier in this text.

8.5 Auditing principle

'The auditor should ensure that the engagement letter documents and confirms the auditor's acceptance of the appointment, and includes a summary of the responsibilities of those charged with governance and of the auditor, the scope of the engagement and the form of any reports.'

Explanation

The contents of an engagement letter are best studied by examining an example. Study the example below carefully, although please note that you would never be asked to reproduce anything as lengthy as this in the exam.

Example of an audit engagement letter

Note: This form of letter has been drafted to apply to limited company clients. It is not necessarily comprehensive or appropriate for use in relation to every company; it must be tailored to specific circumstances – for example, to the special reporting requirements of regulated entities or of small companies to which certain exemptions are given.

To the directors of. . . .

The purpose of this letter is to set out the basis on which we (are to) act as auditors of the company (and its subsidiary undertakings) and the respective areas of responsibility of the directors and of ourselves.

Responsibilities of directors and auditors

As directors of the above company, you are responsible for ensuring that the company maintains proper accounting records and for preparing financial statements which give a true and fair view and have been prepared in accordance with the Companies Act 1985 *(or other relevant legislation).* You are also responsible for making available to us, as and when required, all the company's accounting records and all other relevant records and related information, including minutes of all management and shareholders' meetings.

We have a statutory responsibility to report to the members whether in our opinion the financial statements give a true and fair view and whether they have been properly prepared in accordance with the Companies Act 1985 *(or other relevant legislation).* In arriving at our opinion, we are required to consider the following matters, and to report on any in respect of which we are not satisfied:

- whether proper accounting records have been kept by the company and proper returns adequate for our audit have been received from branches not visited by us
- whether the company's balance sheet and profit and loss account are in agreement with the accounting records and returns
- whether we have obtained all the information and explanations which we consider necessary for the purposes of our audit
- whether the information given in the directors' report is consistent with the financial statements.

In addition, there are certain other matters which, according to the circumstances, may need to be dealt with in our report. For example, where the financial statements do not give details of directors' remuneration or of their transactions with the company, the Companies Act 1985 requires us to disclose such matters in our report.

We have a professional responsibility to report if the financial statements do not comply in any material respect with applicable accounting standards, unless in our opinion the non-compliance is justified in the circumstances. In determining whether or not the departure is justified we consider:

- whether the departure is required in order for the financial statements to give a true and fair view; and
- whether adequate disclosure has been made concerning the departure.

Our professional responsibilities also include:

- including in our report a description of the directors' responsibilities for the financial statements where the financial statements or accompanying information do not include such a description; and
- considering whether other information in documents containing audited financial statements is consistent with those financial statements.

Scope of audit

Our audit will be conducted in accordance with the Auditing Standards issued by the Auditing Practices Board, and will include such tests of transactions and of the existence, ownership and valuation of assets and liabilities as we consider necessary.

We shall obtain an understanding of the accounting and internal control systems in order to assess their adequacy as a basis for the preparation of the financial statements and to establish whether proper accounting records have been maintained by the company. We shall expect to obtain such appropriate evidence as we consider sufficient to enable us to draw reasonable conclusions therefrom.

The nature and extent of our procedures will vary according to our assessment of the company's accounting system and, where we wish to place reliance on it, the internal control system, and may cover any aspect of the business's operations that we consider appropriate. Our audit is not designed to identify all significant weaknesses in the company's systems but, if such weaknesses come to our notice during the course of our audit which we think should be brought to your attention, we shall report them to you. Any such report may not be provided to third parties without our prior written consent. Such consent will be granted only on the basis that such reports are not prepared with the interests of anyone other than the company in mind and that we accept no duty or responsibility to any other party as concerns the reports.

As part of our normal audit procedures, we may request you to provide written confirmation of certain oral representations which we have received from you during the course of the audit on matters having a material effect on the financial statements. In connection with representations and the supply of information to us generally, we draw your attention to Section 389A of the Companies Act 1985 under which it is an offence for an officer of the company to mislead the auditors.

In order to assist us with the examination of your financial statements, we shall request sight of all documents or statements, including the chairman's statement, operating and financial review and the directors' report, which are due to be issued with the financial statements. We are also entitled to attend all general meetings of the company and to receive notice of all such meetings.

The responsibility for safeguarding the assets of the company and for the prevention and detection of fraud, error and non-compliance with law or regulations rests with yourselves. However, we shall endeavour to plan our audit so that we have a reasonable expectation of detecting material misstatements in the financial statements or accounting records (including those resulting from fraud, error or non-compliance with law or regulations). However, our examination should not be relied upon to disclose all such material misstatements or frauds, errors or instances of non-compliance as may exist.

We shall not be treated as having notice, for the purposes of our audit responsibilities, of information provided to members of our firm other than those engaged on the audit (for example information provided in connection with accounting, taxation and other services).

Once we have issued our report we have no further direct responsibility in relation to the financial statements for that financial year. However, we expect that you will inform us of any material event occurring between the date of our report and that of the Annual General Meeting which may affect the financial statements.

Other services

You have requested that we provide other services in respect of . . . .The terms under which we provide these other services are dealt with in a separate letter.

Fees

Our fees are computed on the basis of the time spent on your affairs by the partners and our staff and on the levels of skill and responsibility involved. Unless otherwise agreed, our fees will be billed at appropriate intervals during the course of the year and will be due on presentation.

Applicable law

This (engagement letter) shall be governed by, and construed in accordance with, (English) law. The Courts of (England) shall have exclusive jurisdiction in relation to any claim, dispute or difference concerning the (engagement letter) and any matter arising from it. Each party irrevocably waives any right it may have to object to an action being brought in those Courts, to claim that the action has been brought in an inconvenient forum, or to claim that those Courts do not have jurisdiction.

Agreement of terms

Once it has been agreed, this letter will remain effective, from one audit appointment to another, until it is replaced. We shall be grateful if you could confirm in writing your agreement to these terms by signing and returning the enclosed copy of this letter, or let us know if they are not in accordance with your understanding of our terms of engagement.

Yours faithfully

We agree to the terms of this letter.

Signed for and on behalf of (company) ___________________________________

Conclusion

The APB is now responsible for setting ethical standards in relation to audit, for example in the areas of independence, objectivity and integrity; the professional bodies are still responsible for setting their own rules of conduct. The POBA has responsibility for overseeing the ethical agenda.

Auditors must make a commercial decision as to whether to accept a new appointment. In addition, they are subject to ethical considerations before they can accept an appointment.

The letter of engagement is essential in order to set out the various duties and requirements of the parties involved.

SELF-TEST QUESTIONS

The ethical base of auditing

1 What are the five fundamental principles identified in the ACCA Code of Ethics? (1.1)

Integrity, objectivity and independence

2 Which persons are regarded as closely connected with a person? (2.2)

3 Which persons are regarded as closely connected with a practice? (2.2)

4 What happens if goods and services are provided free to a practice from an audit client? (2.2)

5 Can an audit firm supply other services to a client? (2.2)

Confidentiality

6 What should the auditor do if the client does not make full disclosure to them? (3.2)

7 What is whistle-blowing? (3.4, 3.7)

The auditor's responsibility in relation to detection of fraud and error

8 What are the responsibilities of internal and external auditors in the detection of fraud and error? (5)

Client screening

9 List factors indicating that a potential audit client may be high risk. (6.4)

The engagement letter

10 What steps should an auditor follow before agreeing to accept a new appointment? (8.3)

EXAM-TYPE QUESTIONS

Question 1: Regulation of independence

(a) State seven elements of the ACCA's Rules of Professional Conduct which strengthen the independence of the auditor. **(7 marks)**

(b) Briefly suggest how the independence of the auditor might be further strengthened and improved. **(7 marks)**

(Total: 14 marks)

Question 2: Billington Travel

Professional ethics are relevant to both external auditors and internal auditors.

You work for a medium-sized firm of Chartered Certified Accountants with seven offices and 150 employees. You firm has been asked to tender for the provision of statutory audit and other services to Billington Travel, a private company providing discounted package holiday services in the Mediterranean. The company is growing fast and would represent a substantial amount of fee income for your firm. The finance director has explained to you that the company would like the successful firm to provide a number of different services. These include the statutory audit and assistance with the preparation of the financial statements. The company is also struggling with a new computer system and the finance director considers that a systems review by your firm may be helpful. Your firm does not have much experience in the travel sector.

Required:

(a) Explain why it is necessary for external auditors to be and be seen to be independent of their audit clients. **(3 marks)**

(b) With reference to the ACCA's *Rules of Professional Conduct*, describe the ethical matters that should be considered in deciding on whether your firm should tender for:

(i) the statutory audit of Billington Travel **(4 marks)**

(ii) the provision of other services to Billington Travel. **(4 marks)**

You are a student Chartered Certified Accountant and you are one of four assistant internal auditors in a large manufacturing company. You report to the chief internal auditor. You have been working on the review of the creditors system and you have discovered what you consider to be several serious deficiencies in the structure and operation of the system. You have reported these matters in writing to the chief internal auditor, but you are aware that none of these matters have been covered in his final report on the system which is due to be presented to management.

Required:

(c) List the actions you might take in these circumstances. **(6 marks)**

(d) Explain the dangers of doing nothing in these circumstances. **(3 marks)**

(Total: 20 marks)

For answers to these questions, see the 'Answers' section at the end of the book.

FEEDBACK TO ACTIVITY 1

The general ethical principle is that objectivity may be threatened by the acceptance of hospitality from a client and thus the acceptance of 'undue hospitality' poses a threat to the objectivity principle.

However, this does not preclude *all* hospitality, but only excessive hospitality. In the circumstances outlined, it is reasonable to conclude that the invitation can be accepted. The auditor should always make a judgement based on the circumstances in question. Essentially it is vital that he is not placed in a compromising position which could affect his independence and objectivity.

FEEDBACK TO ACTIVITY 2

The acceptance of the nomination to replace the present auditor will be dependent upon the following considerations.

(a) **Legal**

S389 CA 1985 prohibits officers or servants of the company or partners or employees of an officer or servant of the company from accepting the position of auditor to the company.

The auditor must be a member of a recognised supervisory body (RSB) and eligible under the rules of that body. An RSB must only deem persons eligible for appointment who are appropriately qualified, or a member of a firm controlled by a qualified person.

(b) **Ethical**

If the fees from this appointment would exceed 10% of the gross fees of the practice then the appointment should not be accepted.

Any personal relationship (kinship, friendship or mutual business interest) with an officer or employee of the company would be considered unethical.

Any financial involvement with the company (such as a shareholding or a loan to or from the company) would also be regarded as unethical.

Finally, any conflict of interest should be avoided, such as advising two clients who were in dispute with each other.

(c) **Practical**

It may be impossible for the appointment to be accepted because the practice is not sufficiently large to audit the company satisfactorily or is heavily engaged in other audits at the time the client would need the audit to be carried out.

Also, the firm may not have the necessary expertise, for example in computing or international trade, to provide a satisfactory service to the client.

Finally, it may be that the level of fees is not considered sufficient, particularly if the client is considered high risk. In all situations, an appointment should be declined if there is no way in which the problem can be circumvented.

Chapter 4

INTERNAL AUDIT AND REVIEW: I

CHAPTER CONTENTS

Internal audit is going through a significant period of change, both in the UK and globally. The nature of internal audit and the approach to internal activity is increasingly under review. As with any other department, there are pressures on the internal audit function to add value to an organisation. The importance of corporate governance has resulted in a greater focus on providing managers and directors with required assurance. There is also a trend towards closer links with the risk management industry. In the light of these ongoing trends, it is important that you keep abreast of the latest developments in the internal audit world.

Objectives

By the time you have finished this chapter you should be able to:

- explain the regulatory environment for internal audit and review
- explain the role of internal audit and review in the following areas:
  - corporate governance
  - risk management
  - organisational control
  - achieving corporate objectives
- describe the development and changing role of internal audit
- summarise the relative merits of outsourcing internal audit and internal review services to external auditors and others, and the associated problems
- explain the differences between the roles of external and internal audit.

1 Corporate governance

DEFINITION

Corporate governance concerns the way that a company is operated and controlled, and in particular encompasses the operation of the board and audit committee, as well as the overall control and risk management framework.

Corporate governance is defined as the internal means by which a company is operated and controlled. It concerns such matters as the responsibilities of directors, the appropriate composition of the board of directors, and the necessity for internal and external audit.

The topic became important in the UK in the 1980s, following the high profile collapses of a number of large companies (Maxwell, Polly Peck, BCCI, etc) where poor standards of corporate governance had led to insufficient controls being in place to prevent wrongdoing. The topic became important in the US in the 1990s following the collapses at Enron and WorldCom.

The authorities internationally have now been working for a number of years to tighten up standards of corporate governance. This chapter reviews the progress that has been made, especially as it affects audit.

KEY POINT

Corporate governance is a key area for auditors, since this now provides impetus to the role of internal and external audit.

Corporate governance is a key area for auditors to understand since recent developments provide impetus to the role of internal and external audit. Failure to meet corporate governance requirements can result in a major risk to the reputation of any company. Even companies for which the requirements are not compulsory may well seek to comply in order to ensure that their reputation does not suffer.

The first work in the UK to tighten up standards of corporate governance was carried out by a committee under the chairmanship of Sir Adrian Cadbury.

1.1 The Cadbury Committee

The Cadbury Committee was set up in 1991 by the FRC, the Stock Exchange and the accountancy profession to examine the reporting and control functions of boards of directors and the role of auditors and shareholders. Its full title was *'The Committee on the Financial Aspects of Corporate Governance'*. In the wake of a number of large company disasters, a better title might have been *'The Committee on How to Stop Fraud'*.

The report entitled *'The Financial Aspects of Corporate Governance'* was issued in 1992. It contained a recommended code of best practice for company directors.

1.2 Developments following Cadbury

The Cadbury Report was welcomed, and was followed by a number of further reports:

- the Greenbury Report considered the determination and disclosure of directors' remuneration
- the Hampel Report consolidated all the existing rules and regulations into a single Combined Code on Corporate Governance, which was presented to the Stock Exchange for their approval. The Financial Services Authority (FSA), as the body responsible for setting the rules that listed companies must follow, has now ruled that listed companies must follow the Combined Code, or else explain their non-compliance
- the Turnbull Report provided guidance to assist listed companies in implementing the requirements in the Code relating to internal control
- the Higgs Report considered the role and effectiveness of non-executive directors
- the Smith Report considered the role of audit committees.

In 2003 a revised Combined Code was published by the FRC, which is responsible for revising the Code when necessary. The revised Code incorporates all of the reports described above, and represents today's best practice in corporate governance. All listed companies are required to disclose in their annual report how they have applied the principles of the Code, and whether they have complied with the provisions of the Code. Listed companies must explain the circumstances of non-compliance with the Code's provisions.

1.3 Codes of governance versus legislation

The UK's approach to corporate governance improvement has been for the profession to develop a Combined Code of Practice, with which listed companies must 'comply or explain'. The Code can be regularly revised as necessary by the FRC in the light of developments.

This voluntary code approach is very different from the statutory approach followed by the US. Public confidence in financial reporting was so low in the US following Enron and other collapses that the US authorities decided that firm action had to be taken quickly. The Sarbanes-Oxley Act 2002 was passed to show that the authorities meant business.

KEY POINT

The principles of good governance cover five areas: the board of directors, directors' remuneration, accountability and audit, relations with shareholders, and institutional shareholders.

1.4 The Combined Code

The principles of good governance in the Combined Code cover five areas:

- the board of directors
- directors' remuneration
- accountability and audit
- relations with shareholders
- institutional shareholders.

EXAM HINT

The principle which is most relevant for Paper 2.6 is **accountability and audit**.

Whilst all aspects of good governance are important to the auditor, it is the area of accountability and audit that is most relevant to this exam, along with the supporting guidance on internal control. The Code requires following three principles. A company's board must:

- present a balanced and understandable assessment of the company's position and prospects
- maintain a sound system of internal control to safeguard the shareholders' investment and the company's assets
- establish formal and transparent arrangements for considering how they should apply the financial reporting and internal control principles and for maintaining an appropriate relationship with the company's auditors.

The Code contains the following provisions to back up these principles:

- in the annual report, both the directors and the auditors should explain their responsibilities
- the directors should report that the business is a going concern, with qualifications as necessary
- the board should, at least annually, conduct a review of the effectiveness of the group's system of internal controls and should report to shareholders that they have done so
- the board should establish an audit committee of at least three, or in the case of smaller companies two, members who should all be independent non-executive directors. At least one member of the audit committee should have recent financial experience.

KEY POINTS

The 2003 **Combined Code** states the auditor's responsibilities in the area of corporate governance. It also recommends that the directors review the effectiveness of the group's system of internal controls, and the Turnbull Report (1999) provided extra guidance in this area.

In 2004, the APB issued a Bulletin *The Combined Code on Corporate Governance: Requirements of auditors under the Listing Rules of the Financial Services Authority* to clarify the auditor's responsibilities in the area of corporate governance. As stated above, the Combined Code recommends that the directors should review the effectiveness of the group's system of internal controls and should report to shareholders that they have done so. The review must cover all controls, including financial, operational and compliance controls and risk management systems.

A working party under the chairmanship of Nigel Turnbull issued the **Turnbull Report** in September 1999 giving guidance to directors on how to carry out their responsibilities for the internal control review described above. This remains part of the 2003 Combined Code.

Turnbull requires that listed companies (i.e. public companies whose shares are listed on the London Stock Exchange) should 'be required to confirm that there is an ongoing process for identifying, evaluating and managing the company's key risks and that it is regularly reviewed by the board and accords with the guidance'.

KEY POINT

Turnbull emphasises the need for a **sound system of internal control**. A risk review should be performed and the system should be monitored.

There is a clear recognition within Turnbull that companies' objectives, internal organisation and the organisational environment are continually evolving and therefore risks will evolve. There is emphasis on the need for a sound system of internal control, requiring a thorough and regular evaluation of the nature and extent of the risks to which the organisation is exposed. Turnbull also requires monitoring of the system of internal control by individuals with the required skills, technical knowledge and objectivity.

Turnbull is key for the internal auditor because internal auditors are seen as able to provide much of the corporate governance assurance required.

Clearly, the Combined Code also affects the external auditor, who is required to audit the company accounts for listed companies. The audit report for such companies must include a statement on meeting the corporate governance requirements. Some companies are struggling more than others to grapple with an increasingly demanding corporate governance environment. The need for an ongoing mechanism or process for managing risks also presents challenges for the organisation. It is no longer enough to send a checklist around once a year to meet corporate governance requirements. There must be evidence of an appropriate control culture and evidence of ongoing review. This has resulted in increased importance of audit committees and the need for greater information to be available to the Board and to the audit committee. The challenge for external auditors is how best to confirm that the company complies with these requirements, which means that there must be increasing attention by external auditors on the way that organisations evaluate risk, establish controls and report on corporate governance.

KEY POINT

Corporate governance requirements place a greater burden on both internal and external audit, but they also provide more opportunity to all auditors in the way that they perform their role.

Whilst corporate governance requirements place a greater burden on both internal and external audit, they also provide more opportunity to all auditors in the way that they perform their role.

The APB Bulletin gives guidance to auditors when reviewing the directors' report to shareholders concerning the directors' review of the effectiveness of internal control. The APB believes that a separate auditor's report dealing with their review of corporate governance matters is unnecessary. Auditors are encouraged to include a full description of their responsibilities within the auditor's report on the financial statements; this is illustrated in later chapters dealing with ISA 700 and audit reports.

The auditor of a listed company therefore has different responsibilities concerning the different components that make up the annual report. The auditor must:

- conduct a full audit of the financial statements
- review the company's compliance with the Combined Code
- read all other information in the annual report (see ISA 720), so that the credibility of the audited financial statements is not undermined by inconsistencies between the financial statements and the other information provided.

1.5 Audit committees

KEY POINT

The Combined Code requires that listed companies must have an **audit committee** of at least three non-executive directors (two for smaller companies), to apply the financial reporting and internal control principles and for maintaining an appropriate relationship with the company's auditors.

An audit committee can be defined as a committee consisting of non-executive directors which is able to view a company's affairs in a detached and independent way and liaise effectively between the main board of directors and the external auditors.

In 2002, the FRC set up a committee under the chairmanship of Sir Robert Smith to clarify the role and responsibilities of audit committees, especially in reinforcing the independence of auditors. The Smith Report was issued in January 2003 and its provisions were included in the revised Combined Code issued later in 2003.

The Combined Code now requires that listed companies must have an audit committee of at least three non-executive directors (or in the case of smaller companies, two members), to review the financial reporting and internal control principles and for maintaining an appropriate relationship with the company's auditors. The board should satisfy itself that at least one member of the audit committee has recent and relevant financial experience.

Objectives and advantages

Three main objectives are usually associated with audit committees.

- increasing public confidence in the credibility and objectivity of published financial information (including unaudited interim statements)
- assisting directors (particularly non-executive directors) in meeting their responsibilities in respect of financial reporting
- strengthening the independent position of a company's external auditor by providing an additional channel of communication.

Additional advantages may include the following:

- They may improve the quality of management accounting, as they are better placed to criticise internal functions.
- They should lead to better communication between the directors, external auditors and management.

Disadvantages

Audit committees may lead to:

- fear that their purpose is to catch management out
- non-executive directors being over-burdened with detail
- a 'two-tier' board of directors.

Finally, there is undoubtedly additional cost in terms of, at least, time involved.

The functions of an audit committee

The Combined Code sets out the main role and responsibilities of the audit committee, which must be set out in written terms of reference. These include:

- monitoring the integrity of financial statements
- reviewing the company's internal financial controls
- monitoring and reviewing the effectiveness of the internal audit function
- making recommendations in relation to appointment and removal of the external auditor and their remuneration
- reviewing and monitoring the external auditor's independence and objectivity and the effectiveness of the audit process
- developing and implementing policy on the engagement of the external auditor to supply non-audit services
- review arrangements for confidential reporting by employees and investigation of possible improprieties.

In respect of the internal audit function, the Smith guidance on audit committees requires the audit committee to:

- ensure the internal auditor has direct access to the board chairman and to the audit committee and is accountable to the audit committee
- review and assess the annual internal audit work plan
- receive periodic reports on the results of internal audit work
- review and monitor management's responsiveness to the internal auditors' findings and recommendations
- meet with the head of internal audit at least once a year without the presence of management
- monitor and assess the effectiveness of internal audit in the overall context of the company's risk management system.

1.6 Risk management

KEY POINT

Many companies have changed or at least formalised the ways that they identify, assess and manage risk. Risk management and control should be embedded within organisations and processes.

Many companies have changed or at least formalised the ways that they identify, assess and manage risk. Risk management has become increasingly important within organisations and to internal auditors. Traditionally there has been a fragmented approach to risk management, which contributed to some well publicised corporate failures. Therefore boards have had to take greater ownership of risk. The Combined Code emphasises that risk management and internal control should be embedded within organisations and processes. Whilst internal auditors can play an important role in the framework for risk management, ownership resides with management.

The Institute of Internal Auditors has published several position statements on internal audit and risk including 'embedding risk management' and 'the role of the internal auditor in risk management'. The Institute suggest a range of involvement, depending on the organisation's needs but it can include the following:

From
Focusing audit work on significant risks & auditing the risk management processes across the organisation – giving assurance

To
Providing active support & involvement in the risk management process

To
Training & educating line staff in risk management & control

To
Co-ordinating risk reporting to the board, audit committee & risk committee

2 Internal audit and corporate governance

2.1 History and background of corporate governance

To understand the requirements of corporate governance, it is useful to look at the key guidelines (or 'building blocks') of corporate governance published during the last 15 years (the period in which this issue has come to prominence).

Date	*Standard*	*Stock Exchange Requirement – building blocks of corporate governance*
2003	Smith Report Higgs Report	Updating the Combined Code to reflect reviews of the roles of non-executive directors and audit committees.
1999	Turnbull Report	Building on the Combined Code
1998	Combined Code	Bringing together previous guidance
1996	Hampel	Extending requirements to cover operational controls
1995	Greenbury	Conduct/remuneration of directors
1992	Rutteman	Existence and effectiveness of financial controls
	Cadbury	Existence of financial controls
Pre – 1992	None	Informal guidance

In the early days, guidance was very much on an informal basis. The first set of guidance concentrated on the need for financial controls, initially their existence and then their effectiveness. The Greenbury Report looked at the conduct and remuneration of directors, a specific area of corporate governance. Hampel then extended requirements to cover not just financial controls but also operational controls. By the late 1990s, corporate governance was increasing in importance and the decision was made to publish the Combined Code, which brought together the previous guidance. With the Turnbull Report publishing greater guidance the emphasis is much more on risk, rather than just controls. The risk assessment concept is covered in a later chapter.

KEY POINT

The history of corporate governance mirrors that of internal audit, with a move from an accountancy-type, financial role to one that covers operational controls and risk-based auditing.

The history of corporate governance to some extent mirrors that of internal audit. Internal audit used to be seen purely as an accountancy-type, financial role, but has developed to cover operational controls and many organisations now operate risk-based auditing. However, there has been concerns that the advance of internal auditing has meant the neglect of the importance of financial risk.

2.2 Impact of corporate governance on internal audit and review

The Turnbull Report emphasises the importance of internal audit. It states that: 'An objective and adequately resourced internal audit function should be in a position to provide the Board with much of the assurance it requires regarding the effectiveness of the system of internal control.'

KEY POINT

Internal audit can contribute to good corporate governance by advising management on how a proper system of internal control can be maintained.

The main role of internal audit according to Turnbull is normally to evaluate risk and monitor the effectiveness of the system of internal control. Turnbull sets out the requirements for an organisation and these have a key bearing on how internal audit should operate. In particular, effective corporate governance should be concerned with the following areas:

- risk requirements
- the nature and extent of the risks regarded as acceptable
- the threat of such risks realising
- the ability to reduce incidence and impact if risks arise
- costs and benefits relating to operating relevant controls.

KEY POINT

According to Turnbull, effective corporate governance should be concerned with:

- risk requirements
- the nature and extent of the risks regarded as acceptable
- the threat of such risks realising
- reducing incidence and impact if risks arise
- costs and benefits relating to operating relevant controls.

The Combined Code also requires listed companies which do not have an internal audit function to review the need for one annually. If there is no internal audit function and there has not been a review of the need for one, the board must disclose this in their annual report. The reason for the absence of such a function should also be explained in the annual report. This requirement increases the importance and profile of internal auditing, since if there is no internal audit function, management need to apply other monitoring processes to assure itself and the board that the system of internal control is functioning as intended.

Where there is an internal audit function, the board should review annually:

- the scope of work of the internal audit function
- the resources allocated to the function
- the authority of the function.

Following the failure of WorldCom, a study was commissioned to investigate allegations including fraud, mismanagement and irregularities within the company. The subsequent report highlighted weaknesses in internal audit processes, including the lack of independence in the internal audit structure, which was not challenged by the audit committee or external auditors. Internal auditing was viewed as focusing primarily on maximising revenue, reducing costs, and improving efficiencies, including performing audits and projects that would be seen as adding value to the company, rather than monitoring the adequacy of internal controls to reduce risk.

3 Similarities between internal and external audit

KEY POINT

The **internal** and **external auditor** should **work closely together** to ensure that the most efficient and effective use is made of both functions.

Chapter 1 set out the differences between internal and external auditing, covering their objectives, legal basis, scope, approach and responsibility. Clearly, external auditors are required to provide an opinion on whether financial statements provide a true and fair view, whereas the scope for internal auditors is much more broad. However, external auditors increasingly take a broader view to more robustly examine all controls within an organisation and to use risk as a way of directing resource effectively. There is therefore a lot of common ground. The internal and external auditor should work closely together to ensure that the most efficient and effective use is made of both functions. This will include co-ordination of planning activity and sharing results of audits.

4 Outsourcing of internal audit

KEY POINT

Both in the UK and elsewhere in the world, an increased trend is towards the **outsourcing** of **internal audit**, either wholly or in part.

Both in the UK and elsewhere in the world, an increased trend is towards the outsourcing of internal audit, either wholly or in part. In local government, the pressures to provide 'best value' and to adopt competitive tendering have resulted in internal audit departments facing challenges to the provision of an in-house service. There are a number of advantages and disadvantages of outsourcing of internal audit.

Refer to an article on 'Outsourcing internal audit' by Carol Masters in the ACCA *Students Newsletter* in October 2000. This provides a helpful outline of the benefits and disadvantages of outsourcing as well as the procedures for outsourcing. Also refer to the ACCA internal audit bulletin in January 2004 which discusses the issue of internal audit and related services provided by accounting firms as a threat to independence.

4.1 Advantages of outsourcing internal audit

- There is greater focus on cost and efficiency of the internal audit function.
- Internal audit staff can be used from a broader source of expertise, e.g. professional firms that may specialise in the particular type of organisation.
- It reduces the risk of high turnover or loss of staff from the internal audit department.
- External sources are useful for providing specialist, expensive skills such as IT or treasury, that an in-house department may find difficult to recruit or retain.
- Skills required for only a short time each year can be provided without incurring excessive costs of maintaining an in-house expertise.
- Contracting out could increase independence, since staff from an external firm will need to comply with robust ethical guidelines and are more likely to be rotated to avoid close working relationships building up.
- Outsourcing could provide access to new market place techniques without the need for significant levels of investment or in-house development. For example, outsourcing may include the use of audit methodology software that an in-house team would have to buy or develop.
- With a professional outsourced department, less management time is required on internal audit, e.g. in appraisals, training and development.

4.2 Disadvantages of outsourcing internal audit

- Conflict of interest may arise if the outsourced internal audit service is being provided by the external auditors.
- There may be pressure on independence arising from the cost associated with the provision of internal audit. The outsourced department may experience pressure from management, either through a threat not to renew the outsourcing contract, or by withholding payment.

- There is the risk of lack of knowledge or awareness of the organisational objectives, culture or business.
- There is the increased cost of an outsourced service, with less time spent on internal audit.
- An outsourced department may not be able to provide the same flexibility or ready staff availability, particularly where problems arise, since they do not have a permanent presence.
- Standards of service may fall once the contract has been secured and the previous team disbanded.
- There is a risk of blurring roles between internal and external audit, resulting in less credibility for both.

4.3 Procedures for outsourcing

Where outsourcing is carried out, some general procedures to minimise the risks and disadvantages are appropriate including:

- controls over acceptance of internal audit contracts to ensure no impact on independence or ethical issues
- regular reviews of the quality of internal audit work performed
- separate departments covering internal and external audit
- clearly agreed scope, responsibilities and reporting lines
- performance measures, management information and risk reporting
- procedure manuals for internal audit.

KEY POINT

Increasingly, there is a trend towards a **partnership approach**, where specialist skills are outsourced, whilst the core internal audit department remains in-house.

As a general rule, official guidance (as in Ethical Standard ES 5, for example) suggests that external auditors should think very carefully before also providing internal audit services to the same client.

Increasingly, there is a trend towards a partnership approach, where specialist skills are provided by consultants or are outsourced, whilst the core internal audit department remains in-house.

5 The future role of internal auditing

KEY POINT

Internal audit is facing a number of challenges for the future, and needs to be clear about the role it is providing and how it links with other control and risk functions.

Internal audit is facing a number of challenges for the future. It needs to be clear about the role it is providing and how it links with other control and risk functions.
In particular, it needs to respond to a number of key challenges:

- To remain viable, the internal audit profession needs to be perceived as adding value to organisations. The difficulty for internal audit is demonstrating how added value is achieved and balancing this against the need to provide robust independent assurance.
- The response and link to the risk management profession and how far internal audit should be an internal risk function. This may mean a merged internal audit and risk function, risk and audit working in partnership or a distinct independence from the risk profession. Internal audit can play a role in embedding risk management across the organisation and ensuring a joined up approach to risk management.
- In the financial services industry, some integration of audit, risk and compliance is taking place but this presents challenges about the degree of independence of internal audit.
- Internal audits need to adopt the perspective of the entire value chain, taking a broader view of organisations.
- The structure and concept of internal audit must reach beyond its own inherent processes to reflect organisational service drivers and organisational objectives.

- Standards and other professional guidance must not only lead the profession but must also symbolise distinctive quality in the industry.

KEY POINT

One challenge for internal audit is to educate management and boards that internal auditors have appropriate skills to operate in business risk management.

Internal audit is increasingly moving away from the traditional financial risk and control focus, but the challenge is to educate management and boards that internal auditors have appropriate skills to operate in business risk management. The ICA booklet on the value added by internal audit suggests that boards, audit committees and senior management should recognise the value of the internal auditors' knowledge of the company, its systems and its processes and their skills in:

- systematically analysing business processes
- objectively assessing the effectiveness of processes
- independently reporting to improve the effectiveness of processes
- using their knowledge to help spread good practices throughout the organisation.

Conclusion

Internal audit is going through a significant period of change, which provides a number of challenges and opportunities. Corporate governance developments have provided much focus on the role of internal audit and auditors need to demonstrate the right skills, knowledge and understanding of corporate objectives to provide support in this important area.

There are a number of differences between internal and external audit although both are interested in identifying risk and understanding the organisation's system of internal control.

There are a number of advantages and disadvantages to the increasing trend of outsourcing internal audit.

SELF-TEST QUESTIONS

Corporate governance

1 What is meant by corporate governance? (1)

2 What topic did the Higgs Report consider? (1.2)

3 What body is responsible for future revisions of the Combined Code? (1.2)

4 Does the directors' annual review of the effectiveness of controls only cover the financial controls, or must it include all controls? (1.4)

5 State five functions of an audit committee. (1.5)

Internal audit and corporate governance

6 If a listed company does not have an internal audit department, how often must it review the need for one? (2.2)

Outsourcing of internal audit

7 List four advantages and four disadvantages of outsourcing of internal audit. (4.1, 4.2)

The future role of internal auditing

8 Name three areas for internal audit to address for the future. (5)

EXAM-TYPE QUESTION

Internal v External auditors

There are similarities and differences between the responsibilities of internal and external auditors. Both internal and external auditors have responsibilities relating to the prevention, detection and reporting of fraud, for example, but their responsibilities are not the same. Both internal and external audit are part of an organisation's overall corporate governance arrangements. Sometimes, the responsibilities of internal auditors are out-sourced to external organisations.

Required:

(a) Explain the difference between the responsibilities of internal auditors and external auditors for the prevention, detection and reporting of fraud and error.

(5 marks)

(b) Explain the role of internal audit in the context of:

(i) corporate governance;

(ii) risk management;

(iii) organisational control. **(10 marks)**

Your answer should include one example of how an internal audit department in a manufacturing company might fulfil its role under each of the headings above.

(c) Outline the issues that should be considered when an organisation decides to out-source the internal audit function. **(5 marks)**

(Total: 20 marks)

For the answer to this question, see the 'Answers' section at the end of the book.

Chapter 5
INTERNAL AUDIT AND REVIEW: II

CHAPTER CONTENTS

The previous chapter provided an overview of the developing role of internal audit. This chapter explores the nature and role of internal audit in more detail, with practical examples of types of internal audit and review assignments.

Objectives

By the time you have finished this chapter you should be able to:

- describe the scope of internal audit work and the limitations of the internal audit function
- discuss the nature and purpose of internal audit and internal review assignments including value for money, best value, IT and finance
- explain and analyse the nature and purpose of operational internal audit and review assignments.

1 Scope of and limitations on internal audit work

1.1 Scope of internal audit work

KEY POINT

An **internal audit charter**, approved by the board, the audit committee or some other senior executive committee should be in place, setting out the objectives, scope and authority of internal audit.

The internal audit function is responsible for evaluating and commenting on the effectiveness of risk management, control and corporate governance processes. However, management remains responsible for identifying and managing risk, reporting on risk and ensuring that the right policies, procedures and practices are in place.

An internal audit charter, approved by the board, the audit committee or some other senior executive committee should be in place, setting out the objectives, scope and authority of internal audit. This should include a statement granting access to everywhere in the organisation.

Internal audit should provide an independent and objective function, but there are increasing pressures to add value within the organisation and for this reason the function cannot be truly independent of the organisation in which it operates. Internal audit is part of the overall control framework of the organisation.

1.2 Limitations of the internal audit function

Independence

KEY POINT

The **independence** of internal audit can be compromised, particularly where reporting lines are through to operational areas which they are required to review and report on.

Internal audit should be an independent and objective function. However, this independence can be compromised, particularly where reporting lines are through to operational areas which they are required to review and report on.

For example, the traditional reporting line was through to Finance and in some instances this is still the case. If an auditor with such a reporting line is required to provide critical comment on Finance itself, there may be pressure to avoid confrontation and either soften or omit such comment. The standards for the Institute of Internal Auditors require that independent oversight is provided where internal audit is responsible for an operational area.

Where internal auditors have moved to the Internal Audit department from an operational area, they should not be involved in audits of that department for a minimum of a year. Whilst they might be seen to have excellent knowledge of the area, their independence could be compromised.

Relationship between internal and external audit

Internal and external audit should work closely together, with reliance by external audit on the work of internal audit. This is dependent on the two functions having a common understanding of the organisation's needs and is not always effective. This reliance is explored in more detail in Chapter 7.

Variation of standards

Approaches to internal audit vary significantly across the industry. Whilst some are moving to a more consultancy-type approach, others continue to perform a 'tick and check' approach.

Relatively new profession

Internal audit is still a relatively new profession, which has been changing significantly over the years. A wide variety of backgrounds are attracted into internal audit.

Expectations gap

There is a balance to be achieved between added value work and 'checking' work, and a potential skills and expectations gap between consultancy and compliance.

Organisations are increasingly subject to change in objectives, systems and procedures, which affect the company risk profile. Internal auditors may not always be geared up for such constant change which affects both the scope of work carried out and the skills required.

KEY POINT

There is generally **poor understanding** of the function of internal audit, with many people viewing it as a negative, policing activity.

Understanding of internal audit

There is generally poor understanding of the function of internal audit. It is still seen as a negative 'policing' activity, checking for compliance. There is therefore a significant education exercise for internal auditors within an organisation to aid understanding of risks, controls and internal auditing.

ACTIVITY 1

What are the limitations of internal audit?

Feedback to this activity is at the end of the chapter.

2 Nature and purpose of internal audit assignments

There are a number of approaches to internal audit assignments which you should be aware of. These tend to have their origins in the public sector but may be useful in commercial organisations.

2.1 Value for money

DEFINITION

Value for money (VFM) auditing is concerned with obtaining the best possible combination of services for the least resources. It is, therefore, the pursuit of economy, efficiency and effectiveness.

Value for money auditing had its origins in the local authority public sector in the early 1980s as a route for controlling the volume of expenditure and ensuring that money was spent efficiently. Its success led to its use in central government departments, nationalised industries and the private sector. It has increasingly become a consideration of all auditing, including operational auditing.

- **Economy** **Least cost**
  Accomplishes objectives and goals at a cost commensurate with the risk.

- **Effectiveness** **Best results**
  Providing assurance that the organisation objectives will be achieved.

- **Efficiency** **Best use of resources**
  Accomplishes goals and objectives in an accurate and timely fashion with minimal use of resources.

2.2 Best value

DEFINITION

Best value is a requirement for local authorities to demonstrate achievement of the **'4C' principles** (see below), as well as demonstrating service delivery and meeting customer needs through effective performance management systems.

Best value is a requirement for local authorities to demonstrate achievement of the '4C' principles (challenge, compare, consult and compete), as well as demonstrating service delivery and meeting customer needs through effective performance management systems.

Reviewing best value is a major trend within local government, following an increasing focus on tendering for contracts and ensuring 'best value' through regulation and political pressures. Best value is changing the local government operating environment and affecting all services and activities. It cannot, therefore, be ignored by internal audit; in fact, auditors can play a major role in providing assurance on best value.

These approaches differ in detail and emphasis but they share an important common theme – that of assisting the organisation to achieve its objectives by identifying and managing the risks to which it may be exposed. These risks may inhibit the achievement of objectives.

DEFINITION

The 4Cs:

- challenge
- compare
- consult
- compete.

The 4Cs

- **Challenge** – review internally the different options for providing services and question the status quo.
- **Compare** – compare with other service providers to review options for improving performance.
- **Consult** – consult all users of services and those affected by services.
- **Compete** – demonstrate through performance management and continuous improvement that the most efficient and effective service is being provided.

The 4Cs apply equally to internal auditors, who must demonstrate best value in the provision of their own service, including appropriate consultations with customers and effective performance management information.

DEFINITIONS

Audit of information technology: a specialist type of internal auditing, reviewing and reporting on all aspects of systems, including hardware, applications, IT environment and systems developments.

Project auditing: a specialist type of internal audit review, examining and evaluating the way that change is managed within an organisation.

2.3 Audit of information technology

Information technology is a specialist type of internal auditing, reviewing and reporting on all aspects of systems, including hardware, applications, IT environment and systems developments. This includes identifying risks associated with IT and reporting all input, output and processing controls. With ever expanding technology and automation of processes, all auditors need to understand how to audit IT systems or how best to work closely with specialists in carrying out audits. When auditing an operation, the system at the centre of that operation cannot be ignored. When planning an audit, it is important to consider the nature of systems involved, where specialist expertise might be required, where computer assisted audit techniques are appropriate or when an integrated IT and operational audit will be necessary.

The pervasive nature of computer systems throughout business today means that the above points must be stressed. It is no longer acceptable for internal auditors to act in ignorance of their organisation's IT set-up. The risks associated with IT demand specialist attention from internal auditors.

2.4 Project auditing

Project auditing can be seen as one type of IT auditing or as a type of internal audit in its own right. Increasingly, as organisations change, they do so through projects or work. Sometimes this is through a programme of work (i.e. a number of projects that together form a larger project called a programme). Internal auditors increasingly have a role to play in auditing such projects and their involvement could help to improve effectiveness. This can be done in two ways:

- reviewing the way that the project has been managed
- reviewing the risks and controls associated with the project and ensuring that these are adequately addressed.

Sometimes a risk and control workshop approach can help the management and development of projects, in particular by bringing together IT staff, users and managers to create greater awareness of each area's needs and by focusing on the risks and controls of the project. Internal audit can play a part in such workshops as facilitators although overall responsibility for managing risks and implementing controls lies with the management.

ACTIVITY **2**

Your organisation has announced that it is implementing a new integrated HR and Finance system. What should internal audit's role be in this implementation?

Feedback to this activity is at the end of the chapter.

2.5 Financial internal audit

DEFINITIONS

Financial internal audit: examining records and evidence to support financial and management reporting.

Operational internal audit covers examination and review of a business operation, including the control procedures and whether they are being adhered to.

Financial auditing was traditionally the main area of work for the internal audit department. It embraces the conventional tasks of examining records and evidence to support financial and management reporting in order to detect errors and prevent fraud. It would include analysing information, identifying trends and potential significant variations from the norm.

2.6 Operational internal audit

Operational auditing covers examination and review of a business operation, including the control procedures and whether they are being adhered to. The audit would also identify areas for improvement in efficiency and performance including improving operational **economy**, **efficiency** and **effectiveness** – the **three Es** of value for money auditing.

3 Operational and internal audit assignments

This section deals with operational and internal audit assignments in relation to a number of major business functions, i.e.:

- procurement
- marketing
- treasury
- human resources.

In all cases, the audit work should be based on an approval which starts by identifying the objectives of the audit. These should focus, for each of the above areas, on the identification of the principal business risks involved which may prevent the organisation achieving its objectives, and the assessment of the extent to which controls are in place and are operating effectively in order to manage these risks. To achieve this latter objective, appropriate control tests will need to be performed. The outcome of each assignment should be a report to management which appraises the control systems which are currently in place and which makes appropriate recommendations for improvement. This reporting aspect is dealt with later.

Detailed audit procedures are set out in 3.1 to 3.4 below. As an overview these involve:

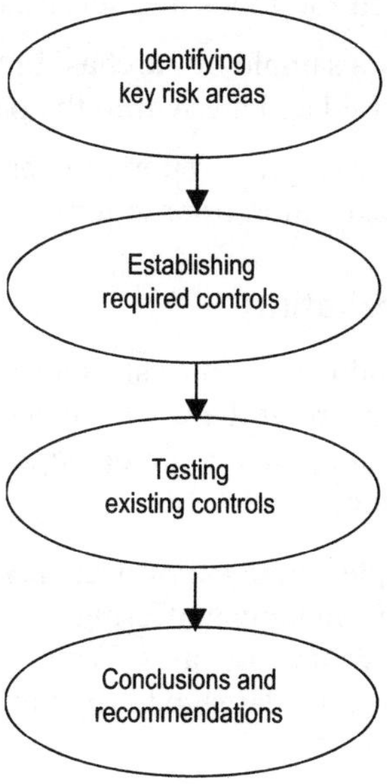

3.1 Procurement

DEFINITION

Procurement: the process of purchasing goods and services.

Organisations can spend significant amounts of money on goods and services, and this must be effectively controlled to minimise the risk of financial loss, fraud or damage to company reputation.

***Main areas of risk exposure*:**

- fraudulent payments to suppliers
- excessive fees for goods or services
- inaccurate payments for goods or services
- delays in paying for purchases resulting in damage to company reputation
- breach of regulatory, legal or company requirements.

***Control procedure*:**

- established policy and procedures for procurement, communicated to all levels of management
- authorisation and approval procedures for procurement, with different levels covering different cost levels
- procedures for negotiating the best deals in the market place for specific bulk purchases – in some instances, this may be through a dedicated procurement section, in which case all procurement requests should be made through this unit to maximise the benefit of any negotiated deals
- approved list of suppliers, with no purchases made outside that list without prior authorisation
- effective payment procedures
- exception reports showing where transactions have not been authorised, where they fall outside of the established procedures.

***Tests of controls*:**

- conduct a walk-through test to ensure that procedures are being followed in practice

- trace orders for goods and services through the system, confirming use of authorised suppliers, correct pricing, appropriate terms and accurate amounts invoiced for goods and services received
- review a sample of purchasing transactions to ensure that they have been correctly authorised and are within the parameters set by the organisation
- review exception reports to ensure that they have been actioned and trace through some exception transactions.

3.2 Marketing

DEFINITION

Marketing encompasses all aspects of the promotion and branding of an organisation, including branding and image management, product promotion and advertising and pricing.

Internal audit sometimes shys away from reviewing areas like marketing because of the 'artistic' nature of the work carried out. However, there are significant risks associated with marketing that could damage the finances and/or reputation of the company or organisation.

For example, some major organisations have been significantly caught out by marketing campaigns offering free or reduced travel that have far outweighed the increased volume of sales. When organisations cannot meet the needs of such promotions, the damage to reputation can be enormous, as well as the impact on the bottom line.

***Main areas of risk exposure*:**

- breach of regulatory requirements - this could be a particular risk in marketing campaigns that could result in fines or censure
- shareholder value lost or damage to reputation through poor brand image
- financial loss arising from poor cost control
- fraudulent practices
- excessive or inappropriate use of marketing entertainment.

***Control procedure*:**

- marketing strategy in place, agreed and documented
- approved policy and procedures
- authorisation of key activities, decisions and financial commitments
- appropriate skills and training of staff
- cost/benefit analysis or other financial case produced for marketing campaigns
- approved agents used only.

***Tests of controls*:**

- walk through tests of marketing campaign and confirm operation of procedures
- review marketing strategy
- review any exception reports – have non-approved agents been used?
- review sample of marketing campaigns and confirm that appropriate cost/benefit cases have been prepared
- review training plans.

3.3 Treasury

DEFINITION

Treasury management: the process of managing cashflow and investments within an organisation to maximise the use of available finances.

Key areas of treasury management include dealing and settlement,

Treasury is a high-risk area for many organisations but frequently an area where internal audit lacks specialist skills. There are some standard risks, controls and tests that will form part of any treasury review.

Normally, treasury units would be subject to frequent review (e.g. annually) because of the nature and complexity of the area and the potential impact on the company if the treasury is uncontrolled. There have been a number of highly publicised cases of companies making very heavy financial losses because of poor controls over treasury.

investments, accounting.

This can make the company very vulnerable, ranging from complete financial collapse, to takeover threats through to financial loss and damage to company reputation.

***Main areas of risk exposure*:**

- exposure to significant financial loss, in particular where deals executed outside of trading limits
- lack of record of deals or trading positions resulting in financial loss or damage to reputation
- failure to have agreements with counterparties
- inaccurate market risk monitoring and reporting
- securities lost or misappropriated
- future cashflows are inaccurate or incomplete resulting in errors in settlements and deal valuations
- duplicate transactions or settlements
- inaccurate or incomplete valuations
- errors in accounting and deal records
- errors in management, statutory and regulatory reporting
- unauthorised access to treasury systems or lack of reliability or robustness of systems resulting in vulnerability to financial loss
- poor investment performance.

***Control procedure*:**

- settlements
- data maintenance controls
- valuations
- cash flow management
- market risk monitoring
- systems controls, including security, access, segregation of duties and output reports
- levels of staff, training and expertise.

***Tests of controls*:**

- confirm current level and type of exposures
- check sample of reconciliations and confirm that these have been completed in a timely manner, that there are no long-standing items and that they have been independently reviewed
- review trends in performance and dealing activity to identify any potential areas of concern
- check agreements with counterparties
- check monitoring undertaken and exception reports
- review valuations
- confirm segregation of duties operates effectively
- confirm organisation set-up and procedures are adequate.

Key areas to review with a treasury audit are that the appropriate control culture and organisation framework are in place.

3.4 Human resources

HR consists of a number of key areas:

- policy
- recruitment
- pay and benefits administration
- performance management
- training and development
- disciplinary and grievance
- leavers.

It is sometimes easy to focus on the financial areas such as payroll administration, but other areas of HR can be equally or more important to the future of the company.

***Main areas of risk exposure*:**

- failure to identify and recruit the right skills
- setting up of 'ghost' employees
- inappropriate means of recruitment
- excessive reliance on consultants or contractors resulting in high costs and financial loss
- failure to document decision making on candidates for interview resulting in vulnerability to challenge or legal action
- inaccurate or incomplete standing data on staff, resulting in failure to maximise potential of individuals
- failure to provide feedback to staff on performance
- over-reliance on small number of key staff or loss of key staff
- failure to provide training and development of staff
- inappropriate training and development
- incorrect or fraudulent payments to leavers
- leavers do not return company property on departure
- failure to understand reasons for leaving and address any underlying problems of staff morale
- inappropriate payments made to staff through fraud or error
- disciplinary procedures not carried out appropriately or in line with company or legal requirements - this could lead to an individual taking legal action resulting in damage to reputation and financial loss.

***Control procedure*:**

- policy and procedures manuals - these should be up-to-date, reflect all current policy and have been formally approved and documented
- training of HR to ensure delivery of agreed policy
- authority and approval procedures
- systems access controls
- audit trail of key actions and decisions
- management and supervisory review
- exception reports.

Tests of controls:

- walk through tests of key procedures
- confirmation that procedures are operating effectively
- review of exception reports
- review of reconciliations undertaken
- review of access and security to HR systems and that there is adequate segregation of duties
- review sample of key transactions to ensure that they have been processed accurately, promptly and appropriately, with clear evidence of management review.

KEY POINT

Human resources may not be reviewed in a single exercise, but instead as a series of small reviews, concentrating on key areas.

Overall, HR is a broad scope review. It may be that HR is not reviewed in a single exercise, but instead as a series of small reviews, concentrating on key areas such as training or recruitment.

ACTIVITY **3**

Are there common areas of risks, controls and tests for the different types of operational and internal audit review?

Feedback to this activity is at the end of the chapter.

Conclusion

From this chapter, you should understand the different types of internal audit approach and how an internal audit should be conducted for a number of specialist areas.

Important overall messages to remember are as follows:

- The internal audit function should include in its scope all types of risk and controls, not just financial.
- Internal auditing should include a review of operational objectives, risks within the review, controls in place to minimise risks, directed testing to the areas of risk and control vulnerability and reporting.

SELF-TEST QUESTIONS

Scope of and limitations on internal audit work

1 What is the scope of internal audit? (1.1)

Nature and purpose of internal audit assignments

2 What is value for money? (2.1)

3 Define the 3Es. (2.1)

4 What is best value and what do the 4Cs represent? (2.2)

5 Define IT auditing and project auditing and explain any differences. (2.3, 2.4)

6 What is the difference between financial and operational auditing? (2.5, 2.6)

Operational and internal audit assignments

7 List five key risks of procurement. (3.1)

8 Why is marketing an important area for internal audit or review? (3.2)

9 How often is treasury normally audited? (3.3)

10 List six key areas of HR for operational review. Would these areas all be reviewed at the same time? (3.4)

EXAM-TYPE QUESTION

Roxy Hotels (Part 1)

Roxy Hotels is a listed company which runs a chain of some 40 hotels. The company has an established internal audit department which is based at the head office and which makes regular visits to the hotels.

The hotels provide business and tourist class accommodation. They also provide restaurants, bars, conference and leisure facilities which are open to the general public as well as residents. The company operates a computerised central booking and billing system and a stock and asset control system, both of which can be accessed via terminals in the hotels. Access to the system is restricted by the use of passwords and all significant expenditure is authorised through head office. The payroll is operated through head office. Hotel and regional managers are actively involved in the setting of budgets and cash flow forecasting. On average, throughout the year, the chain has a 65% occupancy rate.

Required:

(a) Describe six areas in which the internal audit department at Roxy Hotels might check detailed transactions and balances. **(6 marks)**

(b) Describe four areas in which the internal audit department at Roxy Hotels might perform reviews of system or operational performance. **(4 marks)**

(Total: 10 marks)

(ACCA Pilot Paper Dec 01)

For the answer to this question, see the 'Answers' section at the end of the book.

FEEDBACK TO ACTIVITY 1

There are a number of possible limitations of internal audit, although the limitations will primarily arise out of the approach and style of the function itself, as well as the organisation. Key limitations are as follows:

- relationship with other review functions, including external audit
- independence
- variation of standards
- relatively new nature of the profession
- understanding of internal audit, particularly by management
- expectations gap and willingness of internal audit to change and adapt to the changes within an organisation.

FEEDBACK TO ACTIVITY 2

The system crosses over the boundaries between key areas of the organisation and could present a significant level of risk. Therefore, involvement in the development and implementation should be key.

Example risks to the project are as follows:

- lack of business case for the new system, resulting in unnecessary expenditure
- poor project management, resulting in financial loss, waste of resources, failure to maximise the benefits of the system, delays and overruns
- failure to obtain buy-in to the new system, resulting in users not effectively using the system and retaining alternative systems, manual processes or spreadsheet.

Specific risks associated with the system itself could be as follows:

- failure to understand and document how the HR and Finance systems and processes link, resulting in corruption of data, financial loss and damage to reputation
- loss of systems resulting in failure to pay staff, suppliers, customers, etc.
- potential for fraudulent transactions on both the HR and Finance elements of the system.

Internal audit may look to the potential for facilitating a workshop with management, to help identify the risks that need to be managed and confirm the controls required to manage the risks.

Some key areas for internal audit to review are as follows:

- Objectives of the system – Have they been clearly established?
- Costs and benefits – Has a calculation of costs versus benefits been carried out? Has a clear business case been established?
- Project management structure and approach – Is the project following clearly established project management methodology and have the roles and responsibilities for the project been agreed and communicated?
- Is there a process for establishing risks and issues of the project and managing them?
- Are all users involved in the project and have they agreed requirements?
- Are there adequate timescales set aside for the project?
- Is there sufficient time set aside for different levels of testing for the project? Have types, parameters and conditions for testing been agreed, along with objectives and expected outcomes?
- Is there a clear decision making process if problems are found with the system and for final decision on when and how to implement?
- Are there mechanisms for managing and communicating faults that arise?
- Are there processes for post implementation review, including confirming that the desired benefits have been achieved?

FEEDBACK TO ACTIVITY 3

It is clear from a review of the different types of internal and operational audit that there are common areas of control and tests.

There are a number of common types of risks, e.g. fraud, errors in processing resulting in financial loss, damage to reputation.

Common controls

- policy and procedures
- management and supervision checks
- segregation of duties
- reconciliations
- exception reporting.

Common tests

- walk-through tests
- compliance tests
- review of sample of transactions, including checking for evidence of independent review
- review of exception reports
- review of systems controls, including access and security.

Chapter 6

PLANNING AND RECORDING THE AUDIT

Many of the principles and techniques of audit planning and recording apply equally to external and internal audit. However, this chapter deals with 'additional' points relevant for internal audit.

CHAPTER CONTENTS

Audit planning is a vital area of the audit, conducted primarily at the beginning of the audit process. The plan developed will be revised as necessary during the course of the audit. For internal auditors, the need for a high-level audit plan is particularly important, based on an assessment of risks within the organisation. This will form the basis for individual audit assignment planning.

In undertaking effective planning, the auditor needs to understand the different stages of the audit and make judgements on the level and detail of work to be undertaken. This chapter also considers the working papers and files used to record audit work.

The documentation of the audit is a fairly straightforward area of knowledge.

This chapter also sets out a framework for the use of testing and the balance to be applied between tests of control and substantive procedures. The detailed testing procedures in both these areas are extensively covered in later chapters. However, you always need to bear in mind the objectives of the testing.

Objectives

By the time you have finished this chapter you should be able to:

- describe the sources and nature of information gathered in planning audit and review assignments
- describe the purpose of analytical procedures and risk analysis in the planning stage and illustrate the application of such procedures
- understand the components of risk and how information technology is used in risk analysis
- define and illustrate the concepts of materiality and tolerable error
- distinguish between risk-based, procedural and other approaches to audit and review work
- describe and illustrate the contents of work plans and work programmes
- explain the importance of audit documentation and describe the nature of documentation required for different types of assignment
- explain and show how information technology is used in preparing work programs and work plans.

1 General principles of external audit

1.1 Primary objectives

The primary objectives of an audit, which were discussed in Chapter 1, are:

- the expression, in an audit report, of an expert and independent opinion on the truth and fairness of the information contained in the annual financial statements

- the ascertainment and evaluation of the reliability of the accounting systems as a basis for the preparation of the financial statements.

Remember that it is the directors' responsibility to prepare financial statements that show a true and fair view of the state of the company's affairs, and that company legislation requires companies to keep such records as will be sufficient to show the nature of all transactions and disclose, at any time, the financial position at that time. Auditing procedures will be designed to ensure that auditors can satisfy themselves that the company has kept proper accounting records, and to allow them to form an opinion on the financial statements.

KEY POINT

ISA 200 states that auditors should carry out an audit in accordance with ISAs (and ethical principles) to determine with reasonable confidence whether the financial statements are free from material misstatement.

ISA 200 *Objective and general principles governing an audit of financial statements* states that auditors should carry out an audit in accordance with ISAs (and ethical principles) to determine with reasonable confidence whether the financial statements are free from material misstatement.

It requires them to evaluate the overall presentation of the financial statements to ensure that they have been prepared in accordance with relevant legislation and accounting standards, and to issue a report with a clear opinion on the financial statements.

It points out that auditors can only be expected to obtain *reasonable* assurance.

1.2 Extent of audit work

KEY POINT

It is for auditors to decide on the extent of audit work they consider necessary in order to support their opinion.

It is for auditors to decide on the extent of audit work they consider necessary in order to support their opinion. They may decide to conduct an extensive review of the accounting systems by carrying out detailed tests on a large number of transactions, documents, records, etc. On the other hand, they may wish to rely on the internal controls which are in operation to justify a reduction in the level of audit testing on those items.

2 Audit planning, knowledge of the business and analytical procedures

2.1 Planning

In all walks of life it is necessary to plan actions before those actions are performed. The complexity of the enterprise, its form, its commercial environment, etc., will all affect the nature of the planning required.

ISA 300 *Planning an audit of financial statements* states that the main objective of planning is to enable the audit to be performed in an effective manner.

KEY POINT

The **purposes of planning** are:

- to ensure that appropriate attention is paid to the different areas of the audit
- to ensure that potential problem areas are identified
- to facilitate review.

The purposes of planning are as follows:

- To ensure that appropriate attention is paid to the different areas of the audit. This involves, for example, ensuring that adequate time is devoted to the audit of inventories, which are usually higher risk, and that petty cash, which is usually lower risk, is not over-audited. Similarly, for internal auditors, planning will help direct attention to the areas of greatest risk both in deciding on audit assignments to be undertaken and within audit assignments.
- To ensure that potential problem areas are identified, such as weaknesses in the control over creditors, which might lead to a material understatement. For internal auditors, planning will also identify potential problem areas requiring evaluation, assessment and reporting.
- To facilitate review.

Planning also assists in the proper allocation of work to the audit team and the coordination of work done by other auditors and experts.

2.2 ISA 300 key points

- Auditors should plan the audit work so as to perform the audit in an effective manner.
- Auditors should establish the overall audit strategy for the audit.
- Auditors should develop and document an overall audit plan describing the expected scope and conduct of the audit, in order to reduce audit risk to an acceptably low level.
- Auditors should develop and document the nature, timing and extent of planned audit procedures required to implement the overall audit plan.

The audit work planned should be reviewed and, if necessary, revised during the course of the audit.

Note the terminology used by ISA 300.

Audit strategy ⟶ Audit plan ⟶ Audit procedures

When planning an audit, the auditor must first establish the overall audit strategy, setting the scope, timing and direction of the audit, and guiding the development of the more detailed audit plan. The audit strategy will consider:

- scope
  - what is the applicable financial reporting framework?
  - what industry-specific factors are relevant?
- timing
  - what are the deadlines for completion of the audit?
- direction
  - what areas are likely to have the highest risks?
  - is internal control likely to be effective?

Once the audit strategy has been established, the auditor can then start developing a more detailed audit plan addressing the various matters, identified in the audit strategy. The purpose of the audit plan is to ensure that the audit objectives can be achieved through efficient use of the auditor's resources while reducing audit risk to an acceptably low level. The audit plan will include:

- a description of the planned risk assessment procedures designed to assess the risks of material misstatement (see ISA 315)
- a description of the planned substantive audit procedures judged necessary depending on the risks assessed. This leads from the relative emphasis expected to be placed on tests of control as opposed to substantive procedures
- other matters required to be carried out under the audit, such as any additional reports that are required by statute.

The planned audit procedures that the auditor intends to carry out can be described as a work plan. The auditor may use standard audit programmes (work programmes) or audit completion checklists to document the procedures to be carried out, but the auditor must be confirm that they are tailored if necessary to the particular circumstances of the audit.

KEY POINT

Planning procedures vary from one audit to the next, but auditors should take an **organised, step-by-step approach** to the planning process.

2.3 Typical planning procedures

Although the auditor's planning procedures will vary from one audit to the next the following are typical:

- Consider the **background** to the client's or department's business and attempt to ascertain any problem for that sector of industry or commerce which may affect the audit work.

- Consider an **outline plan** of the audit including the extent to which the auditor may wish to rely upon internal controls and the extent to which work can be allocated to interim or final audit stages.
- Review matters raised in the **audit of the previous year**, by examining the files and discussing points with staff previously involved in the audit to ascertain those facts which may have relevance to the current year.
- Assess the effect of any **changes in legislation** or **accounting practice** on the financial statements of the client. ISA 250A requires auditors to recognise that non-compliance with laws and regulations may have a material effect on the financial statements.
- Review any **management** or **interim accounts** which the client may have prepared, as these may indicate areas of concern in their audit.
- **Meet the senior management** of the client to identify problem areas, e.g. material variances between budgeted and actual results, and significant changes in the client's accounting procedures.
- Consider the **timing** of significant phases in the preparation of the financial statements, e.g. dates of stocktaking, balancing of personal ledgers, posting of nominal ledgers, preparation of trial balance and draft accounts.
- Consider the extent to which the **client's employees** may be able to analyse and summarise the financial data, and the relevance to the audit of work carried out by the client's internal auditors.
- Consider the need for **expert help** and the involvement of other auditors in auditing other branches or divisions.
- Determine the **number and grade of audit staff** to be allocated to each stage of the audit. Staffing is considered in more detail later in this chapter.
- Consult members of the **audit team** to discuss any foreseeable problems. Often the partners will consult the manager, who then becomes responsible for communication with other personnel used on that particular job. The preparation of a memorandum setting out the outline audit approach may be helpful.
- A **budget** should be prepared allocating the time of each member (or grade) of the audit team. This budget should be used to control the time spent on that audit and any major variation (time both under- and over-spent) should be investigated by the manager. The use of the budget for the previous year should prove a valuable aid in the preparation of this year's budget.
- The client should be informed of the **expected date of attendance** by the auditor's staff and their agreement obtained.

KEY POINT

The main failings in the planning process arise from:

- starting work before finishing planning
- inadequate documentation
- lack of understanding of the business.

The main failings in the planning process for auditors arise from:

- the auditor starting detailed testing before completing the planning work, resulting in omissions, unnecessary work and misunderstandings with the client
- inadequate documentation (see below)
- lack of a proper understanding of the business.

We referred in an earlier chapter to ISA 315, which requires auditors to obtain a knowledge of the business, sufficient to enable them to identify and understand those issues that may have a significant impact on the financial statements.

We said that knowledge is obtained both before accepting the client and after, and should cover general economic factors, industry conditions affecting the client's business, the entity itself, the entity's products, market, suppliers, expenses and operations, the entity's financial performance and condition and the reporting environment.

ACTIVITY **1**

What are the various sources of evidence available to the auditor in obtaining the requisite knowledge of the business?

Feedback to this activity is at the end of the chapter.

2.4 Analytical review procedures

We have already seen references to the use of analytical procedures in the planning stage, as a part of the substantive testing , and in the final overall review of the financial statements. This section brings together these various elements and covers in detail ISA 520 *Analytical procedures.*

Note: In this area auditors have to exercise their professional judgement. It is particularly difficult to adopt a standardised approach to analytical review – every company differs in certain respects. Some firms do have standard working papers which help the preparer decide which figures/ratios, etc. could be calculated, but the auditor must then interpret those figures.

Definitions and explanation

DEFINITION

Analytical procedures means the analysis of relationships between different types of financial information, and also non-financial information.

Analytical procedures means the analysis of relationships:

- between items of financial data and also between non-financial data deriving from the same period
- between comparable financial information deriving from different periods or different entities – to identify consistencies, predicted patterns or significant fluctuations, unexpected relationships, and the results of investigations thereof.

They are used at the planning, detailed substantive, and review stages of the audit.

When intending to apply analytical procedures as substantive procedures, the auditor should consider the following issues.

KEY POINT

When intending to apply analytical procedures as substantive procedures, auditors should consider:

- the **plausibility** and **predictability of relationships** identified
- the degree to which information can be **disaggregated**
- the **availability** of information
- the **relevance** of the information
- the **comparability** of information
- the **auditor's own knowledge** of the business.

- The **plausibility** and **predictability of relationships** identified for comparison and evaluation – there is usually a strong relationship between sales and commissions, for example.
- The degree to which information can be **disaggregated** – generally the more disaggregation, the better.

  In the case of diversified enterprises analytical review procedures are more effective when applied to financial information from individual business segments rather than to the financial statements of the entity as a whole. For example, it would be appropriate in the audit of a retail chain to apply analytical review procedures to individual outlets because in the aggregated figures, the trends and fluctuations of some outlets may be hidden by those of others.
- The **availability** of both financial and non-financial information

  If auditors are using financial information, they may already have tested its validity. They must take care in using non-financial information, and whether or not it is sufficiently reliable. This may have been prepared by management and could be biased. If the auditor wished to use internally generated production statistics to 'prove' the cost of sales figure in the financial statements, it would first be necessary to verify independently the non-financial information.
- The **relevance** of the information, for example whether budgets reflect expectations, or goals to be achieved.
- The **comparability** of information.
- The **auditor's own knowledge** of the business.

Analytical procedures obviously need to be cost-effective, and the results will be more credible if other audit work supports those conclusions, and if patterns are well established and can be accurately predicted.

In some enterprises, where accounting ratios and trends remain constant, analytical review is an efficient test. In a rapidly growing company exhibiting variable trends, it may well be a complete waste of time! As ever, auditors must choose the most cost effective selection of audit procedures.

Carrying out analytical review procedures

Analytical review procedures range from simple comparisons (e.g. current period amounts or ratios with earlier years' figures) to more sophisticated methods using computer audit software and advanced statistical techniques (e.g. multiple regression analysis).

Note the wide-ranging nature of analytical review procedures. Essentially, analytical review involves comparison. The auditor wishes to ensure that the various items making up the financial statements are consistent with:

- each other (for example, the relationship between receivables and sales, or between current assets and current liabilities)
- known trends (for example, the likely effects of government restraints on a hire purchase business) – such trends may be predictions produced by the auditor
- the auditor's own knowledge of the business.

The auditor should ask the following key questions:

- What data, ratios and statistics exist which are of significance for the business?
- With what should they compare?

The position may be summarised as follows:

Types of data, ratios, etc.	*Comparison with*
Financial data (e.g. items in annual statements, management accounts, budgets, account balances)	• Preceding period • Budgets and forecasts
Non-financial data (e.g. production and employment statistics)	• Entries in accounting records • Other financial data
Ratios and percentages (developed from financial and non-financial data, e.g. inventory turnover ratios)	• Preceding period • Budgets and forecasts • Industry statistics

Procedures

KEY POINT

Steps in carrying out analytical procedures:

1 Obtain an **understanding** of the business.
2 Identify relevant and credible **relationships**.
3 Establish the **validity** of any data to be used.
4 Predict a likely **range** of **expected values.**

The procedures remain the same whatever the stage of the audit. A series of steps are identified which are summarised and commented on below.

1 Obtain an **understanding** of the business.
2 Identify relevant and credible **relationships** – For example, the gross profit percentage expresses the relationship between sales and cost of sales. In many businesses this ratio may fluctuate widely and may be of little use to auditors, but for companies in the retail industry, for example, this ratio would generally remain constant.
3 Establish the **validity** of any data to be used – Auditors may decide to use their client's constant gross profit percentage in their analytical review techniques. They could independently verify cost of sales, and then apply the percentage to it.

5 Compare predictions with actual and consider the implications of any variances.

6 Seek explanations for any variances and corroborate those explanations.

4 Predict a likely **range** of **expected values** – The audited cost of sales percentage can be used to predict the value of sales. Auditors must take all their knowledge of the business into account in making this prediction. For example, they may know of a factor in this particular accounting period affecting the gross profit percentage and should adjust their calculations accordingly.

Auditors should allow for the effect of:

- general inflation (as measured by a suitable index)
- specific price changes (goods and services used by the enterprise)
- seasonal factors
- industrial disputes, including those affecting key suppliers
- changes in the level of business activity in the economy as a whole
- technological changes making products or services obsolete
- changes in management policy, e.g. expanding or contracting operations (this should be apparent from a review of management or directors' minutes).

5 **Compare predictions** with actual and consider the implications of any variances, remember that there are two points to look out for:
  - the changes which *do* occur but which differ significantly from those *expected*
  - the changes which would normally be *expected* to occur but which *fail to do so.*

  Auditors should investigate both categories fully.

6 **Seek explanations** for the above and corroborate those explanations – Auditors should never just take management's word for why a change has happened or failed to happen.

Analytical review procedures can be a good audit technique where there are identifiable and consistent relationships between figures. But avoid making the mistake of imputing validity to two figures simply on the basis that the relationship between them appears reasonable.

For example, there may indeed be the usual relationship between sales and cost of sales – perhaps a 20% gross profit. But if selling prices have remained constant and supplies have become increasingly expensive, it may be that 20% is no longer reasonable. Procedure **4** above avoids this problem.

Auditors can use such analytical review techniques at various stages of the audit:

At the planning stage

Analytical procedures at the planning stage should assist in determining the nature and extent of appropriate audit procedures to be carried out. The procedures can be used at this stage of the audit to help highlight potentially high risk areas. For example, if based on interim or draft financial statements, the auditor discovers that turnover has increased, but distribution costs have fallen, there is the possibility of a misstatement in these areas. You should note that analytical procedures are also useful at later stages in the audit, as indicated below.

At the detailed testing stage

In most cases, analytical review procedures will be used in conjunction with other substantive tests. However, there may be circumstances in which analytical review procedures by themselves can provide the required level of assurance. One example would be where the value of one item can be verified directly by reference to another item of data, the validity of which has already been established (for example, where commission paid to the sales force is a known percentage of the value of sales, this expense item can be verified directly by reference to the audited figure for sales). This procedure is sometimes referred to as 'proof in total'.

KEY POINT

Where the explanations received for material unexpected variations cannot be substantiated, auditors will need to obtain sufficient evidence using **alternative procedures**.

Where the explanations received for material unexpected variations cannot be substantiated, the auditor will need to obtain sufficient evidence using alternative procedures (e.g. by increasing the extent of other substantive tests). Where they indicate the possibility of misstatement, the auditor should conduct a thorough investigation to determine whether in fact a misstatement has occurred and, if so, its full extent and its effect on the financial statements.

For example:

- If there has been a significant increase in the repairs and maintenance expense account balances, the auditor should consider additional vouching of the constituent items – this might disclose misclassified (e.g. capital) or improper expenditure.
- If there has been an increase in stock in relation to sales or a reduction in gross profit percentages, this might cause the auditor to extend the tests with respect to the realisability and market value of stock.

If tests cannot be extended or where alternative forms of evidence are not available, auditors will need to consider qualifying their audit opinion. Similarly, if the results of the analytical review procedures indicate that material error probably exists, but cannot be rectified because its exact extent cannot be quantified, this may cause auditors to consider qualifying their opinion.

At the review of financial statements stage

At the final stage of the audit, the auditor should carry out an overall review of the information in the financial statements and compare it with other available data. This should not reveal material unexpected variations, as these should normally have been detected at an earlier stage of the audit. If however, any anomalies are identified, these should be investigated and resolved.

ACTIVITY 2

Analytical review procedures are used by the auditor for a number of purposes. Describe briefly the nature of these procedures during the audit and the circumstances in which they will be used by the auditor.

Feedback to this activity is at the end of the chapter.

2.5 Stakeholder dialogue

KEY POINT

Auditors should communicate with the stakeholders to identify any risks arising from the organisation's interfaces between its various parts.

A key aspect of planning is to understand all potential stakeholders of the audit. Stakeholders are those groups who have an interest in the organisation and who are affected by its actions and decisions. In addition to shareholders/owners, stakeholders may also include present and former employees, customers, suppliers and society as a whole.

It is important to talk to stakeholders because risks often occur in the interfaces between different parts of organisations, and in relationships between internal and external stakeholders. Therefore, discussions will help identify how risks are being managed and whether there are any specific problems that will require further investigation.

During the planning stage of the audit, the auditor needs to identify the stakeholders and the inputs, outputs and measurables involved. Stakeholders may also have key requirements from the audit that need to be factored into the audit plan.

3 The overall audit plan

3.1 Designing, documenting and recording of the audit plan

ISA 300 requires that auditors must document the overall audit plan to cover the following areas:

- the auditor's knowledge of the business
- risk and materiality
- the nature, timing and extent of procedures
- coordination, direction, supervision and review.

3.2 The timing of audit work

KEY POINT

Auditing may be:

- performed **at** or **after the year end**
- divided into **interim** and **final** audits
- **continuous**.

The timing of audit work must be planned to suit the nature of the business being audited. There are three main possibilities:

- All the audit work is done **at** or **after the year end**. This is likely to be the case when the business being audited is small.
- The work is divided into **interim** and **final audits**, planning and tests of controls taking place at the interim stage and the substantive balance sheet audit taking place at the final stage.
- The third possibility is **continuous audits**, where the client is so large that the auditor is present throughout the year.

KEY POINT

The work of planning is a **continuous process** throughout the audit.

Although the planning memorandum (the document containing the audit plan) will be prepared before detailed audit work commences, it is important to bear in mind the fact that the planning stage does not end there.

There will inevitably be adjustments to the original plan which can only be discovered later. A significant breakdown in internal control may entail more work; a change in the timing of physical stocktaking may mean rescheduling the audit. The work of planning is, therefore, a continuous process throughout the audit.

Similarly, internal auditors will also produce an audit planning memorandum or terms of reference, setting out the scope, objectives, approach, key risks and timescales of the review.

Effective system based project control techniques can aid the planning of audits, in particular by scheduling the stages of audits, factoring in resources available and taking account of other audit commitments.

3.3 Developing the audit plan to meet the audit objectives

KEY POINT

A 'Planning Memorandum' should be used to record decisions and prevent key areas from being missed during the audit.

Most practising firms and internal audit departments have formalised the planning exercise for all but the very small audit assignment by using a **Standard Planning Memorandum** in which evidence of initial decisions as to the appropriate procedures relevant to each assignment is recorded, together with adjustments and additions to those procedures resulting from audit tests and review processes. The following is an example of such a checklist designed to achieve planning and control objectives. Do not be too concerned by references to ideas we have not yet covered; they will be covered in later sections of the text.

Prepared by:
Date:
Reviewed by:
Date:

Planning Memorandum

1 Job timetable Give provisional dates of timing of audit work: – Planning meeting with client – Commencement of interim audit – Conclusion of interim audit – Management letter (interim) – Debtors/creditors circularisation.	*Planned date*	*Actual date*
2 Changes since previous audit 2(a) In the nature of the client's business (for example, changes in product range, terms of sales, etc.). 2(b) In the management structure or key financial/accounting personnel. 2(c) In the accounting system (including those resulting from previous management letters). 2(d) In external requirements (for example, accounting standards, legislation, rules, etc.).	*Detailed comments*	
3 Planning decisions 3(a) The main changes in the audit programme from the previous period are (give both changes in tests and in sample sizes). 3(b) Indicate on an audit area basis whether it is intended to seek reliance on internal controls: – Sales and debtors – Purchases and creditors – Stock and work-in-progress – Salaries and wages – Bank and cash – Fixed assets – Other (specify). 3(c) Indicate those areas in which material errors have been identified in previous periods and audit emphasis to be placed thereon 3(d) The following systems areas are to be (re-) flowcharted. 3(e) The following sections of the permanent file are to be created/updated. 3(f) Specialist assistance required (specify). 3(g) Indicate whether an audit committee meeting is mandatory for this client prior to signing of the audit report.	*Detailed comments*	

3(h)	Prepare a summary of schedules and other details that client staff will provide for us.	
3(i)	Where we provide accountancy services, indicate whether: (i) our accountancy and audit work has been planned to avoid duplication of work (ii) staff engaged on the accountancy work have been briefed as to the assurance that will be placed on their work and the audit objectives that are relevant.	
3(j)	State briefly other services we provide for the client and their impact on nature and timing of audit.	
4	**Internal audit department**	*Detailed comments*
4(a)	Indicate to what extent we are able to reduce the level of our audit tests by relying on relevant internal audit work.	
4(b)	State briefly the liaison with the internal auditors: (i) at the planning stage of the audit (ii) during the transactions audit (iii) at the final stage.	
5	**Briefing instructions**	***Date*** ***Name*** ***Level***
5(a)	State any particular sequence in which the work is to be carried out.	
5(b)	State any specific points which require particular attention or parts to be done by a specific person.	
5(c)	Insert date when briefing meeting with audit team held and names and levels of staff briefed.	
6	**Supervision and review**	***Date*** ***Name*** ***Level***
6(a)	State any particular stages (or areas of difficulty) at which the senior is to refer back to the manager.	
6(b)	State how, and at what stages, it is proposed to supervise and review the transactions audit.	

7	**Financial ratios**	***Previous year (actual) %***	***Budget for year %***	***Management accounts to ... %***
7(a)	From the most recent management information, extract the following ratios (if management information not reliable or available include such observations in 7(b) below): – Gross profit: sales – Distribution costs: sales – Administrative costs: sales – Net profit before tax: sales – Net profit before tax: total net assets/liabilities – Rate of stock turnover – Number of weeks debtors			

	– Number of weeks creditors – Current assets (excluding stock): current liabilities – Shareholders' funds: total assets.
7(b)	State the conclusions drawn and steps to be taken in the light of 7(a).
8	**Time budget** State briefly the reasons for significant variances in the current year budget with the budget and actual time of previous year.

Whilst the internal audit planning memorandum may have different steps, the same principles apply. The auditor will have a schedule of work or planning memorandum covering key stages of the audit and 'planned versus actual' timescales and capture of key decisions.

3.4 In the exam

In answering a question in the exam on planning, it is possible that you would have to put together an audit plan document. The examiner is unlikely to provide you with a standard form and the marks will not allow scope for anything as ambitious as the above!

The examiner will be looking for two things:

- that you can demonstrate your knowledge of the relevant ISAs for external auditors
- that you have spotted the potential problems with this client and suggested in outline how they might be dealt with.

A good question on this area would give you details about a client for whom you have to formulate an audit plan. To show your knowledge of the relevant ISA, you could structure your answer around the planning procedures noted earlier.

ACTIVITY 3

Outline **six** typical planning procedures.

Feedback to this activity is at the end of the chapter.

4 Audit risk

4.1 Introduction

KEY POINT

There may be a significant **risk** involved in auditing some clients; the 'riskier' the client is, the more work the auditor will plan to perform.

The ways in which risk models are used can be linked to the objectives of the audit. External auditors are principally concerned with the risk that the financial statements contain misstatements that they may not detect. Internal auditors are concerned with the risks that the organisation will not achieve its objectives and hence will consider all the risks which could be financial, operational, or compliance in nature.

(a) **Risk models** are discussed later in this chapter as an internal audit tool to determine the risks associated with different areas of an organisation in order to prioritise audit resources and assist in long term planning. In the case of the internal auditor there is the potential to decide that the audit should not take place at all as the risk model indicates low risk. External auditors use client screening procedures which include an assessment of the risks associated with a potential client **before** a decision is made to accept the assignment. Unlike internal auditors if the risk assessment is high the audit is more likely to be rejected.

(b) **Risk-based** audit is primarily (but not exclusively) used by external auditors to identify the high risk areas of a client's business and hence focus the audit effort. Consequently this is used for short-term planning on a particular audit **after** the decision has been made to accept the assignment (explained in more detail below).

4.2 Alternative approaches to an external audit

KEY POINT

There are two main ways of gathering the evidence needed to meet audit objectives:

- systems approach
- direct verification approach.

In order to achieve the audit objectives, evidence is required. In practice, there are two main ways this evidence is acquired:

- **Systems approach** – The evaluation of the system of internal control forms the basis of the audit. Detailed testing of items in the financial statements is kept to a minimum.
- **Direct verification approach** – More detailed testing of items in the financial statements is carried out. The opinion is based upon the ability of the auditor to obtain sufficient appropriate evidence from a number of sources. This approach will be used if the auditor cannot rely on systems of internal control.

In most situations, the systems based approach is used, as it is the most efficient method of arriving at an audit opinion.

4.3 Risk-based audit

KEY POINT

Risk-based audit is used by auditors to focus resources on high-risk clients and on high-risk areas of a client's business.

The risk-based audit is a development of the systems based audit. It is used by auditors in order to concentrate on high-risk clients and on high-risk areas of a client's business, rather than performing detailed audit tests on all areas of a client's business. It enables a cost effective audit to be achieved, and is dealt with in ISA 315 *Understanding the entity and its environment and assessing the risks of material misstatement.* This points out that auditors require an *understanding* of the accounting and internal control systems, sufficient to plan the audit and develop an effective audit approach.

KEY POINT

Audit confidence is measured here as 100% minus audit risk.

Audit risk can be set at any level. It is usually set at 4 to 6%.

Auditors aim to ensure that there is no more than, say, a 5% risk that their opinion on the financial statements is incorrect. Or, in other words, they are ensuring that they are 95% certain that their opinion on the financial statements is correct. (**Audit confidence** is measured here as 100% minus audit risk.) The percentage used (here 95%) is one of convention only. It implies (correctly) that we can never be 100% sure of any conclusion. This is known as **audit risk** and means that auditors accept that 5 in every 100 reports issued may be incorrect. Audit risk can be set at any level. If auditors set it at 100%, there is no need to do any work at all, but there is a high risk of being found negligent! Auditors in practice 'set' audit risk at 4 to 6% and tailor their audit procedures accordingly.

KEY POINT

Total audit risk comprises:

- **inherent risk** (or IR)
- **control risk** (or CR)
- **detection risk** (or DR).

$AR = IR \times CR \times DR$

Total audit risk, the risk of giving an inappropriate opinion when financial statements are materially misstated, has three components:

- inherent risk (or IR)
- control risk (or CR)
- detection risk (or DR).

These three risks multiplied together give total audit risk. Thus:

$$AR = IR \times CR \times DR$$

These risks are explained below. Remember though that it is the auditor's judgement that is always used to determine the value to be placed on these items – there is no hard and fast rule that the auditor can follow.

KEY POINT

The lower the risk level required, the greater the audit work required.

Broadly, the lower the risk level required, the greater the audit work required.

In most cases, internal auditors will operate a risk-based approach to auditing, making decisions based on the impact and probability of risks occurring and therefore directing attention towards highest impact and highest probability risks:

- **Impact of risk** – If the risk materialised, what would be the scale of effect, i.e. how far could it affect the area under review? For example, if the company breached regulatory requirements resulting in fines and negative publicity, that could be assessed as high impact because of the adverse effect on profit and reputation.
- **Probability of risk** – This looks at how likely the risk is to materialise. A risk may have a high impact (e.g. complete loss of a building due to fire), but much lower probability.

Assessing impact and probability helps prioritisation and understanding of the nature of the risks involved.

4.4 Determining the areas of audit risk

DEFINITION

Inherent risk: the susceptibility of an account balance or class of transactions to material misstatement, irrespective of related internal controls.

(a) *Inherent risk*

Inherent risk is assessed at both the financial statement (entity) level, and at the level of individual balances and transactions. At the entity level, inherent risk will be affected by such items as how much the company is subject to market forces, the cash situation of the company, the trading history of the company, and the nature and incidence of unusual transactions. A business in the construction industry is more risky than a food retailer as it is more volatile.

At the account balance or class of transactions level factors affecting inherent risk will include the susceptibility to misappropriation, the complexity of the underlying transactions or the degree of judgement involved in determining account balances.

Inventory, for example is more inherently risky than cash as there is greater scope for manipulation and error.

DEFINITION

Control risk: the risk that material misstatement could occur in an account balance or class of transaction which would not be prevented or detected by the accounting or internal control systems.

(b) *Control risk*

Control risk will be affected by such factors as the control environment at the company including, for example, the integrity of the staff operating the system, the extent of supervisory controls, and the strength of controls in particular account areas.

The preliminary assessment of control risk should always be high unless the auditor can either identify controls that are likely to prevent or detect misstatements in each area, or plans to perform tests of control to support the assessment.

The accounting and internal control system should be fully documented by the auditor. The auditor's assessment of control risk should be clearly stated.

Evidence should be obtained through tests of control to support any assessment of control risk that is less than high; the lower the assessment of control risk, the more evidence is needed to show that systems are suitably designed and operating effectively.

When tests of control are complete, auditors should review their preliminary assessment of control risk.

DEFINITION

Detection risk: the risk that auditors' substantive procedures do not detect a material misstatement in an account balance or class of transaction.

(c) *Detection risk*

This is the 'variable' and is determined by re-arranging the audit risk equation.

$$DR = AR \div (IR \times CR)$$

The auditor determines the level of total audit risk that is acceptable and estimates the inherent and control risks by assessing the factors referred to previously. Detection risk can then be calculated as shown in the following example:

AR = 5% IR = 50% CR = 20%

$$DR = 0.05 \div (0.5 \times 0.2) = 0.5 \text{ i.e. } 50\%$$

4.5 Client risk evaluation questionnaire

Many auditors use formal procedures at the planning stage of the audit in order to assess inherent and control risk. Such questionnaires will include the factors that affect inherent risk at the financial statement and account balance levels. Questions on control risk will cover the control environment and the existence of specific controls. Audit software could be used to record the answers to the questions and provide guidance on the level of testing required. Use of audit software is discussed later in this text.

5 Planning materiality

5.1 Concept of materiality

The concept of materiality was examined in an earlier chapter. There, we concluded that an item is material if its omission or misstatement would reasonably influence the decisions of users of the financial statements.

KEY POINT

In planning the audit, the auditor needs to establish **materiality levels** to ensure that any material misstatement or omissions in the accounting records are discovered.

In planning the audit, the auditor therefore needs to establish **materiality levels** to ensure that any material misstatement or omissions in the accounting records are discovered.

Materiality will also be relevant to the internal auditor, although more from quantifying risk exposure of general findings to management rather than from the point of view of the financial statements.

5.2 Establishing materiality levels

Materiality levels are used in two ways in an audit:

- in the overview of the financial statements
- in calculating sample sizes for testing of transactions.

KEY POINT

An **overall materiality level** is set based on the evaluation of client risk; the materiality for sampling purposes is then usually derived from overall materiality.

Firstly, an overall materiality level is set based on the evaluation of client risk. When detailed audit work is undertaken on various types of transactions, the materiality for sampling purposes is usually derived from overall materiality. It may well be that for a risky area of the audit, the sampling materiality level is set well below the overall materiality level.

Different measures of materiality can be used in practice. The most common bases used are a percentage of turnover, pre-tax profit or asset values.

Clearly the lower the materiality level, the larger the sample size will be in the class of transactions being tested. The use of sampling techniques in auditing is covered in chapter 16 of this text.

6 Audit programmes

6.1 Designing the audit programme

ISA 300 requires auditors to develop and document the nature, timing and extent of planned audit procedures required to implement the overall audit plan.

KEY POINT

The **audit programme** is essentially a record of the audit testing. It should specify audit objectives for each area and time budgets.

The audit programme is essentially a record of the audit testing. It specifies the nature and extent of the checking, and the members of staff who have carried out the work. It also contains evidence of review of work.

The audit programme serves as:

- a set of instructions to the audit team
- a means to control and record the proper execution of the audit work

- a record of the audit procedures to be adopted, the audit objectives, timing, sample size and basis of selection for each area.

The audit programme is an important part of the auditor's working papers and records a significant part of the audit evidence required to justify the audit opinion.

Audit programmes should be constructed carefully. They should not stifle initiative, and the work specified should be regarded as a minimum and not a maximum.

EXAM HINT

You are unlikely to be asked to produce an audit programme, but rather a list of specific tests.

You are unlikely to be asked to produce an audit programme, but rather a list of specific tests. However, an example of an audit programme is reproduced below as this does bring together all the objectives and tests for one area.

Example of an audit programme

AUDIT PROGRAMME — Prepared by:

AUDIT AREA: Wages and Salaries — Date:

Client: — Reviewed by:

Period: — Date:

Tests of control

Control objectives

To establish that:

(a) the computation of wages and salaries is only in respect of the client's employees and at authorised rates of pay

(b) wages and salaries are in accordance with records of work performed, e.g. time, output, commissions on sales

(c) payrolls are calculated accurately

(d) payments are only made to the correct employees

(e) payroll deductions are correctly accounted for and paid to the appropriate third parties

(f) all transactions related to wages and salaries are accurately entered in the accounting records.

Tests of control to be carried out

(a) Test sample of time sheets, clock cards or other records, for approval by responsible official. Pay particular attention to the approval of overtime.

(b) Test authority for payment of casual labour, particularly if in cash.

(c) Observe wages distribution for adherence to procedures ensuring employees sign for wages, that unclaimed wages are rebanked, etc.

(d) Test authorisation for payroll amendments by reference to personnel records.

(e) Test control over payroll amendments.

(f) Examine evidence of checking of payroll calculations (e.g. a signature of the financial controller).

(g) Examine evidence of approval of payrolls by a responsible official.

(h) Examine evidence of independent checks of payrolls (e.g. by internal audit).

(i) Inspect payroll reconciliations.

(j) Examine explanations for payroll expense variances.

(k) Test authorities for payroll deductions.

(l) Test controls over unclaimed wages.

Substantive procedures

(a) Select sample of time records, etc. and test casts and calculations.

(b) Test sample of personnel records for:

  (i) rates of pay

  (ii) authorisation of changes in rates of pay

  (iii) leavers' and joiners' personal details.

(c) Select payrolls and:

  (i) check to time records, etc. to ensure employees are only paid for work done

  (ii) test to personnel records to ensure employees exist and are being paid at the correct rate

  (iii) test casts and calculations with reference to tax, national insurance and other tables

  (iv) check deductions are paid over to the tax authorities on time and that no unrecorded penalties may arise.

(d) If a payroll control account is maintained, check this to the nominal ledger.

(e) Test totals of cheques drawn to net pay due to employees and tax authorities.

(f) Test postings of payrolls to nominal ledger accounts.

6.2 Standardised audit programmes and professional judgement

DEFINITION

A **standardised audit programme** is a pre-prepared listing of objectives and tests which can be used on any audit.

Standardised audit programmes are common in practice and are often drawn from a database of procedures in large firms.

Their advantages are that they streamline work and act as a checklist to ensure that all important areas are considered. They improve the efficiency of the audit and facilitate delegation and control.

However, they have a disadvantage in that, if used slavishly, they may stifle professional judgement. Auditors need to use professional judgement in their work as all audits will be different, and tests therefore need to be designed that take account of the different circumstances found in each audit.

A middle way is used by some firms who, in their audit manual, will suggest the items to be included in an audit programme rather than requiring a standard form to be filled in.

The internal auditor may also use standardised audit programmes for certain types of audits. The same dilemma is faced in balancing use of judgement against making best use of information already there. In general, consistency of approach will be important to the internal auditor (i.e. same steps, standards and requirements), but this will not normally be a set programme of audits, except in the routine areas. For example, branch auditors may have a standard set of audit objectives and tests. However, a completely new area under review would need to follow the appropriate audit principles, including understanding risks, assessing controls, identifying objectives, but this would be less clearly defined.

Having the right computer system to support the audit process can help generate consistent, efficient but flexible audit programmes for internal or external auditors, providing an ease of tailoring to match the risk of the area.

7 Staffing and training issues

KEY POINT

Planning procedures should include the appropriate **staffing** of the audit.

7.1 Staffing

We noted earlier in the chapter that planning procedures include the appropriate staffing of the audit. Planning needs to cover such points as:

- number of staff required
- level of expertise required
- length of time each member of staff will be needed
- exact timing of their work.

To assist in the allocation of staff to each stage of the audit, larger firms will designate job titles to each member of the audit team.

Job title	*Job description as regards the audit*
Partner	• Agree fees with client. • Review audit. • Sign audit report (after approval of accounts by directors).
Manager	• Set broad time limits to job. • Assign staff to job. • Agree detailed timetable with supervisor or senior. • Review staff requirements and timetable at various stages. • Review audit in detail at end of interim and final audits.
Supervisor or junior manager	• Take charge of large jobs, e.g. a large diversified company, where each branch or division is audited by a senior.
Senior	• Take charge of the audit. • Agree audit timetable with client, and manager or supervisor. • Decide on detailed audit work.
Clerks, semi-seniors and juniors	• Compile audit working papers. • Perform detailed audit work assigned by seniors.

For internal auditors, the same decisions will need to be made on the level of staffing and expertise. However, the roles will be less rigid and dependent on what the auditor can bring to any particular review. There may be a need for specialist auditors to be involved (e.g. IT or Treasury) and, in this case, the lead auditor will need to ensure that such expertise is available during the appropriate timescales of the review.

7.2 Training

KEY POINT

Auditors should undertake CPD to ensure their knowledge is up to date.

We saw in an earlier chapter that membership via qualification with an RQB is a prerequisite of membership of an RSB and hence entitlement to audit. Training requirements include the setting of examinations and practical training. The practical training does not stop when an auditor has qualified. The practical training continues through the requirement to undertake **continuing professional development (CPD)**.

From January 2005 the ACCA is introducing, on a phased timetable, compulsory CPD for all members, under an initiative called 'ACCA Realise'. Four areas of activity are recognised as relevant CPD:

- e-learning, e.g. on-line learning, or learning from CD-ROMs or audio tapes
- work-based, e.g. participating in mentoring or coaching activities

- research/reading/presenting, e.g. reading technical journals
- courses/events, e.g. attending courses and conferences.

All ACCA members (except those who are fully retired) must undertake annual CPD and must make a CPD return annually. Participation is being phased in, based on date of entry to membership. The table below shows the starting year for each category.

Phase 1: members admitted since 1 Jan 2001, and all members holding Practising Certificates or Insolvency Licences	CPD period 1 Jan 2005 to 31 Dec 2005, submission deadline 1 Jan 2006
Phase 2: members admitted between 1 Jan 1995 and 31 Dec 2000	CPD period 1 Jan 2006 to 31 Dec 2006, submission deadline 1 Jan 2007
Phase 3: all remaining members who registered before 1995	CPD period 1 Jan 2007 to 31 Dec 2007, submission deadline 1 Jan 2008

Any member can opt to begin earlier than scheduled; indeed the ACCA encourages early adoption.

Members can complete their CPD in one of two ways, either via their employer (if their employer has an approved CPD scheme) or the 'unit scheme' route. Under the unit scheme route, a member must complete and record 40 units of CPD annually, each unit equating to one hour of qualifying activity. Every member must complete a CPD return annually, confirming that they either have participated in an approved employer's scheme, or that they have achieved the necessary number of units.

Large firms run internal training courses to satisfy the CPD requirement; smaller firms are often members of a training consortium which provides equivalent courses.

7.3 Recognising the needs for the use of experts

ISA 620 *Using the work of an expert* recognises that an auditor has a general knowledge of business, but cannot be expected to have a detailed knowledge in all disciplines. During the course of an audit, therefore, the auditor may need to consider audit evidence from specialists in arriving at an audit opinion. This is considered in detail in a later chapter.

8 Recording the audit process

8.1 Working papers

ISA 230 *Documentation* states that working papers are the record of planning, performance, supervision and review of an audit, as well as of the evidence obtained to support the audit report.

KEY POINT

Auditors should record their reasoning on significant matters that require the exercise of judgement.

Auditors are required to record all matters which are important in supporting the report and in particular their reasoning on all significant matters that require the exercise of judgement. It is in areas such as these that the auditor may subsequently be questioned, often with the benefit of hindsight, and it is important for auditors to be able to show what they knew at the time.

Working papers should enable an experienced auditor with no previous connection with the audit to understand the work performed and the basis of decisions taken.

Working papers should not be made available to third parties without client consent. Extracts from the papers can be made available to the client entirely at the discretion of the auditor. However the auditor's working papers are not a substitute for proper accounting records!

If the auditor is required to defend their audit opinion in a court of law, then clearly it is important that the working paper files are clear, logical and concise and adequately support this audit opinion.

Internal auditors should also clearly document evidence obtained during the audit to support their findings and conclusions.

The detailed contents and structure of typical audit files are considered below.

8.2 Contents of working papers

Working papers should include the following:

- information likely to be of continuing importance, ie *permanent file information* such as Memorandum or Articles of Association and other information concerning the legal and organisational structure of the entity
- auditing planning information, e.g. time budgets and details of client's stocktaking
- details of the internal control and the accounting systems of the business, including the auditor's evaluation and assessment of risk
- details of audit work carried out, including notes of errors, action taken and conclusions drawn, including work carried out by other auditors
- evidence of review of audit work
- supporting schedules to financial statements
- audit summary including significant and unusual matters
- copies of approved financial statements and auditors' reports, letters of representation and other correspondence with management.

The structure of internal audit working papers may be different but the same obligations apply. Key requirements include the following:

- permanent file information
- planning information, including timescales, time budgets, planning memorandums and assessment of risks at the planning stage
- risk and control evaluations
- testing work papers and records of other detailed work
- conclusions from tests and risks evaluations
- audit findings, recommendations and management comment
- draft and final audit reports
- evidence of audit management review.

8.3 Standardisation of working papers

KEY POINT

Standardisation of working papers offers several advantages, but an element of flexibility is essential.

Standardisation of working papers offers several advantages:

- It improves the efficiency of the preparation and review of working papers.
- It facilitates the delegation of work.
- It helps to maintain quality control.
- It is useful for routine documentation such as checklists for financial reporting standards, statements of standard accounting practice and specimen letters.
- It can make best use of readily available technology to provide a central store of information related to the audit, providing accessible and clear documentation.

However, a certain amount of flexibility is essential, and it is important that the auditor should always remember the need to exercise professional judgement. It is never appropriate to follow a standard approach mechanically.

8.4 General guidelines

The following general guidelines may be useful.

- For manual documents, permanent ink should be used (although there is currently some debate over this as it has been proved scientifically that it is harder to destroy all traces of pencil).
- Descriptions should be given of audit symbols used.
- All working papers must be prepared neatly and tidily so that they clearly, concisely and logically show the schedules, results of tests, etc. They should each be headed with:
  - client's name and file number
  - period end or date
  - subject of working paper
  - reference of working paper within current or permanent file (see below)
  - initials of preparer and date of preparation
  - initials of reviewer and date of review.

All working papers which record tests must be concluded by the person undertaking the test, with a summary of the result of the test and a conclusion (or opinion) on its effectiveness.

Schedules supporting a figure in the balance sheet or profit and loss account should:

- consist of a **summarised schedule** (a lead schedule) showing the make-up of the figure in the balance sheet, and be supported by backing schedules showing the make-up of those figures on the lead schedule
- have extensive **cross-referencing** between the backing schedules, lead schedules and the accounts themselves to facilitate explanation of any figure in the accounts or working paper
- give **comparative figures** for the previous year so that the auditor can explain and satisfy himself on movement/differences between the years
- **be adjusted** if any final adjustments are made to the accounts
- show the **tests** carried out to verify the figures on the schedules.

KEY POINT

If the client has prepared an accounting schedule, this should be made available to the auditor.

The client may already have prepared a schedule which the auditor requires for the audit. In order to save audit time and costs, arrangements should be made for copies to be available to the auditor (who needs to be satisfied as to their reliability). If the client does not, but could, prepare schedules, they should be encouraged to do so.

Internal audit should similarly retain appropriate working papers, and cross-referenced to any decisions or conclusions made.

All records of matters raised during the audit must show the reply received to the query and the fact that the query has been cleared for audit purposes.

KEY POINT

Auditing working papers are usually filed in two separate files:

- permanent file
- current file.

8.5 Filing of audit working papers

Auditing working papers are usually filed in two separate files:

- permanent file
- current file.

The contents are considered in detail below.

8.6 The permanent audit file (PAF)

The purposes of the permanent audit file are:

- to document information which is of recurring value regarding items appearing in the financial statements
- to document information of a permanent nature regarding the client's business
- to give audit staff new to the audit information regarding the client's affairs and the nature of the audit.

The following table illustrates a typical permanent audit file's contents. You do not need to memorise this table, but it will give you an idea of the type of and examples of information held on this file.

Typical contents of Permanent Audit File

Section	*Title*		*Information contained*		
1	**Index**	–			
2	**Constitution**		Copies of:		
		(a)	Company's initial founding documents or	–	detailing legal form, business objects, borrowing powers
		(b)	Partnership agreement or		
		(c)	Trust deed		
3	**Background and organisation**	(a)	Nature and history of the business		
		(b)	Ownership		
		(c)	Registered office		
		(d)	Management structure	–	including organisation chart
		(e)	Industry	–	client's size, economic factors affecting the industry, seasonal fluctuations and demands
		(f)	Premises and plant	–	locations, extent of facilities, owned or leased, age, capital expenditure budgets
		(g)	Products		
		(h)	Purchasing	–	volumes, main suppliers
		(i)	Sales	–	volumes, main customers, methods of distribution, pricing policies, exports
		(j)	Personnel	–	numbers, analyses by departments or function, method of remuneration, contracts, union agreements, pension schemes
4	**Systems**	(a)	Details of methods of accounting	–	manual, IT, costing systems
	(For larger audits this section could be held on a separate file)	(b)	List of accounting records and where kept		
		(c)	Flowcharts and specimens of accounting documents and accounting codes		
		(d)	Accounting manuals		
		(e)	Statistical information	–	composition of reserves, how they arose and movements

				–	a 5-year comparison of *performance indicators* (major accounting ratios)
				–	industry statistics
5	**Contracts, agreements, minutes**	(a)	Leases	–	extracts
		(b)	Title deeds inspected annually by auditor	–	details
		(c)	Royalty agreements	–	extracts
		(d)	Minutes of continuing importance	–	directors' meetings
				–	members' meetings
		(e)	Prospectuses	–	copies
		(f)	Stock Exchange undertakings	–	copy
6	**Group**	(a)	Group structure		
		(b)	Auditors of all group companies		
7	**Taxation**	(a)	Special concessions with Inland Revenue		
		(b)	VAT information		
		(c)	Group elections		
8	**Other Professional Advisors**	(a)	Bankers		
		(b)	Lawyers		
		(c)	Stockbrokers		
		(d)	Registrars		
9	**Job administration**	(a)	Letter of engagement	–	time budgets and costings
		(b)	Letters of authority		
		(c)	Job administration		
10	**Control**	(a)	Control schedule of *rotational tests*		
		(b)	Control over branch and site visits		
		(c)	Deed examination		
		(d)	Review of other auditors on group audits		
		(e)	Copies of management letters		
11	**Miscellaneous**		Details of other client information of a permanent nature		

KEY POINT

The **current audit file** should:

- provide a record of the work planned
- detail the work performed
- enable *any* person to satisfy themselves that an adequate examination for audit purposes has been made of the client's affairs.

Internal auditors will have similar permanent files to capture relevant information for audit reviews. This could include the same type of background information but will be primarily an ongoing reference point for internal auditors and so will be what is appropriate to the organisation.

8.7 The current audit file (CAF)

The purposes of the current audit file are:

- to provide a record of the work planned
- to detail the work performed including:
  - procedures followed
  - tests performed

  - information obtained
  - conclusions reached

- to enable *any* person – but especially the reporting partner reviewing the audit – to satisfy themselves that an adequate examination for audit purposes has been made of the client's affairs.

The following table shows a typical current audit file's contents. Again, there is no need for you to memorise this, but take it as illustrative of the type of information held on this file.

Typical contents of Current Audit File

Section	*Title*		*Information contained*
1	**Index**	-	
2	**Financial statements**	(a)	Copy of draft accounts
		(b)	Copy of final signed accounts
3	**Reports and final papers**	(a)	Copies of all draft and final reports issued to client
		(b)	Comments received from client and Letter of Representation
		(c)	Points on accounts and points carried forward to next year
		(d)	Management Letters
		(e)	Final journal entries
		(f)	Company accounts checklist
		(g)	Reporting partner review
		(h)	Audit completion report
4	**Job administration and planning**	(a)	Planning programme
		(b)	Budget and fee estimate
		(c)	Time and cost summary
		(d)	Briefing notes
		(e)	Copy of planning letter to client
		(f)	Points forward from previous year
5	**Balance sheet, income statement and cash flow statement audit**	(a)	Lead schedules
		(b)	Audit programmes
		(c)	Detailed working papers and conclusions
		(d)	Company accounts and accounting standard checklists
		(e)	Queries raised and explanations received
		(f)	Third party confirmations and certificates
6	**Systems audit**	(a)	Audit programmes (Tests of control and Substantive)
		(b)	Detailed working papers and conclusions
		(c)	Queries raised and explanations received
		(d)	Weaknesses identified and copy of Letter of Weakness sent to client
7	**Accounts preparation**	(a)	Schedules
		(b)	Trial balance
		(c)	Cross-reference to audit work performed
8	**Extracts from minutes**	(a)	Directors' meetings
		(b)	Members' meetings

9	**Statistical information**	*Performance indicators* collected which have a bearing on the extent, nature, timing of substantive tests (PAF should be updated accordingly)

The internal audit file is more likely to contain the following key areas:

- index
- management review
- planning and organisation
- risk and control evaluations
- working papers/testing
- reporting.

8.8 Electronic working papers

Increasingly, the main contents of the audit file will be held electronically, although there is still a requirement to retain evidence which may be manual. Some audit departments have an objective of a "paperless" office, with all information held electronically but it is still currently inevitable that some working papers will only be available manually, in particular where manual signature evidence is required. However, there is increasing use of digital signatures and some companies have moved to the use of document image processing, so that all documents are held in a central database store. Auditors should be aware of the changing technology and the impact on the planning and documentation of audits.

8.9 Benefits and problems of electronic working papers

Although benefits can be identified arising from an audit firm's use of electronic working papers (improved legibility, rapid search facility, reduction in bulk), it is important that tight controls are implemented to ensure confidentiality and safe custody. These controls are covered in chapter 16 of this text.

ACTIVITY **4**

Outline six uses of technology in the planning of audits.

Feedback to this activity is at the end of the chapter.

9 Small company audits

Small companies possess many characteristics similar to those of partnerships and sole traders. The major audit problems which arise are:

- The business employs very few staff and hence there is very little scope for division of responsibilities.
- The accounting systems are often relatively unsophisticated and possibly dominated by one person.
- The owners of the business are frequently heavily involved in the day-to-day running of the business.

KEY POINT

Internal control of small businesses is **constrained** by:

- the restricted scope for segregation of duties
- the domination of the business by senior management.

9.1 Internal control

There are two major constraints on the effective internal control of small businesses:

- the restricted scope for division of responsibilities owing to the small number of employees
- the domination of the accounting function by one person.

A further factor is the *nature* of the internal controls. The extent of management supervision in day-to-day operations is critical. Management supervision is itself an important element of internal control, but the difficulty from the auditor's viewpoint is that little evidence of its effective operation is available at a subsequent date.

Although the auditor can obtain representations from management, the basic difficulty still remains. A further point is that while day-to-day supervision is an important check by management on employees, there is little check on management itself. This is not usually so in the case of large companies, because of the existence of effective internal audit functions and sophisticated reporting systems.

Finally, the most difficult situation of all from the auditor's viewpoint comes about in the case of a small, but rapidly expanding, business. So much of the proprietor's time is taken up with steering the business along an expansion path, that the extent and effectiveness of day-to-day supervision is very much reduced.

Practice Note 13 (PN 13) was introduced by the APB in July 1997 and examines each of the SASs then in force, outlining to what extent it should be applied to the audit of small organisations.

9.2 External auditing aspects

These may be summarised as follows.

KEY POINT

The **engagement letter** is important to prevent misunderstandings about the auditor's role and responsibilities.

Engagement letter

This is of particular importance for two reasons:

- In a situation where the relationship with the client is likely to be less formal than for larger businesses, it removes any misconceptions the client may have as to the auditor's responsibilities.
- In circumstances where accounting work is often undertaken, it makes clear the distinction between audit and accountancy.

KEY POINT

With small companies, the emphasis of audit testing will be on substantive testing.

Substantive procedures

In the audit of small companies, the emphasis of audit testing will be aimed towards substantive testing as opposed to tests of control. In particular, tests on debtors and stock verification will be very much intensified.

However, if internal control is very poor, *no amount of substantive procedures will offer the auditor the necessary assurance*. For example, if a business receives a large proportion of its income in the form of cash and internal control over this area is poor, no amount of audit testing will satisfy the auditor that the accounting records are complete and accurate and reflect all the transactions. The auditor may then be unable to express an opinion as to truth and fairness.

KEY POINT

Auditors cannot rely *solely* on **management representations**.

Management representations

Letters of representation will be relied on to a far greater extent for small businesses than for large businesses. The auditor will have to decide to what extent the representations of management are backed up by supporting evidence, such as the auditor's knowledge of the business and its records, as well as significant ratios.

Overall review

An overall review is not of itself a sufficient basis for expressing an audit opinion on the financial statements. However, the review does provide valuable support for conclusions reached from other audit work.

There is a limit on the extent to which analytical procedures may be applied to the financial statements of small businesses. Accounting records may be fairly simple and management information, such as monthly accounts and budgets, non-existent. Weaknesses in internal control may cast severe doubts on the completeness and accuracy of the financial statements.

9.3 Auditing techniques and small companies

Planning and recording

Obviously, planning and recording are simpler with a small client, but they are nevertheless needed. The need to record the work done and evidence obtained is just as great as with a large client.

Accounting system

The small client is less likely to have a well-developed accounting system. The auditor will have to judge whether in the context of the business the system of gathering and recording the data is adequate.

Internal control

Auditing standards make it clear that the auditor does not have to rely on the system of internal control. In the case of small businesses, internal control will usually be provided by the proprietor. The lack of evidence of such control will mean the auditor cannot rely upon it.

Audit evidence

Audit evidence is essential for an unqualified audit report. However, evidence will be harder to obtain in the case of a small client.

Review of financial statements

The financial statements need to be reviewed as much as those of a large concern to ensure compliance with accounting and statutory regulations.

9.4 Auditor independence and small companies

KEY POINT

Areas of the small company audit where the auditor's independence might be compromised are:

- involvement of auditor with management
- cost pressures.

There are two particular areas of the small company audit where the auditor's independence might be compromised:

- Involvement of auditor with management – Inevitably, the small company is likely to look to its auditors for professional advice and guidance. It is also likely that the accounting firm may be involved in the preparation of the accounts, and taxation matters.
- Cost pressures – The audit fee is likely to be relatively larger for a small client than a large client. The auditor will be under pressure to restrict costs, and hence audit time.

It is, however, the auditor's professional duty to overcome these problems and maintain their independence.

9.5 The small company audit issue

KEY POINT

The statutory audit of small companies was abolished in 1994. Before this time, the UK was almost the only country in the world to have an audit requirement for all companies.

The statutory audit of small companies was abolished in 1994. The detailed rules and recent regulations to widen the exemption from audit are discussed in a later chapter of this text. Before 1994, the UK was almost the only country in the world to have an audit requirement for all companies and was severely out of line with international practice in this respect. Nevertheless, forms of business medium are different in the UK from those abroad, particularly from those in Europe, and the ACCA opposed the abolition of the small company audit requirement. The various arguments for and against abolition are set out below.

Arguments for abolition

- Audited accounts for many smaller companies serve only a compliance function and add little to management's knowledge and understanding of the business.

- The resources expended by the company on the audit could be used to obtain more useful financial advice.
- Banks and other financiers are generally in a position to make specific conditions for providing finance, and therefore have little need for a statutory audit.
- Abbreviated accounts filed ten months after the year end are of little value to trade suppliers and customers in establishing a trading relationship.

Arguments against abolition

- Most auditors consider that it is perfectly possible to audit a small company and produce a satisfactory audit report.
- If banks and other creditors required their own independent audit, the result might be to increase, not reduce, the costs of a small company.
- The audit is necessary to protect creditors which is important in view of the limited liability of the shareholders.
- Shareholders, particularly minority shareholders, are entitled to full and reliable information about the position of their company.

10 Engagements to review financial statements

KEY POINT

Review engagements are NOT full audits but provide a degree of assurance.

External auditors may be required to carry out a review of financial statements – work falling short of the standard of a full audit, but nevertheless providing some assurance as to the financial statements. This is referred to as '**negative assurance**'.

Planning procedures for, and proper documentation of, review engagements are equally important as for audits. Much of the work for this type of assignment will be concerned with the performance of analytical procedures and other review procedures. Other detailed verification work normally associated with an audit will not normally be carried out or would be done so only on a very restricted basis.

Small companies, not required to have an audit commonly, may choose to have such a review to provide a degree of assurance to external parties.

Because there is little established guidance in the UK, the principles covered here are based on the International Standard on Review Engagement, ISRE 2400 *Engagements to review financial statements*.

10.1 Objective of a review engagement

ISRE 2400 defines the objective of a review engagement as follows:

'The objective of a review of financial statements is to enable an auditor to state whether, on the basis of procedures which do not provide all the evidence that would be required in an audit, anything has come to the auditor's attention that causes the auditor to believe that the financial statements are not prepared, in all material respects, in accordance with an identified financial reporting framework (negative assurance).'

10.2 The work of the review

Principles of the engagement

- The auditor should plan and perform the review with an attitude of professional scepticism recognising that circumstances may exist that cause the financial statements to be materially misstated.
- The auditor should obtain or update a knowledge of all aspects of the business under review.
- The auditor should obtain sufficient appropriate evidence, mainly through enquiry and analytical procedures, to be able to draw conclusions.

Detailed procedures

Procedures for the review of financial statements will ordinarily include:

- Obtaining an understanding of the entity's business and the industry in which it operates.
- Inquiries concerning the entity's accounting principles and practices.
- Inquiries concerning the entity's procedures for recording, classifying and summarising transactions, accumulating information for disclosure in the financial statements and preparing financial statements.
- Inquiries concerning all material assertions in the financial statements.
- Analytical procedures designed to identify relationships and individual items that appear unusual. Such procedures would include:
  - comparison of the financial statements with statements for prior periods
  - comparison of the financial statements with anticipated results and financial position
  - study of the relationships of the elements of the financial statements that would be expected to conform to a predictable pattern based on the entity's experience or industry norm.

11 Internal audit planning

The audit planning procedures dealt with earlier in this chapter can, in general, be applied to internal audit.

11.1 Risk management and internal audit

Risk management

DEFINITION

Risk is the probability that an event or action may adversely affect the organisation or activity under audit.

Risk management is the process of evaluating and controlling risk to ensure that the organisation is managed as effectively as possible.

A separate risk management industry exists, but there are increasingly close links between internal audit and risk. In some organisations, there are integrated risk and audit functions.

Risk management is the process of evaluating and controlling risk to ensure that the organisation is managed as effectively as possible. This does not mean that organisations avoid risk, because taking risks can result in financial profit or other significant benefits to the organisation. However, it means that the level of risk exposure is factored into decisions made against a clear understanding of the appetite for risk and potential impact of any risk.

Risk management is in itself a line management role. Risk management functions can exist within organisations to identify, monitor and measure risk and to publish risk management policies. Line management will implement policies and exercise control over their exposure to risk. Internal audit can ensure that it best adds value by using a risk-based approach that maximises the benefits to the organisation and by using language that line management can understand. This means explaining why controls are important on the basis of how they can prevent or minimise the impact of things going wrong and risks materialising.

ACTIVITY 5

You lead a small internal audit and review team for Advance Lead, a company listed on the stock exchange. Advance Lead has just announced that they are setting up a risk department in response to the corporate governance guidance from Turnbull. You are concerned about how your role will fit in respect to the new risk management function. Highlight the points you would need to consider in deciding how you would approach this development.

Feedback to this activity is at the end of the chapter.

DEFINITION

Risk-based internal auditing means assessing, evaluating and prioritising risk in order to direct attention effectively.

Risk-based internal auditing

Risk-based internal auditing provides the opportunity to target limited resources on key risks and allows the auditor to discuss plans and reports in business oriented terms. By considering risks, internal auditors can answer "why" controls are required. The latest definition of internal audit from the IIA places greater emphasis on risk management and many departments have moved towards such a risk-based approach.

Risk-based internal audit involves the following activities:

- identifying risks in relation to business objectives
- assessing and prioritising risks in terms of probability and timing
- deciding how to deal with risks
- monitoring risk management.

Risks can often be usefully assessed by a 'matrix' or 'grid' approach which evaluates risks in terms of their positioning on a 'high/low' scale. The simple matrix below uses the two variables of 'risk impact' and 'risk likelihood'.

Risk matrix

Risk	Impact	Likelihood
1	High	High
2	High	Low
3	Low	High
4	Low	Low

The auditor would pay more attention to Risks 1 and 2, and a lower level of attention to Risks 3 and 4.

In terms of dealing with risks, a number of standard techniques are available. The auditor may advise management on the technique which is most appropriate for a particular risk. The appropriate technique may be related to the risk assessment matrix approach referred to above. Standard techniques for dealing with risks together with their possible applications are summarised below:

Technique	Application
• Accept the risk	Low impact, low likelihood risk, where action is not justified on a cost-benefit basis
• Reduce the risk	Institute improved internal control procedures
• Avoid the risk	Avoid the situation/activity generating the risk
• Transfer the risk	Insurance or third party indemnity

11.2 Organisational control

KEY POINT

It is important for organisations to have a common **internal control framework** to achieve effective management of risk and to demonstrate compliance with corporate governance requirements.

Organisational control is central to corporate governance guidance and the role of internal audit. It is important for organisations to have a common internal control framework to achieve effective management of risk and to demonstrate compliance with corporate governance requirements. It is also useful for internal auditors to apply such a framework or control model to the way that they report the results of their work. In this way, a common picture of the level of control across the organisation can be built up and used for reporting purposes.

The control environment includes the following key requirements:

- organisational culture and values
- management operational style and approach
- organisational structure
- authority and responsibility
- operating policy and procedures
- human resources policies and practices.

11.3 Corporate objectives

KEY POINT

Internal audit can help with the setting of corporate objectives and in monitoring achievement of corporate objectives and the level of performance and delivery.

To provide added value, internal auditors must be attuned to the overall corporate objectives. Any effective assessment of risk should be undertaken in the context of corporate objectives. These are of fundamental importance to the success and survival of an organisation, especially in a changing and increasingly competitive world.

Internal audit objectives will to an extent follow the corporate objectives to ensure maximum added value. A major risk to the organisation will be that their objectives will not be met, which could damage reputation and result in financial loss.

Internal audit can help with the setting of corporate objectives and in monitoring achievement of corporate objectives and the level of performance and delivery. They can also assist the board and management by examining the effectiveness of the processes by which risks are identified, prioritised, controlled and reported. However, internal auditors do not have a role to judge the appropriateness of the corporate objectives or the board's strategies to achieve them.

ACTIVITY 6

Why is it important for internal audit to understand corporate objectives?

Feedback to this activity is at the end of the chapter.

11.4 Internal audit objectives and principles

We have set out the objectives of **internal audit**, including the provision of independent and objective consulting activity, providing assurance to management. Internal auditors also have to use their judgement in deciding the extent of audit work required to establish risk and to confirm the operation of controls.

KEY POINT

The **Institute of Internal Auditors (IIA)** sets out the standards that internal auditors should apply, including the need for effective planning – an essential part of the process.

The **Institute of Internal Auditors (IIA)** sets out the standards that internal auditors should apply, including the need for effective planning. The chief internal auditor should establish plans to carry out the responsibilities of the department and internal auditors should plan each audit.

Effective planning is essential to ensure that the internal audit is properly conducted and meets the required objectives. An up-front time commitment is worthwhile to ensure that the audit resource is directed towards areas of greatest risk, and that information and experience already available is maximised.

11.5 Audit universe and high-level plans

KEY POINT

For internal auditors, there will normally be an '**audit universe**', consisting of details of all the potential audits in the organisation, which they can use to formulate a plan.

All auditors need to plan their work effectively, but there also needs to be an overall plan that provides the necessary direction and allocation of work.

For internal auditors, there will normally be an '**audit universe**', consisting of details of all the potential audits in the organisation. From the list of all potential audits, a plan can then be formulated and work then assigned to auditors.

Departments vary in the type, frequency and level of planning undertaken. Traditionally, a longer-term plan was put in place showing how and when the audit of the complete audit universe would be undertaken, with annual plans showing assignments to be completed each year.

Increasingly, internal audit departments are moving away from this, with more focus on risk assessment of the audit universe and a more flexible short-term approach to producing plans and allocating work. This is particularly the case where an organisation is going through substantial change and the auditor needs to be able to react to changing risks as they occur. There also tends to be more breadth of work within an audit plan, to reflect the altered nature and scope of audit work.

A method and frequency of audit planning needs to be agreed and, where an annual plan is produced, this needs to be subject to review as other potential high-risk audits arise and to be supported by quarterly work plans.

Technology is a very powerful tool for effective management of the audit universe and development of audit plans. Internal audit departments can use different types of systems for planning, including off-the-shelf packages, a readily available spreadsheet package, database system or a system tailored to meet specific department needs. As with any system, it is important that the planning tool is compatible with other systems used, that it is flexible and readily updated as the audit universe or risks change. Plans need to be presented to Management, Boards and Audit Committees and therefore the capability of the system to produce clear reports will be a key consideration.

11.6 Risk assessment and risk models

KEY POINT

To support the development of high-level plans, auditors need to identify and prioritise **risks** across the organisation.

To support the development of high-level plans, internal auditors need to identify and prioritise risks across the organisation. In some cases, this will be through a very simple, judgmental model, with each entity within the audit universe rated according to perceived risk, for example in ratings 1–5 or High/Medium/Low.

Risk models can also be developed to support the identification, sizing and prioritisation of risk across the organisation. The advantages of using risk models are:

- a more scientific basis can be demonstrated in the development of audit plans
- they can help in developing a common understanding of risk with senior management in the organisation
- they can be used to prioritise within plans

However, the scientific basis of risk models cannot always be substantiated and they cannot take away from the need for audit senior managers to make judgements on the areas that need to be audited.

KEY POINT

Risk models need to be appropriate to the organisation.

Risk models need to be appropriate to the organisation. There are some common types of factors that could be used in risk models including:

- financial risk, including assessment of profit, assets, revenue
- other volumes (e.g. number of claims, policies, customers)
- regulatory risk (type and scale of legal requirements for the area)
- complexity of processes and procedures
- robustness of control environment

- change – extent and size of change within the area, including staffing, systems and procedures
- IT
- time since last audit
- geographical factors, including location or international barriers.

Where sophisticated risk models are necessary for the organisation, technology can be an important enabler. Statistical analysis of risks and trends can only really be efficiently and effectively carried out with the right systems. Automation can however drive the auditor down a more scientific, technical route that may not be appropriate to the organisation. Therefore careful consideration of the most effective risk analysis techniques is required before making a decision on the right system to be used, which needs to be compatible with other systems and will help drive the audit plan.

Technology can also aid risk analysis in real time auditing scenarios. Some organisations have chosen to implement modern techniques through the use of ongoing monitoring techniques that measure and identify risk. In this way, audit can react quickly to changing or deteriorating risk situations and have clear evidence available more quickly. A requirement for such systems is an automated interface with the organisation's computer systems. Real time auditing lends itself to a highly financial risk environment for example retail banking, where credit risks can be analysed automatically through links to the systems. However, the downside of this tool is that in some cases the type of auditing carried out should be undertaken by management.

11.7 Residual risk

DEFINITION

Residual risk: the level of risk vulnerability after taking account of the application of controls to manage the total potential impact / scale of risk.

The risk factors listed above are made up of a number of different types. Some relate to the potential impact of any risk materialising; others are factors that will affect the ability to control or manage the risk and therefore the probability of such a risk materialising. Overall, the intention of an audit plan is to work out the potential residual risk.

Any risk model used by the audit team needs to be simple, easy to use and easy to maintain.

11.8 Stakeholder dialogue

Audit plans need to be coordinated with other review bodies; in particular, internal and external auditors need to coordinate their coverage to ensure effective review of risks and controls. See Chapter 7 for material on the auditor's reliance on the work of others.

Discussions with appropriate senior managers and executives within the organisation can be valuable in identifying potential issues that may impact the assessment and evaluation of risk. In compiling audit plans, therefore, discussions should be held with each of the main areas to discuss major changes planned and agree the types of risk important in each area.

KEY POINT

Plans should be agreed with senior management, the board and the audit committee.

Plans should be agreed with senior management, the board and the audit committee, so that they understand what audits will be covered and the assurance that can be provided to support corporate governance requirements. Where a risk-based audit plan has been compiled, there may be a mismatch between the amount of audit resource available (audit staff) and the number and scale of audits required. The chief internal auditor will need to justify decisions either to reduce the audit plan required or to increase the number of staff used, e.g. through secondments or consultancy.

11.9 Risk workshops

KEY POINT

Risk workshops can be a useful planning tool: the auditor facilitates a structured brainstorming of the risks associated with the areas and an assessment of the importance of the risks.

Risk workshops can be a useful planning tool. In some organisations, workshops replace a lot of the planning and even much of the audit. Risk workshops will usually involve the key managers of the areas under review and the audit team or audit representatives. The auditor facilitates a structured brainstorming of the risks associated with the areas and an assessment of the importance of the risks, including impact and probability associated with the risks. The workshop could also be extended to cover key controls in operation. In this way, internal audit use the knowledge and experience of management and also help raise the awareness of management about the risks that they face.

Risk workshops can use simple manual techniques or take advantage of advances in technology. Sophisticated information capture and anonymous voting systems can help prioritise risks identified and rate confidence in controls, then provide an automatically generated risk analysis for the auditor.

Conclusion

This is an important chapter that covers the need for properly documented planning and risk analysis and the production of an overall audit plan and audit programme.

Analytical procedures are an important tool for audit planning. Audit evidence needs to be sufficient and appropriate. Working papers are important as they record the various elements of audit evidence obtained.

Control of the audit is required at all stages and includes a review of the audit after it has been completed.

Tests of control determine whether controls operate effectively. Substantive procedures involve testing of transactions and balances. The extent of substantive testing is dependent on the assessment of control risk.

Technology can aid all stages of the planning, risk analysis and control of audits but should be an enabling tool rather than a driver in itself.

Small companies pose special problems of audit; recent legislation continues to extend the exemption of small companies from the requirement to appoint auditors.

It is equally important to carry out proper planning for review engagements by external auditors, and for the work of internal auditors.

SELF-TEST QUESTIONS

General principles of external audit

1 What are the primary objectives of an audit? (1.1)

Audit planning, knowledge of the business and analytical procedures

2 What is the difference between an audit strategy and an audit plan? (2.2)

Audit risk

3 What is a systems approach to auditing? (4.2)

4 What do risk impact and risk probability mean? (4.3)

5 What is inherent risk? (4.4)

Planning materiality

6 An item is material if its X or Y is likely to distort the view given by the financial statements. What are X and Y? (5.1)

Audit programmes

7 What is an audit programme? (6.1)

Recording the audit process

8 What are the reasons for preparing working papers? (8.1)

9 What are the purposes of a permanent audit file? (8.6)

Small company audits

10 What are the problems associated with audits of small companies? (9)

Internal audit planning

11 What are 'risk workshops'? (11.9)

EXAM-TYPE QUESTIONS

Question 1: Koala Limited

Koala Limited is a medium-sized company operating as a manufacturer and wholesaler of soft toys, with a small factory in Basingstoke, a travelling sales force of six representatives and an accounts department consisting of a qualified chief accountant (Helen Jones) and two accounts clerks.

You were the manager in charge of the audit last year and have recently carried out your preliminary planning for this year's audit (to 30 September 20X7). From discussions with Helen Jones, you have discovered that on her appointment in late 20X6, new systems were introduced and you expect to be able to rely from 1 January on the internal controls of the new system in all areas. Previously you were unable to rely on internal control over purchases, wages or salesmen's expenses, and carried out very extensive detailed testing in these areas.

You are required to draft a memorandum setting out the intended means of approaching the audit, to ensure attention is devoted to all critical aspects and to assist in direction and control of the audit. **(15 marks)**

Question 2: EWheels.com

Your firm has recently been appointed as external auditor to EWheels. EWheels is a private 'dot.com' company that operates an internet auction service for the sale of used motor vehicles. You are planning the audit of the financial statements. The company has been in existence for four years and has grown rapidly. It was founded by three individuals: a former car auctioneer, an internet specialist with an interest in cars, and an accountant. The company now has three offices and some 100 employees. The on-line car auction market is very competitive. The company is the biggest provider of the service in the south of the country, but the directors have ambitious plans which include an aggressive marketing campaign, the take-over of a number of target competitors, and additional office space and staff, all of which will require considerable additional finance.

The company is financed partly by private capital brought in by the three founders, and partly by bank loans. The three founders were all directors, but the accountant resigned six months ago and has started a legal action against the company for a considerable amount of money, claiming that he has effectively been excluded from management by the other two directors. The company's balance sheet shows net liabilities. The company has not yet made a profit, although preliminary figures indicate that it has reached break-even point in the current year. Your firm has discovered that the previous auditors were not re-appointed because they refused to issue an unqualified audit opinion on the previous year's financial statements, and instead made reference to the going concern status of the company in their audit report.

The director who resigned six months ago was responsible for the day-to-day accounting function and for the preparation of the financial and management accounts.

The company has been unsuccessful in recruiting a permanent replacement and has used a number of temporary accountants. Your initial investigations have highlighted a number of weaknesses in the operation of the accounting and internal control systems.

Required:

(a) Explain your understanding of audit risk. **(4 marks)**

(b) Describe the risks associated with the audit of EWheels. **(7 marks)**

(Total: 11 marks)

Question 3: Role of small company auditors

Discuss the possible future roles of the existing auditor of a small company now that the requirement for a statutory audit of such a company has been removed. **(12 marks)**

Question 4: BLD Risk Model

BLD Ltd is a building consultants company, with a fast growing business working with major companies in the industry. They have a network of offices working in 10 major cities and have recently moved into the international arena. They have 8 divisions consisting of:

Support Division	*Type of operation*	*Operating budget £m*	*No. of staff*
IT and Operations	Support including IT, HR and Administration, covering all major cities	1.8	20
Finance	Support, based in head office covering all regions.	0.4	5
Sales and Marketing	Support sales and marketing, based regionally and in head office	1.5	12

Customer Facing Divisions	*Type of operation*	*Income £m*	*Profit £m*	*No. of contracts p.a.*	*No. of staff*
Consultancy and Design	Provide consultancy and design services to other divisions and externally	3.9	0.4	60	15
Major Commercial Contracts	Deal with all major contracts in excess of £1m	35	4.1	30	40
Fast Track installations	Deals with all fast track installations where speed of contract implementation is critical, with tight project management required to ensure no fines for delays	11	1.5	20	25
International Contracts	Dealing with cross border and international contracts	8	-1.5	27	5
Domestic Buildings	Operates all non-commercial activity, primarily in new housing	1.1	0.3	85	15

Figures for staffing are permanent staff. High use of contractor staff is required to deliver projects in each of the areas, particularly major commercial, fast track and international contracts.

Each of the five customer facing divisions operate as independent profit centres, with business channelled to them through sales and marketing, figures being submitted to Finance on a monthly basis and with IT being supplied, developed and supported centrally.

You are working with the newly appointed Head of Risk and Audit, who has asked your advice on establishing an appropriate risk model for assessing and comparing risk across the organisation. This would help the audit and risk team direct their overall work and planning for individual assignments.

You are required to:

(a) Discuss the advantages and limitations of risk modelling and explain how a risk model could operate for BLD. **(6 marks)**

(b) Explain the attributes of a good risk model. **(4 marks)**

(c) Describe the types of risk factors that could be considered by BLD in setting up their risk model, with examples of how these would operate. **(10 marks)**

(Total: 20 marks)

Question 5: Roxy Hotels (Part 2)

Roxy Hotels is a listed company which runs a chain of some 40 hotels. The company has an established internal audit department which is based at the head office and which makes regular visits to the hotels.

The hotels provide business and tourist class accommodation. They also provide restaurants, bars, conference and leisure facilities which are open to the general public as well as to residents. The company operates a computerised central booking and billing system and a stock and asset control system, both of which can be accessed via terminals in the hotels. Access to the system is restricted by the use of passwords and all significant expenditure is authorised through head office. The payroll is operated through head office. Hotel and regional managers are actively involved in the setting of budgets and cash flow forecasting. On average, throughout the year, the chain has a 65% occupancy rate.

Required:

(a) Describe the role of internal audit in ensuring that organisations achieve their corporate objectives. **(5 marks)**

(b) List the types of activities normally carried out by internal audit departments. **(5 marks)**

(Total: 10 marks)

(ACCA Pilot Paper Dec 01)

Question 6: Hardy Stores

Hardy Stores Ltd has a branch of 100 outlets across the country selling items related to country pursuits including rifles, fishing, clothing and footwear. They have an established internal audit function, which currently operates on a traditional, inspection type basis. The inspectors visit each outlet once every 3 years and check ordering, stocktaking and cash controls.

The new Head of Internal Audit is keen to modernise the approach to internal audit and has asked you to prepare a paper helping to take this forward.

Required:

(a) Describe the challenges facing a modern internal audit department. **(5 marks)**

(b) Describe the benefits and impact of a risk-based approach to internal auditing for Hardy Stores, including the key changes required. **(9 marks)**

(c) Explain the importance of corporate objectives and control culture in making decisions on the new role of internal audit. **(6 marks)**

(Total: 20 marks)

For the answer to these questions, see the 'Answers' section at the end of the book.

FEEDBACK TO ACTIVITY 1

This knowledge will be obtained from:

- the previous auditor
- prior year working papers
- industry statistics
- press reports
- bankers and other advisers
- prior year financial statements
- management information and reports
- research papers
- the client or department itself.

FEEDBACK TO ACTIVITY 2

Analytical review procedures should be used during the planning stage, during field work and in the auditor's review of the financial statements, to isolate account areas which merit further investigation or trends which seem unusual. Procedures will include ratio analysis, exception reporting and comparison with industry and competitor standards. The auditor will consider current and historical data and trends. The reconciliation of purchases, sales and stock by volume and quantity can be a useful technique.

The review forms part of the basis for the auditor's conclusion on the financial statements, as well as useful and time-saving information to assist in the planning and conduct of future audits.

FEEDBACK TO ACTIVITY 3

Typical planning procedures include:

- review points raised in previous year's audit
- assess the effects of changes in legislation or accounting practice
- review management accounts
- review significant changes in systems
- prepare a timetable of audit work and a budget
- consider the extent to which client's staff or internal audit can assist in accounting matters.

FEEDBACK TO ACTIVITY 4

Uses of technology in planning include:

- risk analysis
- preparation of high level audit plans and presentation to Management, the Board and the Audit Committee
- capturing and maintaining the audit universe to support the planning process
- preparing audit programmes, whether standardised or specific for the audit
- scheduling of audits - allocating both staff and time
- real time auditing, to capture risks as they occur by analysing information downloaded through an automated interface.

FEEDBACK TO ACTIVITY **5**

The establishment of a risk management function may give a greater opportunity for internal audit to play a more influential role in the assessment and evaluation of risk. The key area to understand is how it is proposed that the risk department operates:

- Will it be a risk monitoring function?
- Will it do a line role?
- Will it be a risk information function?
- Will it be performing a line management activity?

In some organisations, risk management and internal audit are working increasingly closer together or have actually merged. Where they remain separate, it is important for the two areas to understand the lines of responsibility and accountability, to liaise very closely over activity and to share information obtained. The corporate governance guidance from Turnbull clearly says that internal audit is in a position to play a powerful role in the provision of assurance to management on corporate governance issues. Therefore, this important role needs to be recognised within the company and used to complement the risk management activity.

FEEDBACK TO ACTIVITY **6**

Corporate objectives are the drive behind the organisation and failure to achieve corporate objectives is a major risk to the organisation. Failure to achieve objectives can cause damage to company reputation and hit shareholder value.

Internal audit will be failing in their role if they do not understand these objectives. They need to be aware because of the impact on future audit work. Additionally, audit objectives need to mirror those of the organisation. If the organisation wants to reduce cost and be more customer-focused, then internal audit cannot distance itself from these same goals. The reputation of internal audit would be damaged if the function were seen to increase costs significantly at the time of a substantial decrease in the organisation as a whole.

Understanding objectives can help to direct audit work and prioritise activities. Objectives are important to the corporate culture and framework of the organisation and therefore can be an important contributor to corporate governance.

In order to achieve objectives, boards and line management must identify and manage risks facing their organisation. Internal auditors can provide support in this activity by examining the effectiveness of the processes by which risks are identified, prioritised, managed, controlled and reported.

Chapter 7

RELIANCE ON THE WORK OF OTHERS IN THE AUDIT

CHAPTER CONTENTS

External auditors are not expected to have the expertise needed for specialist areas (e.g. engineering) and therefore have to assess the need to use experts in order to obtain sufficient evidence. Both internal and external auditors need to ensure the most efficient and effective use of their time and need to therefore understand how they can rely on each other and the work of other review functions. This chapter considers the factors the auditor must assess when relying on evidence of experts.

This chapter also deals with the increasing trend in outsourcing functions to service organisations and the impact on the auditor's work.

Objectives

By the time you have finished this chapter you should be able to:

- explain the extent to which external auditors are able to rely on the work of internal audit, independent experts and service organisations
- explain the extent to which internal auditors are able to rely on the work of independent experts and service organisations
- describe the conditions that must be met before reliance can be placed on the work of others, and the planning considerations in coordinating the work of others
- explain the extent to which reference to the work of others can be made in audit and review reports.

1 The external auditor and reliance on experts

When auditors are planning the audit they must be aware of any areas which may require the use of an expert, and must take the necessary steps to ensure that such persons are used in a controlled manner and that their work can be relied upon.

1.1 Recognising the need for the use of experts

KEY POINT

During the course of an audit the auditor may need to consider audit evidence from **specialists** in arriving at an audit opinion.

ISA 620 *Using the work of an expert* recognises that auditors have a general knowledge of business, but they cannot be expected to have a detailed knowledge in all disciplines. During the course of an audit, therefore, the auditor may need to consider audit evidence from **specialists** in arriving at an audit opinion.

Determining the need to use the work of an expert

One element of the planning of an audit would be the consideration of whether specialist evidence (from lawyers, stockbrokers, geologists, actuaries, etc.) may be necessary for the auditors to form their opinion. Factors affecting this decision would include the materiality of the item concerned, the risk of misstatement and the quantity and quality of alternative sources of evidence available.

If it is decided that expert evidence is needed, the expert should be appointed either by the client, or by the auditors with the consent of the client. If the client refuses, for whatever reason, and there is no other source of evidence for the item concerned, the auditors should qualify their audit report.

The scope of the expert's work

KEY POINT

The auditor must be satisfied that the expert is independent and competent.

In order to be able to rely on the evidence provided by the expert, the auditors must be satisfied that the expert is **competent** and **objective**. If the auditors are in any doubt, they should discuss the problem with the client management. Competence would be evidenced by membership of an appropriate **professional body**, and suitable experience.

Once a specialist is appointed, there should be a consultation between auditor, client and specialist to determine the scope of the expert's work. This should clarify the objectives of the expert's work, sources of available information, the form and content of the report required, etc.

Assessing the work of the expert and the assumptions and methods used

KEY POINT

It is essential that the evidence produced by the expert is sufficient to support the work performed.

The auditors will need to evaluate the expert's findings with respect to the adequacy of the audit evidence. They should, therefore, examine the specialist's report and determine if it is acceptable in the light of other work performed and the auditor's knowledge of the business. If the auditors are not satisfied with the expert's work, they should discuss the problem with the client's management and with the expert. It may occasionally be necessary to obtain the opinion of a second expert.

Where the auditors have used an expert to perform part of the work within the audit, they must evaluate it (as detailed above) in order to fully satisfy themselves that they are happy with the results of the work performed and that the evidence produced by the expert is sufficient, relevant and reliable for the purposes of the audit. In performing this review the auditors are essentially taking responsibility for the work completed and do not make any reference in their audit report to the fact that an expert has been used. This is why it is essential that the review they perform is satisfactory and that the evidence produced by the expert is sufficient to support the work performed if it is challenged by the client or in a court of law.

ACTIVITY **1**

During your audit of LA Insurance, it became apparent that technically difficult issues needed the expertise of an actuary. Your firm did not currently have in-house expertise and therefore following discussion with LAI it was agreed that an expert would be employed to perform the necessary work. The actuary has now completed the work but you have found out that this actuary has worked very closely with LAI on a recent acquisition as well as providing ad-hoc consultancy work. You have been asked to evaluate whether you can rely on the work conducted.

Required:

Explain the importance of reliance on the work of the expert and factors you will consider in making a recommendation on reliance.

Feedback to this activity is at the end of the chapter.

2 The external auditor and reliance on internal audit

2.1 ISA 610: *Considering the work of internal audit*

KEY POINT

External auditors have been subject to pressure by some organisations to place reliance on the work of internal auditors.

The background to this ISA is particularly interesting, as it is coloured by the different ways in which internal audit is perceived.

Internal auditors tend to regard their subject these days as no longer a branch of accountancy, but rather as a multi-disciplined function with an identity all its own. They see the scope of their work as extremely wide, and are keen to do other things besides those normally associated with external audit activities.

Many external auditors, it is fair to say, regard internal audit as a variable commodity, and are often reluctant to place reliance on internal audit work. In recent years, however, external auditors have been subject to pressure by the management of some client organisations to place reliance on the work of internal auditors to reduce the cost of the audit.

2.2 Mutual cooperation in the work of the internal and external auditors

KEY POINT

Cooperation between internal and external auditors is usually desirable.

Modern practice acts as a bridge between these different attitudes:

- A number of the objectives of internal audit may be similar to those of external audit, and procedures similar to those carried out during an external audit may therefore be followed.
- The scope and objectives of internal audit vary widely and are dependent on the responsibilities assigned to the department by management, the size and structure of the enterprise and the skills and experience of the internal auditors.
- Where reliance is placed on the work of internal audit, the external auditors will need to take into account the internal audit's programme of work and amend the extent of their own audit work accordingly.
- The auditors may agree with management that internal audit may render them direct assistance, by performing certain procedures necessary to accomplish the objectives of the external audit, under the control of the chief internal auditor.
- A decision to provide direct assistance by substituting the work of internal audit could affect the internal audit's own work programme, and should include an assessment of the relative costs of using internal and external audit.

2.3 Assessment of internal audit

KEY POINT

The external auditors must obtain a sufficient understanding of the internal audit function to plan an effective audit approach.

KEY POINT

In assessing internal audit, their **organisational status**, **scope**, **professional care**, **technical competence** and **relationships** should be considered.

ISA 610 requires that the external auditors must obtain a sufficient understanding of the internal audit function to assist in the planning and development of an effective audit approach, and to determine whether it is possible and desirable to rely on internal audit work. This assessment will in any case have an effect on the auditor's assessment of the control environment and audit risk. Factors to be considered in deciding whether or not it is appropriate to rely on the work of Internal Audit include the following:

The organisational status of internal audit

The auditors should:

- be able to plan and carry out their work as they wish
- have access to the highest level of management (i.e. the board of directors or audit committee)
- be free of any operating responsibility
- be able to communicate fully with the external auditor
- have an audit charter that clearly sets out role, responsibilities and rights of access.

The scope of the internal audit function

Normally internal audit should include examining and evaluating the whole system of internal controls not just the financial control. Therefore the scope should include the following:

- **corporate** – business planning and corporate governance
- **financial** – e.g. payroll and accounts payable
- **support** – such as IT and Human Resources management
- **other** operations, which could include marketing, and research and development.

Due professional care

The work of internal audit should be properly planned, controlled, recorded and reviewed as evidenced by adequate audit manuals and work programmes and papers. The internal audit department should measure their value and produce reports on their performance.

The technical competence of the internal auditors

The internal audit department should be appropriately staffed in terms of numbers, grades, qualifications and experience to achieve responsibilities and objectives. The department should have the right people with the right core competencies. The external auditors should document their general assessment and conclusions, and should update their assessment year by year. In addition, they should let management know in writing of significant weaknesses in the internal audit function which come to their attention.

The relationships of the internal auditors

The internal auditors should demonstrate constructive working relationships and mutual understanding with management, with external auditors, the audit committee and other review agencies.

2.4 Extent of reliance on, and evaluation of, internal audit work

The following steps are recommended where the external auditors decide they can place reliance on internal audit:

- Discussion with the client's internal auditor about the audit plans, risk assessments, timing of internal work, test levels, sample selection and the form of documentation to be used.
- Consideration of:
  - the materiality of the areas or items to be tested, and also of the information that can be obtained from internal audit
  - the level of audit risk inherent in the areas or items to be tested, or in the information to be obtained
  - the level of judgement required
  - the sufficiency of complementary audit evidence
  - specialist skills possessed by internal audit staff.
- Setting out the extent of planned reliance on internal audit, together with reasons for deciding on that extent, in a planning memorandum.
- Consideration of sending management a letter to confirm the overall arrangements made.
- Review of the manner in which the internal audit work is being controlled. In particular, the auditors should:
  - consider whether work has been properly supervised, and also reviewed in detail when it has been completed
  - compare the results of the work with those of the external auditor's staff on similar audit areas or items
  - satisfy themselves that any exceptions or unusual matters that have come to light as a result of the work have been properly resolved
  - examine reports relating to the work produced by internal audit and management's response to those reports
  - from time to time, determine whether internal audit will be able to complete the programme that it has agreed to undertake, and, if not, make appropriate arrangements.

- Ensuring that the working papers relating to the work of internal audit are up to an acceptable standard.

ACTIVITY **2**

Kiosk plc operate a large number of small retail outlets selling newspapers, sweets, cigarettes and similar articles. The internal control system provides for all the accounting records to be kept at head office with a branch stock account at selling price. Each outlet is required to bank takings daily and to make a weekly stock report. All stock other than newspapers and magazines required by an outlet must be ordered from the company's central warehouse and is delivered twice weekly. Each outlet receives daily deliveries of newspapers and magazines direct from the supplier.

There are usually two members of staff on duty at each outlet at any one time with a considerable number of the staff being employed on a part-time basis.

Kiosk plc employ a small internal audit department who aim to visit each outlet at least twice a year.

Required:

State and explain *three* criteria which should be employed in assessing the likely effectiveness and the relevance of the internal audit function.

Feedback to this activity is at the end of the chapter.

3 The external auditor and reliance on service organisations

ISA 402 *Audit considerations relating to entities using service organisations* provides guidance to the auditor as to planning and performing audit procedures, to ensure he obtains sufficient evidence where an organisation uses service organisations.

3.1 Planning the audit

KEY POINT

External auditors should identify at the planning stages whether **service organisations** are used.

The external auditor should identify at the planning stages of the audit whether or not an organisation uses **service organisations** to assist them, for example in areas such as:

- information processing
- maintenance of accounting records or payroll
- facilities management
- maintenance of safe custody of assets, such as investments
- initiation or execution of transactions on behalf of the other organisation.

The service organisation may provide services to many organisations or may be solely dedicated to the one organisation. The auditor needs to assess the type and range of service provided and the terms on which the services are provided; such information is necessary for the auditor's assessment of audit risk. The auditor should fully understand and document:

- the terms on which the service is provided (which may be oral or documented in writing)
- how the organisation ensures that the service organisation is meeting its contractual and, where relevant, legal terms.

It is important to remember that the auditors still need to obtain sufficient, relevant and reliable evidence in such cases; they must be able to state that the financial statements are free from material misstatement in order to give an unqualified opinion. It should also be stressed that use of a service organisation does not reduce the directors' responsibility for the satisfactory running of their business (i.e. safeguarding the assets, maintaining proper accounting records and preparing accurate and informative financial statements).

3.2 Audit risk

KEY POINT

The auditors need to consider the effect of relevant activities in the assessment of **inherent risk**.

The auditors need to determine the effect of relevant activities on their assessment of inherent risk and the organisation, and the organisation's control environment. The auditor's assessment of **inherent risk** will be affected by the following factors:

- the nature of the services provided
- the degree to which authority is delegated to the service organisation
- the arrangements for ensuring quality of the service provided
- whether the activities involve assets which are susceptible to loss or misappropriation
- the integrity of those responsible for the management and direction of the service organisation
- the financial status of the service organisation (if the organisation has financial pressures then they are more susceptible to fraud and misrepresentation).

KEY POINT

If auditors expect to rely on an organisation's controls to reduce **substantive testing**, a thorough risk assessment should be made.

If the auditors determine that they expect to be able to rely on the controls within the organisation being audited to reduce their **substantive testing** they should perform a thorough assessment of control risk, including:

- the extent and nature of controls operated by the auditee's staff
- the extent to which the service organisation operates an adequate system of internal controls
- the actual occurrence of errors detected by the auditee in output from the service organisation
- the adequacy with which the service organisation ensures that it complies with relevant legislation and regulations
- what information the service organisation provides to the auditee in respect of demonstrating its compliance with controls
- whether the service organisation has its own external auditors who provide the auditee with relevant information on the adequacy of controls within the service organisation
- the skills and knowledge of staff within the service organisation
- what quality assurances processes are used by the service organisation.

The auditors then need to consider whether **sufficient**, **relevant**, **reliable** evidence is available from the service organisation's records, and need to determine what procedures are necessary to obtain evidence for the audit. Possible procedures are listed below:

- inspecting documents and records held by the auditee (e.g. do they maintain submission and confirmation transaction data?)
- assessing the effectiveness of controls at the auditee (for monitoring the performance of the service organisation) and at the service organisation's premises
- obtaining written representation from the service organisation in respect of confirmation of balances and transactions
- performing analytical review procedures on the auditee's records and information received from the service organisation
- requesting the service organisation's auditor or the auditee's internal audit function to perform specific procedures
- reviewing reports/information produced by the service organisation and its auditors regarding the design and operation of its control systems.

It is worth reiterating at this point that the auditors do not just rely on the information produced by the service organisation; they must assess the internal audit staff in terms of reliability and consider factors such as skills, qualifications, experience, resources. Prior to using information they also need to review each set of data produced and consider whether it is appropriate for audit purposes.

KEY POINT

If information required from the service organisation is not available, auditors need to consider their audit opinion.

If the auditors decide that information is required as part of their audit evidence from the service organisation for their audit but that information is not available, then they need to take **appropriate action**:

- They should include a description of the factors leading to the lack of evidence in the 'basis of opinion' section of their report.
- They should qualify their opinion or issue a disclaimer of opinion on the financial statements.

ISA 402 includes a table in the appendix of 'factors relating to activities undertaken by service organisations which may increase the risk of material misstatements'. This has been included in the text below for information, and it is worth noting the specific examples given as these may appear in examination questions.

ISA 402 – Appendix

Outsourced accounting functions

Degree of risk	*Characteristics*	*Examples*
High	Complex transactions Those undertaking accounting work need extensive business or specialist knowledge Delegated authority to initiate and execute transactions Effective controls only possible on 'real time' basis Reversal of outsourcing costly/difficult High cost of performance failure (e.g. misleading management reports leading to poor decision-making) High proportion of finance functions outsourced	Maintenance of both accounting records and preparation of budgets and control reports Accounting records of retail business
Medium	Some business knowledge needed but parameters for necessary judgements can be identified and agreed in advance Transactions can be initiated but execution requires approval from user entity Execution of transactions on instruction from user entity Analytical techniques insufficient for adequate degree of control Discrete functions outsourced	Outsourcing of accounting records by a supplier of raw materials Credit control Leasing arrangements
Low	Little requirement for judgement in processing transactions Non-complex transactions Little business knowledge required Analytical control techniques effective Effects of failure can be contained Easy to rearrange/find alternative service organisations Low proportion of discrete functions outsourced	Processing salary payments Preparation of invoices Data entry

Outsourced investment custody and management

Degree of risk	*Characteristics*	*Examples*
High	Transactions can be initiated on a discretionary basis User entity does not maintain and cannot generate independent records of assets and interest, dividends or other income Complex financial instruments Custody and investment management undertaken by two separate entities but records are not independently generated, or one combined report is provided to the user entity	Discretionary trading, same custodian
Medium	Combination of custody and execution of transactions/collection of income but user entity maintains or can generate (for example, by reference to Extel) independent records of income Custody and investment management undertaken by two unrelated entities which maintain independently generated records (i.e. derived from different source data) and report separately direct to the user entity	Custodian responsible for collection of dividends and reporting of income; user entity reviews information Independent custodian and investment manager
Low	User entity initiates and maintains records of transactions Separation of execution and custody functions Low frequency of transactions and/or counterparties Non-complex financial instruments Analytical control techniques effective	Custody of assets only Execution of investment transactions pursuant to user entity's instructions

4 Reliance on the work of others by internal audit

KEY POINT

Internal auditors should liaise closely with service providers that assess risk and controls.

In the same way that external auditors rely on the work of internal auditors and other service providers, internal auditors also work with other areas of the organisation and other service providers. Internal auditors may also need to rely on experts, for exactly the same reasons as external auditors. It is always important that the internal auditor liaises closely with any area providing a service that assesses risk and controls and provides reports.

There are two main reasons for this:

- managers become very concerned if they feel that different bodies of auditors or reviewers are asking the same questions, and then can become frustrated and even uncooperative
- internal auditors can provide a better service if they are aware of other work undertaken and the types of risks being raised elsewhere.

Types of bodies that internal audit might rely on include the following:

- **Compliance departments** that might review regulatory risk and conduct monitoring.
- **External auditors** – internal audit might choose to rely on external audit to carry out financial accounting work and do very little in this area themselves. Their work should be coordinated to maximise the review of risk and assessment of control and therefore reliance will work in both directions.
- Other **risk departments** (e.g. insurance risk, operational risk).

- Other **review bodies** (e.g. other types of audit, risk, compliance or management review).

KEY POINT

Internal audit should evaluate controls, particularly to assess **corporate governance**.

Internal audit should properly plan their work to ensure that they avoid doing a review at the same time as other review bodies and should have access to the results of other risk assessment and review work. They should spend time evaluating the work and updating their overall views of the organisation's risks and controls. This is particularly important where they have a role in assessing **corporate governance**.

Internal auditors can provide much of the assurance required by the Audit Committee or the Board on corporate governance. Particularly valuable is for the internal audit department to provide a report on the whole of the organisation's internal control system in addition to the traditional audit reports. To provide an effective report in this way, internal audit needs to understand other work, reviewing or commenting on the internal control system, emphasising the importance of maintaining up-to-date information.

KEY POINT

If **joint reviews** are performed, responsibilities should be agreed to maximise effectiveness.

In certain cases, internal audit may want to do **joint reviews** with other bodies, where both parties can bring certain expertise and maximise coverage and knowledge. For example, internal auditors wanting to review regulatory risk within a heavily regulated environment may choose to do a joint review with the compliance department. Where this is the case, it is important that the respective roles, responsibilities and reporting methods are agreed at the start of the review to ensure that the maximum effectiveness is obtained. The internal auditor also needs to remember that internal specialists may be the subject of audit themselves as well as providing expertise on specific audits and therefore there may need to be an independence consideration.

Conclusion

This chapter covers the important issues that the auditor should consider when performing an audit where the organisation uses service organisations to assist it. It identifies that the auditor should assess the effect on their audit procedures when considering what audit evidence is required in order to give reasonable assurance that the financial statements are free from material misstatement. The chapter also considers the approach of both internal and external auditors to the reliance on each other, experts and other review functions. It is important that both internal and external audit properly plan their work and understand the requirements for reliance.

SELF-TEST QUESTIONS

The external auditor and reliance on experts

1 If it is decided that expert evidence is required, who should appoint the expert? (1.1)

2 How does the auditor assess the expert's work? (1.1)

3 Why is it important that the auditor ensures the competence of the work carried out by an expert? (1.1)

The external auditor and reliance on internal audit

4 How does the auditor assess the work of internal audit? (2.3)

The external auditor and reliance on service organisations

5 Give three typical functions that a service organisation might perform for a business entity. (3.1)

6 Give three examples of factors relating to activities undertaken by service organisations which may indicate an increased risk of material misstatements. (3.2)

Reliance on the work of others by internal audit

7 Provide examples of how internal auditors may rely on other review bodies and explain why this might be appropriate. (4)

EXAM-TYPE QUESTION

Peters & Co

Tarranty & Partners is a firm of accountants which has just taken on the audit of Peters & Co. Peters & Co is a medium sized limited company which has a small internal audit department comprising 3 staff, i.e. an audit manager and two senior auditors. The department reports directly to the finance director, to whom all the audit reports are addressed. The audit manager is a recently qualified accountant (ACCA) and started working for Peters & Co six months ago. The two senior auditors are accounting technicians (AAT) who qualified 10 years ago and have always worked for Peters & Co. The audit manager has recently started preparing an audit plan, which the department has never had before as they performed audits as required by the finance director. The audit manager also wants to introduce an audit methodology, as up until now the department has never had standard working papers, and prepared audit files on an ad-hoc basis. All audit working paper files are currently manually prepared, and are filed in the finance department.

You are an audit senior working for Tarranty & Partners who is assisting the audit manager in charge of the audit of Peters & Co, who has asked you to review the internal audit department to enable you to decide whether or not you will be able to rely on their work for the purposes of your audit.

Required:

(a) Prepare a working paper stating what factors you would consider when deciding whether or not to use the work produced by the internal audit department of Peters and Co during the 20X2/20X3 financial year, and conclude on whether you would use their work. **(10 marks)**

(b) Write a letter to the internal audit manager of Peters & Co making recommendations as to how they could improve their controls. **(10 marks)**

(Total: 20 marks)

For the answer to this question, see the 'Answers' section at the end of the book.

FEEDBACK TO ACTIVITY **1**

(***Tutorial note***: Remember to answer the question in full, i.e. cover the two aspects in the question – the importance and factors to consider in deciding on reliance.)

Reliance on the expert is important because the firm will be taking responsibility for the conclusions drawn in making their report and therefore the firm's credibility, integrity and reputation could be at stake.

Factors to consider in deciding whether to place reliance include:

Conflict of interest: Establish the extent of any potential conflict of interest of the actuary in relation to previous consultancy and acquisition work. In particular, was the actuary involved in the work undertaken that is now being evaluated? The actuary must be objective and independent in carrying out the work and there will be doubts over this in view of the previous close contact with LAI.

Professional expertise: In selecting the expert, someone with the right skills, competence and qualifications should have been selected that was a qualified member of the appropriate professional body (in this case, for example the Institute of Actuaries) and therefore signed up to the code of conduct (honesty, professional integrity etc).

Evidence: Has the actuary obtained sufficient, relevant and reliable evidence to support the work undertaken? Can the evidence be supported in a court of law.

Business understanding: Do the conclusions of the actuary fit to your business knowledge and understanding of LAI?

Meeting requirements: Does the report of the actuary meet the requirements established on appointment, including scope and objectives of the work, format and type of report?

If there is any doubt over the reliability of the work performed, the firm will need to discuss with LAI and if necessary obtain a second opinion.

FEEDBACK TO ACTIVITY 2

(***Tutorial note***: Remember to answer the question in full, i.e. state and explain, effectiveness and relevance, etc.)

The following criteria should be employed in assessing the likely effectiveness and relevance of an internal audit function.

Independence – the internal auditors will be employed by the company and will not, therefore, be entirely independent. However, the internal auditors should be free to plan their work as they wish, and should not be involved in setting up systems on which they must later objectively comment. The internal auditors should report to the highest level of management so that they are not reporting directly to those on whom they are required to comment.

Qualifications and experience – internal auditors will have qualifications appropriate to the organisation and do not necessarily have to be professionally qualified. However, the better qualified and experienced the auditor, the more effective and reliable the internal audit function is likely to be. The internal audit department should specify the types of qualifications and experience required to fulfil their objectives and responsibilities and demonstrate how they have fulfilled these requirements.

Scope and authority – the scope of the internal auditors' work is agreed by management but should include examining and evaluating the whole system of internal controls established by management and not just financial controls. Similarly, the level of authority given to the internal auditors to enable them to carry out their tests is agreed by management and should be set out in an Audit charter. The internal auditors should be granted sufficient authority to enable them to obtain all relevant information necessary to fulfil their function. The scope of work should include a review of the risks associated with the company, evaluating of controls including the accounting and other control systems, detailed testing of balances and transactions, etc.

Chapter 8
INTERNAL CONTROL SYSTEMS

CHAPTER CONTENTS

As discussed in an earlier chapter, auditors may take a systems based approach, relying on internal controls to reduce the volume of substantive testing. The internal control system is also an important aspect of the internal auditor's work.

In this chapter we will consider in more detail the nature of internal controls. Consider your practical experience as much as possible.

Objectives

By the time you have finished this chapter you should be able to:

- describe the objectives of internal control systems and the responsibility for internal control systems in the context of organisational objectives
- describe the importance of internal control to auditors
- describe and illustrate the limitations of internal control systems in the context of fraud and error
- state the types of internal controls that can exist in any system
- summarise the methods used to ascertain and record systems
- discuss whether reliance should be placed on the systems to reduce the total amount of testing.

1 Internal control

1.1 Definition of internal control system

DEFINITION

ISA 315 defines the internal control system as comprising the **control environment** and **control procedures**.

ISA 315 *Understanding the entity and its environment and assessing the risks of material misstatement* defines the internal control system as comprising all the policies and procedures adopted by the directors and management of an entity to assist in their objective of achieving, as far as practicable, the orderly and efficient conduct of the business, including adherence to internal policies, the safeguarding of assets, the prevention and detection of fraud and error, the accuracy and completeness of the accounting records, and the timely preparation of reliable financial information.

ISA 315 states that the internal control system consists of the following components:

(a) the control environment

(b) the entity's risk assessment process

(c) the information system, including the related business processes, relevant to financial reporting and communication

(d) control activities

(e) monitoring of controls.

Traditionally in the UK items (b) to (e) have been termed 'control procedures'.

DEFINITION

Control environment means the overall attitude, awareness and actions of management regarding internal controls.

Control environment means the overall attitude, awareness and actions of management regarding internal controls and their importance. It encompasses management style, corporate culture, values, philosophy and operating style, the organisational structure, personnel policies and procedures. The control environment is a key part of the overall corporate governance framework of the organisation.

Personnel policies and procedures, for example, would include those covering recruitment, retention and dismissal. The organisational structure should have clear lines of reporting responsibility; the maintenance of an internal audit function and audit committee demonstrates a commitment to high level controls. The use of management accounts for the purposes of variance analysis is also a high level control.

The control environment provides a background to detailed control procedures. It does not of itself, of course, ensure the effectiveness of the internal control system as a whole.

It should be noted that the existence of an adequate control environment is becoming increasingly important as business organisations and structures become generally larger and more complex. In particular, many control processes which were previously 'manual' are now automated and based on computer systems. Moreover, the growth of the desktop personal computer (PC) has led to a greater level of empowerment in many organisations and a decrease of specialist, centralised controls. These developments mean that more reliance needs to be placed on the general control environment to ensure that organisational objectives are met. This needs to be borne in mind when dealing with the material in this chapter and in Chapters 9-15 which follow.

DEFINITION

Control procedures are those established to achieve the entity's specific objectives.

Control procedures are those established to achieve the entity's specific objectives. These objectives in an accounting context include proper authorisation, timely and accurate recording of transactions in the correct period, safeguarding of assets and ensuring the existence of assets recorded. They include particular procedures to prevent, detect and correct errors. They differ from entity to entity and are affected by the size of the entity. We will look at these in greater detail later in this chapter.

In practice, the choice of controls may reflect a comparison of the cost of operating individual controls against the benefits expected to be derived from them.

DEFINITION

Internal control is 'all means designed to promote, govern and check upon various activities for the purpose of seeing that enterprise objectives are met'. IIA

Many of the internal controls which would be relevant to the larger enterprise are not practical, appropriate or necessary in the small enterprise. Managers of small enterprises have less need to depend on formal internal controls for the reliability of the records and other information, because of their personal contact with, or involvement in, the operation of the enterprise itself.

The Institute of Internal Auditors defines internal control as 'all means designed to promote, govern and check upon various activities for the purpose of seeing that enterprise objectives are met'. Therefore both for internal and external audit, internal controls and the internal control system are much broader than the accounting systems alone.

1.2 Why do companies need internal controls?

KEY POINT

Internal controls exist to prevent **risks** occurring or to minimise their impact.

Internal controls are there to prevent **risks** occurring or to minimise the impact of risks (i.e. to help prevent things going wrong). Even when controls are in place documents may still get lost or portable assets may go missing. The level and extent of internal controls required depends on what the risks are if such controls fail. It is particularly important that stringent controls exist where there are associated legal requirements.

Documents are batched and prenumbered so staff can check that there are none missing. If any **sales invoices go missing** debts may not be collected and income may be understated; cash flow would therefore also be affected resulting in payment difficulties.

If **purchase invoices go missing** we would be overstating profits and if we spent money owing to those creditors cash flow problems could result.

KEY POINT

The larger the organisation, the tighter the controls have to be to prevent significant errors.

But what if the amounts involved are small? Does one invoice really matter? Experience shows that if one invoice has gone missing it is highly likely that several more are also missing, and the larger the organisation gets, the bigger the numbers get, and the tighter the controls have to be to prevent significant errors.

Authorisation controls are another type of internal control and are particularly important. For example, suppose that a clerk routinely authorises false purchase invoices raised by a friend outside the company. The company pays the invoices and the friend and the clerk share the proceeds. This is a very common type of fraud. Controls to prevent this require payments to be authorised only with reference to purchase invoices that are attached to goods received notes, or authorisations for the receipt of services by managers completely unconnected with the accounting function.

1.3 Why internal control interests the external auditor

At an early stage in their work the auditors will have to decide the extent to which they wish to place reliance on the internal controls of the enterprise. As the audit proceeds, that decision will be kept under review and, depending on the results of their examination, they may decide to place more or less reliance on these controls.

KEY POINT

Auditors rely on internal control to reduce the amount of **substantive testing** required.

The principal reason why internal control interests the auditors is that reliance on internal control will reduce the amount of **substantive testing** of transactions and resultant balances in the ledger accounts required.

The operation of internal controls should ensure the completeness and accuracy of the accounting records. If the auditors are satisfied that the internal control system is functioning, there is therefore a reduced risk of error in the accounting records.

It is very important to the auditor, therefore, to establish what internal control system exists and then to test that system to ensure that it is working properly.

Another reason that the auditor needs to consider the adequacy of the accounting system is that the auditor has an additional responsibility under the CA 1985 to form an opinion as to whether proper accounting records have been kept. This implies the operation of a sound system of internal control.

By recording the accounting system and checking its operation by tests of control, the auditor can reduce the amount of substantive procedures. The total amount of work is reduced as a result. ISA 330 *The auditor's procedures in response to assessed risks* provides useful guidance in this area.

1.4 Why internal control interests the internal auditor

A key objective of the internal auditor is to review the organisation's system of internal control and to provide assurance that the corporate governance requirements are being met. Therefore internal controls are fundamental to the work of the internal auditor. Like external auditors, internal auditors have to make decisions on the extent of reliance on controls to manage risks and therefore the level of testing to be carried out.

ACTIVITY 1

Summarise the key reasons that internal controls are of interest to both the internal and external auditor.

Feedback to this activity is at the end of the chapter.

KEY POINT

Internal audit should be able to provide the Board with assurance regarding the **effectiveness** of the **system of internal control**.

Chapter 4 set out in more detail the role and definition of internal audit. However, it is worth reiterating the corporate governance guidance that: 'An objective and adequately resourced internal audit function should be in a position to provide the Board with much of the assurance it requires regarding the **effectiveness** of the **system of internal control**.'

Therefore, both the internal and external auditors have a common interest in confirming the system of internal control.

To provide assurance, internal audit need to check:

- that the controls in place are adequate to guard against the risks identified
- that the controls are operating effectively.

This requires a decision on whether the right controls are in place for the type and level of risk identified. The auditor will be interested not just in whether there are sufficient controls but in examples of over-control and inefficiencies. Traditionally, internal audit staff were seen as 'business prevention', because they were seen as adding in additional 'unnecessary' controls. However, increasingly internal auditors need to be adding value and therefore will review the cost effectiveness as well as the adequacy of controls.

1.5 Types of internal control

KEY POINT

Preventative, **detective** and **corrective** controls all should be considered by an auditor but preventative controls are the most powerful.

There are three key types of control that any auditor should consider.

Preventative controls

These are controls that prevent risks occurring. For example, authorisation controls should prevent fraudulent or erroneous transactions taking place. Other preventative controls include segregation of duties, recruiting and training the right staff and having an effective control culture.

Detective controls

These are controls that detect if any problems have occurred. They are designed to pick up errors that have not been prevented. These could be exception reports that reveal that controls have been circumvented (for example, large amounts paid without being authorised). Other examples could include reconciliations, supervision and internal checks.

Corrective controls

These are controls that address any problems that have occurred. So where problems are identified, the controls ensure that they are properly rectified. Examples of corrective controls include follow up procedures and management action.

Clearly the most powerful type of control is **preventative**. It is more effective to have a control that stops problems occurring rather than to detect or correct them once they have occurred. There is always a possibility that it is too late to sort out the problem.

1.6 Specific control procedures

- Approval and control of **documents and transactions of importance** – in a purchases system, for example, there should be pre-set authority limits. An order up to the value of £1,000 could be approved by a department head, up to £5,000 by any one director, and beyond this by the Board as a whole.
- Controls over **computerised applications** and the IT environment – these are dealt with later in the text.
- Checking the **arithmetical accuracy** of the records - such controls include checking the casts on a purchase invoice, and recalculating the VAT on sales invoices.
- Maintaining and reviewing **control accounts** and **trial balances** – Control accounts include sales and purchase ledger control accounts, bank reconciliations and fixed asset registers.
- Comparing the results of **cash**, **security** and **stock counts** with the accounting records
- Comparing **internal data** with **external sources** of information – this might include supplier statement reconciliations.
- Comparing and analysing the financial results with budgeted amounts.
- Producing and reviewing **exception reports** – e.g. lists of purchasing transactions above certain limits or payments made without a purchase order.

- **Limiting direct physical access** to assets and records – An important general principle with respect to assets and records is that of **segregation of duties**. In particular there should be a division of responsibilities for:
  - **authorising** or initiating the transaction
  - the physical **custody** and control of assets involved
  - **recording** the transaction.

  No one person should be in a position both to misappropriate an asset and to conceal the act by falsifying the records. For example, in a sales system the duties of receiving money from debtors and writing up the sales ledger should be separated. If not, money could be misappropriated and the records falsified to cover this.

2 Understanding the system

2.1 Accounting and internal control systems

KEY POINT

ISA 315 requires auditors to obtain an understanding of the **internal control system** sufficient to determine their audit approach.

ISA 315 requires that auditors obtain and document an understanding of the **accounting system** and **control environment** sufficient to determine their audit approach, whether that be a **systems-based approach**, or a **substantive approach**. It also helps with the assessment of inherent and control risk. If control risk is to be assessed as less than high, the justification for that assessment must be documented.

An important implication of this requirement is that auditors need to develop, or have access to, the necessary technical skills where computer based accounting systems are in operation.

This understanding can be updated year on year and auditors often perform '**walk through**' tests, to confirm that their understanding and documentation of the system are correct. This simply involves taking a transaction through the system from source to destination and can often 'double' as a test of control and as a substantive procedure, depending on which elements of the transaction are checked. Such tests are particularly useful where the auditor is relying on the client's documentation of the system.

Remember that all limited companies are under a legal obligation to keep proper accounting records under S222 CA 1985 and that auditors are required to form an opinion as to whether they have done so.

The accounting records must be sufficient to show and explain the company transactions and must be such as to:

- disclose with reasonable accuracy, at any time, the financial position of the company at that time, and
- enable the directors to ensure that any balance sheet and profit and loss account comply with the requirements of the Act as to their form, content and otherwise.

The accounting records must, in particular, contain:

- daily entries of all money received and expended by the company, and the relevant details in respect of the receipts and expenditures
- a record of the assets and liabilities of the company.

In addition, where the company deals in goods, the accounting records must contain:

- statements of stock held by the company at the end of each financial year
- all statements of stocktakings from which any such statement of stock has been or is to be prepared, and
- except in the case of goods sold by way of ordinary retail trade, statements of all goods sold and purchased, showing the goods and the buyers and sellers in sufficient detail to enable all these to be identified.

Accounting records must be retained for **three years** by a private company and for **six years** by a public company. The period is calculated from the date on which the records were made. This does not apply to the various registers which the Act requires a company to maintain (for example, the register of directors' interests in shares and debentures of the company) which must generally be retained indefinitely.

KEY POINT

An **accounting system** should provide orderly information and analyses to enable financial statements to be prepared.

An **accounting system** should provide for the orderly assembly of accounting information and appropriate analyses to enable financial statements to be prepared. What constitutes an adequate accounting system will depend on the size, nature and complexity of the enterprise. In its simplest form for a small business dealing primarily with cash sales and with only a few suppliers the accounting system may only need to consist of an analysed cash book and a list of unpaid invoices. In contrast, a company manufacturing several different products and operating through a number of dispersed locations may need a complex accounting system to enable information required for financial statements to be assembled.

3 Documenting the system

The various methods of ascertaining and recording the system may be summarised as follows:

Ascertaining	*Recording*
Examining previous audit work	Narrative notes
Client's or department's own documentation of the system	Organisation chart
Interviews with client's or department's staff	Internal control questionnaires (ICQs) or checklists
Tracing transactions/walk throughs	Flowcharts and other diagrammatic representations
Examining client's/department's documents	
Observation of procedures	

These are appropriate methods for ascertaining and recording systems whether for internal or external audit, although more detailed and broader documentation will be required for internal audit. The different methods are examined in more detail below.

3.1 Methods of ascertaining the system

KEY POINT

Systems may be ascertained by examining **previous audits** or the **client's documentation**, **tracing transactions** or by **interview** and **observation**.

Examining previous audit work

In any situation except the first audit, the audit files should contain a record of the system as it operated at the last audit date. Unless there have been major changes, this will only require updating. Thus, the systems examination is work largely carried out at the first audit of a new client.

For internal audit, previous audit work will still be a valuable source of reference. If a previous audit has been undertaken, this should have documented the procedures, processes, key controls and risks. However, this may have changed significantly since the last review and therefore will need checking and revising.

Client's or department's own documentation of the system

Some organisations will have manuals of procedures. These will provide a valuable source of information. For internal audit, areas under review will normally have some form of procedures manuals or other documentation which will be a useful source of information on the intended operation of the system. It is worth checking how recently the procedures have been produced and confirming whether the procedures operate in practice. In particular, local customs sometimes develop outside of the procedures manual. Procedures manuals are also occasionally seen as something to be on the shelves for auditors or because it is a requirement rather than as a meaningful record of actual procedures.

Interviews with staff

For external audit, at various stages during the examination of the system, the auditor will need to sit down with members of the client's staff and find out how they carry out their functions.

For internal audit, interviews with staff are an essential tool for ascertaining and understanding the system. These tend to reveal actual procedures in place and give an early indication of potential problems.

EXAM HINT

Walk through tests are frequently confused by students in exams. Make sure you clearly understand what they are. They involve tracing a very few transactions through a system, to check that a process operates as believed.

Tracing transactions (walk through checks)

In order to follow a particular sequence relating to a single transaction, it may be best to follow through a few typical transactions. Walk through tests are valuable for internal and external audit. They may allow internal auditors to identify any examples of actual procedures varying from intended procedures. They will also aid understanding of the whole process and identify risks.

Examining client's or department's documents

There may be other documentation available that will aid the auditors in their review. For example, if there are communication or management meetings, the minutes of these may reveal any control issues that require further investigation. Steering group meetings should be held for any significant system changes and documentation of these will be a useful source of information.

Observation of procedures

It will often be useful to watch staff carrying out procedures such as wages payout and opening of the post; it enables the auditor to see what actually happens in practice.

3.2 Recording the system

The main ways of recording the system are outlined below; in practice the auditor will use a combination of these methods rather than just one.

KEY POINT

The system may be recorded using **narrative notes**, **organisation charts**, **internal control questionnaires** and **flowcharts**.

Narrative notes

This is a simple and apparently convenient way of describing systems. However, this method suffers from several disadvantages of a practical nature:

- it is cumbersome; systems notes can take up a disproportionate amount of space
- notes may be difficult to interpret and review
- it is difficult to make a note of changes in the system
- it may be difficult to see if part of the system has been missed out altogether.

This method is suitable for small businesses and particular aspects of large businesses where relatively few transactions are involved.

Organisation charts

The organisation chart provides a convenient way of describing the relationships between individuals in an organisation. However it does not specify the precise duties of the individuals concerned and it only describes the **formal** relationships between them. In practice, **informal** relationships may have important implications for the auditor. An example of an organisation chart is set out below:

Organisation chart

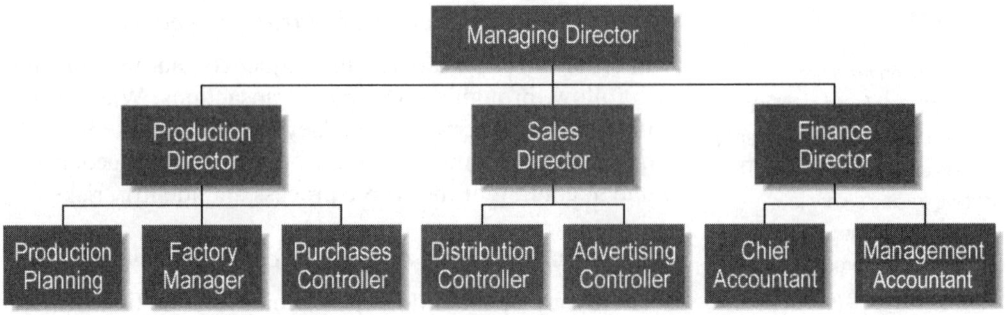

An alternative to the traditional organisation chart is the use of a context diagram to show relationships between different areas.

Internal control questionnaires (ICQs)

ICQs are usually regarded as documents for *evaluating* rather than *recording.* However the various questions making up the ICQs can be constructed in such a way as to require answers in the form of descriptive notes on the system. In this way they can fulfil both functions. ICQs are considered in more detail later.

Flowcharts

Flowcharts are also used by the auditor to document the system, however, this area is not currently examinable and is therefore not included in this textbook.

4 Evaluating the internal control system

As discussed above, having recorded the system, the auditor needs to make a preliminary evaluation of the system in order to make a final decision as to whether to rely on internal controls and adopt a systems approach to testing.

4.1 Internal control evaluation questions (ICEs)

KEY POINT

The ICE is answered using knowledge of the system obtained from the flowchart or ICQ. They are often referred to as Key or Control questions.

The ICE is designed to determine whether desirable controls are present that prevent particular errors or omissions and are answered using knowledge of the system obtained from the flowchart or ICQ. They are often referred to as **key** or **control** questions and require the exercise of the auditor's judgement.

An example of a question from a sales system **ICE** would be: 'Can goods be despatched without being invoiced?'

The answer 'No' to the ICE implies the system is strong as controls exist to prevent the specified problem. A compliance test (test of control) will be required to ensure the controls are operating satisfactorily.

The answer 'Yes' to the ICE question implies that a weakness has been identified and a substantive test (test of detail) will be required to quantify the effect of any errors that may have occurred.

Comprehensive examples of compliance and substantive tests on the revenue and expenditure systems are given in the following chapters.

4.2 Control objectives

KEY POINT

Control objectives seek to establish if controls exist to meet the specified objective.

ICEs seek to establish if controls exist to prevent a specified error or omission.

Instead of focusing on particular errors or omissions the evaluation questions can ask if controls exist to ensure that a particular control objective is achieved.

For example:

ICE – 'Can goods be purchased without proper authority?'

Control objective – 'To ensure that purchases are ordered under proper authority.'

They are effectively addressing the same problem and you should be prepared to deal with questions that ask about risks in a specified area or the control objectives.

4.3 Internal control questions (ICQs)

KEY POINT

ICQs are objective questions which focus on specific controls. They form the subsidiary or criteria questions for answering the ICE.

These are objective questions which focus on specific controls and the information obtained in completing the ICQs are used to answer the relevant ICE.

Consequently they are often referred to as **subsidiary** or **criteria** questions.

Underlying their construction, internal control questionnaires have a number of objectives:

- to **ascertain a client's system** of accounting and internal control
- to **record the client's system**
- to **identify controls (or the absence of controls)** and hence
- to **assist the evaluation of the system** as explained above.

4.4 The link between ICEs and ICQs

EXAM HINT

Ensure you are clear in your mind of the difference between internal control **objectives** and **procedures**.

The distinction between these two questions often causes confusion as they are sometimes shown together on questionnaires. However the **key ICEs** are usually shown in bold type or italics with the **subsidiary ICQs** underneath, e.g.

ICE 'Can goods be purchased without proper authority?'

- Are purchase orders and requisitions approved? (ICQ)
- Are there limits on each buyer's authority to order goods? (ICQ)
- Is purchasing segregated from receiving, accounts payable and inventory records? (ICQ)

A more comprehensive list of purchases system ICEs and ICQs is shown as follows.

Example of part of an ICE adopted by a practising firm

INTERNAL CONTROL EVALUATION

CHECKLIST	Prepared by:	________________
PURCHASES – CREDITORS – PAYMENTS	Date:	________________
CLIENT:	Reviewed by:	________________
PERIOD:	Date:	________________

1 Purchases — Comments — Reference

1.1 *Can goods be purchased without authority?*

(a) purchase requisitions and order approvals?

(b) limit of buyers' authority to order?

(c) purchasing segregated from receiving, accounts payable and stock records?

(d) unissued orders safeguarded against loss?

1.2 *Can liabilities be incurred although goods not received?*

(a) receiving segregated from purchasing, accounts payable and stock records?

(b) are all goods passed directly to stores?

(c) GRNs or equivalent prepared independently?

(d) adequate comparison with order, claims for short shipment, etc.?

(e) invoices, GRNs, direct to accounts payable not purchasing?

(f) invoices checked to order and GRNs, prices checked?

(g) check of extensions, additions, discounts?

(h) documents cancelled to prevent re-use?

(i) unmatched documents investigated regularly?

(j) freight checked, bills matched to consignments?

(k) purchase returns and allowances controlled – follow-up?

(l) forward purchases controlled?

1.3 *Can cut-off errors occur?*

(a) time lapse from receipt of goods to invoice processing?

(b) valuation of unmatched GRNs?

(c) adequate control and recording of receipts?

1.4 *Can invoices be wrongly allocated?*

(a) nominal ledger analysis?

(b) analysis independently checked?

(c) staff purchases controlled?

(d) independent and regular review?

1.5 Can liabilities be recorded for goods or services not ordered?

(a) goods received without authority?

2 Trade payables

2.1 *Can liabilities be incurred but not recorded?*

(a) creditors agreed periodically?

(b) suppliers' statements independently reconciled?

(c) invoice register?

(d) forward contracts?

(e) order backlog follow up?

(f) debit balances controlled?

3 Payments

3.1 *Can payments be made if not properly supported?*

(a) discounts taken?

(b) control over invoices before validating complete?

(c) cheque signatories independent of purchasing, receiving, accounts payable and cheque preparation?

(d) signatories examine support for payment, check completeness, cancel support?

(e) control over signature plates or pre-signed cheques?

(f) control where one signature?

(g) frequency with which cheques mailed?

(h) independent regular bank reconciliation, with cheques directly from bank and review reconciliation?

(i) cheques crossed *account payee only*, continuity accounted for, control over unused cheques?

(j) bank transfers controlled – standing orders?

(k) issue of bearer or 'cash' cheques?

(l) advances and loans controlled?

(m) giro payments, trader's credits, direct debits?

3.2 *Can payments for non-routine purchases be made if not authorised or properly supported?*

(a) services, expense accounts, taxation payments in advance, staff purchases and goods on consignment?

3.3 *Can non-current assets be acquired or removed without proper authorisation and recording?*

(a) approved work orders for fixed assets and major repairs?

(b) approval of cost over-runs?

(c) reporting of scrapping or disposals?

(d) detailed fixed asset register, regular physical inspection and review of values?

(e) periodic insurance appraisals, adequate coverage?

(f) control over loose tools?

5 Computer-based systems

KEY POINT

The features of **computer-based systems** must be recognised and considered by the auditor.

There are a number of distinguishing features of **computer-based systems** which must be recognised and considered by the auditor, whether internal or external auditor. The main features are as follows:

- concentration of controls in the computer department
- lack of primary records
- encoded data
- loss of audit trail
- data needed for audit purposes may be overwritten
- program controls may be important to ensure the completeness and accuracy of accounting records
- the need for specialist expertise
- availability of computer time.

Concentration of controls in the computer department

The need to standardise procedures and utilise the computer resources of a business has led to a concentration of controls in the computer department. You should recognise that such a concentration represents a potential weakness. There is a danger of inadvertent or deliberate corruption of data of which other departments are unaware.

KEY POINT

Data corruption can be minimised by ensuring tight controls are in place.

Most computer users minimise this danger by adopting control procedures which apportion responsibilities within the computer department and allow other (user) departments to check the accuracy of processed data. The auditor's work, particularly at the planning stage, will involve identifying the extent of controls. Clearly if such controls are concentrated in the computer department the adequate functioning of the department will be fundamental to the audit.

The recent reduction in costs of computer hardware has led to the dispersal of both processing and controls in some systems. This enables the users to be more closely involved with the data processing function but may lead to an absence of standardisation of controls. It is a problem considered in more detail later.

Lack of primary records

KEY POINT

As not all computer systems create **primary records**, some transactions may not be traceable to an **originating document**.

In some systems conventional day books will not be maintained. In others an originating document may not be created. In an on-line system for example an operator may receive an order by telephone and use a terminal to key in the relevant data immediately The system creates despatch and invoice documentation and updates stock and customer files. The auditor would be unable to trace these transactions back to an **originating document**.

Such problems are relevant to both management and auditors and should be considered at the time the system is designed. It would be essential for computer generated reports to be provided and reviewed carefully by management.

Encoded data

There is always a danger of transposition errors arising at the encoding stage. The auditor's procedures should take into account the existence of checking procedures (e.g. check digits, data validation) particularly on amendments to standing data items and on the conversion from one system to another.

KEY POINT

Where control is implemented by **exception reporting** there may not be a **visible audit trail**.

Loss of audit trail

Modern systems are usually designed to limit the volume of printed data. Control is implemented by **exception reporting** principles so that detailed printouts of magnetically stored data are not available. The auditor is therefore unable to trace an individual transaction through the system from originating document to financial statements (or vice versa) in the traditional way. There is said to be a loss of (**visible**) **audit trail.**

The auditor must assess the implications of this at the planning stage. It may result in a need to use computer-assisted auditing techniques (CAATs) to obtain appropriate evidence that controls have functioned adequately.

Data needed for audit purposes may be overwritten

The auditors will need to plan audit testing to ensure that the appropriate data is available to them as it may be overwritten during the period. They may need to make frequent visits to their client's premises to ensure that they cover an adequate spread of transactions during the year.

Program controls may be important to ensure the completeness and accuracy of accounting records

The auditors must test controls upon which they wish to rely. This means that they will need to test programmed controls. To do this they will inevitably have to use CAATs.

A further complication which often arises is that the program controls are regularly amended by the client. Old programs may be overwritten and may be unavailable at the accounting year end. The implication is that once again the auditors must be prepared to review and test controls regularly during the year so that they can obtain adequate evidence regarding the functioning of controls during the whole period.

KEY POINT

Increasingly, all auditors need to be capable of auditing systems that are computerised.

The need for specialist expertise

Increasingly, all auditors need to become computer auditors in the sense that they are capable of auditing systems which are computerised. As automation of all activities continues, so auditors need a generic level of skills to ensure that they review all risks. However, it is no longer realistic to expect all staff to have the competence to conduct all audits. Computer specialists are being increasingly used to perform audit work, this trend may spread to external audits as audit competence is put together on a team basis.

There is a major problem for external auditors in that employing and training special computer staff is expensive. This may be a particular problem for smaller practices who do not at present have an extensive portfolio of clients with computer-based accounting systems. It should be impressed upon clients that the installation of a cheap computer system does not necessarily decrease audit costs and may well increase them.

In internal auditing, there is a real shortage of specialist IT auditors, which has led to increasing reliance on outsourced IT functions.

Availability of computer time

The use of CAATs involves the use of the client's computer facilities. There may be a need to organise such facilities well ahead of the required dates.

6 Auditing in a computer environment

6.1 Introduction

While ISA 315 and ISA 330 give general guidance to the auditor in determining the information systems used by the client, these standards do not give detailed advice about auditing in a computer environment. UK auditors could turn to the old Auditing Guideline 407 *Auditing in a computer environment,* although this was formally withdrawn in 2000. Alternatively UK auditors could study ISA 401 *Auditing in a computer information systems environment.*

These documents contain the following major features:

KEY POINT

The principles of an audit in a computer environment are the same as in other circumstances.

- The message is strongly conveyed that the principles of an audit in a computer environment are the same as in other circumstances.
- The Guideline includes in the preface a clear 'health warning' that detailed practical guidance should be obtained by those who are unaccustomed to auditing in a computer environment.
- Emphasis is laid on the knowledge and skills that an auditor will need when auditing in a computer environment. In particular, auditors are recommended that they should develop a basic understanding of the fundamentals of data processing, and attain a level of technical computer knowledge and skills commensurate with the particular circumstances of the audit.
- Smaller computers are discussed. The basic message is that, with the introduction of smaller computers, there is a greater likelihood of weak internal controls, and this will normally lead to greater emphasis being placed on substantive testing of transactions and balances, and on other procedures such as analytical review, rather than on tests of control.
- An explanation is given of audit techniques performed by computer, but the point is made that, where there is a computer-based accounting system, many of the auditor's procedures may still be carried out manually.
- Account is given of the two major types of controls over computer-based accounting systems ('general controls' and 'application controls'), and of the interrelationship between them.

KEY POINT

Guidance is given on the use of third party service organisations to maintain enterprises' accounting records and procedures.

- Guidance is given on the situation where third party service organisations (such as computer service bureaux or software houses) are used for the purpose of maintaining part or all of an enterprise's accounting records and procedures. It is explained that the auditors may encounter practical obstacles, as the enterprise may be placing some reliance on the proper operation of internal controls exercised by the third party. It is recommended that, where the auditors find it impracticable to obtain all the information and explanations that they require from the enterprise itself, they should carry out other procedures. These may include taking steps they consider necessary to enable them to rely on the work performed by other auditors, or carrying out procedures at the premises of the third party.

The details of these documents (and much more!) are incorporated into the following sections of this chapter.

ACTIVITY **2**

List the **eight** special features of computer-based accounting systems which the auditor must address.

Feedback to this activity is at the end of the chapter.

7 Internal control in computer-based systems

A sound appreciation of controls required in these systems is of prime importance to the auditor. As was mentioned earlier, the control environment of most organisations involves the use of automated processing methods and computer based accounting systems.

7.1 Classification of controls

KEY POINT

ISA 315 recognises **application** and **general** controls.

This section of the text uses the classification of controls identified in ISA 315 (and in the earlier Auditing Guideline). ISA 315 recognises only two types of controls:

- **application controls**
- **general controls.**

Both ISA 315 and the Guideline are very general in approach, containing little detail, and no distinction is drawn between large and small systems. This section serves to add detail where it is considered to be necessary.

7.2 Application controls

KEY POINT

Application controls are those which are specific to individual applications.

Application controls cover the transactions and master files which are specific to an individual application.

They are applicable to both computer and manual processing and will therefore consist of both manual and automated controls.

KEY POINT

Application controls comprise **completeness**, **accuracy** and **authorisation** of inputs and controls over **processing**, **outputs** and the **master files**.

Their objective is to ensure the completeness and accuracy of all processing and the validity of the accounting entries made. They fall under the following six main headings and the control *objectives* for each are given below.

Completeness of input

- to ensure that a document is raised for every transaction
- to ensure that each document is input in timely fashion.

Accuracy of input

- to identify the accuracy of data fields on input transactions.

Authorisation of input

- to ensure that each transaction is authorised
- to ensure that the individual who authorised the transaction was empowered to do so.

Controls over processing (updating)

- to ensure that all input data is processed
- to ensure that the correct versions of master files and standing data files are used
- to ensure that the processing of each transaction is accurate to produce accurately updated master files.

Control over output

- to ensure that output is checked for completeness and accuracy
- to ensure that output is properly distributed and actioned.

Controls over master files

- to ensure that all data held on master files is accurate and up-to-date
- to ensure that any amendment to standing data is properly authorised.

The control *techniques* for application controls under the six headings are shown below.

Control techniques for application controls

Processing	*Output*	*Master file*
• Batch reconciliation • Run to run totals to ensure no data lost • Summary processing, e.g. check total depreciation equal to summary of elements • External file labels • Internal file labels	• Check batch control outputs to inputs • Summary of totals • 'End of Report' message • Checklist for distribution of output • Follow up exception reports	• Check amendments on a one to one basis • Periodic printout and checks • Record counts checked • Independent control totals

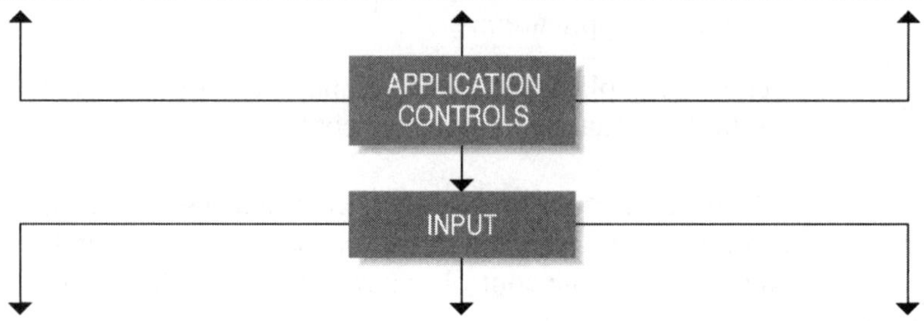

Processing	*Output*	*Master file*
• One to one checks, i.e. each input checked to output • Batch control totals • Hash totals • Document counts • Sequence checks • Matching each master file record to a transaction record	• Check digits • Reasonableness checks to ensure data within certain ranges • Existence checks, e.g. to check that customer account exists • Manual controls, e.g. batch controls and arithmetic checks	• Manual authorisation • Clerical review of transactions • One to one checking of amendments to standing data • Programmed checks on authorisation limits

It should be appreciated that techniques which control the accuracy of input and processing will help to control master file data. As master file standing data items are used many times over in processing they take on a greater importance than transaction data and more costly controls such as one-to-one checks may be justified.

7.3 General controls

KEY POINT

General controls cover the general environment within which application controls operate and are relevant to all applications.

These controls cover the general environment within which application controls operate. Such controls can be expected to be relevant to all applications.

The objective of such controls is to ensure the integrity of application development and implementation and to ensure that computer operations are properly administered to protect hardware, programs and data files.

ISA 315 states that general controls commonly include controls over the following:

- datacentre and network operations
- system software acquisition, change and maintenance
- access security
- application system acquisition, development and maintenance.

Typical controls (with associated control objectives) are listed below.

Controls over systems development (application development)

- to ensure developments are fully authorised
- to ensure proper standards are followed during development
- to ensure changes are properly tested and documented.

Controls to prevent/detect errors during program execution

- to ensure any errors arising are noted and resolved.

Controls to prevent/detect changes to data files

- to ensure changes are authorised
- to ensure changes are made accurately.

Controls to ensure continuity of operations

- to ensure the system can continue to function in the event of disaster or breakdown.

Errors during program execution	*Changes to data files*	*Continuity of operations*
• Systems software should report errors, e.g. wrong file, hardware malfunction • Detailed operations • Job scheduling	• Prior authorisation • Password protection • Back up files • Record of amendments for subsequent checking • Physical protection of files	• Back up procedures • Standby arrangements • Testing back up procedures • Protection against fire and theft • Maintenance agreements • Insurance • Copy of files

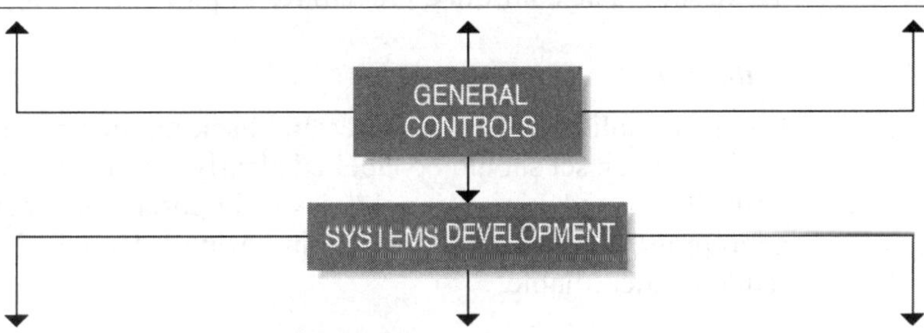

Application development	*Program changes*	*Installation, maintenance and documentation*
• Systems design standards • Programming standards • Testing procedures • Full documentation • Approval by users before implementation • Internal audit involvement • Segregation of duties between development and operations	• Supervision and training • Authorisation of changes • Documentation of changes • Password protection to prevent unauthorised access • Back up of programs • Physical protection of files • Rotation of duties • Thorough testing • Approval of changes	• Testing and documentation • Protection of systems software (read only) • Segregation of duties (programmers, operators, users) • Good quality documentation

8 Further examples of selected controls

Some of the controls in the previous section may be unfamiliar to you. Further details are given here.

8.1 Manual controls

KEY POINT

Manual controls include the physical protection of data stores, keeping back-up media and data properly filed and documented.

Physical controls

Many of the simpler controls are largely a matter of common sense, for example limiting access to the computer room, keeping it locked and allowing keys only to specified people. The computer room should be a controlled environment to minimise risk of damage.

Magnetic media can also be damaged by direct sunlight, extremely cold temperatures and a damp atmosphere. It is important, therefore, to plan both the situation of the room to be used for electronic data processing and the positioning of computers and media within the room with great care.

Adequate fire precautions should exist, and an arrangement made with, perhaps, another firm to utilise its equipment in an emergency. Service agreements with computer manufacturers frequently provide a useful emergency system. Such agreements enable machines to be exchanged, so that an operating machine remains in the department while the original one is repaired. All emergency measures should be clearly documented in a contingency plan.

Back-up media

The back up media should be stored in a place entirely separate from where the main media is kept. This covers not only local damage to one or a few items, but more drastic circumstances such as a fire in the computer room that destroys all the media kept there.

Having created a back-up copy of a disk, it is essential that back ups are taken regularly to enable the data to be restored if there is a system failure.

There should be controlled procedures in place regarding version control of the disks.

Data filing

Having established a set of source and back-up media, the need for a filing system is obvious. Each set should be labelled clearly, so that the data can be identified immediately and minimising the risk of important data being overwritten. It may be appropriate to print labels, thereby imposing a degree of control on how each media is rendered identifiable.

The labelled media should be filed in special boxes to provide a degree of protection against damage and possible data corruption.

Since many sets will be collected over a period of time, it is important to file them efficiently so that any set is easy to find at any given moment. (Naturally, this is applicable to the back-up media too.) The appointment of a media librarian to control the filing and movement of media is necessary in larger organisations.

Documentation

Each process should also be documented and a job sheet, clearly explaining the tasks that are to be done, should pass to the person responsible for completing them.

As data is stored on media, further useful documentation can be provided by creating an information file for each set. A list of all the files on the media and their contents, as well as the dates on which the files were originated and updated and the name of the persons responsible for this, can be recorded on an information file, as well as any further notes likely to be of use later. This file would be automatically generated.

Staff training

In addition to these control measures, it is important that all staff involved with automated data processing are adequately trained so that they understand the system and the reasoning behind the controls to which they should adhere. They must be aware too of the need for careful handling of the disks themselves.

Proofing

In some cases the data may be checked manually by a different person after keying, or the data can be keyed twice by two different people. In this way any errors would be identified and corrected prior to processing. This process should be carried out after data has been keyed onto the disk for the first time. Mistakes identified during proofing should be corrected and then the corrections proofed.

8.2 Programmed controls

KEY POINT

Programmed controls include using **passwords**, date/time stamps and programmed prompts and checks.

Passwords

The more sophisticated the program, the more in-built controls it is likely to have. This is particularly true of the control known as **data-hiding**. When a disk contains information that should not be widely available (for example, data concerning salaries on personnel files) it is possible to **hide it**, while making other information on the same disk less difficult to obtain. This may be done by **passwords**.

A program that operates through passwords will prevent access to either all or specific items of data to any user who is not aware of the relevant password. Where relevant, a hierarchy of passwords will exist such that extremely sensitive data may only be accessible by a small number of personnel.

Passwords can also be applied in such a way that read-only access to a file is available without the appropriate password. It is possible to impose a password on a disk drive (this is particularly relevant to computers with only one disk drive and hard disk storage). It is, however, not highly advisable, because to forget the password is to render access to the computer totally impossible.

Care should be taken when applying passwords to ensure that if passwords are forgotten the data can still be accessed via emergency procedures. Such procedures would require proper high level authorisation.

Prompts

The deletion of any created file is often controlled by a stage at which the computer pauses and asks the users if they are sure that the deletion command was intentional. Similarly, any attempt to exit the program or retrieve another file without storing work done previously, is checked by a similar pause and query that provides users with the opportunity to go back and save the data if it is required.

The same type of program prevents two files being created with identical names on the same disk and asks, when storing data, the name of the file on which it is to be stored.

Check digits

Check digits are a means of control in that they ascertain whether or not a number (for example, an International Standard Book Number) is valid. A formula is used to calculate the digit which is attached to the end of the number itself.

Modulus 11 is a common system and works as follows:

number, say	32153
multiply by weightings (see below)	65432
results	18/10/4/15/6
results total	53
results total ÷ modulus	53 ÷ 11 = 4
remainder	9
modulus minus remainder	11 – 9 = 2
check digit	2
number now becomes	321532

The weightings to use are in ascending order starting on the right. The check digit will be assigned weighting 1 so start with weight 2 at the first stage above.

If there is no remainder the check digit is 0, if the remainder is 10 the check digit is shown as X.

The check digit is initially calculated by the computer and then becomes an integral part of the number. The example above could be a customer account number.

The computer will then detect if the number is ever input incorrectly, e.g. a transposition error resulting in 231532. The computer performs the modulus 11 calculation on 23153 and gets a check digit of 11 – 8 = 3 (check it yourself to confirm this) instead of 2. An error message will then be sent to the operator.

Batch totals and hash totals

These controls are often used in batch processing systems whereby documents are grouped (batched) together and processed in a single block.

A batch (or control) total is the sum of one of the numerical fields on the documents in the batch, e.g. total of the sales invoice values. This total is calculated manually and the documents are then input to the computer. The computer then calculates the batch total and this is compared with the manually calculated total. If they are different then an error has occurred: perhaps an invoice value has been mis-keyed or a document may have been omitted from input altogether. The input clerk is alerted to the error and can then investigate it.

A hash total works in exactly the same way as a batch total but a different type of field is used. A typical hash total would be the total of customer account numbers: unlike the batch total the value of the hash total is meaningless but it is still useful for control purposes to detect errors on input or omissions.

Reasonableness checks

The program will check to ensure that the data input is reasonable given the type of input it is. An example on a payroll system would be to check that hours recorded for the week fall within the range 30–50.

Existence checks

The computer will check to ensure that the data input is valid by checking that the entity already exists on the system, e.g. check to ensure that an employee number input already exists on the system.

Dependency checks

In some cases, data input fields can be compared with other fields for reasonableness, e.g. when inputting a purchase invoice the operator keys in the net amount and the VAT amount and the computer will check that the VAT is a sensible amount as compared with the net amount.

9 Small ('stand-alone') computer systems

9.1 Description

DEFINITION

Personal computers are economical, powerful, self-contained general purpose computers used either as part of a computer-based accounting system, or alone.

Personal computers, PCs can be defined as economical, powerful, self-contained general purpose computers used either as part of a computer-based accounting system, or alone.

PCs are easily portable and controls associated with larger systems may not be practicable. The operating system and applications software are often purchased as a package from third-party vendors and they may not contain as many control and security features as would be found in a larger environment. Data and program files can be stored on removable media such as disks as well as on non-removable hard disks.

Problems include the following:

- the danger of errors or loss of data on conversion to a new system – the process should be fully documented and record counts and control totals should be used
- the danger of badly made and poorly documented amendments to programs
- a lack of proper audit trail.

KEY POINT

PCs can be used as stand-alone workstations or as part of a network, which allows for sharing of resources.

PCs can be used as stand-alone workstations operated by one or many users at different times, as workstations which are part of local area networks (LANs), or as workstations connected to central computers as part of distributed accounting systems.

A local area network typically has one PC acting as a file server which manages the network. The arrangement allows for sharing of resources such as storage facilities, printers, data and programs.

This section is concerned with the second and third type of system. It should be appreciated that such systems are now extremely powerful and have widespread applications within many organisations.

9.2 Problems associated with small computer systems

KEY POINT

The use of non-specialist staff may lead to control problems in small computer systems.

The reduction in the cost of small computers in recent years may lead the company to believe that controls are not needed or may be implemented at low cost. The auditors must encourage their client to appreciate that it is the value of the data not the cost of the computer that should dictate the time and money spent implementing control.

There is normally only a limited division of duties in a mini-computer system. The same person may be responsible for preparation of input data, computer operations and distribution of output. It is important to implement clerical application controls outside the computer department to counter the limited segregation of duties within it.

The client may be a first-time computer user and may not implement a wide range of application controls. In any case the system may not be fully documented and the supplier of a package may not be prepared to release full details. The auditor may need to rely largely on substantive testing to obtain adequate audit evidence.

There may be unrestricted access to terminals or data. This should be controlled by:

- nominating specified personnel to use terminals
- physical access restrictions
- password protection
- proper supervision by senior officials
- user logs to record the use of terminals and attempts to gain unauthorised access.

Many small systems operate on a real-time basis. Controls may include detailed editing of transactions, the maintenance of transaction logs and control accounts and full review of output by officials outside the computer department. The auditor should check that editing and authorisation extend to changes in standing data as well as routine transactions.

There are dangers of errors or loss of data on the conversion to a new small computer system. The conversion process should be fully documented and controls such as maintaining record counts and control totals should be used. If possible the auditor should become involved prior to and during the conversion process.

There are dangers that program changes are made that are unauthorised or badly designed by the client's staff. In addition the client's staff may neglect other managerial duties in spending time attempting to program the computer.

The client should attempt to segregate operations staff from programmers. It is often cost-effective for the client to employ a consultant to design and amend programs. The object programs may be held in machine code only and so are much more difficult for staff to amend. Back-up versions of programs should be maintained.

There is finally a general problem that such systems may not provide a visible audit trail. The auditor may wish to use audit interrogation packages but the writing of a one-off program may not be cost-effective. The use of a manufacturer's own enquiry programs may not be cost-effective unless the portfolio of clients using that type of equipment is large.

The result is that a substantive-based approach is likely to dominate this type of audit until computer-assisted techniques which are reasonably priced and which can be applied to a wide range of small systems become available.

10 Limitations on the effectiveness of internal controls

KEY POINT

All internal control systems have inherent limitations and are subject to abuse or human error.

As we have seen, it is possible to reduce the volume of substantive procedures required, but not to eliminate the requirement altogether. This is because all systems have inherent limitations such as:

- the need to balance the cost of the control with its benefits
- the fact that internal controls are applied to systematic transactions, not one-off year-end adjustments, which are often large and subject to error
- the potential for human error – any system of control is dependent on the people operating the control
- the possibility of fraudulent collusion designed to 'get round' controls that segregate duties (for example, the supervisor responsible for checking and authorising overtime claims could collude with employees, to enable excess overtime payments to be claimed)
- the abuse of authority and override of controls (abuse of authority might involve ordering personal goods through the firm - it is very easy for directors and managers of organisations of any size to instruct staff to bypass normal procedures, such as the requirement for authorisation for payments)
- the obsolescence of controls.

11 Reliance by the auditor on system internal controls

Having considered in detail examples of both application controls and general controls, the question arises as to what extent the auditor should rely upon such controls. Inevitably there is no easy answer to such a question.

KEY POINT

ISA 500 requires auditors to obtain reliable evidence sufficient to draw reasonable conclusions.

ISA 500 requires auditors to obtain sufficient appropriate audit evidence to be able to draw reasonable conclusions on which to base the audit opinion. The relationship between tests of control and substantive procedures holds in a computer-based accounting system: if the auditors obtain reasonable assurance from testing the controls they can limit their substantive work.

11.1 The relationship between application and general controls

It may be appropriate for the auditors to concentrate upon application controls before deciding how far to proceed with examining general controls. The reasons for this are as follows:

- application controls can be more easily related to a specific control objective, and therefore a specific audit objective, than can general controls
- application controls can be more easily tested by using specific transactions to act as a medium for the test which is then performed either clerically or by using computer-assisted audit techniques
- as a result of the above two reasons, the testing of application controls may be more effective than general controls.

KEY POINT

General controls can be highly relevant to the auditor, however it may be appropriate to concentrate on application controls first.

There are, however, certain reasons for still considering general controls to be highly relevant to the auditor:

- if application controls become concentrated in the computer department, the environment within which the application controls function will be fundamental
- if certain application controls are lacking the auditors may attempt to limit their substantive testing by placing more reliance on general controls.

Auditors can follow three basic rules relating to audit testing of controls:

- the auditors can test and rely on general controls alone without having to test application controls
- the auditors can test and rely on manual application controls alone without having to test general controls
- in order to rely on programmed application controls the auditors must first be satisfied with general controls - this is because if the controls covering the whole computer environment are poor, then the programmed application controls within it will be worthless.

11.2 Audit documentation

KEY POINT

Control documentation may be in the form of audit or systems files or internal control questionnaires.

You have seen that the auditors are likely to wish to rely upon controls as a source of audit evidence. To do so they must obtain a record of the system and carry out a preliminary evaluation. Their work will be assisted by the use of documentation to help identify the internal controls on which they may wish to place reliance.

The documentation may take a variety of forms but two particular methods will often form an important part of the audit documentation.

Audit control file or systems file

This file contains important details of both clerical and programmed procedures. It must be reviewed and updated regularly. The auditors should arrange to have their name on distribution lists to receive notification from the client of all procedural changes. The file might typically contain the following items:

- copies of documents used in the system with details of checks performed on them
- description of how source documents are converted into input with control procedures
- detailed application controls in each area of the system
- flowcharts
- details of all data files including storage media, organisation, labelling, storage arrangements, back-up facilities
- details and copies of output documents
- the results of the auditor's review of the system and the effectiveness of the controls within it.

Internal control questionnaire (ICQ)

The ascertainment and evaluation of both application and general controls will be assisted by the use of specially designed ICQs. The ICQ would include questions covering both clerical and programmed controls as both types are likely to be relied upon by the auditor.

Conclusion

It is the responsibility of management to ensure the operation of a sound system of internal control but the auditor must examine the system as well. There are many types of control that could be introduced but the costs of additional controls must be weighed against the expected benefits.

There are a number of ways the internal control system can be ascertained and recorded.

Computer-based systems have a number of special features which must be recognised and considered by the auditor.

Internal controls in computer-based systems are conventionally divided into application controls and general controls. The auditor should look at application controls before general controls.

SELF-TEST QUESTIONS

Internal control

1 What is the definition of an internal control system? (1.1)

2 Explain the three main types of internal control. (1.5)

3 List seven examples of internal control procedures. (1.6)

Documenting the system

4 What methods can be used to ascertain a system of internal control? (3)

5 What are walk through checks? (3.1)

Evaluating the internal control system

6 What is the difference between an ICQ and an ICE? (4.4)

Internal control in computer–based systems

7 Give a definition of application controls. (7.2)

8 State four application controls appropriate for data output. (7.2)

9 Give a definition of general controls. (7.3)

10 State four general controls appropriate for program changes. (7.3)

Limitations on the effectiveness of internal controls

11 List four major limitations of control systems in general. (10)

EXAM-TYPE QUESTIONS

Question 1: Internal controls

You have read that: 'If auditors wish to place reliance on any internal controls, they should ascertain and evaluate those controls and perform tests on their operation'.

Required:

(a) What are the major objectives of a system of internal control? **(4 marks)**

(b) Explain briefly the major categories of internal control. **(5 marks)**

(Total: 9 marks)

Question 2: Rothwell Ltd

On making arrangements to commence the final audit work at Rothwell Ltd, the company accountant informs you that the company has acquired a new system for processing transactions and preparing financial statements. The company accountant had not seen fit to discuss the matter with you, as the computer salesman had run a demonstration which seemed to show that the introduction of the PC-based system would cause very few problems. However, while you are carrying out your final audit tests, you are informed that the computerised accounting data cannot be accessed. The only response which the company accountant is able to receive from the computerised system is that 'the system is active'. You say that this means that the data disks have been corrupted either because of a malfunction in the software or because of a 'user error'.

Required:

(a) Describe the audit implications of the introduction of the PC-based system in the period between the interim audit visit and the year-end date. **(6 marks)**

(b) Describe the controls which the company should have installed in order to ensure that this corruption of the data files did not cause a major accounting breakdown. **(8 marks)**

(c) Describe the audit implications in the year that the corruption of data files has taken place, assuming that the company has not maintained adequate safeguards over computer-generated data. **(6 marks)**

(Total: 20 marks)

For the answers to these questions, see the 'Answers' section at the end of the book.

FEEDBACK TO ACTIVITY 1

Reasons that internal controls are of interest to both the internal and external auditor include the following:

- To fulfil the objectives of auditors. In the case of internal auditors, a key objective is to review the organisation's system of internal control and to provide assurance that the corporate governance requirements are being met. For external auditors, internal controls should ensure the completeness and accuracy of the accounting records which generate the financial statements upon which they have to provide an opinion.
- Internal controls are used to manage risks and therefore all auditors need to understand how internal controls are operating in the management of risk.
- Both internal and external audit need to decide on the extent of reliance on internal controls and therefore the amount of testing required.
- Reliance on internal controls reduces the amount of substantive testing required by both internal and external audit.

- The internal control environment can be an important indicator of the control culture of the organisation and therefore how effectively the organisation is being governed.

FEEDBACK TO ACTIVITY 2

The eight special features of computer-based accounting systems are:

- concentration of controls in the computer department
- lack of primary records
- encoded data
- loss of audit trail
- data needed for audit purposes may be overwritten
- program controls may be important to ensure the completeness and accuracy of accounting records
- the need for specialist expertise
- availability of computer time.

Chapter 9

INTERNAL CONTROL – SALES AND PURCHASES

CHAPTER CONTENTS

This chapter builds on the earlier chapters on principles of **internal control**, evidence and testing by reviewing how we apply these techniques to the specific area of **sales** and **purchases**.

Internal and external auditors will both be involved in reviewing sales and purchases transactions and the types of risks and controls will be very similar. The main difference between the two types of audits will be the overall objectives and purpose of the review, with internal auditors carrying out a more detailed, broader review to provide assurance to management.

For external auditors, many organisations' audits are not split into interim and final stages, with both tests of control and substantive procedures being carried out at the year end. Where an interim audit is performed some months before the year end, the emphasis is on tests of controls.

It is far better, and easier in the long run, if you can relate general principles to each audit area rather than learning long lists of tests.

This chapter considers tests of control *and* the substantive tests that are performed in respect of sales and purchases.

You should note that it is possible that examination questions in this area (as with others) may be set in a computer based context. You should always bear this in mind.

Objectives

By the time you have finished this chapter you should be able to:

- understand the key risks associated with sales and purchases
- understand the typical control objectives for the sales cycle
- detail tests of controls and substantive tests which may be appropriate for the sales system and sales total
- understand the typical control objectives for the purchases cycle
- detail tests of controls and substantive tests which may be appropriate for the purchases system and purchases total.

1 General

1.1 Control objectives, procedures, and tests of control

KEY POINT

Poor internal controls in the sales and purchases systems would result in serious financial implications.

Why do we need internal controls in the sales and purchases system?

Consider what might happen if controls did not exist:

- If sales orders are not prenumbered – they may get lost and goods not despatched, or they may be raised more than once.
- If despatches are not matched with invoices – invoices may not be issued, or invoices may be incorrect.

Such control failures would result in poor customer relations, possible loss of income, inaccurate accounting records and high administrative costs to correct the problems.

- If batch controls are not used for processing invoices – invoices may get lost and when payment is made by the customer this could not be allocated against an invoice. Or, if the customer doesn't pay, the invoice would not be chased for payment as it had never been processed.
- If individual debtor and creditor accounts are not maintained in sales and purchase ledgers – it will be difficult to identify who owes what monies, and would make it difficult to monitor overdue amounts and would be far less efficient when dealing with any debtor and creditor queries. Reconciliation to control accounts would not be possible.

All these factors would result in lack of management knowledge and control of the business.

It is not practical to go into detail on the exact reason for every control that is commonly used, but as you go through this section, try and think of reasons *why* the control is in operation, think about what might happen if the control were *not* there, what assets could be lost, what records would be incorrect, and how the business would be damaged or made inefficient and unprofitable.

Remember that control **objectives** for all systems are in outline as follows:

That only *authorised* transactions are *promptly* recorded at the *correct* amount in the *appropriate* accounts in the proper *accounting period*, that *access* to assets is only in accordance with proper authorisation and that recorded assets are *compared* with existing assets.

KEY POINT

Control procedures include sequential document **numbering**, maintaining **batch** and **control accounts** and **authorisation**.

Detailed **control procedures** are often similar across sales, purchases and other areas and include for example:

- **sequential numbering** of documents with subsequent checking of the sequence for completeness
- the maintenance of **batch** and other control totals at the input stage with subsequent checking to output for completeness and accuracy
- the maintenance of **control accounts** which are checked to ensure that they reconcile to the ledgers
- **authorisation**, evidenced by the signature of responsible officials for the raising, input and distribution of documents.

Tests of control by the auditor involve auditors ensuring that the procedures above have been applied, by looking for evidence of, for example, the checking of sequences, batch totals, control account reconciliations and authorisation. Often the auditors are simply looking for a signature, to show that the control procedure has been performed. They will also sometimes re-perform the task to ensure that, for example, the reconciliation has been performed correctly rather than the document simply having been signed. Reperformance of a control procedure will often also serve as a substantive procedure.

ACTIVITY 1

Outline four common control procedures for sales and purchases and four common tests of control.

Feedback to this activity is at the end of the chapter.

You must distinguish carefully between control **objectives**, control **procedures** (both of which are the responsibility of the client) and **tests of control** (which are the responsibility of the auditor).

KEY POINT

For every audit, consider the specific **risks** relevant and their impact and probability.

1.2 Risks associated with sales and purchases

In understanding why we need to audit sales and purchases, we already have an idea of the level and types of **risks** involved. For every audit undertaken, we need to consider in more detail the specific relevant risks and the impact and probability of such risks materialising. In this way, the auditor can prioritise work on the areas of greatest risk. It is therefore worth summarising the key risks associated with sales and purchases, as follows:

- sales and purchases failing to meet the control objectives of the organisation, resulting in financial loss and damage to reputation
- inappropriate or expensive goods purchased resulting in missed budgets and financial loss
- failure to purchase goods or services at the right time and therefore failure to meet required deadlines
- fraudulent purchase or sales transactions resulting in financial loss or damage to reputation
- poor quality of goods received and despatched, resulting in claims against the company, failure to deliver company objectives and damage to reputation
- failure to agree appropriate terms and conditions with suppliers or customers resulting in disputes over sales and purchases
- failure to meet regulatory requirements for goods sold or purchased.

ACTIVITY 2

List separately four risks associated with sales and four risks associated with purchases.

Feedback to this activity is at the end of the chapter.

2 Sales system

2.1 Control objectives

How do the control objectives noted above translate into 'real life' objectives for sales?

KEY POINT

Where sales are made on credit, the sales cycle includes control objectives for **debtors**.

For many businesses, sales are made on credit and thus the **sales cycle** includes control objectives for **debtors**. These control objectives include the following:

- sales are made in accordance with company objectives, with agreements in place with all customers
- customers' orders should be authorised, controlled and recorded in order to execute them promptly and determine any provision required for losses arising from unfulfilled commitments
- goods shipped and work completed should be controlled to ensure that invoices are issued and revenue recorded for all sales
- goods returned and claims by customers should be controlled in order to determine the liability for goods returned and claims received but not entered in the debtors' records
- invoices and credits should be appropriately checked as being accurate and authorised before being entered in the debtors' records
- validated debtors' transactions, and only those transactions, should be accurately entered in the accounting records
- there should be procedures to ensure that sales invoices are subsequently paid and that doubtful amounts are identified in order to determine any provisions required.

2.2 Achievement of objectives

KEY POINT

The achievement of sales control objectives involves **segregation of duties**. **Receipt**, **despatch** and **invoicing** should be segregated.

In order to achieve these objectives there should be good **segregation of duties**. There are three distinct processes in the sales system which should be segregated and performed by different staff in order to ensure effective internal controls.

Accepting customers' orders

Sequence-controlled documents should be used to acknowledge all orders received. Any uncompleted orders should be regularly reviewed.

Credit limits should be checked by the credit control department. Selling prices, special discounts and delivery dates should be fixed by senior members of the sales department – never by the accounts staff.

Despatch department

Sequence-controlled documents should be used (goods outwards or despatch notes) for all goods leaving the premises. These should be completed by the gatekeeper or the despatch department – never by the accounts staff.

Invoicing the goods

Sequence-controlled invoices should be raised by the sales department and then passed to the accounts department for recording. Independent checks should be made to ensure that invoices have been raised for all goods outwards notes.

In addition strict control of credit notes is essential to ensure that they are raised by proper authority in the sales department against goods received notes. It is not uncommon for credit notes to be raised to 'hide' what are in fact bad debts. Credit notes can also be used to cancel out fictitious sales invoices which have been raised in order to boost sales figures artificially.

2.3 Control procedures over sales and debtors

KEY POINT

The controls in the sales cycle reflect its importance to the business and the fraudulent opportunities that exist.

There are a large number of controls that may be required in the sales cycle owing to the importance of this area in any business and the possible fraudulent opportunities that exist for diverting sales away from the business and other persons benefiting.

Orders

- The orders should be checked against the customer's account; this should be evidenced by initialling. Any new customer should be referred to the credit control department before the order is accepted to ensure agreements are in place prior to processing of any sales orders.
- Existing customers should be allocated a credit limit and it should be ascertained whether this limit is to be exceeded if the new order is accepted. If so the matter should be referred to credit control.
- All orders received should be recorded on pre-numbered sales order documents.
- All orders should be authorised before any goods are despatched.
- The sales order should be used to produce a despatch note for the goods outwards department. No goods may be despatched without a despatch note.
- Discount should be within procedures and clearly authorised, with monitoring by management on the level, type and reason for discounts.

Despatch

- Despatch notes should be pre-numbered and a register kept of them to relate to sales invoices and orders.
- Goods despatched notes should be authorised as goods leave and checked periodically to ensure they are complete and that all have been invoiced.

Invoicing and credit notes

- Sales invoices should be authorised by a responsible official and referenced to the original authorised order and despatch note.
- All invoices and credit notes should be entered in sales day book records, the sales ledger, and sales ledger control account. Batch totals should be maintained for this purpose.
- Sales invoices and credit notes should be checked for prices, casts and calculations by a person other than the one preparing the invoice.
- All invoices and credit notes should be serially pre-numbered and regular sequence checks should be carried out.
- Credit notes should be authorised by someone unconnected with despatch or sales ledger functions.
- Copies of cancelled invoices should be retained.
- Any invoice cancellation should lead to a cancellation of the appropriate despatch note.
- Cancelled and free of charge invoices should be signed by a responsible official.
- Each invoice should distinguish between different types of sales and VAT. Any coding of invoices should be periodically checked independently.

Returns

- Any goods returned by the customer should be checked for obvious damage and, when accepted, a document should be raised.
- All goods returned should be used to prepare appropriate credit notes.

Debtors

- A sales ledger control account should be prepared regularly and checked to individual sales ledger balances by an independent official.
- Sales ledger personnel should be independent of despatch and cash receipt functions.
- Statements should be sent regularly to customers.
- Formal procedures should exist for following up overdue debts which should be highlighted either by the preparation of an aged list of balances or in the preparation of statements to customers.
- Letters should be sent to customers for collection of overdue debts.

Bad debts

- The authority to write off a bad debt should be given in writing and adjustments made to the sales ledger.
- The use of court action or the writing-off of a bad debt should be authorised by an official independent of the cash receipt function.

KEY POINT

Sales procedures need to be communicated to all affected parts of the organisation.

General

- Authorised and documented sales policies and procedures need to be implemented and communicated to all affected parts of the organisation, and should be maintained up to date.
- Accurate, complete and timely management information should be in place to record trends in sales, impact on stock and forecasts of future requirements to support the development of future sales and stock strategy.
- Commission payments to salespeople should be authorised and in line with agreed company procedures.

2.4 Tests of control

You should by now be familiar with the meaning of 'tests of control', namely that they are tests performed to obtain audit evidence about the operating effectiveness of controls in preventing, or detecting and correcting, material misstatements.

KEY POINT

Tests of control should check that sales control procedures and objectives are being applied and achieved.

Tests of control should be designed to check that the control procedures are being applied and that objectives are being achieved. Tests may be appropriate under the following broad headings.

Sequence test checks

Carry out *sequence test checks* on invoices, credit notes, despatch notes and orders. Ensure that all items are included and that there are no omissions or duplications.

Authorisation

Check the *authorisation* for the:

- acceptance of the order (the creditworthiness check)
- discounts applied to orders
- despatch of goods
- raising of the invoice or credit note
- pricing and discounts
- write-off of bad debts.

Check both that the relevant signature exists and that the control has been applied, e.g. check pricing for accuracy and credit limits to ensure that they have not been exceeded. This last test will also serve as a substantive procedure.

Arithmetical accuracy

Seek evidence of checking of the arithmetical accuracy of:

- invoices
- credit notes
- VAT.

This is often done by means of a 'grid stamp' containing several signatures on the face of the invoice. Ensure that the control has in fact been applied by checking the accuracy of such invoices and credit notes. This last test will also serve as a substantive procedure.

Despatch notes

Check *despatch notes* and goods returned notes to ensure that they are *referenced* to *invoices* and credit notes and vice versa.

Control account reconciliations

Check that *control account reconciliations* have been *performed and reviewed.* Re-perform the control by checking the reconciliation to source documentation.

Ensure that *batch total controls* have been *applied* by seeking signatures and tracing batches from input to output.

Check that *exception* and *management* information *reporting* on sales have been produced and reviewed, with evidence of action taken on unusual trends or level of discounts or unusual prices.

In all cases, tests should be performed on a *sample* basis. The auditor should investigate errors and consider the need for further testing to obtain comfort on the proper application of the control procedure.

If the auditor finds significant weaknesses in the controls over the sales system, he should communicate his findings promptly to management, in accordance with ISA 260 (see next chapter of this text).

2.5 Substantive procedures

You should also be confident about the meaning of 'substantive procedures', namely audit procedures performed to obtain audit evidence to detect material misstatements in the financial statements. They include:

- tests of details of transactions, balances and disclosures; and
- analytical procedures.

KEY POINT

Substantive procedures may be applied to accounting records, invoices and credit notes, stock records and control accounts.

Accounting records

- Check additions and cross-casts of the sales day book and sales returns day book.
- Check the postings of individual invoices to the nominal ledger and the control account.
- Check entries in the sales day book and sales returns day book back to original invoices, credit notes and despatch notes, and vice versa.

Invoices and credit notes

- Check numerical sequence of invoices enquiring into missing numbers and inspecting all copies of cancelled invoices.
- Check copy sales invoices and credit notes with the sales day books and debtors' ledger accounts, checking analysis of sales day books where appropriate and authorisation of credit notes.
- Compare invoiced prices with authorised, up to date price lists, quotations and correspondence.
- Check calculations and additions of invoices and credit notes.
- Scrutinise credit notes for large or unusual items.

Stock records

The risks and internal controls associated with stock are covered in more detail later in the text. However, there are a number of key controls worth stating here:

- Check goods despatched notes or goods outwards records to the copy sales invoices.
- Trace goods outwards from invoice to despatch note to stock records.
- Trace goods returned from returns documentation to stock records and credit note.

General

Where returns or allowances affect the calculations of commissions, ensure that adjustments have been made properly.

Control accounts

Test control account reconciliations checking back to source documentation such as sales invoices, cash and returns records. Ensure that any reconciling items are dealt with properly. The external auditor will be particularly interested in the year end control account reconciliation.

Analytical procedures

KEY POINT

Analytical procedures may be applied to fluctuations in sales levels and cut-off problems.

Examine fluctuations in sales levels - fluctuations, particularly around the year end, can be identified by comparing levels of sales throughout the year on a month by month basis, or by comparing the sales in the last month of the year to sales in the first month of the next year.

Significant fluctuations from month to month may indicate misclassification between months or the omission of sales or the incidence of a few individual sales of large amounts. The auditor could consider vouching large individual sales.

Checking budgets to actual figures can also be worthwhile as significant variances can identify problems.

Cut-off problems - An increase in sales just before the year end with low sales just after the year end may indicate that the client has tried to effect as many deliveries as possible prior to the year end in order to maximise reported profits. The auditor should consider identifying and checking large items in the last month and the first month of the next period to ensure delivery did take place before the year end.

Disclosure

Turnover must be disclosed by class of business and geographical market.

You may have noted that the tests of controls and substantive procedures noted above sometimes appear to be very similar. Remember that we have said that one test can serve *both* as a test of controls and as a substantive procedure. Where, for example, an invoice is checked for authorisation (test of control), it can also be checked for the accuracy of pricing (substantive procedure). This does *not* mean that tests of controls and substantive procedures are interchangeable. It is vital that you understand the conceptual difference between the two types of test. Refer back to previous chapters, if necessary.

3 Purchases system

3.1 Control objectives

KEY POINT

As purchases can be made on credit, the **purchases cycle** includes control objectives for **creditors**.

For all businesses, purchases can be made on credit and thus the **purchases cycle** includes control objectives for **creditors**. You also need to bear in mind that 'purchases' has a wide meaning in terms of the purchases cycle as purchases will include all types of expense and the purchase of fixed assets. The ultimate destination of the purchases is therefore not confined to cost of sales and stock.

Purchasing processes and systems will be relevant to, and present significant risks to, most organisations and will therefore be a common subject of investigation by internal audit. The type and extent of audit will clearly depend on the organisation itself. The internal audit of purchasing was covered in Chapter 4 and you should also consider the appropriate risks and controls outlined there.

KEY POINT

Purchasing control objectives are to ensure proper order **authority**, **documentation**, **recording** and **goods inspection**.

In detail, the control objectives are to ensure that:

- purchased goods/services are ordered under proper authorities and procedures
- purchased goods/services are only ordered as necessary for the proper conduct of the business operations and are ordered from suitable suppliers
- goods/services received are effectively inspected for quality, quantity and condition
- invoices and related documentation are properly checked and approved as being valid before being entered as trade creditors
- all valid transactions relating to trade creditors (suppliers' invoices, credit notes and adjustments), and only those transactions, should be accurately recorded in the accounting records.

3.2 Control procedures over purchases and creditors

KEY POINT

Purchase controls encompass **orders**, **goods receipt**, **invoicing** and **returns** and **purchase ledger** and **supplies**.

As with the sales system, there are a large number of controls that may be required in the purchases cycle owing to the importance of this area in any business. The following list is classified by type of control.

Orders

- Requisition notes for purchases should be authorised.
- All orders should be authorised by a responsible official whose authority limits should be pre-defined.
- Major items, e.g. capital expenditure, should be authorised by the board.
- All orders should be recorded on official documents showing suppliers' names, quantities ordered and price.
- Copies of orders should be retained as a method of following up late deliveries by suppliers.
- Re-order levels and quantities should be pre-set and preferably recorded in advance on the requisition note.

Receipt of goods

- Goods inwards centres should be identified to deal with the receipt of all goods.
- All goods should be checked for quantity and quality. Goods received notes (GRNs) should be raised for all goods accepted. The GRN should be signed by a responsible official.
- GRNs should be checked against purchase orders and procedures should exist to notify the supplier of under or over-deliveries. GRNs should be sequentially numbered and checked periodically for completeness.

Invoicing and returns

- Purchase invoices received should be stamped with an approval grid and given a unique serial number to ensure purchase invoices do not go astray.
- Purchase invoices should be matched with goods received notes and should not be processed until this is done.
- The invoice should be checked against the order and the GRN, and casts and extensions should also be checked.
- The invoices should be signed as approved for payment by a responsible official independent of the ordering and receipt of goods functions.
- Invoice sequential numbers should be checked against purchase day book details.
- Input VAT should be separated from the expense.

- Invoices should be properly allocated to the nominal ledger accounts, perhaps by allocating expenditure codes. A portion of such coding should be checked independently.
- Batch controls should be maintained over the posting of invoices to the purchases day book, nominal ledger and purchase ledger.
- A record of goods returned should be kept and checked to the credit notes received from suppliers.

Purchase ledger and suppliers

- A purchase ledger control account should be maintained and regularly checked against balances in the ledger by an independent official.
- Purchase ledger records should be kept by persons independent of the receiving of goods, invoice authorisation and payment routines.
- Statements from suppliers should be checked against the purchase ledger account.

ACTIVITY **3**

PKS have recently installed a central purchasing system, that allows all staff to automatically select and order necessary products for delivery. You have been asked to identify the key risks associated with this system and the control procedures that should operate.

You should summarise five key risks and control procedures to manage the risks.

Feedback to this activity is at the end of the chapter.

3.3 Tests of control

KEY POINT

Tests of control should check that control procedures and objectives are being applied and achieved.

As already noted, tests of control should be drawn up so as to check that control procedures are being applied and to achieve control objectives. One suggested way to design tests of control for a particular situation is to list the documents in a transaction cycle and generate appropriate tests of control for each document.

Purchase order	Test for: • evidence of a sequence check • evidence of approval • adherence to authority limits.
Goods received note	Test for evidence of a sequence check.
Goods returned note	Test for evidence of a sequence check.
Purchase invoice	Test for: • serial numbering • evidence of a sequence check • evidence of matching purchase invoices with goods received notes and purchase orders • evidence of checking casts, extensions and VAT treatment • evidence of account coding • initialling of invoice grid for work done • approval of purchase invoice for further processing.
Credit note	Test for evidence of matching credit notes to goods returned notes.
Purchase ledger	Test for evidence of authorisation of adjustments to purchase ledger.
Purchase ledger control account	Test for: • evidence of review of reconciliation of purchase ledger listing • evidence of authoristaion of adjustments to purchase ledger control account.

The internal auditor will also be looking for a number of high-level organisation and management controls. Here are some examples:

- Appropriate, authorised, communicated and documented purchasing procedures, in particular setting out how, when and who can make purchases, particularly since sometimes purchasing can be made across departments in organisations. These procedures must be maintained up to date to ensure their continued usefulness.
- Management information and reporting of purchasing levels and trends, with clear evidence of review and action taken on any exceptions (i.e. purchases made from unauthorised suppliers).

3.4 Substantive procedures

KEY POINT

Substantive procedures may cover accounting records, invoices and credit notes, stock records and control accounts.

Substantive procedures might include the following:

Accounting records

- Check additions and cross-casts of the purchase day book and purchase returns day book.
- Check postings from the day books to the nominal ledger accounts and to the control accounts.
- Vouch purchase day book and purchase returns day book to invoices and credit notes.
- Scrutinise the records for large or unusual transactions and vouch these items checking postings to the accounts.

Invoices and credit notes

- Check invoices and credit notes with the day books, ensuring that the analysis is correct and check to creditors' ledger. Make sure that the invoices have been approved for payment.
- Vouch invoices to orders.
- Agree prices charged on invoices and credit notes to suppliers' price lists, agreements or other evidence.
- Check calculations and additions on invoices and credit notes.

Stock records

- Vouch invoices with goods received records.
- Trace goods into stock records.

Control accounts

Test the year end control account reconciliation checking back to source documentation such as sales invoices, cash and returns records. Ensure that any reconciling items are dealt with properly.

Analytical procedures

KEY POINT

Analytical procedures may be used to identify unusual purchasing trends or purchasing outside agreed limits.

Although review procedures can be applied to the external audit of purchases, generally the purchases figure is verified and then used to compute a sales figure for use in analytical review procedures.

For internal auditors, **analytical review** may be appropriate to identify unusual trends in purchasing, levels of purchasing outside of agreed limits or non-authorised suppliers.

Conclusion

To test sales and the sales cycle, the control objectives and the control procedures for the particular business need to be established. Tests of control and substantive procedures which may be appropriate for the sales system and sales can then be designed.

Similar principles apply to the purchases system and purchases.

SELF-TEST QUESTIONS

General

1 What are the key risks associated with sales and purchases? (1.2)

Sales system

2 What are the control objectives for the return of goods by a customer? (2.1)

3 What are the control objectives for valid debtors' transactions? (2.1)

4 What are the three distinct processes in the sales system where there should be good segregation of duties? (2.2)

5 What are the substantive tests to be applied on sales invoices? (2.5)

Purchases system

6 What are the control objectives for the purchase of goods by the business? (3.1)

7 What are the substantive tests to be applied on purchase invoices? (3.4)

EXAM-TYPE QUESTIONS

Question 1: Sticky Bar Chocolates Limited

Sticky Bar Chocolates Limited employs 46 salespeople in the United Kingdom, each with a defined geographical area to cover. Each salesperson is supplied with a new car, changed every three years. At the end of each week, each salesperson submits a claim on a pre-printed form for expenses with supporting vouchers. Expenditure is on petrol, repairs and servicing of the car, hotels, lunches and entertaining. Each claim is scrutinised by Mr Jones who is deputy chief accountant. He verifies that the claims are supported by vouchers. He clears any inconsistencies with the salespeople concerned and makes out cheques for signature by two directors of the company. The total amount paid out by the company in the year to 30 April 20X7 was £320,000. The company made a profit in that year of £1.5 million.

Required:

(a) Identify the shortcomings of this system and suggest ways of improving the system. **(6 marks)**

(b) Describe tests of control and list the tests of control that the auditor would perform on this system. **(3 marks)**

(c) Describe substantive procedures and tabulate the substantive procedures that the auditor would perform on the item 'salesmen's expenses'. **(4 marks)**

(d) During the audit, the auditor discovered that the salesperson in one area was submitting false claims for entertaining customers. Explain any further action that the auditor should take. **(3 marks)**

(Total: 16 marks)

Question 2: Howden plc

Howden plc is a manufacturing company which has grown considerably in recent years. Following your audit of the company for the year ended 31 May 20X7 you issued a memorandum on internal control in which you brought certain weaknesses in internal control to the attention of management. The chief accountant of Howden plc agrees that the company has grown too large for the internal control systems that have been in force for some years and has asked your advice on the sort of control you would wish to see in force in a purchases and trade creditors system.

Required:

(a) Inform the chief accountant of the basic division of duties which you would expect to find in any internal control system, giving your reasoning. **(4 marks)**

(b) Advise the chief accountant of the main internal control features you would expect to find in the following functions of the purchases and trade creditors system of Howden plc:

- buying **(4 marks)**
- receipt of goods **(4 marks)**
- accounting for purchases **(4 marks)**
- payment of outstanding balances. **(4 marks)**

(Total: 20 marks)

For the answers to these questions, see the 'Answers' section at the end of the book.

FEEDBACK TO ACTIVITY **1**

Common control procedures for sales and purchases:

- Sequential numbering of documents
- Maintenance of batch or other control totals and checking to output for completeness and accuracy
- Maintenance of control accounts and reconciliation to the ledgers
- Authorisation of transactions, evidenced through signature.

Common tests of control:

- Check evidence of checking of sequences
- Review evidence of checking of batch totals
- Review evidence of authorisation (through signature)
- Confirm control account reconciliation performed correctly and authorisation.

FEEDBACK TO ACTIVITY **2**

Key risks for sales:

- Fraudulent sales transactions resulting in financial loss or damage to reputation
- Poor quality of goods sold, resulting in compensation claims against the company and damage to reputation
- Breach of regulatory requirements for sales, resulting in damage to reputation
- Failure to agree appropriate terms and conditions with customers, resulting in non-payment or dispute over goods or service supplied.

Key risks for purchases:

- Goods purchased that do not meet needs or purchases at higher than necessary cost, resulting in inability to deliver company objectives, missed deadlines or financial loss
- Fraudulent or duplicate purchases resulting in financial loss and potential for damaging publicity
- Failure to agree appropriate terms and conditions with suppliers resulting in damaging or costly disputes
- Failure to purchase goods or services at the right time and therefore failure to meet required deadlines.

FEEDBACK TO ACTIVITY **3**

PKS central purchasing system

Key risks:

- Excessive or duplicate ordering of products, with multiple ordering across departments or teams
- Fraudulent purchasing through the system
- Lack of flexibility with the system resulting in staff bypassing automated system (e.g. if PKS only allow limited products to be purchased)
- Failure to obtain value for money for purchases made
- Products not received, incorrect products or poor quality goods received.

Control procedures

- On-line authorisation of purchases, with system designated levels of authority
- Authorised list of suppliers, with responsibility for adding and deleting suppliers
- On-line information on products already held in the organisation
- Reconciliation of goods ordered and goods received
- Payment made only for goods authorised on the system, with automatic generation of invoices
- Goods received checks and listing of returns due to poor quality of goods delivered.

Chapter 10

INTERNAL CONTROL – PAYROLL AND OTHER AREAS; REPORTS TO MANAGEMENT

CHAPTER CONTENTS

The practical testing of internal controls, accounting systems and financial statements is continued in this chapter. Staff costs are significant in any business and thus substantive procedures are also covered. Internal controls over the cash system and other systems are dealt with in this chapter, prior to greater analysis in subsequent chapters.

Payroll is a key area of review by internal and external auditors, since it presents a significant level of risks to the organisation. In particular, for many organisations, people are seen as the company's greatest asset and therefore accurate, timely and effective payment to them is seen as key. Payroll will be a regular audit for internal auditors and a key area of substantive testing for external auditors. It is important that both types of auditors liaise closely together and rely on respective work carried out.

Again, payroll is an area where computer based systems are utilised. Here, in particular, processing may be outsourced.

We will also look at reports to management which deal with weaknesses the auditors discover in internal control systems.

Objectives

By the time you have finished this chapter you should be able to:

- understand the typical control objectives for the wages cycle
- understand the risks associated with payroll
- list tests of control and substantive procedures which may be appropriate for the wages system and wages total
- understand the typical control objectives for the cash cycle and list appropriate tests of control
- understand the typical control objectives for the other accounting systems
- state the contents of and prepare a management letter.

1 Introduction

Why do we need internal controls for payroll, cash, fixed assets and stocks? With cash, fixed assets and stocks, one objective is clear: we need to safeguard them as assets.

With payroll, we need to be sure that we are paying only for work that has been done, at the correct rates and that our liabilities to the tax authorities are accurate, to avoid fines and penalties. It is possible for payroll records to be falsified so that the company pays for work that has not been done. Overtime needs to be authorised, because if it is not, employees can put in fictional claims and whilst the accounting may be correct, the business suffers.

Payroll calculations need to be checked, especially where produced manually and also when produced by a computer, because if tax or social security rates are too high, employee relations suffer and we incur administrative costs in sorting the problem out; if they are too low, we are still liable to the tax authorities, but we cannot reclaim the amounts that are due from employees.

KEY POINT

Cash transactions should be checked by at least two people - one of whom deals with the cash, and the other who records the transaction.

Most cash transactions involve checking by at least two people, one of whom deals with the cash, and the other who deals with the records (segregation of duties). For example, when cash comes in from customers, if the same person opens the mail and updates the cash book and the sales ledger, that person could steal the cash (or part of it) and then claim that no cash was received. If there are two people opening the mail, there is a reduced chance of this happening. If two individuals supervise the opening, there is of course the possibility that they will collude to steal the cash, falsify the records and split the proceeds between them. This is an example of an inherent limitation in a control system; no system is perfect as people can always 'get around' it by collusion.

KEY POINT

Stock and fixed assets are often more easily stolen than cash, as it is not possible to have two people present every time stock is dealt with.

Stock and fixed assets are often more easily stolen than cash. The bulk of theft in shops in the UK is believed to be not theft by 'customers', but theft by employees. It is not possible to have two people present every time stock is dealt with; stock has to be controlled by means of counting it regularly, reconciling it to stock, sales and purchases records and trying to establish reasons for differences. If there are always large discrepancies in the food section of a department store, and many of those discrepancies often relate to cheese, it may be appropriate to move staff around. Fixed assets are less portable than stock but it is surprising how often companies do not know what fixed assets they have or where they are. A fixed assets register that shows names, numbers and descriptions of fixed assets, which is regularly checked to the assets themselves, helps here, and discourages the assets from 'walking'.

2 Payroll

2.1 Procedures

KEY POINT

Wages and **salaries** systems generally cover **employment** records, **attendance**, **payroll** functions and salaries analysis.

Systems in force with regard to wages and salaries vary considerably with the size and nature of the business but the procedures involved generally fall into the following broad categories:

- engagements, promotions, transfers and discharges of employees
- time attendance and job recording
- preparation of payroll and analysis of wages and salaries
- payments of wages and salaries.

The external auditor will be particularly interested in the overall payment procedures for payroll but the internal auditor will need to do more extensive planning of the audit and review the overall management and control environment for payroll.

2.2 Control objectives

KEY POINT

Control systems for wages and salaries should include payment accuracy and proper recording for the **tax** and **National Insurance**.

The control objectives of a sound system of internal control for wages and salaries are as follows:

- The computation of wages and salaries should be only in respect of the client's employees and at authorised rates of pay.
- Wages and salaries should be in accordance with records of work performed, e.g. time, output, commissions on sales.
- Payrolls should be calculated accurately.
- Payment should be made to the correct employees.
- Liabilities to the tax authorities for PAYE and NI should be properly recorded.

2.3 Risks associated with payroll

KEY POINT

Administrative risks of the payroll include **inaccurate** or **delayed** payments, **error** or **fraud**.

Administrative risks associated with the payroll include:

- invalid or unauthorised payments to staff, including **fraudulent payments** or payments that staff are not entitled to, resulting in financial loss
- failure to make payments on a timely basis resulting in staff dissatisfaction
- delays or errors in amendments, additions and deletions to payroll records resulting in inaccurate payments, staff dissatisfaction, potential financial loss and management decisions being made on the basis of inaccurate information
- corrupt data uploaded to, or downloaded from, the payroll system resulting in errors and discrepancies
- unauthorised access to the payroll system resulting in manipulation or **fraud**
- incorrect calculation and payments to the tax authorities resulting in censure or fines
- unauthorised, inaccurate or delayed bonus or one-off payments resulting in financial loss or staff dissatisfaction
- incorrect or fraudulent payments to leavers resulting in financial loss
- payments made to staff who do not exist.

2.4 Control procedures – payroll and wages

KEY POINT

Wage control procedures centre on **written authorisation**.

Approval and control of documents

- There should be written authorisation to employ or dismiss any employee, in accordance with company procedures and legal requirements.
- Changes in rates of pay or salary should be authorised in writing by an official outside the wages department. This may be through a standard form for authorisation of changes to payroll details.
- Overtime worked should be authorised by the works manager or employee's manager or someone outside of payroll and be in accordance with company procedures. Some staff may not be entitled to overtime because of their level or type of employment and therefore appropriate mechanisms for ensuring only authorised staff receive overtime should exist.
- An independent official should check the payroll and sign it.
- The wages cheque should be signed by two signatories evidenced against the signed payroll. Cheques should have two signatories and should be checked against an approved payroll entry.
- Where pay relates to hours at work, some form of time recording should be used, such as time keys or automatic entry swipe card systems, or other clock cards should be used. There should be supervision of the time-recording system or cards, and the timing devices, particularly when employees are clocking-on or off. There is a clear risk that staff can manipulate systems to obtain additional hours and therefore additional payments. This could include getting other staff to clock in or out for them. The manager or supervisor should know the hours worked by staff and check outputs to ensure that expected and actual hours tally.
- When an employee has been absent for a significant period, their entitlement to salary should be checked against personnel details.
- Cheques should have two signatories and should be checked against an approved payroll entry.
- Direct bank transfers should also be signed and checked regularly against details on personnel files.

- Personnel records should be kept for each employee, giving details of engagement, retirement, dismissal or resignation, rates of pay, holidays, etc. with a specimen signature of the employee.
- A wages supervisor should be appointed who could perform some of the authorisation duties listed above.

Arithmetical accuracy

- Where relevant, payroll should be prepared from time-recording systems, clock cards, job cards, etc., and a sample checked for accuracy against current rates of pay.
- Payroll details should provide for the accurate calculation of deductions, e.g. PAYE, NI, pensions, trade union subscriptions, etc., which should be checked periodically.

Control accounts

- Control accounts should be maintained in respect of each of the deductions showing amounts paid periodically to the Revenue, trade unions, etc.
- Overall checks should be carried out to highlight major discrepancies, e.g. check against budgets, changes in amounts paid over a period of time, check against personnel records.
- Management should exercise overall control within the payroll department.

Access to assets and records

Where employees are paid in cash, there are a number of specific control procedures as follows:

KEY POINT

Employees should sign for their wages. The wages department should separate or rotate duties.

- Employees should sign for their wages.
- No employee should be allowed to take the wages of another employee.
- When wages are claimed late, the employee should sign for the wage packet and the release of the packet should be authorised.
- The system should preferably allow the wages to be checked by the employee before the packet is opened, by using specially designed wage packets.
- The wages department should preferably be a separate department with their personnel not involved with receipts or payments functions.
- The duties of the wages staff should preferably be rotated during the year, so as to ensure that no employee is responsible for all the functions in respect of any particular department.
- The employee making up the pay packets should not be the employee who prepares the payroll.
- A surprise attendance at the pay-out should be made periodically by an independent official.
- Unclaimed wages should be recorded in a register and held by someone outside the wages department until claimed or until a predefined period after which the money should be re-banked. An official should investigate the reason for unclaimed wages as soon as possible.

Clearly different procedures apply where salaries are paid by direct transmission (e.g. BACS), including independent checking and authorisation prior to submission.

The types of controls shown here build on the earlier internal control chapters. It may help you to come up with ideas for a system with which you are not familiar. The following parts of this section illustrate controls expected in other major areas. These are not classified by type.

Try generating a couple of these areas yourself and then review the controls suggested. There is no *necessity* to learn these lists, but you should practise the technique to generate them, and use the rest of the section for reference.

2.5 Control procedures – salaries

- Personnel records should be kept similar to those for hourly paid employees.
- Written authority should be required to employ or dismiss an employee or change salary rate.
- Overtime should be authorised by someone outside the payroll department.
- The usual checks on deductions are required.
- When an employee has been absent for a significant period, their entitlement to salary should be checked against personnel details.
- Cheques should have two signatories and should be checked against an approved payroll entry.
- Direct bank transfers should also be signed and checked regularly against details on personnel files.

2.6 Control tests – payroll and wages

KEY POINT

Control tests should be applied to ensure payment accuracy.

The programme of tests should ensure that the following key controls are in existence and working efficiently:

- Employees can be paid only for work done.
- Employees are paid at the correct rate.
- Errors cannot occur in the calculation of the payroll or the deductions from gross pay.
- Only valid employees are paid.

A suggested programme of tests of control is as follows:

- Test sample of time sheets, clock cards or other records, for approval by responsible official. Pay particular attention to the approval of overtime.
- Test authority for payment of casual labour, particularly if in cash.
- Observe wages distribution for adherence to procedures ensuring employees sign for wages, that unclaimed wages are re-banked, etc.
- Test authorisation for payroll amendments by reference to personnel records.
- Test control over payroll amendments.
- Examine evidence of checking of payroll calculations (e.g. a signature of the financial controller).
- Examine evidence of approval of payrolls by a responsible official.
- Examine evidence of independent checks of payrolls (e.g. by internal audit).
- Inspect payroll reconciliations.
- Examine explanations for payroll expense variances.
- Test authorities for payroll deductions.
- Test controls over unclaimed wages.
- Test controls over calculation of bonus and one-off payments to ensure evidence of authorisation.
- Check exception reporting to ensure evidence of review and action taken to investigate and redress any discrepancies.

2.7 Substantive procedures – wages and salaries

KEY POINT

Substantive control procedures involve testing and checking samples of records and calculations.

Substantive testing procedures include the following:

- Select sample of time records, etc. and test casts and calculations.
- Test sample of personnel records for:
  - rates of pay
  - authorisation of changes in rates of pay
  - leavers' and joiners' personal details
  - to actual personnel to ensure existence.
- Select payrolls and:
  - check to time records, etc. to ensure employees are only paid for work done
  - test to personnel records to ensure employees exist and are being paid at the correct rate
  - test casts and calculations with reference to tax, national insurance and other tables
  - check deductions are paid over to the tax authorities on time and that no unrecorded penalties may arise.
- If a payroll control account is maintained, check this to the nominal ledger.
- Test totals of cheques drawn to net pay due to employees and tax authorities.
- Test postings of payrolls to nominal ledger accounts.

ACTIVITY **1**

People Solutions

You are undertaking an audit of payroll for People Solutions. They have an off-the-shelf payroll system and all staff are paid on a monthly basis by cheque. You have completed the planning and initial work for this audit and have established that the following controls are in place:

- New staff and leavers are captured via a standard form, signed off by the line manager and keyed into the system.
- Overtime has to be authorised by the line manager.
- A card swipe time recording is in operation for some but not all staff.
- Total value and number of payroll cheques are reconciled to staff records and to time recording records on an infrequent basis.
- There is no separate payroll function, since payroll is located within the General Finance team, who deal with all payments and receipts.

Three major risks have materialised in the last six months:

- Inland Revenue payments have been late and inaccurate, resulting in a pending investigation of controls over tax.
- Two leavers were recently discovered to be still on the payroll three months after leaving the organisation.
- Overtime has exceeded the budget by 500%.

Explain the controls that may have prevented the risks materialising and explain the further work that you would undertake.

Feedback to this activity is at the end of the chapter.

3 Cash system

3.1 Control objectives

KEY POINT

Cash control is of prime importance; **receipts** and **payments** should be recorded promptly and accurately.

The **control of cash** is clearly of prime importance in any business. The central objectives are that:

- all sums are received and subsequently accounted for
- no payments are made which should not be made, and all are authorised by the appropriate person
- all **receipts** and **payments** are promptly and accurately recorded.

Beyond this, it is better to consider detailed controls for each area of the business dealing with cash. In reality there is not one 'cash system', in the same way as there is a sales cycle for example; there are a number of systems which have their own considerations as to control due to the specific circumstances of that part of the business.

You should also appreciate that the cash system also refers to cheque receipts and payments. Businesses should try as much as possible to conduct all their cash transactions by means of cheques or other forms of bank transfers, as controls over cheque transactions are easier to establish and maintain.

Controls are set out below for various cash systems. In considering the controls, you should consider the nature and type of risks of the systems. You should also refer to the later chapter on the audit of cash and bank. Again, also be aware of the need to apply the general principles of internal control.

3.2 Controls over cash receipts by post

KEY POINT

There should be strict controls over the receipt and opening of postal cash receipts to minimise the risk of unauthorised 'manipulation'.

- The company should safeguard against possible interceptions between the receipt and opening of the post, e.g. by using a locked mail box and restricting access to the keys.
- The opening of the post should be supervised by a responsible official and where the volume of mail is significant, at least two persons should be present when the mail is opened.
- All cheques and postal orders should be restrictively crossed 'Account payee only, not negotiable' as soon as the mail is opened.
- A record should be made at the time of the opening of the post of:
  - cheques and postal orders received
  - cash received.

This record may be in the form of a rough cash book, adding machine list or copies of remittance advices. It provides control over the eventual sums banked and entered into the cash book.

- The cashier and sales ledger personnel should not have access to the receipts before this record is made.
- Post should be date stamped. It provides evidence of when remittances are received and can periodically be checked against the date of banking. This helps to prevent cash received one day being banked as representing different receipts on a later day (a process known as 'teeming and lading').

3.3 Controls over cash collected by travelling sales personnel

Where an organisation employs travelling sales personnel who are responsible for collecting cash from customers strict control procedures should operate. If possible, cash sales should be avoided.

Typical control procedures are as follows:

KEY POINT

Salespeople should be required to remit cash and report sales regularly; periodically their own receipt books should be checked against cash book entries.

- Authority to collect cash should be clearly defined.
- **Salespeople** should be required to remit cash and report sales at regular intervals which should be formally notified to nominated employees.
- A responsible official should quickly follow up salespeople who do not submit returns as required.
- Collections should be recorded when received, e.g. in a rough cash book or copies of receipts which should be given to the salespeople.
- The collector's cash receipts should be reconciled to the eventual banking.
- Periodically, a responsible official should check the salespeople's own receipt books with cash book entries.
- If salespeople hold stocks of goods, an independent reconciliation of stock with sales and cash received should be made.

3.4 Controls over cash sales

KEY POINT

Cash sale records should be recorded at the time of sale, and independently reconciled daily with **cash received**.

- **Cash sales** should be recorded when the sale is made normally by means of a cash till or the use of **cash sale invoices**.
- If cash sale invoices are used they should be pre-numbered, a register should be maintained of cash sale invoice books and copies should be retained.
- **Cash received** should be reconciled daily with either the till roll or the invoice totals.
- This reconciliation should be carried out by someone independent of those receiving the cash and recording the sale.
- Daily banking should be checked against the till roll or invoice total and differences investigated.
- A responsible official should sign cancelled cash sale invoices at the time of cancellation. All such invoices should be checked periodically for sequential numbering.

3.5 Controls over banking

KEY POINT

Receipts should be **banked** intact daily and recorded promptly in the **cash book**.

- Receipts should be **banked** intact daily.
- Each day's receipts should be recorded promptly in the **cash book**.
- Sales ledger personnel should have no access to the cash or the preparation of the paying-in slip.
- Periodically a comparison should be made between the split of cash and cheques
  - received (and recorded in rough cash book)
  - banked (and recorded on paying-in slip).

3.6 Controls over cheque payments

KEY POINT

Cheque **signatories** should be restricted with ideally two signatures being required. **Cheque preparation** and **purchase** or **sales ledger** should be separate duties.

- Unused cheques should be held in a secure place.
- The person who prepares cheques should have no responsibility over **purchase ledger** or **sales ledger**.
- Cheques should be signed only when evidence of a properly approved transaction is available. Such evidence may take the form of invoices, payroll, petty cash book, etc. This check should be evidenced by signing the supporting documentation.
- In a large organisation those approving the original document should be independent of those signing cheques.

- Cheque signatories should be restricted to the minimum practical number.
- Two signatories at least should be required except perhaps for cheques of small amounts.
- The signing of blank cheques and cheques in favour of the signatory should be prohibited.
- Cheques should be crossed before being signed.
- Supporting documents should be cancelled as paid to prevent their use to support further cheque payments. This cancellation could be done by the cashier before the cheque is signed (provided the cancellation identifies the cheque number) or by the cheque signatory at the time of signing the cheque.
- Cheques should preferably be despatched immediately. If not, they should be held in a secure place.
- Returned cheques may be obtained from the bank and a sample checked against cash book entries and supporting documentation.
- There should be clearly defined levels of authorisation in respect of cheque values.
- Cancelled cheques should be retained as evidence of cancellation with supporting documentation.

3.7 Bank reconciliations

- Bank reconciliations should be prepared at least monthly and signed and dated by the person who completed the reconciliation to indicate performance of the control.
- The person responsible for preparation should be independent of the receipts and payments function or, alternatively, an independent person should check the reconciliation.
- If the reconciliation is prepared by an independent person he or she should obtain bank statements directly from the bank and hold them until the reconciliation is completed.
- The preparation should preferably include a check of at least a sample of receipts and payments against items on the bank statement.

3.8 Controls over petty cash

KEY POINT

There should be restricted access to the **petty cash floats**; the '**imprest**' system should be used to reimburse these.

- The level and location of **cash floats** should be laid down formally.
- There should be restricted access to the floats.
- Cash should be securely held, e.g. in a locked drawer, with restricted access to keys.
- All expenditure should require a voucher signed by a responsible official, not the petty cashier.
- The **imprest** system should be used to reimburse the float, i.e. at any time the total cash and value of vouchers not reimbursed equals a set amount.
- Vouchers should be produced before the cheque is signed for reimbursement.
- Vouchers should be cancelled once reimbursement has taken place.
- A maximum amount should be placed on a petty cash payment to discourage normal purchase procedures being by-passed e.g. such as £25.
- Periodically, the petty cash should be reconciled by an independent person.
- Rules should exist preferably preventing the issue of IOUs or the cashing of cheques.

3.9 Tests of control

KEY POINT

Tests of control should cover **cash receipts** and **payments**, **bank reconciliations** and **petty cash**.

The following tests could be included in a work programme for the bank and cash section of the audit:

Cash receipts

- Attend mail opening and ensure procedures are adhered to.
- Test independent check of cash receipts to bank lodgements.
- Test for evidence of a sequence check on any pre-numbered receipts for cash.
- Test authorisation of cash receipts.
- Test for evidence of arithmetical check on cash received records.

Cash payments

- Inspect current cheque books for:
  - sequential use of cheques
  - controlled custody of unused cheques
  - any signatures on blank cheques.
- Test (to avoid double payment) to ensure that paid invoices are marked 'paid'.
- Test for evidence of arithmetical check on cash payments records, including cashbook.
- Examine evidence of authority for current standing orders and direct debits.

Bank reconciliations

- Examine evidence of regular bank reconciliations (usually one per month).
- Examine evidence of independent check of bank reconciliations (e.g. a signature).
- Examine evidence of follow-up of outstanding items on bank reconciliations. Pay particular attention to old outstanding reconciling items that should be written back such as old, unpresented cheques.

Petty cash

- Test petty cash vouchers for approval.
- Test cancellation of paid petty cash vouchers.
- Test for evidence of arithmetical check on petty cash records.
- Examine evidence of independent check of petty cash balance.

ACTIVITY 2

Car Park Company

Your firm of accountants audits a company which deals in properties. Among its properties is a vacant city centre site which, owing to local planning regulations, will not be developed for at least three years. The directors of the company have decided to use the vacant site (which they have enclosed) as a car park for up to 200 vehicles at any one time. Your firm has been asked to prepare a report on systems of control which would be appropriate in the operation of such a car park.

The company intends to operate the car park as follows:

Hours of business

Monday to Saturday 0600 hours to 2200 hours (site locked with exits and entrances barred between 2200 hours and 0600 hours and all day Sunday).

Charges

Length of stay	*Scale of charges*
Up to 1 hour	£0.20
1–2 hours	£0.40
2–3 hours	£0.60
Up to maximum of 16 hours	£3.20
Overnight stay	£2.00

Staffing

Number of attendants – four with only one attendant working at any one time on one shift either 0600–1400 or 1400–2200 hours. (Each attendant normally works 4 days per week, thus allowing for holidays and illness.)

Operating details

All cars to enter past one automatic barrier and machine which issues a date and time-stamped entry ticket to the car driver.

All cars to leave through one manned exit barrier after paying the attendant the correct fee.

Staff work routine

Members of staff on early shift must ensure:

- that there are sufficient pre-numbered tickets in the ticket machine
- that the correct date and time are being printed by the ticket machine
- that the correct cash float (£20) is in the pay booth till.

When cars leave, duration of stay and fee are calculated and entered by the staff member on the pre-numbered ticket issued by the ticket machine.

The correct fee is received by the attendant, who retains the pre-numbered ticket.

At the end of the shift all cash received should be either banked (day shift) or deposited in the night safe (night shift) by the appropriate attendant and cash float of £20 retained. The pay booth must be securely locked when the car park is closed and during any short absence of an attendant.

During the afternoon a member of the accounts department staff from head office collects all used tickets and records of cash banked. All accounting records are maintained at head office.

Required:

- Explain what is meant by the two following objectives which management might hope to achieve from a good system of control over the operation of the car park:

  – completeness of income

  – safe custody of assets.
- Describe three internal controls (i.e. *six* controls in total), which are or might be used to achieve each of the above objectives, stating why each control would lead to the control objectives being met.
- Outline two tests of controls that you would perform when auditing the internal control which would ensure completeness of income, stating why the tests would give assurance.

Feedback to this activity is at the end of the chapter.

4 Reports to management

4.1 Principles

KEY POINT

The auditor uses a 'management letter' to report internal control weaknesses (with recommendations) to management.

ISA 260 *Communication of audit matters with those charged with governance* states that the **management letter** will normally be a natural by-product of the audit, and the auditor should incorporate the need to issue the letter in the planning of the audit.

The management letter is sometimes called the **letter of weakness**, the **internal control memorandum**, the **letter of recommendations** or the **constructive service letter**.

It should be normal practice at the end of the interim audit, and at the end of the final audit, to send a letter to the client setting out material *weaknesses* in the system of internal control.

4.2 Action on weaknesses found during the audit

The weaknesses will arise out of the examination of the accounting systems, the initial ascertainment of the system and after testing of controls has been carried out. The testing may reveal that certain controls which should have existed have not in fact operated. It then may be appropriate to suggest alternative controls which have a better chance of being operated.

The report to management covers three main areas:

- **material weaknesses** in the design as well as the operation of the accounting and internal control system together with constructive **recommendations for improvement**
- other constructive advice on **economies** and **efficiencies**
- comments on **accounting policies** and **unadjusted errors** in the financial statements.

4.3 Other points

KEY POINT

The management letter should be drafted as soon as possible after completion of the audit procedures.

To be effective, the letter should be drafted as soon as possible after completion of the audit procedures giving rise to the need to comment.

It is preferable to discuss all the points in the letter with management before the letter is issued. It is essential that the contents of the letter are considered by the management. The auditor should, therefore, ask the management to reply to the letter. A copy of the letter with replies should be kept on the files. Points made in previous years should be reviewed by the auditor and checked to ascertain whether corrective action has been taken.

In practice, the auditor has little control over what happens to the report once it has been despatched. Occasionally, management may provide third parties, e.g. their bankers, with copies of the report.

The auditor can use a disclaimer of liability against unforeseen liability to third parties, but this may not give full protection from liability where the auditor knows or ought to know that a report to management may be passed to a third party who would rely on it.

An example of a management letter which uses an appendix to indicate the detailed points is shown in the following pages.

4.4 Example of a management letter

The ISA does not give a suggested format. There are other acceptable layouts which you may have seen in practice; columnar formats with the headings 'weakness', 'implication' and 'recommendation' are common. Again, it is not necessary to learn this example, as the points would not be appropriate for all enterprises. Note, however, the type of points made.

In addition, it is important that 'feedback' is obtained, in the form of a response from the client itemising comments, references and proposed action plans. Space for this could be provided by including an additional column in the layout.

Private and confidential

The Directors,
Upper plc,
Lower Court,
London

15 May 20X7

Dear Sirs

Upper plc
Audit for the year ended 31 December 20X6

In accordance with our normal practice, we are writing to you with regard to matters arising out of our audit for the year ended 31 December 20X6 which we consider should be brought to your attention.

Our responsibilities as auditors are governed by the Companies Act and principally require us to report on the accounts laid before the company in general meeting.

This report has been prepared for the sole use of the directors of Upper plc. None of its contents may be disclosed to third parties without our written consent. Bloggs & Co. assumes no liability to any other persons.

The matters detailed in this report reflect matters coming to our attention during the course of our audit. They are not intended to be a comprehensive statement of all weaknesses that may exist or of all improvements that could be made. We set out below those matters which we consider to be of fundamental importance. Other matters of lesser significance, but which nevertheless require your attention, are dealt with in note form in the attached Appendix.

Management reporting

A fundamental requirement to allow proper control over your business is the regular and timely preparation of accurate management accounts. Preferably these should be prepared monthly, compared with budgets and submitted for formal consideration and adoption by the full board of directors. At the moment no such system exists.

Internal control – accounting system

- The company exercises no control over the input, processing or output of information processed by the computer bureau. Reliance is placed on the computer bureau to ensure complete and accurate processing of accounting information. In our opinion the directors should ensure that the company effects proper control over the completeness and accuracy of information processed.
- There are other areas covering aspects of stocks, fixed assets and debtors where control is lacking or inadequate which are dealt with in the Appendix attached.
- Our audit work was made considerably more difficult by the absence of care in filing supporting documentation which was therefore difficult to trace. The proper maintenance of records is not only a requirement of the Companies Act but is also necessary for the efficient running of your business.

Preparation of accounts

- The quality of the draft statutory accounts submitted to us for audit was poor.
- The accounts were produced late without proper support. When support was provided, in some cases it failed to agree with the amounts stated in the draft accounts.
- A number of items required to be disclosed under the Companies Act were omitted. Extensive discussions were necessary with you to ascertain the information to be disclosed in respect of directors' interests and capital expenditure.

To reduce the time spent on the audit, and thus the cost to you, all supporting documentation should agree with the accounts and statutory disclosure information should be assembled prior to our examination.

We would be pleased to discuss these points with you at your convenience.

Yours faithfully

Bloggs & Co.

Appendix

Upper plc:
Year ended 31 December 20X6

Computer processing

Weakness

- Lack of control exercised over computer processing.

Implications

- The completeness, accuracy and validity of the accounting records may be undermined.

Recommendations

- Authorisation of input especially journals not arising from books of prime entry.
- Batch controls using registers over all input in terms of value and number of documents/transactions processed.
- Use of hash totals.
- Management control over master file amendments.
- Reconciliation to control accounts.
- Clear audit trail for the correction and resubmission of any rejected transactions.
- All financial information processed at one location.
- A back-up system should be available if the bureau is unable to process the input.

Payroll

Weakness

- No evidence of approval.

Implications

- Unauthorised changes may occur.

Recommendation

- Management should evidence their approval of the payroll, changes in rates of pay and the employment of new staff.

Stock

Weakness

- Lack of physical and financial control over stocks.
- Cut-off errors were discovered for widgets despatched prior to the year end but uninvoiced.
- Overhead allocation in valuation of widgets lacked support.

Implications

- Stock could be misappropriated.
- The year end stock figure could be misstated.

Recommendations

- A simple system of perpetual stock should be implemented at each location. This should be used to check for the despatch and receipt of stock and would provide good overall control to enable a comparison of:
  - expected use to actual by comparison with orders, and
  - book stock to actual after regular stock checks.
- Improvements should be made to the system of control to facilitate a review of the despatches at the year end to ensure that a proper cut-off is achieved.
- The valuation of widgets depends on the estimated throughput during the year. It is important that the number of widgets produced is properly recorded and that consideration is given to normal production levels to allow compliance with accounting standards.

Fixed assets

Weakness

- Lack of physical control.
- Lack of clear capitalisation policy.
- Assets with nil net book value were subject to a depreciation charge.

Implications

- Portable assets could be misappropriated.
- Items could be incorrectly capitalised.
- The depreciation figures in the accounts could be overstated.

Recommendations

- A register should be introduced to record all assets at cost together with associated depreciation.
- In previous years, capital additions, notably the improvements to the leasehold premises, have been written off. Also, assets scrapped have not been written off. The effect of these cancel out and therefore we have not proposed an adjustment to opening figures. A capitalisation policy should be laid down and adhered to.
- A register would enable the identification of fully depreciated assets and allow them to be excluded from the depreciation calculations.

Weakness

- Lack of proper allocation of costs.
- Lack of supporting documents.
- Lack of control over cheque books.
- Unauthorised charges.
- Poor control over unrecorded liabilities.

Implications

- Purchases in the accounts may be misstated.
- Payables may be understated if unrecorded liabilities are not controlled.

Recommendations

- All charges incurred should be allocated to the relevant cost centre to promote accountability of these centres.
- Proper supporting documents for all payments must be retained and properly filed for easy retrieval.
- Control over payments would be improved if only one cheque book was in use at any one time.
- Documents supporting charges should be authorised by an appropriate level of management.
- A purchase day book should be introduced. Payments should be marked off. This would provide control over unpaid invoices and a means for regular control account reconciliation.

5 Internal audit reporting on payroll and other systems

KEY POINT

Payroll is a key area of review for the internal auditor.

Payroll and other accounting systems are key areas of review for internal auditors because of the level of risk presented by assets and resources of an organisation. Such systems should be considered in the same way as any other areas by the internal audit department. The internal auditor would have planned the audit, identified risks, reviewed internal controls, carried out tests and formed conclusions. The auditor should report findings and make recommendations in the usual manner (see later chapter on internal audit reporting). It is then important that the auditor follows up promptly on recommendations to ensure their implementation, particularly for high-risk areas.

Payroll is seen as a fairly standard audit for the internal auditor and therefore there may be more standardised audit programmes and risk and control schedules, particularly in an organisation that requires an annual audit of payroll. In branch retail environments, there may also be standard audit checklists relating to cash and other assets that may be subject to regular checks. The frequency and type of such regular "inspections" is reducing as internal auditors move towards risk based auditing.

Conclusion

Salaries and wages are a major cost of a business and require controls to ensure amounts paid represent genuine expenses.

The cash system is really a number of detailed sub-systems each with very specific control objectives.

Other systems will probably have their prime functions as the valid purchase of assets and their subsequent safe custody.

All these areas are important for both internal and external auditors who should co-ordinate their audit activity. The standard procedures for auditing are appropriate, including identifying risks, assessing controls, conducting testing, producing reports and communicating with management.

SELF-TEST QUESTIONS

Payroll

1 What are the control objectives for payroll? (2.2)

2 What are the key risks associated with payroll? (2.3)

3 What are the substantive procedures to be applied on personnel records? (2.7)

Cash system

4 What are the central control objectives for any cash system? (3.1)

5 What controls should exist over cash sales? (3.4)

6 What controls should exist over petty cash? (3.8)

7 What are appropriate tests of control for current cheque books? (3.9)

Reports to management

8 What three main areas should a report to management cover? (4.2)

EXAM-TYPE QUESTIONS

Question 1: Quicksand Ltd

Mr A Black has recently acquired the controlling interest in Quicksand Limited, who are importers of sportswear. In his review of the organisational structure of the company Mr Black became aware of weaknesses in the procedures for the signing of cheques and the operations of the petty cash system. Mr Black engages you as the company's auditors and requests that you review the controls over cheque payments and petty cash. He does not wish to be a cheque signatory himself because he feels that such a procedure is an inefficient use of his time. In addition to Mr Black, who is the managing director, the company employs twenty personnel including four other directors, and approximately three hundred cheques are drawn each month. Further the petty cash account normally has a working balance of about £600, and £300 is expended from the fund each month. Mr Black has again indicated that he is unwilling to participate in any internal control procedures which would ensure the efficient operation of the petty cash fund.

Required:

(a) Prepare a letter to Mr Black containing your recommendations for good internal control procedures for:

– cheque payments **(9 marks)**

– petty cash. **(7 marks)**

(Marks will be awarded for the style and layout of the answer.)

(b) Discuss the audit implications, if any, of the unwillingness of Mr Black to participate in the cheque signing procedures and petty cash function. **(4 marks)**

(Total: 20 marks)

Question 2: Management reports

The report to management which in some respects is a report on the ability and effectiveness of management is as useful to shareholders as the financial statements and should be distributed to the members not just to management themselves.

Required:

Discuss this proposition. **(12 marks)**

For answers to these questions, see the 'Answers' section at the end of the book.

FEEDBACK TO ACTIVITY 1

People Solutions

There are no details of controls over the **Inland Revenue** payments but controls that should have been in place include:

- Control accounts in respect of the deductions and amounts paid periodically to the Revenue.

- Independent management checks on the control accounts and Inland Revenue returns should have been carried out to highlight major discrepancies, e.g. check against budgets, changes in amounts paid over a period of time, check against personnel records.
- Control over changes to tax deductions or coding, with system input controls and checks in place.

Additional work includes checking the controls that were in operation. The Inland Revenue is planning an investigation of controls over tax and the company should have already instigated their own review and have implemented improvements in controls. Check what improvements have been put in place and the background to the problems that have occurred and at what point the problems occurred. Also confirm that management have been reconciling payroll deductions, control accounts and returns and that exceptions have been properly and promptly acted upon.

For **leavers**, there are some controls in place, including a standard form signed by the line manager. It is not clear without further detail why the problems occurred but the controls in place must be sufficiently robust for all leavers to be taken off the payroll immediately. The breakdown in controls could be within Payroll or the line manager areas and therefore it would be useful to check what review of controls has taken place and the results of the investigation into the situation.

For **overtime**, there are no details of controls over overtime but controls that should have been in place include:

- Overtime worked should only be paid where authorised by the line manager.
- There should be a budget for overtime, which is independently reviewed and exceptions notified to the area concerned.
- Company policies and procedures for overtime should be in place and adhered to.
- Independent checks should be carried out to ensure that only staff of the appropriate level or type of employment receive overtime.

Further work to be carried out includes reviewing whether there are specific areas that have incurred excess overtime budget, whether any explanations have been provided for the excess and whether the overtime had been independently agreed or authorised.

Further work to be undertaken:

- Review why the payroll department is part of Finance and why they are involved with receipts and payments functions.
- Confirm whether any compensating controls or other risk mitigation is in place.
- Confirm also that staff are rotated regularly.

FEEDBACK TO ACTIVITY **2**

Car Park Company

Completeness of income

Any enterprise would want to have adequate controls to ensure that all income to which the enterprise is entitled has been received and accurately recorded. Although there is no segregation of duties with only one person operating the pay booth and exit barrier at a time, the use of pre-numbered tickets does compensate for this to a certain extent.

Safe custody of assets

The safe custody of assets is of particular importance in the case of valuable and moveable assets such as cash. It is essential that cash is banked, intact regularly. The amount of cash banked per the paying-in slips should agree to that received according to the car park tickets.

Internal controls

Calculations of amount charged for each ticket should be independently checked at head office for accuracy.

Analytical procedures should be performed on parking fees received, and full explanations should be sought for any deviations from expectation.

Physical controls should be instigated to ensure that the ticket machine is not tampered with in any way.

Cash banked should be agreed to the total receipts per tickets by head office personnel. In addition, reconciliations between the cash book and bank statements should be performed on a regular basis.

The cash box should be kept locked when not in use, and during transfer to the bank. There should be adequate security and insurance.

Cash counts should be carried out, without warning, to check that the money held reconciles to the initial float plus the day's takings per the parking tickets.

Tests of controls

For a sample of days, check that parking tickets have been signed as evidence of the fee charged having been checked by head office personnel. The cash banked per the statement should be agreed to the summary of fees taken. These tests would indicate whether all income due had been properly recorded and received.

For a sample of parking tickets, check that the issue from, and subsequent return to, head office was controlled, and that any missing tickets were fully investigated. This test would indicate whether all tickets resulted in income being received and recorded.

Tutorial note: Lots of information here – don't worry. The question does need reading through carefully and perhaps some brief notes made of what will go into each part of the answer laid out in rough. Then answer each part of the question, remembering to bring in the question information. Answers which show thought in planning and use the information given will score much higher than those which are rushed and ignore the question details.

Chapter 11
AUDIT EVIDENCE

CHAPTER CONTENTS

Audit evidence is necessary to support the audit opinion; the auditors therefore need to obtain sufficient, relevant and reliable evidence to satisfy themselves that the objectives of the individual audit tests have been met. Once satisfied, they can arrive at the overall audit opinion in the knowledge that it can be adequately defended, if required, as all the evidence exists to prove how the opinion was arrived at.

The auditors also need to consider when planning the audit what type(s) of audit evidence will be necessary in order to ensure that this is obtained on a timely basis. Certain types of evidence, such as that obtained from a debtors circularisation, needs the involvement and co-operation of others (i.e. the client and their customers). In such cases where the evidence-gathering process is lengthier, it is vital that sufficient planning is carried out.

It is important to consider audit evidence at this stage as the next few chapters will concentrate on the 'balance sheet' audit items and testing of those items, which is principally substantive in nature. The auditors need to consider for each of the balance sheet items what evidence they need to obtain to satisfy themselves that those items are correctly stated in the accounts.

We start by considering the assertions made in the financial statements by the directors. These assertions underlie all items in the financial statements, and so the auditor needs to obtain audit evidence that supports these assertions. The task of answering exam questions is made easier if you can design substantive tests based on these assertions, rather than learning long lists of tests for particular types of assets and liabilities.

You should appreciate that the assertions apply to profit and loss account items as well as balance sheet items but have been included at this stage to show the practical relative emphasis given to the testing of the assertions in the balance sheet audit.

The principles of audit evidence are equally applicable to the internal auditor, who needs to provide sufficient, reliable and relevant evidence and be able to back up audit opinions and conclusions.

Objectives

By the time you have finished this chapter you should be able to:

- describe the sources and relative merits of the different types of evidence available
- describe the financial statement assertions commonly reported on and the principles and objectives of balance and transaction testing
- audit significant accounting estimates
- understand the types of evidence available in the audit of small entities and specific characteristics and difficulties that are encountered with the audit of smaller entities.

1 The assertions contained in the financial statements

KEY POINT

The key financial statement assertions are: **existence, rights and obligations, occurrence, completeness, valuation, measurement, presentation and disclosure.**

1.1 Financial statement assertions

The financial statement assertions that are relevant to the financial statements, and which need to be considered in the context of audit evidence, are normally summarised as follows:

- existence
- rights and obligations
- occurrence
- completeness

- valuation
- accurate measurement
- presentation and disclosure.

These are examined individually in further detail later in the chapter.

2 Audit evidence

KEY POINT

ISA 500 requires auditors to obtain **sufficient appropriate** audit evidence on which to base audit opinions.

ISA 500 *Audit evidence* requires that auditors obtain ***sufficient appropriate** audit evidence* to be able to draw reasonable conclusions on which to base the audit opinion.

'Sufficient' relates to the quantity of evidence, 'appropriate' relates to the quality or reliability and relevance of evidence.

Evidence will normally be sought from a variety of different sources because evidence is persuasive rather than conclusive and auditors seek reasonable, not absolute, assurance.

2.1 Sufficient, appropriate evidence

KEY POINT

To judge what is sufficient appropriate evidence consider the **transaction level**, **materiality** and the information's **reliability**.

The auditor's judgement as to what constitutes sufficient appropriate evidence is influenced by such factors as the following:

- the assessment of risk at the financial statement level and the individual balance or class of **transaction level**
- the nature of the accounting and **internal control systems**
- the **materiality** of the item
- the auditor's knowledge and experience of the business
- the findings of audit procedures
- the source and **reliability** of the information.

We have already noted that the assessment of **risk** affects the amount of evidence required.

KEY POINT

Risk may be specific or general within the financial statements.

Risk may be in a specific area, for example stock or doubtful debt provisions are always subjective and hence high risk areas. Alternatively it may be a risk running through the financial statements as a whole. For example:

- the auditors may have found material errors in the past – they may lack confidence in those preparing the records
- the company may be approaching insolvency and hoping to impress potential financial backers by showing the figures in a better light
- a bonus to be paid to management may be based on reported results.

3 Accounting and internal control systems

3.1 The audit approach and tests of control

KEY POINT

ISA 315 requires auditors to obtain an understanding of the accounting and control systems to determine their audit approach.

ISA 315 requires that auditors obtain and document an understanding of the accounting system and control environment sufficient to determine their audit approach. The audit approach will broadly comprise either:

- a systems based approach, whereby the auditor obtains comfort on the adequacy of the system by means of tests of controls, supplemented by a reduced level of substantive testing
- a wholly substantive approach.

The former is by far the more efficient approach but the latter is often necessary in small businesses where the accounting and internal control systems are weak.

The auditor should make a preliminary assessment of control risk and then plan and perform tests of control to support that assessment.

KEY POINT

Auditors must obtain sufficient appropriate evidence to support the assessed level of **control risk**.

Auditors must obtain sufficient, appropriate evidence to support the assessed level of **control risk**. This will relate to both the design and the operation of the accounting and internal control system.

So, for example, if the preliminary assessment of controls over creditors is low risk (i.e. the system of controls over creditors appears to be good at the planning stage) and tests of controls show that the controls are in fact good (i.e. postings to creditors are properly checked and authorised etc.), it may be possible to reduce the sample of creditors selected for circularisation or reconciliation at the year end.

Note that where control risk is assessed as less than high, auditors must document the basis for that conclusion. Note also that it is often necessary to assess inherent risk and control risk together.

Deviations from prescribed controls may result from changes in personnel, human error or changes in the volume of transactions. The idea of an '**exception**' is an important one. The auditor cannot excuse failure of a control on the grounds that the amounts involved were small. If a control can fail in respect of a small monetary amount, it is as likely to fail with a significant amount.

The auditors will not be able to take comfort from the operation of controls if they have found any exceptions – *unless* they can satisfy themselves that the exception is an isolated departure. An example of this could be an error made on a day when a temporary clerk was employed where there are no errors in any other time periods. The auditors may have to take that day and test it more extensively (i.e. not rely on internal controls), but they could rely on controls over the remaining period. They are effectively splitting the year into two populations, taking a reliance approach for one, a substantive approach for the other. If substantially different controls are used at different times during the period, auditors need to consider each separately.

KEY POINT

Where control **exceptions** are high, a reassessment of the control risk may be required.

Where the exceptions found are unacceptably high, the effect is to require a reassessment of the control risk, i.e. the internal control system cannot be relied upon to the extent originally envisaged. Control risk is therefore increased and therefore the substantive testing will need to be increased. In addition the nature of the errors found may result in the auditors concluding that their initial assessment of the inherent risk is incorrect. You need to appreciate that the auditors in planning the audit are not in possession of detailed facts about the company's operations and the testing procedures provide them with further information that may be at variance with their original opinion.

Bear in mind that in practice it can be difficult to distinguish between a series of isolated deviations from the application of a control procedure and the non-functioning of that procedure as a whole. Consider the following: 'Our regular member of staff was off sick in March, in April we employed a temporary clerk, in May we had a reorganisation and in June we had a full systems failure and spent all of our time reinputting information, for these reasons only half of your sample of credit notes have been authorised.' On the assumption that credit notes were authorised for the rest of the period, do you consider the procedure to have been operating effectively, or has it broken down? It is of course a matter of professional judgement.

3.2 Substantive procedures – relevance

Management are responsible for the fair presentation of financial statements. In representing that the financial statements give a true and fair view, management are making assertions about the various elements of the financial statements.

KEY POINT

To form an opinion on the financial statements, the auditors need to obtain evidence supporting the **financial statement assertions**.

The relevance of the audit evidence should be considered in relation to the overall audit objective of forming an opinion and reporting on the financial statements. To achieve this objective the auditor needs to obtain evidence to support the following financial statement '**assertions**':

(a) Assertions about transactions and events for the period:

- **occurrence** – a transaction or event pertaining to the entity occurred during the relevant accounting period (i.e. the transactions are not *overstated*)
- **completeness** – there are no unrecorded transactions or events (i.e. the transactions are not *understated*)
- **accuracy** – transactions and events have been measured and recorded accurately
- **cut-off** – transactions and events have been recorded in the correct accounting period
- **classification** – transactions and events have been recorded in the correct accounts

(b) Assertions about account balances at the period end:

- **existence** – assets and liabilities exist
- **rights and obligations** – an asset or liability pertains (i.e. belongs) to the entity (i.e. the entity has legal or other rights or obligations relating to the asset or liability)

  The auditor must ensure that it is the business which owns the asset at the balance sheet date. There are many situations where an asset could be on the business premises but belong to someone else. Stock, for example, may have been sold but not yet delivered. In a small business, some of the assets may belong to the major shareholder.
- **completeness** – there are no unrecorded assets or liabilities
- **valuation and allocation** – assets and liabilities have been measured at appropriate amounts, and any resulting valuation or allocation adjustments have been appropriately recorded

(c) **Assertions about presentation and disclosure**

- **occurrence and rights and obligations** – all disclosed events, transactions and other matters have occurred and pertain to the entity
- **completeness** – there are no unrecorded disclosures
- **classification and understandability** – financial information has been appropriately presented, and disclosures are clearly expressed
- **accuracy and valuation** – all information has been disclosed fairly and at appropriate amounts.

It is traditional to summarise the above assertions into completeness, occurrence, valuation, existence, rights and obligations, measurement, and presentation and disclosure. You may find this summarised approach useful in the exam.

EXAM HINT

Devise a mnemonic to remember these assertions: '**COVER MP**' or '**MORE PVC**' are examples.

You should devise a mnemonic to try and remember these assertions: '**COVER MP**' for example. Note that assets and liabilities refer to the balance sheet, transactions refer to the profit and loss account.

Two of the most important assertion tests are for completeness and existence. These are tests going in the 'opposite direction' to each other.

If, for example, the auditors wish to test for the *completeness* of creditors, they should take a sample of source documents such as goods received notes, and trace them through the related invoices, daybooks and ledgers to the financial statements in the form of creditors.

If, on the other hand, they wish to test for the *existence* of debtors, they should start at the other end with a sample of debtors from the financial statements and trace these back through the ledgers, daybooks and invoices to the source documentation, i.e. the orders or despatch notes.

Auditors in practice are concerned about the completeness or understatement of expenses and liabilities, and the existence or overstatement of assets and income. However, remember that if the trial balance balances and the auditors discover an overstated debit there must also be either an overstated credit or an understated debit. If they discover an understated credit there must also be either an understated debit or an overstated credit.

The best test of the existence of an asset is to check its physical existence, if it is tangible, and the entity's document to title if it is not. Just because an asset exists does not mean to say that it belongs to the reporting entity; documentary evidence is needed to prove ownership.

KEY POINT

Substantive tests may be incorporated with other procedures, e.g. tests of control.

Substantive tests may be incorporated with other procedures such as tests of control. An invoice for example is checked for both its accuracy (substantive) and its authorisation (test of control). The same invoice may also be used as part of a 'walk through' test which the auditors will perform as part of their preliminary assessment of internal controls at the planning stage.

ACTIVITY **1**

Define 'tests of control' and 'substantive procedures'.

Feedback to this activity is at the end of the chapter.

ACTIVITY **2**

Indicate which of the following are tests of control, which are substantive tests, and which may be both:

1 checking an approval grid on a purchase invoice for evidence of authorisation
2 performing an analytical review of the draft financial statements
3 checking the physical existence of an expensive new item of plant
4 checking whether management prepare a monthly bank reconciliation
5 checking the bank reconciliation at the year-end
6 attending the client's annual stocktake
7 analysing the age of debtor balances
8 checking a sample of despatch notes to sales invoices
9 checking procedures for control of computer passwords
10 reviewing the minutes of board meetings.

Feedback to this activity is at the end of the chapter.

3.3 Substantive procedures – reliability

Although the reliability of audit evidence is dependent upon the particular circumstances, the following general presumptions may be found helpful:

- evidence obtained from independent external sources is more reliable than that obtained from the entity's records
- evidence obtained from the entity's records is more reliable where the accounting and internal control system operate effectively
- evidence obtained directly by auditors by such means as analysis and physical inspection is more reliable than evidence obtained by or from the entity
- documentary evidence is more reliable than oral evidence
- original documents are more reliable than copies, telexes or faxes.

KEY POINT

Documentary evidence is least reliable if created and held by the entity; most reliable if created by third parties and held by the auditor.

EXAM HINT

Third party evidence is an important source and questions frequently test this area of knowledge.

Documentary evidence is least reliable if created and held by the entity (e.g. invoices). It is more reliable if it is created by third parties and held by the entity (e.g. supplier statements). It is most reliable if it is created by third parties and held by the auditor (e.g. responses to debtor circularisations).

The auditors should consider whether the conclusions drawn from differing types of evidence are consistent with one another. When audit evidence obtained from one source appears inconsistent with that obtained from another, the reliability of each remains in doubt until further work has been done to resolve the inconsistency. However, when the individual items of evidence relating to a particular matter are all consistent, then the auditors may obtain a cumulative degree of assurance higher than that which they obtain from the individual items. This is a form of 'synergy'.

Unfortunately, there are no hard and fast rules against which the reliability of evidence can be measured. It is very much a matter for the auditor's judgement, but note the presumptions above.

The problems of obtaining sufficient, relevant and reliable audit evidence are by their nature difficult, and no quick solution is as yet available. Most of the negligence claims against auditors arise where the quality of audit evidence is weak. Such cases rarely get into court but substantial cash settlements have been made out of court by many firms of auditors.

These settlements give a clear indication of the cost of lack of quality control and consequent weakness of audit evidence. Clearly when things go wrong in a business, a client will consider suing the auditors. The auditors must ensure that they have sufficient evidence to defend themselves against such a claim.

When obtaining confirmation from third parties as a source of evidence the auditor should consider:

- when such evidence is appropriate
- which assertions are satisfied
- how can such evidence be obtained and what use(s) can be made of it.

Typical situations where such evidence is invaluable is with debtor confirmations, bank confirmations, (and in some cases) creditor confirmations.

Where third party evidence relates to specific balances e.g. bank, debtors, creditors then it provides persuasive evidence as to rights and obligations and where relevant ownership of assets.

ACTIVITY **3**

Explain each of the following techniques of gathering audit evidence and give an example of each:

- inspection
- observation
- enquiry
- confirmation
- re-calculation
- re-performance.

Feedback to this activity is at the end of the chapter.

3.4 Analytical procedures as substantive tests

KEY POINT

Analytical procedures can be used as substantive tests when in conjunction with detailed tests or if the amounts are immaterial.

Analytical procedures deal with comparisons of financial and non-financial information and were considered earlier in the context of planning. Analytical procedures used as substantive tests can be used alone where the total amounts involved are immaterial and in conjunction with detailed tests of transactions and balances elsewhere. These procedures provide good 'overall' evidence as to the accuracy of a balance or class of transactions. Examples include the following:

- a comparison of payroll costs on a monthly basis taking account of wage rises, starters and leavers and seasonal work
- a comparison of sales with expenses, on a monthly basis and as a comparison with prior years
- a comparison of the ageing of stock or debtors on a monthly or quarterly basis and calculation of debtor days or stock turnover.

KEY POINT

Analytical procedures are limited by relationships' accuracy and predictability and the availability of relevant, comparable information.

Analytical procedures are used widely but are limited by factors such as the accuracy and predictability of relationships and the availability, relevance and comparability of information. They are also limited by the auditor's knowledge of the business and the availability of other types of evidence. It is common for analytical procedures to be performed on management accounts. These accounts must be reconciled to the financial accounts to avoid the possibility of auditing one set of information and reporting on another.

So, if a volatile business with no established trading record, perhaps a start-up, produces information from systems that are poorly controlled, in a sector with which the auditor is relatively unfamiliar, it is unlikely that analytical procedures will form a substantial part of testing.

A key feature of analytical procedures is the investigation, explanation and corroboration of significant fluctuations and unexpected relationships. This emphasises the need for *predictable* patterns in the business. Bear in mind that explanations may be plausible 'we sold more beer in June because it was hot', but incorrect 'we *recorded* more beer sales in June because a large batch of invoices was posted twice in error!'

ACTIVITY **4**

Backtor plc

During your audit of Backtor plc the following evidential matters have been included in your working papers:

1 flowcharts of the company's payroll routine prepared by your audit assistant backed up by tests of controls

2 an oral statement by the production director that the expected working life of plant acquired during the year is ten years

3 a newspaper report to the effect that new technology is expected to have an adverse effect on the sales of products representing 20% of the company's turnover

4 a letter to the managing director from the company's bank manager indicating that the bank intends to extend overdraft facilities for a period of one year

5 list of items of stock counted by a member of your firm of chartered certified accountants during observation of the company's stock count

6 a letter from a debtor to your firm in reply to a confirmation request indicating agreement with the balance as recorded in the books of Backtor plc.

Required:

In respect of each of the above evidential matters:

- explain its relevance to the overall audit objective of forming an opinion and reporting on the financial statements
- state, giving reasons, how reliable you judge the evidence to be
- describe one additional item of audit evidence you would seek to support the matter described.

If any of the items of evidence referred to above were inconsistent with other evidence collected by you (e.g. in relation to expected plant life, if working lives in the past for the kind of plant referred to have been seven years and not ten years), what steps would you take?

Feedback to this activity is at the end of the chapter.

3.5 Audit working paper files

KEY POINT

Audit files are a prime source of audit evidence and thus must be capable of supporting the audit opinion in a court of law.

Types of **audit files** and **working papers** were considered in detail in an earlier chapter at the planning stage of the audit. It is worth reiterating at this point however, that audit files are a prime source of audit evidence and thus must be capable of supporting the audit opinion in a court of law.

In addition **ISA 230** *Documentation* states that working papers are the record of the planning, performance, supervision and review of an audit as well as of *the evidence* obtained to support the audit report.

4 The use of accounting estimates

KEY POINT

In some cases, amounts in the financial statements can only be **estimated** as it is not possible to state a definite value for them.

In some cases, amounts in the financial statements can only be estimated as it is not possible to state a definite value for them, for example legal claims against the company or those being pursued by the company against others.

Accounting estimates also include estimates of provisions for depreciation, deferred tax, write-downs to net realisable value such as doubtful debt and obsolescence provisions, profit and loss recognition on long-term contracts, warranties, guarantee or rectification provisions, contingent liabilities as well as the usual accruals and prepayments, and other areas in which a significant element of judgement is required. Such items are inherently more risky than non-judgemental items and control risk is usually higher as these are non-routine transactions. The auditor therefore should follow the principles contained within **ISA 540** *Audit of accounting estimates* when auditing any estimated values contained in the financial statements.

Essentially, the principles to be followed are any or all of:

- review and test the process used by management to develop the estimate
- use an independent estimate (generated by the auditor) to compare with management's estimate
- consider the use of an expert in the relevant field to obtain an independent view as to whether or not the estimate is accurate
- review subsequent events.

Where, in the case of contingent liabilities, subsequent events 'crystallise' the liability, there will be no need to review management's processes or use independent estimates.

The auditor will normally test the calculations of the estimate, assess the assumptions made (e.g. the court is 90% likely to find in our favour), compare estimates with those made in previous periods and ensure that the estimate is in accordance with the auditor's knowledge of the business and the other audit evidence obtained.

These principles and some of the problems involved can be illustrated by considering the following example.

Example

The Dynamic Diesel Engine Company manufactures two distinct ranges of engines, both used in power boats.

The Estoeng range is well established, having been on the market for ten years. The Novoeng is a newly introduced product using innovative technology patented by the company. The company gives a two-year warranty on all their sales. During the accounting period just ended approximately the same number of both ranges were sold.

The auditor would need to assess the adequacy of the warranty provision which will, of course, be an estimated amount. It should be noted that the audit problem will be greater in the case of the Novoeng because of the lack of previous experience with warranty claims.

In the case of the Estoeng, the auditor can make use of warranty claim statistics and costs from previous years, adjusting for any known divergences from previous patterns (e.g. cost increases, known production defects). This is not available for the Novoeng range.

Key audit procedures in relation to the warranty provision in respect of these engines might include:

- discussions with management (including technical manager) on the reliability of the new technology
- identification of the level of costs which may be involved in possible rectification work
- a careful review of actual warranty claims relating to the engines received to date
- possibly discussion with industry experts on the general reliability of the technology involved
- an assessment of the possible materiality of any misstatement in the provision to the financial statements of the company.

5 Small company audit issues

KEY POINT

Obtaining **independent** evidence can be difficult when auditing small companies.

The audit of **small companies** creates additional issues for the auditor when it comes to obtaining *independent* audit evidence. This is principally due to the very nature of small companies, and the fact that control is often centralised in the form of the managing director. There are also issues surrounding segregation of duties in small companies, as clearly it is often more difficult to ensure such effective controls exist. In some cases, normally where the accounting system is less sophisticated (for example a significant proportion of income arises from cash sales), it may be difficult to verify the completeness of sales income. It is important to be aware of potential problems and what effect these can have on the auditor's work.

Conclusion

Audit evidence needs to be sufficient and appropriate. It can be obtained from a variety of sources including inspection, observation, enquiry and computation.

Working papers are important as they record the various elements of audit evidence obtained.

Small companies pose special problems in respect of obtaining sufficient, appropriate audit evidence; independent audit evidence is harder to obtain when undertaking a small company audit – the auditor has to decide what is necessary in the individual circumstances.

SELF-TEST QUESTIONS

The assertions contained in the financial statements

1 What are the seven traditionally identified financial statement assertions? (1.1)

Audit evidence

2 What factors should the auditor bear in mind as to what constitutes suitable audit evidence? (2)

EXAM-TYPE QUESTION

Rolfe Enterprises

You are an audit senior in the firm of Diggers & Partners, working on the audit of Rolfe Enterprises Limited. You have been told by the audit manager to conduct a review of the client's board minutes. The audit junior who is working for you on the audit has told you that she doesn't understand why you have to perform that task as she thought you obtained all your evidence from the tests that you performed, and surely the minutes might not be independent anyway.

Required:

(a) Draft an e-mail to the audit junior explaining why the auditor should conduct a review of the board minutes as part of the audit and give five examples of information that you would normally expect to find in the minutes. Comment on the statement that the minutes are not a reliable source of evidence. **(7 marks)**

(b) The Company Secretary has just called you to inform you that you shall not be permitted access to the minutes, as there is a considerable amount of confidential information contained within them, and that you will have to obtain your evidence from other sources. Write a letter to the Company Secretary in response to this. **(7 marks)**

(c) Following your letter and further discussions, you have now been permitted access to the minutes and have identified that an asset of considerable value (10% of balance sheet total) was purchased in the year. However, there is no evidence of approval of this transaction. What action would you take? **(6 marks)**

(Total: 20 marks)

For the answer to this question, see the 'Answers' section at the end of the book.

FEEDBACK TO ACTIVITY 1

Tests of control are those tests which seek to provide audit evidence that internal control procedures are being properly applied throughout the period under review.

Substantive procedures are those tests of transactions and balances, and other procedures such as analytical review, which seek to provide audit evidence as to financial statement assertions such as completeness, existence, valuation, presentation and disclosures, etc.

FEEDBACK TO ACTIVITY 2

1 test of authorisation controls

2 substantive procedure as to whether results appear reasonable

3 substantive procedure

4 test to see if control is in existence

5 substantive procedure performed on bank balance

6 both – test on control procedures adopted at the stocktake and substantive procedure relating to the existence and condition of stock

7 substantive procedure which helps in assessing the need for a doubtful debt provision

8 both – test of control, that goods despatched are invoiced but also assists in ensuring that invalid sales are not included (substantive procedure)

9 test on control environment

10 both – could include checks on authorisation of major capital expenditure and substantiation of capital commitments, directors' remuneration, etc.

FEEDBACK TO ACTIVITY **3**

- **Inspection** – this covers the physical review or examination of records, documents and tangible assets. An example of a test of controls is examining copy sales invoices for authorisation. An example of a substantive procedure would be checking the physical existence of a tangible asset. Additional work may be required to determine ownership, valuation and contractual obligations.
- **Observation** – this technique involves looking at a process or procedure being performed. However, this observation may not be typical of the usual conduct of the procedure. An example is the distribution of wage packets to see that internal control procedures are adhered to or the observation by auditors of stock being counted in accordance with stocktaking instructions.
- **Enquiry** – seeking relevant information from knowledgeable persons inside or outside the enterprise, whether formally or informally, orally or in writing. The reliability of this technique depends on the qualification and integrity of the source. An example is the seeking of formal representations from management on the value of a material subsidiary company in an overseas country.
- **Confirmation** – seeking to corroborate information in the accounting records (e.g. confirmation of debtor balances).
- **Recalculation** – checking the arithmetical accuracy of records or performing independent calculations (e.g. checking the addition of the trial balance).
- **Reperformance** – of controls such as the bank reconciliation to ensure they were performed correctly.

Note: All of the above can be used as a test of control or as substantive procedures.

FEEDBACK TO ACTIVITY **4**

Backtor plc

1 Flowcharts provide evidence of the system in operation and, as they were prepared by the audit staff, the value of the evidence is good. The tests of control have demonstrated that the system does in fact operate as recorded and, if it is felt necessary, this could be further substantiated by walk through tests.

2 The statement provides evidence as to the accuracy of the depreciation charge in the profit and loss account, and the net book value of plant in the balance sheet. As it is oral evidence from someone from within the enterprise, it is not particularly reliable. Further evidence could be obtained by considering the useful lives of similar items of plant in the past or consulting trade journals which may detail the relevant information.

3 The newspaper report provides evidence that the auditors may wish to consider when carrying out their overall review of the financial statements of the enterprise. It is also of importance in considering the continuing commercial viability of the company. As the evidence is from a source independent of the company, it is considered to be reliable, but it must be borne in mind that newspaper reports can be based upon hearsay and not just fact. The quality of the evidence could be improved by discussing the matter with management or considering volumes of sales in recent months.

4 The letter provides evidence that the company is a going concern. As the evidence is from a source external to the company, it is reliable, but would be more so if the letter had been sent direct to the auditors. To substantiate the evidence, the normal bank letter would be sent.

5 Attendance at a client's stocktake and performance of test counts provide evidence as to the existence and valuation of stock. As the evidence is documentary, was prepared by a member of the audit firm, and is based on physical inspection, it is very reliable. To support the evidence obtained, the items would need to be traced through to the final stock valuation.

6 Direct confirmation from a debtor provides evidence as to the accuracy of the debtors' figure included in the balance sheet. As the evidence is documentary, and from a source external to the company, it is reliable. To further support the evidence, the receipt of cash from the debtor, after the year-end, could be checked.

If items of evidence are inconsistent, then the reliability of each remains in doubt until the inconsistency has been resolved. With respect to the example given, the auditor would need to find evidence to explain the increased useful life from, for example, trade journals, etc.

Working papers should enable an experienced auditor with no previous connection with the audit to understand the work performed and the basis of decisions taken.

Chapter 12
THE AUDIT OF FIXED ASSETS

CHAPTER CONTENTS

This chapter considers the fixed assets element and categories of the balance sheet audit. Investments may be fixed or current assets depending on whether they are held for the long or short term. It is important to keep in mind the financial statement assertions when you are considering any aspect of the balance sheet audit. If you can't remember them you should refer back to the previous chapter to remind yourself. The assertions underlie all the items in the financial statements and therefore the auditor needs to obtain audit evidence to support those assertions. When answering examination questions you should design tests based on the assertions rather than learning long lists of tests for particular types of assets and liabilities. You should appreciate that the assertions do apply to the profit and loss account as well as the balance sheet.

The techniques and procedures performed by the external auditor, as described in this chapter will apply equally to the internal auditor.

As usual, the possible impact of computer based systems (e.g. fixed asset register) should be recognised.

Objectives

By the time you have finished this chapter you should be able to:

- describe and tabulate for inclusion in a work programme the substantive procedures used in obtaining evidence in relation to tangible and intangible fixed assets and investments
- explain the purpose of substantive procedures in relation to financial statement assertions concerning tangible and intangible fixed assets and investments.

1 Fixed assets

1.1 Definition of fixed assets

DEFINITION

Fixed assets (intangible, tangible and **investments)** are assets held for continuing use, not resale.

Fixed assets have the fundamental characteristic that they are held for continuing use in the business and not for resale.

Under the Companies Act requirements fixed assets are subdivided in the following way:

Categories of fixed assets

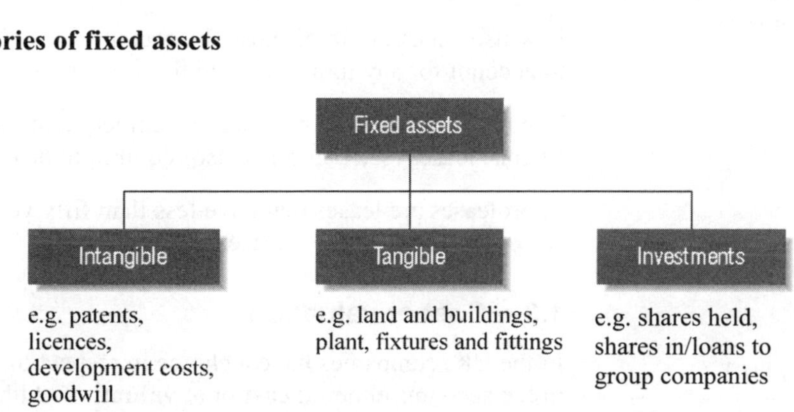

Any assets not intended for continuing use are treated as current assets regardless of when they will be realised.

1.2 Tangible assets – statutory disclosure requirements

The statutory requirements are contained in Schedule 4 CA85. They are most easily explained by a schedule which would contain the minimum statutory information.

Statutory information requirements for tangible assets

	Land and buildings	*Plant and machinery*	*Fixtures, fittings, tools and equipment*	*Payments on account and assets in course of construction*	*Total*
Cost or valuation	£	£	£	£	£
At beginning of year	X	X	X	X	X
Additions	X	X	X	X	X
Disposals	(X)	(X)	(X)	(X)	(X)
At end of year	X	X	X	X	X
Accumulated depreciation					
At beginning of year	X	X	X	X	X
Eliminated on disposals	(X)	(X)	(X)	(X)	(X)
Provisions for the year	X	X	X	X	X
At end of year	X	X	X	X	X
Net book amount					
At end of year	X	X	X	X	X
At beginning of year	X	X	X	X	X

The net book amount of land and buildings comprises:

	20X5	*20X4*
	£	£
Freehold	X	X
Long leaseholds	X	X
Short leaseholds	X	X
	X	X

KEY POINT

Statutory disclosures for tangible assets cover their valuation and the accounting policies for **depreciation** and **impairment in value**.

Where tangible assets are included at a valuation the notes must disclose:

- the years in which the valuation took place and, for each year, the value of those assets
- for any valuation during the year the names of the valuers, or their qualifications, and the bases of valuation adopted.

It is also necessary to disclose the accounting policies as regards the **depreciation** and to account for any impairment in the value of assets.

The net book value of plant and machinery and fixtures and fittings that are held under finance leases (see below) is also required to be disclosed separately.

Short leases are leases that have less than fifty years to run at the balance sheet date. All other leases are long leases.

1.3 Cost or valuation

KEY POINT

In the UK, companies have a choice of incorporating tangible assets in the accounts either at **cost** or at **valuation**.

In the UK, companies have a choice in respect of tangible assets of incorporating them in the accounts either at **cost** or at **valuation**. Although valuation is available for any tangible assets, it is normally applied only to property, frequently valued every five years by professional valuers.

The following points should be noted:

- The basis used, cost or valuation, must be disclosed in the accounts.
- Any surplus on revaluation should be credited direct to **revaluation reserve**.
- Assets need not be revalued simply because their current market value has fallen below cost. Because the assets are held for use in the business their current market value is not of great significance, unless there has been an **impairment in value** in which case the asset must be written down in the balance sheet. The debit should go to profit and loss account, but can be taken to revaluation reserves in certain circumstances.
- Depreciation should be based on the *revalued* amount and current estimates of useful life.

1.4 FRS 15 *Tangible fixed assets*

FRS 15 sets out the principles of accounting for the measurement, valuation and depreciation of tangible fixed assets. It does not apply to investment properties which are covered by SSAP 19.

KEY POINT

FRS 15 covers assessment of depreciation, estimated **useful life**, and profit/loss on disposal.

The following points from **FRS 15** should be noted:

- Assessment of depreciation, and its allocation to accounting periods, involves the consideration of three factors:
  - cost (or valuation when an asset has been revalued in the financial statements)
  - the nature of the asset and the length of its expected useful life to the business having due regard to the incidence of obsolescence
  - estimated residual value of the asset at the end of its useful economic life in the business of the enterprise.
- If the asset's estimated **useful life** has been revised, charge the remaining NBV (net book value) over the new estimated life.
- Profit/loss on disposal to be disclosed, if material.
- Assets must be depreciated even if market value exceeds NBV.
- Freehold land need not normally be depreciated.
- Buildings on freehold land should be depreciated.
- The method by which depreciation is calculated for each category of assets should be disclosed in the accounts together with the effective useful lives assumed.

1.5 SSAP 21 *Accounting for leases and hire purchase contracts*

KEY POINT

Operating leases are expensed through the profit and loss account. **Finance leases** are capitalised in the balance sheet.

Under **SSAP 21**, certain assets which are leased are required to be capitalised in the lessess's balance sheet, i.e. shown as fixed assets, rather than the rental payments being expensed through the profit and loss account. **Operating leases** are expensed through the profit and loss account. **Finance leases** are capitalised in the balance sheet. Finance leases are those that 'transfer substantially all the risks and rewards of ownership'. These are the sort of assets that are held under the lease for most of their useful lives. Normally the lessee is required to insure and maintain the asset. The payments the lessee makes to the lessor amount to the full market price of the asset (or nearly the full price). In short, the lessee *owns* the asset in all but name.

Under the general principle that requires financial statements to show the substance of transactions rather than merely their legal form, assets under finance leases are shown in the balance sheet as belonging to the lessee, along with all of the other assets owned, even though legally they still belong to the lessor.

The value of such assets must be disclosed in the fixed assets note to the accounts.

1.6 Non-depreciation of fixed assets

KEY POINT

Sometimes properties that are maintained to a high standard have an effectively **indefinite useful life**, and are *not* depreciated.

You should note that some companies do not depreciate certain properties such as hotels and supermarkets on the grounds that the asset is constantly maintained to a high standard and that the residual value will always be higher than cost and that the property has an indefinite useful life (e.g. a well kept 500 year old pub). If these arguments are accepted, it follows that any depreciation required would be immaterial.

This argument can be acceptable providing that refurbishment costs are expensed to the profit and loss account in lieu of depreciation, and that the company carries out an annual impairment review to ensure that the carrying value does not need to be written down.

1.7 Internal control over fixed assets

KEY POINT

Records of **fixed assets** should be properly maintained.

Control objectives

The control objectives are to ensure that:

- fixed assets are correctly recorded, adequately secured and properly maintained
- acquisitions and disposals of fixed assets are properly authorised
- acquisitions and disposals of fixed assets are for the most favourable price possible
- fixed assets are properly recorded, appropriately depreciated, and written down where necessary.

KEY POINT

Fixed asset controls focus on **budget control**, **authority procedures**, **physical inspections** and **depreciation**.

Control procedures over fixed assets

- Annual capital expenditure budgets should be prepared by someone directly responsible to the board of directors.
- Such budgets should, if acceptable, be agreed by the board and minuted.
- Applications for authority to incur capital expenditure should be submitted to the board for approval and should contain reasons for the expenditure, estimated cost, and any fixed assets replaced.
- A document should show what is to be acquired and be signed as authorised by the board or an authorised official.
- Capital projects made by the company itself should be separately identifiable in the company's costing records. They should reflect direct costs plus relevant overhead but not include any profit.
- Disposals of fixed assets should be authorised and any proceeds from sale should be related to the authority.
- A register of fixed assets should be maintained for each major group of assets. The register should identify each item within that group and contain details of cost and depreciation.
- A physical inspection of fixed assets should be carried out periodically and checked to the fixed asset register. Any discrepancies should be noted and investigated.
- Assets should be properly maintained and adequately insured.
- Depreciation rates should be authorised and a written statement of policy produced.
- Depreciation should be reviewed annually to assess the need for changes in the light of profits or losses on disposal, new technology, etc.
- The calculation of depreciation should be checked for accuracy.
- Fixed assets should be reviewed for the need for any write-down.

KEY POINT

Tests of controls focus on authorisation for purchase and disposal, physical checks against the **asset register**, and depreciation.

Tests of controls

- Check authorisation of purchase to board minutes, capital expenditure budgets and capital expenditure form.
- Check authorisation for disposals of significant assets.
- Confirm existence of fixed asset register which adequately identifies assets and comments on their current condition. Ensure register reconciles to nominal ledger.
- Test evidence of reconciliation of register to physical checks of existence and condition of assets.
- Check authorisation of depreciation rates, and particularly changes in rates.
- Examine evidence of checking of correct calculations of depreciation.

ACTIVITY 1

What types of controls would you expect to find in a fixed asset system?

Feedback to this activity is at the end of the chapter.

2 Verification procedures

2.1 Verification procedures – general

EXAM HINT

Remember that **verification procedures** are designed to support the **financial statement assertions**.

Remember that **verification procedures** are designed to support the **financial statement assertions**. These can be summarised as:

- existence
- rights and obligations
- occurrence
- completeness
- valuation
- measurement
- presentation and disclosure.

2.2 Freehold and leasehold land and buildings

KEY POINT

Apply the financial statement assertions to freehold and leasehold land and buildings, and plant, machinery, fixtures and fittings.

- Examine a sample of title deeds, land registry certificates, conveyancing documentation from solicitors, and leases. Pay particular attention to any 'encumbrances', i.e. mortgages or other securities held over assets *(ownership, rights and obligations and disclosure).*
- Inspect directors' minute book to ensure all title deeds, conveyances, tenancy agreements and leases are properly authorised *(occurrence).*
- Check a sample of entries in the fixed asset register and trace back to source documentation to ensure properly stated at cost *(valuation).*
- Review company policies for depreciation and ensure appropriate in the light of the useful life of the building (commonly over 50 years) and ensure that land is not depreciated *(valuation and measurement).*
- Check a sample of calculations of depreciation and ensure accurate and in line with company policy *(measurement).*
- Review assets and establish the need for any write-down for impairments in value. Discuss with directors *(valuation).*
- If freehold or leasehold assets are let to third parties, inspect tenancy agreements, and perform analytical procedures on rental income *(rights and obligations).*
- Ensure freehold land and buildings are stated in accordance with Sch 4 CA 1985 at cost or valuation less accumulated depreciation. If a valuation is performed in the year of audit, give the name or qualification of the valuer and the basis of valuation *(disclosure).*

- Ensure assets held under leases are appropriately disclosed as long-term or short-term *(disclosure)*.
- Physically inspect a sample of assets *(existence)*.
- Ensure that the fixed asset register reconciles to the nominal ledger.

2.3 Plant, machinery and fixtures and fittings

- Examine a sample of invoices, contracts, finance leases or other evidence of title to assets including vehicle registration documents *(ownership)*.
- Review company policies for depreciation and ensure appropriate in the light of the useful life of the assets *(measurement)*.
- Check a sample of calculations of depreciation and ensure accurate and in line with company policy *(measurement)*.
- Review assets and establish the need for any write-down for impairments in value. Discuss with directors *(valuation)*.
- Ensure that VAT is appropriately capitalised where it is not recoverable *(valuation)*.
- Ensure assets are stated in accordance with Sch 4 CA 1985 and that the NBV of assets held under finance leases is disclosed separately *(disclosure)*.
- Physically inspect a sample of assets *(existence)*.

2.4 Assets in the course of construction

KEY POINT

For **assets under construction**, ensure the cost allocation system is appropriate and relates to the project.

Such assets are built by the company for itself and can include **plant and machinery** as well as **buildings**. The tests are as above except that there are no title deeds or documents of title to examine. Instead the auditor may perform the following tests on the company's own records:

- Ensure the company's system for allocating costs to the asset is appropriate. Some tests of control may be necessary here. Such costs include raw materials, goods taken from trading stock, costs of labour and sometimes interest costs.
- Ensure that the costs that are included relate to the project by taking a sample of costs included and tracing back to costings and source documentation.

The risk is always that costs which should be expensed through the profit and loss account and reducing profits, are in actual fact being capitalised in the balance sheet, thus turning losses into assets.

2.5 The audit of accounting estimates

The audit of **accounting estimates** is often applicable to asset values, and therefore the auditor will need to test such estimates to ensure that they are 'accurate'. The use of such estimates is considered in the earlier chapter on audit evidence.

3 Intangible fixed assets

3.1 CA 1985

KEY POINT

Intangible fixed assets must be disclosed separately.

Intangible fixed assets must be disclosed separately under the following headings:

- development costs (see below)
- concessions, patents, licences, trade marks and similar rights
- goodwill (if acquired for valuable consideration)
- payments on account for intangible fixed assets.

All movements in the year must be given.

3.2 Research and development expenditure

KEY POINT

SSAP 13 states that **research and development** expenditure comprises **pure** or **applied research** or **development**.

SSAP 13 states that research and development expenditure means expenditure falling into one or more of the following broad categories:

- **Pure** (or basic) **research**: *experimental* or *theoretical* work undertaken primarily to acquire new scientific or technical knowledge for its own sake rather than directed towards any specific aim or application.
- **Applied research**: *original* or *critical investigation* undertaken in order to gain new scientific or technical knowledge and directed towards a specific practical aim or objective.
- **Development**: the use of *scientific* or *technical knowledge* in order to produce new or substantially improved materials, devices, products or services.

KEY POINT

Pure and applied research should be written off as incurred. **Development costs** may be carried forward under certain circumstances.

The cost of **pure and applied research** should be written off as incurred.

Development costs may be carried forward only if:

- There is a clearly defined project.
- The related expenditure is separately identifiable. There should be a project costing system into which all relevant costs are allocated. This would include direct labour and material plus overheads incurred for the development of the project.
- The outcome of the project has been assessed as to its technical feasibility. This is a difficult matter for auditors to assess but they may be able to rely on technical consultants.
- The outcome of the project has been assessed as to its commercial viability. This may be supported by formal market research, advance orders from customers etc.
- Further development costs together with related production, selling and administration costs are expected to be more than covered by related future revenues.

  In other words, the client should have budgeting and forecasting procedures on which to base their decision on the continuation of the development project.
- Adequate resources exist to complete the project. The auditor should ensure that either existing working capital is adequate or that further finance is likely to be available from shareholders, bankers or other sources of capital.

  Once commercial production has commenced development costs should be amortised over the period of production that has benefited from the development expenditure. This may be done on a time basis or using a 'unit of production' method.

  If development costs are capitalised then the reason for doing so must be disclosed in the accounts and also the period over which the costs are being written off.

  Deferred development expenditure should be reviewed at the end of each accounting period and where the circumstances which have justified the deferral of the expenditure no longer apply, the expenditure should be written off immediately.

The main procedures in audit work to verify compliance with SSAP 13 are to check that the conditions noted above have been complied with.

3.3 Trade marks and patents

KEY POINT

Trade marks and **patents** may be capitalised and written off over their useful lives with renewal fees being charged to revenue.

Trade marks and **patents** may be capitalised and then written off over their useful lives with any renewal fees being charged to revenue. If a trade mark or patent is abandoned then the net book amount should be written off immediately. Normally the company should keep a register of all material items which should be checked against the agreements, the accounting records, and third party confirmation from the patent agent of the existence and company's title to the assets. Auditors will need to consider the valuation of the assets. This will include a review of the future income arising from the trade mark and patent to see whether it justifies the value placed on it. In assessing the future income it will be necessary to consider the possibility that income will not arise due, for example, to expiry or changes in the client's business.

3.4 Goodwill

KEY POINT

CA 1985 requires that **goodwill** be written off over a disclosed period not exceeding its economic life. **FRS 10** requires that it be capitalised as an intangible fixed asset and amortised over its economic life.

Sch 4 CA 1985 requires that **purchased goodwill** (i.e. not internally generated) should be written off over a period not exceeding its useful economic life and the reason for choosing that period must be disclosed. This allows goodwill to be written off immediately or capitalised but for the company to justify the treatment.

FRS 10 *Goodwill and intangible assets* requires that purchased goodwill should be capitalised as an intangible fixed asset, and should be amortised over its economic life if this is limited.

There is a rebuttable presumption in FRS 10 that the useful economic life of purchased goodwill is limited and does not exceed 20 years from the date of acquisition. The normal situation is therefore for goodwill to be capitalised and amortised over not more than 20 years.

However, the directors may believe that the useful economic life is greater than 20 years or even indefinite. In such circumstances annual impairment reviews must be performed and if goodwill is considered to be indefinite it need not be amortised. This conflicts with CA85 and therefore should only be adopted for the overriding purpose of giving a true and fair view. The reasons for, and effect of the departure from the CA85 must be clearly stated in the notes.

The auditors must satisfy themselves that the goodwill is calculated correctly and that the period of write-off is a reasonable one. It will be necessary to consider the possibility of an impairment in value below the amount stated in the accounts by reviewing the current position and future trading prospects, if a useful life of more than 20 years is being used.

The auditors will have most work to do if the directors have chosen an amortisation period of longer than 20 years, or zero amortisation. The details of the impairment review must be carefully examined.

3.5 Brand names

KEY POINT

The valuation of **brand names** is shown in the balance sheet.

Some companies in recent years have placed valuations on the **brand names** of the goods that they sell. The valuation is shown in the balance sheet. The reason for doing this is that the brand name is valuable to the company in that it helps to sell the company's goods. For example, many people would rather buy a 'branded' tin of baked beans, rather than the 'own make' offered by a supermarket.

FRS 10 deals with all intangible assets (including brands) as well as goodwill, and requires that:

- an intangible asset purchased separately from a business should be capitalised at its cost
- an intangible asset acquired as part of the acquisition of a business should be capitalised separately from goodwill if its value can be measured reliably on initial recognition
- an internally developed intangible asset may be capitalised only if it has a readily ascertainable market value.

The large majority of internally developed intangible assets (such as self-grown brands) will not have a readily ascertainable market value so cannot be shown on the balance sheet.

The amortisation requirements for intangible assets other than goodwill are identical to those for goodwill identified above. The auditor's responsibilities will be the same, checking the amount capitalised, the acceptability of the chosen amortisation period and the disclosure requirements.

ACTIVITY 2

IFS have recently acquired a major competitor, which has included the trademark and patent relating to 'Hydrospa' the leading brand in the industry. The purchase price included goodwill. Outline the treatment of intangible fixed assets acquired.

Feedback to this activity is at the end of the chapter.

4 Investments

4.1 Classification

KEY POINT

Investments will be treated as **fixed assets** if intended for use on a continuing basis, otherwise it will be a **current asset**.

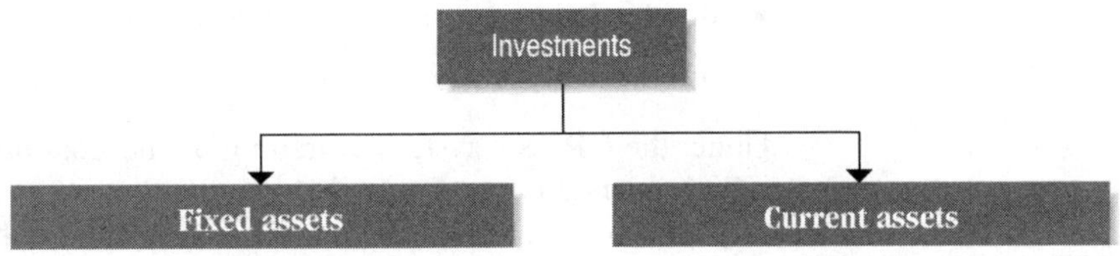

KEY POINT

Fixed asset investments may be stated at **historical cost**, market or other value. **Current asset investments** may be stated at historical or **current cost**.

An **investment** will be treated as a **fixed asset** if it is intended for use on a continuing basis in the company, otherwise it will be a **current asset** regardless of the date of its expected realisation. In practice, fixed assets tend to be those held for more than one year, current assets being those that are held for less.

Fixed asset investments may be stated at **historical cost, market value** or other appropriate value as decided by the directors.

Current asset investments may be stated at **historical cost** or **current cost**.

4.2 Statutory disclosure requirements

KEY POINT

Statutory disclosure for investments covers accounting policies, valuations, share holdings and investment movements.

In general terms, the following items should be disclosed in relation to all investments:

- the accounting policy and valuation method relating to the investment
- the difference between market value and book value of listed investments - if market value is lower there may be a need to consider adjusting for an impairment in value
- details relating to investments consisting of shares in other companies including the proportion of shares held and the country of incorporation
- movements on investments during the year.

4.3 Internal control

KEY POINT

Where there are few investments, systematic **internal controls** are unlikely.

Where a trading concern holds only a few investments, there is unlikely to be any systematic **internal control** system specifically for those investments.

With a larger investment portfolio, there should be a system of internal control which will include:

- authorisation procedures for purchases and sales
- registers reconciled with control accounts
- control over dividend/interest receipts
- proper division of responsibility and supervision.

4.4 Verification procedures

Verification procedures should follow the general approach outlined for tangible fixed assets. However, the following specific points should be noted:

Existence and ownership

Establishment of title and beneficial ownership of investments is not conclusively possible. However, evidence is available in the form of:

- share certificates, correspondence with nominees etc
- payments for securities, brokers 'bought notes' or 'contract notes'
- dividends/interest from securities, dividend 'warrants'
- internal control procedures.

Under the **CREST** system of trading on the London Stock Exchange, some shareholders do not receive share certificates when they buy shares through certain organisations (e.g. stockbrokers, banks) who hold the shares as nominees. Where investments are held through such a nominee, the auditor will need to examine correspondence with the nominees and consider obtaining formal confirmation of investments held from the nominee.

Valuation

Valuation of listed securities is easily confirmed with appropriate financial publications. Directors' valuation of unlisted securities is something on which the auditors report, and the basis of the calculations must therefore be examined. The auditor must also consider whether any provisions for impairment in value are adequate, which may mean examining copies of accounts of companies in which investments are held.

Income

Income from securities can be verified with known interest rates for fixed interest securities, and a share information service (e.g. **Extel**) for listed shares. Unlisted share income must be verified with copies of the accounts.

Conclusion

There are three main categories of fixed asset (tangible, intangible and investments) and the verification procedures for each are similar. It is, however, necessary to bear in mind the special legal and accounting standard provisions which apply to particular types of assets.

SELF-TEST QUESTIONS

Fixed assets

1 State four examples of intangible assets. (1.1, 3.1)

Verification procedures

2 How is ownership verified for freehold land and buildings? (2.2)

Investments

3 Describe verification procedures relating to the existence and ownership of fixed asset investments. (4.4)

EXAM-TYPE QUESTIONS

Question 1: Engineering company

You are part of an audit team engaged upon the audit of an engineering company which has a substantial number of items of plant and machinery in its books.

Required:

(a) Explain how you would establish that the fixed assets which had been purchased during the year had been properly authorised by the directors. **(4 marks)**

(b) Explain the function of a fixed asset register, why it is necessary for the company to maintain such a register and what use you would make of it in the course of your audit. **(4 marks)**

(c) State the procedures you would expect to be in operation concerning the scrapping of plant and machinery. **(4 marks)**

(d) Explain how depreciation rates should be authorised and state how you would satisfy yourself that these rates were adequate. **(4 marks)**

(e) The company does not wish to charge depreciation on assets which are not in use. Explain the basis on which you would decide whether or not this decision was satisfactory. **(4 marks)**

(Total: 20 marks)

Question 2: Stocks and shares

For some companies investments in stocks and shares represent a substantial portion of total assets; for others investments are only temporary assets, or merely reflect incidental aspects of company operations. For the auditor, investments in stocks and shares represent assets with high inherent audit risk.

Required:

(a) List five audit objectives sought by the auditor when examining investments in stocks and shares. **(5 marks)**

(b) Explain what is meant by 'inherent audit risk' and show why investments in stocks and shares represent assets with a high inherent audit risk. **(6 marks)**

(c) Describe the audit procedures which would verify the existence and ownership of investments in stocks and shares. **(5 marks)**

(d) Describe how the auditor would determine that all investment income from stocks and shares had been properly recorded in the accounting records. **(4 marks)**

(Total: 20 marks)

Question 3: Springfield Nurseries

Your firm is the auditor of Springfield Nurseries, a company operating three large garden centres which sell plants, shrubs and trees, garden furniture and gardening equipment (such as lawnmowers and sprinklers) to the general public. You are involved in the audit of the company's fixed assets. The main categories of fixed assets are as follows:

- land and buildings (all of which are owned outright by the company, none of which are leased)
- computers (on which an integrated stock control and sales system is operated)
- a number of large and small motor vehicles, mostly used for the delivery of stock to customers
- equipment for packaging and pricing products.

The company holds records of these assets on a computerised fixed asset register. The depreciation rates used are as follows:

- buildings 5% each year on cost
- computers and motor vehicles 20% each year on the reducing balance basis
- equipment 15% each year on cost.

You are concerned that these depreciation rates may be inappropriate.

Required:

(a) Explain the main risks associated with financial statement assertions relating to fixed assets. **(3 marks)**

(b) List the sources of evidence available to you in verifying the ownership and cost of:

- the land and buildings
- the computers and motor vehicles. **(9 marks)**

(c) List the procedures you would perform to check the appropriateness of the depreciation rates on each of the three categories of fixed asset. **(5 marks)**

(d) Describe the action you would take if you disagreed with any of the depreciation rates used and explain the potential effect of the disagreement on your audit report. **(3 marks)**

(Total: 20 marks)

(ACCA Pilot Paper Dec 01)

For the answers to these questions, see the 'Answers' section at the end of the book.

FEEDBACK TO ACTIVITY 1

Types of controls in a fixed asset system may include the following:

- authorisation limits and procedures, including board approval for major items
- estimates obtained for major items
- all fixed assets recorded in a register which is regularly reconciled with the nominal ledger
- regular physical checking of assets against the register
- procedures for the disposal of fixed assets
- procedures to ensure that depreciation rates are appropriate and correctly calculated
- procedures to ensure that impairments in value are detected and correctly accounted for.

FEEDBACK TO ACTIVITY 2

IFS have acquired a number of intangible fixed assets, which are:

- Goodwill. FRS 10 requires that purchased goodwill should be capitalised as an intangible fixed asset and should be amortised over its economic life. Normally, this is over a period of up to 20 years. The directors will need to decide what the appropriate economic life is and justify the treatment. Annual impairment reviews must be performed if the useful economic life is judged to be greater than 20 years.

- Brand name. Since this has been acquired as part of the acquisition, this can be capitalised separately from goodwill if its value can be measured reliably on initial recognition. In the case of Hydrospa as the leading brand in the industry, there may be a case for saying it can be capitalised separately.

- Trade mark and patents. These may be capitalised and then written off over their useful lives with any renewal fees being charged to revenue. There needs to be third party confirmation from the patent agent of the existence and title to the assets. The directors need to consider future income of the trade mark and therefore the value to be placed on it.

Chapter 13
THE AUDIT OF DEBTORS, PREPAYMENTS, BANK AND CASH

CHAPTER CONTENTS

This chapter examines the audit of debtors, prepayments, bank and cash. For these areas, much reliance is placed on third party confirmation of balances. These are areas that both internal and external auditors will be involved in auditing, and are present within every business. Bank and cash present financial risk to the company or operation under review and for this reason, appropriate controls need to be in place. There are standard procedures to be followed in debtor confirmations and bank reports.

You should bear in mind in the audit of debtors that debtors are a product of the sales cycle and therefore the control objectives of the sales cycle, which were explained in a previous chapter, are relevant.

The audit techniques and procedures shown are equally applicable to the internal auditor, who may also undertake audits of debtors, prepayments, bank and cash. These areas are important areas of risk for the internal auditor to consider and they are likely to form part of larger audits rather than necessarily audited in their own right. The internal auditor will approach the audit in the standard way of planning, evaluating risks, assessing internal controls and conducting testing and substantive procedures. Relevant records may be computer based.

Objectives

By the time you have finished this chapter you should be able to:

- describe, and tabulate for inclusion in a work programme, the substantive procedures used in obtaining evidence in relation to debtors and prepayments, and the related income statement entries
- explain the purpose of substantive procedures in relation to the financial statement assertions concerning debtors and prepayments
- describe and tabulate for inclusion in a work programme the substantive procedures used in obtaining evidence in relation to bank and cash, and the related income statement entries
- explain the purpose of substantive procedures in relation to financial statement assertions concerning bank and cash
- explain the procedures involved in a bank report.

1 Debtors

1.1 Internal control over debtors

This is a revision of previous chapters on controls. The objectives of internal controls over debtors are to ensure that:

- all goods despatched are invoiced
- invoicing is at correct price and discount
- goods are only despatched on credit to approved customers
- invoices are recorded and related to subsequent cash receipts
- debtors balances are controlled and bad debts pursued
- credit notes are approved.

KEY POINT

Internal control over **debtors** should be such that the possibility of any falsification is eliminated.

In addition, the internal control over debtors should be such that the possibility of any falsification of the debtors' accounts is eliminated. An important part of the controls would be to ensure that the cashier does not have access to the sales ledger, and the sales ledger clerk does not have access to cash received. Thus, the possibility of '**teeming** and **lading**' (i.e. the offsetting of one debtor's cash received against another debtor's account to cover up a misappropriation of the first debtor's cash received) could only be brought about by collusion. Collusion, you will remember, is an inherent limitation of any system of internal control.

1.2 The audit of debtors

Substantive procedures consist of the following.

Control account

The auditor should obtain a list of the debtors balances in the sales ledger and agree the total with the control account.

Year end balances

- Reviewing the age of outstanding debts and considering the possibility of future bad debts.
- Checking the authority and correspondence for debts written off.
- Checking contras with the purchase ledger. Contras arise where a company owes money to, and is owed money by, the same third party. The contra nets the two amounts off.
- Checking that the debtor balances are made up of specific invoices relating to recent transactions and enquiring into any balances which appear to be in dispute, or old.
- Direct confirmation of balances with debtors. This will be considered further in the next section.
- Review the individual accounts of major customers and those that appear irregular either by nature, composition or size of the balances or the transactions therein.
- Review and test the year end cut-off procedures for sales.

Analytical procedures

- A comparison of debtor days ratio $\frac{\text{debtors}}{\text{sales}} \times 365$ with budget or prior years to identify and investigate any significant variations.

  Separate computations may be appropriate to take into account different classes of business, varying credit terms and other factors.
- A comparison of the proportion of the debts in different age bands to prior years. This information should be available directly from the client.

KEY POINT

A high incidence of **old debts** may indicate poor economic conditions or credit control.

A high or increasing incidence of **old debts** may indicate either poor or deteriorating economic conditions or credit control. In such instances, the work on bad debts and any year-end doubtful debt provision will become critical.

Bad debts

Audit procedures to confirm the appropriate provision for doubtful debts:

- the company's previous bad debt experiences
- evidence from debtors' circularisation (refer to next section)
- aged analysis of debtors

- post-balance sheet events (see below and later chapters). A key test is for the auditor to review cash received after the year end from debtors at the year end. If the debtor has subsequently paid, then that debt was not bad or doubtful at the year end.

In the light of this information, the auditor will have to consider whether the provision made by management in the accounts is adequate.

KEY POINT

Specific provisions are made for debts known to be bad or very doubtful. **General provisions** are based on past experience.

Both specific and general provisions may be made. Specific provisions are made for those debts which are known to be bad or doubtful. General provisions (usually a percentage of total debtors) are based on past experience.

Returns inwards and credit notes

KEY POINT

Controls over **returns inwards** and **credit notes** should prevent the fraudulent cancellation or hiding of company debts.

There should be strict internal controls over **returns inwards** and **credit notes** issued, to prevent the fraudulent cancellation of a company debt, or to 'hide' bad debts.

From an audit point of view the major problem is likely to be the issue of a substantial volume of credit notes after the year end to cancel false sales made before the year end. This is known as '**window dressing**'. For this reason, both the system, and post-balance sheet events, should be carefully examined.

Goods on sale or return

KEY POINT

Goods on **sale or return** should not be included in sales or debtors, until the right to return the goods has lapsed.

Goods on **sale or return** should not be included in sales or debtors. Instead they form part of the inventories, in customers' hands.

It is very difficult for the auditor to establish whether the goods included in sales do in fact have a right of return. Evidence will be provided by:

- the customs of the trade
- past experience
- any formal written contracts
- the volume of returns.

Prepayments

DEFINITION

Prepayments are amounts paid for in one period which relate to the next period.

Prepayments are commonly made for rent, gas, electricity and telephone standing charges and other items where the expenditure has been paid for in the current period, but relates to the next period. Prepayments are often immaterial and reliance is often placed on analytical procedures. Nevertheless, as year-end adjustments, there are rarely any controls over prepayments and any errors are likely to be those of understatement. Auditors generally are concerned with the overstatement of assets. They will adopt the following procedures:

- considering the client's own system (if any) for accounting for prepayments
- obtaining a schedule of prepayments, ensuring that it is cast correctly and comparing it with prior year prepayments and performing other analytical procedures
- test checking a sample of prepayments for correct calculation, referring to supporting documentation.

Disclosure

EXAM HINT

The three categories relevant to the exam are **trade debtors, other debtors**, and **prepayments and accrued income**.

There are three categories of debtors from the CA 1985 formats relevant to this exam:

- trade debtors
- other debtors
- prepayments and accrued income.

Debtors due within one year and debtors due after one year should be disclosed separately within the notes to the accounts.

2 Verification of debtors by direct circularisation

One of the most effective methods for confirming debtor balances is by the auditor communicating directly with the customers of the client to seek direct confirmation of the amounts outstanding. ISA 505 *External confirmations* provides useful guidance to the auditor in carrying out such an exercise.

2.1 Circularisation

KEY POINT

Circularisation must be carried out on the client's authority, but under the control of the auditor.

This must be carried out on the client's authority and on client headed paper, but under the control of the auditor. Should the client refuse such authorisation, then the auditor will have to consider the adequacy of other evidence in forming their opinion. Clients rarely refuse, as such circularisations are commonplace and are an efficient way of obtaining evidence. If no other evidence is available, the auditor might have to consider qualifying the audit opinion.

The circularisation procedure satisfies a number of objectives:

- strong evidence whether debtors are overstated – customers can usually be relied on to complain if the balance they are supposed to owe is too large
- weaker evidence whether debtors are understated – customers are less likely to complain if the balance is too small
- indirect evidence of the sales figures
- evidence of the functioning of internal controls
- evidence of the efficiency of the cut-off procedures if carried out at the year end
- evidence of the existence of debtors.

Evidence is also obtained as to irregularities such as 'teeming and lading' and 'window dressing' which are referred to above. It does not, however, give evidence as to *recoverability*. Our debtor may agree that they *owe* us a lot of money, but this does not guarantee that they will *pay* us.

If the auditor has significant concerns over the recoverability of a debt he should examine what efforts have been made to obtain payment and examine any correspondence with the client. He should use his judgement to determine whether or not a doubtful debt provision is necessary.

2.2 Timing and form of circularisation

KEY POINT

Ideally, circularisation should be carried out at the year end, as this provides direct evidence of the balance sheet figures.

Ideally, the circularisation should be carried out at the year end, as this provides direct evidence of the balance sheet figures. In practice, pressures to complete the audit by a deadline may mean that the circularisation is carried out one or two months before the year end, and 'rolled forward'.

In the latter case, movements on the control accounts should be reviewed for reasonableness in the period between the circularisation and the year end.

KEY POINT

Positive confirmation asks the customer to agree or disagree with the balance; **negative confirmation** asks for a response only on disagreement.

There are two types of request:

- **positive** – customer is asked to confirm to the auditor direct whether they agree or disagree with the balance
- **negative** – customers only asked to respond if they disagree; this method may be appropriate where there are a large number of small balances, where the system is well controlled.

Positive circularisations are now generally used.

It is useful if the circularisation letter or form is accompanied by a copy of the customer's ledger account in the client's books; this makes it easier for the *customer* to reconcile differences between their records and the audit client's records.

2.3 Control of circularisation

In all cases the circularisation must be controlled by the auditor.

Selection

Customers to be circularised should be selected by the auditor from a sales ledger listing agreed to the nominal ledger control account. The auditor is primarily concerned with the overstatement of debtors. When we come to look at creditors, where we are primarily concerned with understatement, we will see that we will not necessarily select our sample from the year-end list of creditors.

Particular attention should be given to:

- old unpaid accounts
- accounts written off during the period under review
- accounts with credit balances.

The following should not be overlooked:

- accounts with nil balances
- accounts which have been paid by the date of the examination.

If a client is unwilling to circularise a particular balance because, say, there are delicate negotiations in progress, the auditor should establish that the reason is a genuine one (and not an attempt to 'cover up' a problem balance), and then perform alternative procedures such as those noted below.

Despatch

The despatch should be carried out, or supervised, by the auditor. The addresses of customers should be independently checked.

Response

Responses should be sent directly to the auditor. The auditor should check the replies against his schedule. A reminder should be sent where no replies are received.

2.4 Problems

KEY POINT

When customers fail to respond it may be possible to confirm on an individual invoice basis.

Some customers will disagree. All such disagreements must be followed up until the auditor is satisfied, and the results noted on the working papers.

Some customers will fail to respond, even after a reminder. In many cases, customers do not maintain purchase ledgers but use the so-called 'open invoice' system (unpaid invoices are entered in the ledgers, but simply held in a file until paid). In such cases it may be possible to confirm on an individual invoice basis.

If there is no means of eliciting a response, then the auditor will have to apply alternative audit procedures. These will normally involve an examination of post balance sheet events in respect of the sales ledger accounts concerned, i.e. cash received after the balance sheet date, and an inspection of invoices making up the balance together with signed delivery notes.

2.5 Evaluation of circularisation

KEY POINT

The circularisation will form a key part of the evidence in relation to the debtors figure.

After the completion of the circularisation it will form a key part of the evidence in relation to the debtors figure.

The auditor will need to evaluate the results in terms of:

- percentage response
- number of disagreements
- outcome of follow-up of disagreements
- the materiality of the amounts involved.

The evaluation will as usual require the application of the auditor's judgement to the information.

2.6 Examples of requests for third party confirmation

(a) ***Positive method – Example letter***

Swallow Limited
Bird Estate
Highcity
Beds

30 April 20X5

Hugh Allen Limited
Brow Estate
Lowtown
Beds

Dear Sirs

CONFIRMATION OF INDEBTEDNESS

1 In accordance with the request of our auditors, ABC & Co, we shall be obliged if you will confirm directly to them your indebtedness to us at 31 March 20X5 which, according to our records, amounted to £1,457.67, as shown by the enclosed statement.

2 If you are in agreement with the balance shown, please sign this letter in the space provided below and return it intact DIRECTLY TO OUR AUDITORS in the enclosed reply paid envelope.

3 If you disagree with the balance, please notify our auditors, giving full details of the difference.

PLEASE NOTE THAT THIS IS NOT A REQUEST FOR PAYMENT.

We thank you for your co-operation in the above matter.

Yours faithfully

Swallow Limited

Reply to: ABC & Co
Certified Accountants
2 Low Close
Downtown
Beds

The balance shown above is correct/incorrect*.

Signature: ______________________ *Position:* ______________________

Date: ______________________

Details of difference:

____

**Please delete as appropriate.*

(b) ***Negative method – Example letter***

Dear Sirs

CONFIRMATION OF INDEBTEDNESS

(Paragraph 1 per positive method)

(Paragraph 2 omitted)

If you disagree with the balance, please inform our AUDITORS DIRECTLY using the enclosed reply paid envelope, giving full details of the difference by completing the form below . . . .

Yours faithfully

Etc.

The balance shown above is incorrect.

Signature: ______________________ *Position:* ______________________

Date: ______________________

Details of difference:

____

ACTIVITY 1

In carrying out an audit, the auditor appraises and tests the system of internal control in order to ascertain that it is capable of processing transactions or determining quantities and values completely and accurately. The auditor further carries out substantive tests in an attempt to ensure that the transactions, assets and liabilities recorded in the accounting records, upon which the figures in the financial statements are based, are in fact completely and accurately recorded.

You are required to:

List the substantive tests the auditor would carry out to verify the values attributed to trade debtors in a company's financial statements.

Feedback to this activity is at the end of the chapter.

3 Liquid assets

Cash and bank balances are **liquid assets** and include:

- notes and coins
- bank current accounts
- bank deposit accounts.

KEY POINT

Liquid assets are the most vulnerable of the company's assets but they are amongst the most easily verified.

Because of their liquidity, these assets represent the most vulnerable of all the company's assets. On the other hand, they are amongst the most easily verified, because they can be confirmed directly by third parties or by physical counts. Both internal and external auditors will be involved at different stages in verification of cash and bank balances and will follow similar check procedures.

Note

KEY POINT

Cash and bank carry a **primary risk** of financial loss.

Cash and bank are financial assets and there is a primary risk of financial loss because of:

- fraudulent activity or misappropriation of funds, particularly where large amounts of cash are involved or where there are devolved authorities for activities surrounding cash and banking

- inappropriate or inadequate banking arrangements for the area under review resulting in financial loss
- delays in making bankings resulting in financial loss or overdraft
- excessive banking charges resulting in financial loss.

3.1 Internal controls over cash

KEY POINT

Internal control over liquid assets should be very tight.

This is a revision of previous chapters on controls. Internal control over liquid assets should be very tight. Any weaknesses increase the risk of fraud and should be drawn to management's attention. The objectives of internal controls over cash are to ensure that:

- all sums are received and subsequently accounted for
- no payments are made which should not be made
- all receipts and payments are promptly and accurately recorded.

3.2 Verification

KEY POINT

Audit **verification** comprises independent confirmation of **bank balances** and an examination of **bank reconciliations**.

There are two stages of verification:

- confirmation from bank, etc. of the balance – this is considered in detail below
- examination of the bank reconciliations.

The second stage is of great importance. The reconciliation should establish that:

- differences between the bank and the client's records can be specifically identified
- the differences are differences of timing
- any old differences have been cleared
- all major differences are cleared in the post-balance sheet period.

3.3 Example reconciliation

Reconciliations usually start with the balance per the **cash book** and reconcile this to the balance per the *bank statement*, although the reverse is also acceptable.

Bank reconciliation as at 31 July 20X7

	£
Balance per cash book	12,345.22
Add: Unpresented cheques	223.46
Less: Outstanding lodgements	(16.34)
Difference	1.34
Balance per bank statement	12,553.68

Most of the differences above are timing differences. Cheques will have been sent to suppliers on the last day of the period but the suppliers will not have had a chance to take the cheques to the bank and as far as the bank is concerned, no payment has yet been made. These cheques are '**unpresented**'.

'**Outstanding lodgements**' are cheques received by the company and paid into the bank, but not yet credited by the bank.

3.4 Audit of bank reconciliations

The balances per the cash book and the bank statement can be quickly checked to the relevant records. Unpresented cheques and outstanding lodgements can be checked that they appear in one record but not in the other.

KEY POINT

All **unpresented cheques** and outstanding lodgements should be checked to ensure that they do '**clear**' shortly after the period end.

All unpresented cheques and outstanding lodgements should be checked to ensure that they do '**clear**' shortly after the period end by reviewing bank statements just after the period end. Any old items should be considered carefully. If a cheque has not been presented to the bank after six months, it may be that the supplier has lost it or has gone out of business. In any case the cheque will be 'stale' and the bank will not honour it even if it is presented. The auditor should consider the need for the creditor to be reinstated and a new cheque issued, or the need for the cheque to be written back as income.

Unexplained differences, even if small, must be investigated as they may represent large errors in both directions that net each other off.

It is sometimes necessary to adjust the cash book *before* the reconciliation is performed.

	£
Draft balance per cash book as at 31 July 20X7	12,153.32
Add: sundry receipts per bank statement not in cash book	123.45
Less: direct debits per bank statement not in cash book	(21.55)
Add: error in addition of cash book	90.00
Adjusted balance per cash book as at 31 July 20X7	12,345.22

Again, all of the adjusting items need to be checked to their source.

Reconciliations are normally performed by the client on a monthly basis and should show evidence of review. The auditor should check that they are cast correctly.

ACTIVITY **2**

You are undertaking an audit of the liquid assets of RatCo. The company have a petty cash system for small purchases but also deal with a significant level of cash, since much of their income is received in the form of cash payments. RatCo also have three bank accounts used for different purposes but for the same legal entity.

You are required to:

Identify the risks that you would examine for the liquid assets of RatCo and outline the controls that you would expect to be in operation.

Feedback to this activity is at the end of the chapter.

4 Bank reports for audit purposes

KEY POINT

Obtaining a **bank certificate** is an *essential* part of the audit and is encouraged by Practice Note 16; a **standard request letter** has been agreed with the British Bankers Association.

Obtaining a bank certificate is an *essential* part of the audit and is encouraged by Practice Note 16 *Bank reports for audit purposes*. In order to assist the banks in the administration of the letters, a standard request letter has been agreed with the British Bankers Association. The procedure for sending out the standard letter and a copy of the standard letter itself are set out below.

4.1 Procedure

- The standard letter set out in the Appendix to PN 16 should be sent on each occasion *by the auditor* on their *own notepaper* to the manager of the bank branch with which the client has the prime business arrangement. Note that debtors' circularisations are sent out on the client's notepaper.
- Auditors should ensure that the bank receives the client's *authority* to permit disclosure. The clearing banks state that this authority must be evidenced by either:
  - the client's *countersignature* to the standard letter
  - a specific authority contained in an *accompanying letter*

  - a reference in the standard letter to a *standing* written authority given on a specified earlier date, which remains in force. An ongoing standard authority is the preferred approach.
- Wherever possible, the letter should reach the branch manager at least two weeks in advance of the date of the client's financial year end. Special arrangements should be made with the bank if, because of time constraints, a reply is needed within a few days.
- The bank confirmation letter has been simplified by PN 16 and is now restructured into two sections.
  - Information applicable when a client's banking relationship is 'simple'. This is the usual situation.
  - Supplementary information that may be applicable when the banking relationship is more complex.

KEY POINT

The auditor's request must specify whether the auditor is requesting the 'standard' or 'supplementary information'.

The auditor's request must, therefore, specify whether the auditor is requesting the 'standard information' or whether 'supplementary information' is also required. Where supplementary or additional information is requested, banks may charge their customers a fee for providing the information, and responses to auditors are likely to take longer to process.

4.2 Appendices to Practice Note 16

(a) ***Example of confirmation request letter***

To: *XYZ Bank PLC*
25 ABC Street
Warrington
Cheshire
WA1 1XQ

Dear Sirs

In accordance with the agreed practice for provision of information to auditors, please forward information on our mutual client(s) as detailed below on behalf of the bank, its branches and subsidiaries. This request and your response will not create any contractual or other duty with us.

COMPANIES OR OTHER BUSINESS ENTITIES
(attach a separate listing if necessary)

ABC Ltd
DEF Ltd

AUDIT CONFIRMATION DATE *31 December 20X4*

Information required	Tick
Standard	✓
Trade finance	
Derivative and commodity trading	
Custodian arrangements	
Other information (see attached)	

The Authority to Disclose Information signed by your customer is attached/already held by you (delete as appropriate). Please advise us if this Authority is insufficient for you to provide full disclosure of the information requested.

The contact name is [*John Caller*] Telephone [*020 7234 5678*]

Yours faithfully

[*PQR Accountants*]

(b) ***Example of authority to disclose information***

To: *XYZ Bank PLC*
25 ABC Street
Warrington
Cheshire WA1 1XQ

ABC Ltd
DEF Ltd

I/We authorise *XYZ Bank PLC* including all branches and subsidiaries to provide to our auditor *PQR Accountants* any information that they may request from you regarding all and any of our accounts and dealings with you.

____

signature(s)

(c) ***Example of 'standard' request for information***

1 **Account and balance details**

- Give full titles of all Bank accounts including loans (whether in sterling or another currency), together with their account numbers and balances. For accounts closed during the 12 months up to the audit confirmation date give the account details and date of closure.

  Note: Also give details where your customer's name is joined with that of other parties and where the account is in a trade name.

- State if any account or balances are subject to any restriction(s) whatsoever. Indicate the nature and extent of the restriction, e.g. garnishee order.

2 **Facilities**

Give the following details of all loans, overdrafts, and associated guarantees and indemnities:

- term
- repayment frequency and/or review date
- details of period of availability of agreed finance, i.e. finance remaining undrawn
- details of the facility limit.

3 **Securities**

With reference to the facilities detailed in (2) above give the following details:

- Any security formally charged (date, ownership and type of charge). State whether the security supports facilities granted by the Bank to the customer or to another party.

  Note: Give details if a security is limited in amount or to a specific borrowing or if to your knowledge there is a prior, equal or subordinate charge.
- Where there are any arrangements for set-off balances or compensating balances, e.g. back to back loans, give particulars (i.e. date, type of document and accounts covered) of any acknowledgement of set-off, whether given by specific letter of set-off or incorporated in some other document.

4 **Additional banking relationships**

State if you are aware of the customer(s) having any additional relationships with branches or subsidiaries of the Bank not covered by the response. Supply a list of branches, etc.

(d) ***Example of request for 'supplementary' information***

Request for trade finance information

On occasion auditors may request trade finance information. Responses must be given in the order as below and if no information is available then this must be stated as 'None' in the response.

5 **Trade finance**

Give the currencies and amounts of the following:

- Letters of credit
- Acceptances
- Bills discounted with recourse to the customer or any subsidiary or related party of the customer.
- Bonds, guarantees, indemnities or other undertakings given to the Bank by the customer in favour of third parties (including separately any such items in favour of any subsidiary or related party of the customer). Give details of the parties in favour of whom guarantees or undertakings have been given, whether such guarantees or undertakings are written or oral and their nature.
- Bonds, guarantees, indemnities or other undertakings given by you, on your customer's behalf, stating whether there is recourse to your customer and/or to its parent or any other company within the group.
- Other contingent liabilities not already detailed.

Note: For each item state the nature and extent of any facility limits and details of period of availability of agreed facility.

Securities

With reference to the facilities detailed in the above section give the following:

- Details of any security formally charged (date, ownership and type of charge). State whether the security supports facilities granted by the Bank to the customer or to another party.

Note: Give details if a security is limited in amount or to a specific borrowing or if to your knowledge there is prior, equal or subordinate charge.

- Where there are any arrangements for set-off of balances or compensating balances, e.g. back to back loans, give particulars (i.e., date, type of document and accounts covered) of any acknowledgement of set-off, whether given by specific letter of set-off or incorporated in some other document.

EXAM HINT

You should learn the main headings in the standard request letter:

- account and balance details
- facilities
- securities
- additional banking relationships.

4.3 Commentary on the standard letter

You do not need to memorise the contents of these letters, but you should learn the main headings in the standard request letter:

- **Account and balance details** – This refers to all accounts held including loans and joint accounts, and also encompasses accrued charges and the bank's right of set-off (i.e. the bank's right to offset debit and credit balances).
- **Facilities** – This refers to all loans, overdrafts and guarantees given. Such information might lead to the disclosure of contingent liabilities, or might shed light on the going concern status of the client.
- **Securities** – This refers to fixed and floating charges on securities held.
- **Additional banking relationships** – This is where the auditor seeks to find unrecorded assets or liabilities by asking the bank whether it is aware of any other branches where the client holds an account.

Conclusion

Debtors may be a major asset of the company and the main procedure involves the circularisation of debtors to obtain third party evidence.

Bank balances are readily verifiable with a third party. The bank letter can also be used to ask other questions such as about guarantees.

Testing of controls and substantive procedures on debtors and bank and cash balances are equally applicable to internal auditors.

SELF-TEST QUESTIONS

Debtors

1 What substantive tests should the auditor perform in the audit of year end debtor balances? (1.2)

2 How can analytical procedures assist in the audit of debtors? (1.2)

Verification of debtors by direct circularisation

3 What are the two possible methods for drawing up a debtors' circularisation? (2.2)

4 How should an auditor evaluate the results of a debtors' circularisation? (2.5)

Liquid assets

5 What are the two stages of verification of cash and bank balances? (3.2)

Bank reports for audit purposes

6 What will the bank require from the client when it receives a letter from the auditor? (4.1)

EXAM-TYPE QUESTIONS

Question 1: Askwith Limited

A senior audit clerk is briefing an experienced junior auditor who is about to commence the audit of the debtors of Askwith Limited. The sales ledger, says the senior clerk, is maintained by the client on a mainframe computer. Sales invoice and credit note data are fed to the computer via 12 terminals in regional offices. All cash entries, journal entries relating to bad debts and other adjustments, and any other special entries are input via two terminals located at the client's head office. The computer produces, as a monthly routine, an aged debtors' schedule containing on average 3,000 live balances. Your task, the senior clerk tells the junior auditor, is to verify the accuracy of the aged debtors' schedule including arranging for circulars to be sent to a representative sample of debtors. To assist the junior in this task he hands him a copy of the audit programme.

The audit programme contains, among other things, the following:

- for balances over £1,000 at the year-end, use special computer audit program to dump transaction details for one month prior to the year-end and for one month after the year-end
- circularise debtors (seeking a positive response) and follow up those who do not reply
- test cut-off using dumped transactions.

The new junior audit clerk is a little confused by some of the terminology being used, the reasons underlying his senior's requests and the detail of the techniques being used.

Required:

(a) State the steps to be taken by the auditor where no reply is received to the initial circularisation of debtors and explain what alternative procedures might be used to verify the balances. **(5 marks)**

(b) Explain the significance of cut-off tests relating to trade debtors and suggest *THREE* appropriate detailed tests. **(5 marks)**

(Total: 10 marks)

Question 2: Defaulters Limited

You are currently carrying out the interim audit of Defaulters Limited. The audit senior has asked you to carry out the cash audit, and as a part of your work you are about to review the bank reconciliation statement of the company. The cash book showed a debit balance of £37,802 as at 31 May 20X1 which included the previous week's receipts of cash which had not yet been paid into the bank. A receipt of £200 on the bank statement has not yet been entered into the cash book, and the balance per the bank statement was £31,100. You have found that the unpresented cheques were as follows.

Cheque number	*Amount (£)*	*Date*
134	232	1.3.20X1
183	300	2.4.20X1
284	506	12.4.20X1
861	380	31.5.20X1
862	412	31.5.20X1
863	290	31.5.20X1

The cashier has informed you that the receipts not yet deposited with the bank were £7,588 and has given you the following bank reconciliation statement.

			£	£
Balance per cash book 31 May 20X1				37,802
Add:	Unpresented cheque	861	380	
		862	412	
		863	290	
				1,082
				38,884
Less:	Undeposited receipts		7,588	
	Petty cash balance		196	
				7,784
Balance per bank 31 May 20X1				31,100
Deduct unrecorded credit				(200)
Actual cash 31 May 20X1				30,900

You ascertain that the internal auditors had reviewed the cash transactions during the month of May and were satisfied that the cash book balance of £37,802 was, in fact, correct but were not responsible for preparing the bank reconciliation statement. You have not as yet verified the petty cash system which is maintained on an imprest.

Required:

(a) Prepare an audit schedule showing the amount of cash which the cashier may have misappropriated from the company listing the audit work which would be carried out in order to verify this amount. **(9 marks)**

(b) Explain how the cashier had attempted to conceal the possible theft of cash from the company. **(3 marks)**

(c) Describe two weaknesses in internal control which have contributed to the theft of cash by the cashier. **(4 marks)**

(d) Explain the action the auditor should take when he suspects the existence of possible improprieties. **(4 marks)**

(Total: 20 marks)

(ACCA Jun 91)

Question 3: Debtors internal control systems

There are many reasons for maintaining internal control systems. These include the need to ensure that:

- transactions are properly authorised
- transactions are promptly and accurately recorded
- access to assets and records is properly authorised
- recorded assets represent actual assets.

In the absence of internal controls, errors, omissions and misappropriation of assets are likely and external and internal auditors pay particular attention to both the design and operation of internal control systems.

Debtors is an area in which most organisations expect internal controls to be operating effectively.

Required:

(a) In the context of debtors, list and describe the types of error, omission and misappropriation of assets that can occur in practice where internal controls are weak or non-existent. **(4 marks)**

(b) Explain why even a good system of internal control will not necessarily prevent or detect errors, omissions and the misappropriation of assets in a debtors system, and explain why a good system of internal control is important to auditors. **(4 marks)**

(c) List the main internal controls that you would expect to be in operation in the debtors system at a small manufacturing company with a computerised accounting system. **(9 marks)**

(d) Explain why external auditors seek to rely on the proper operation of internal controls wherever possible. **(3 marks)**

(Total: 20 marks)

For answers to these questions, see the 'Answers' section at the end of the book.

FEEDBACK TO ACTIVITY **1**

Substantive tests for the audit of trade debtors:

- Obtain a list of sales ledger balances and agree the total of the balances to the sales ledger control account and the nominal ledger.
- Check the cast on the list of balances.
- Agree a sample of the balances to the individual sales ledger accounts.
- Carry out a debtors' circularisation to obtain direct confirmation of a sample of balances.
- Review the balances for old/disputed debts and ensure that adequate provision has been made for these.
- Ensure that contras with the purchase ledger have been authorised.
- Review after-date cash receipts for a sample of debtors, including doubtful debtors.
- Review after-date credit notes for items which should be reversed.
- Check that the cut-off at the year end between sales and stock is correct.
- Ensure that all debts are collectable and that the disclosure in the financial statements is correct.

FEEDBACK TO ACTIVITY **2**

RatCo liquid assets – Example risks:

- A significant level of RatCo income is received in the form of cash, providing risks of fraud or misappropriation of funds.
- Failure to use petty cash for business purposes, excess holdings of petty cash or loss of petty cash may result in financial loss or inappropriate use of assets.
- Delays may occur in banking of income received, resulting in financial loss.
- Inappropriate or inadequate banking arrangements may be in place, resulting in financial loss.
- Excessive bank charges, resulting in financial loss.
- Confusion or manipulation of the use of the three different bank accounts.

RatCo liquid assets – Example controls:

- Recording of all cash received and cash paid out.
- Procedures for banking all receipts daily.
- Authorisation of payments and receipts.
- Cash receipt books regularly checked and reconciled against bankings.
- Confirmation from the bank of the balance of the accounts.
- Bank reconciliations carried out and independently reviewed, with any exceptions promptly investigated and explained.
- Clearly designated bank accounts, showing title, purpose and use of account.

Chapter 14
THE AUDIT OF STOCKS

CHAPTER CONTENTS

This chapter considers stock, which is one of the principal assets in many companies. You can expect a question on stock in most exam sittings.

Both the internal and external auditor needs to understand and apply appropriate and relevant techniques and procedures when auditing stocks. Internal auditors are more likely to be involved in auditing stocks during the financial year as they will be concerned with internal controls over the stock control system. Whereas the external auditor is principally concerned with ensuring that the stock valuation at year end (and therefore the figure included in the financial statements) is accurate.

Many companies in the modern environment operate computer based stock records, which may be referred to in examination questions.

Objectives

By the time you have finished this chapter you should be able to:

- understand the risks associated with stocks
- discuss the types of internal controls expected
- describe and tabulate for inclusion in a work programme the substantive procedures used in obtaining evidence in relation to stock
- explain the purpose of substantive procedures in relation to financial statement assertions concerning stock.

1 The audit of stocks and work in progress

1.1 The importance of stocks and work in progress

Factors which make this asset important from the audit viewpoint include the following:

KEY POINT

Stock balances have a direct effect on reported **profit**.

- Misstatement of **stock balances** has a direct effect on reported **profit**. It is the easiest asset for management to manipulate and thereby manipulate profits from one accounting period to another.
- Some stocks can be very difficult for an auditor to identify. There may be thousands of different lines of stock; there may be some stock items of a very specialist nature.
- The quantities of stock held at a given moment may be difficult to establish. It may not be possible to cease stock movements during the stocktake and cut-off may be hard to establish with precision.

KEY POINT

Net realisable values for stock may be hard to establish, and **work in progress** balances may be intangible.

- Valuation may be difficult. The problems of specialist stock have already been mentioned; but even for less specialised lines there may be difficulties to do with obsolescence etc, and as a consequence **net realisable values (NRV)** may be hard to establish. The amount of overheads that can be attributed to stock may be subjective in nature.
- Stock losses from pilferage, wastage etc. may be difficult to control.
- Some very significant work in progress (WIP) balances may be intangible in nature (e.g. film production costs).

1.2 Legal and professional requirements

DEFINITION

Stocks and work in progress includes materials, bought in parts, work in progress and finished goods.

There are a variety of official pronouncements in connection with stock:

- **ISA 501** guidance on 'Attendance at physical inventory counting'.
- **SSAP 9** *Stocks and long-term contracts.*
- **Companies Act 1985**, **S222** which requires that proper accounting records are kept. These include statements of stock and statements of stocktaking.

The term **stocks and work in progress** includes raw materials, bought in parts, work in progress (manufactured goods in an incomplete state) and finished goods.

1.3 CA85 Disclosure requirements

KEY POINT

CA85 requires stock to be disclosed under **raw materials**, **WIP**, **finished goods** and **payments on account**.

The Companies Act 1985 requires stock to be disclosed under four categories:

- raw materials and consumables
- work in progress
- finished goods and goods for resale
- payments on account.

All current assets (including stock) must normally be stated at the lower of their **net realisable value** and their **purchase price** or **production cost**.

1.4 SSAP 9 *Stocks and long-term contracts*

KEY POINT

SSAP 9 requires individual items of stock to be stated at the lower of **cost** and **NRV**.

SSAP 9 requires individual items of stock to be stated at the lower of **cost** and **NRV**.

Cost is that expenditure which has been incurred, in the normal course of business, in bringing the product or service to its present location and condition (including appropriate costs of conversion). Conversion costs include direct costs such as labour which relates to WIP and finished goods, and production overheads.

Production overheads cause particular problems in valuation and will be examined later in the chapter.

Net realisable value is the estimated or actual selling price (net of trade discounts but before settlement discounts) less further costs to completion and further costs of marketing, selling or distribution.

Cost flow assumptions as to the items in stock, e.g. FIFO and average cost, are allowed to be used to value the items in stock provided the assumption approximates to real flows into and out of stock.

SSAP 9 gives guidance on practical problems in respect of stock, these are considered later in the chapter.

2 Risks associated with stock

KEY POINT

The risks associated with stock vary depending on the nature of the item and can be significant.

It is worth summarising the key risks associated with stock:

- inadequate or inappropriate stocks held to meet the demands of sales and production
- overstocking resulting in poor cash flow and financial loss
- inaccurate or incomplete record of stock movements resulting in lack of awareness of the stock position and difficulties in meeting customer needs
- lack of security over stocks resulting in loss, theft or misappropriation
- stock inappropriately stored resulting in **damage** or deterioration
- inappropriate or unsatisfactory stock write offs or disposals resulting in financial loss or damage to reputation

- **obsolete** stock held or incorrectly supplied to customers, resulting in financial loss and damage to reputation
- lack of information held on stock holdings resulting in poor decision and inability to meet the demands and objectives of the business.

3 Internal controls

Control objectives

KEY POINT

Stock controls focus on goods movement, authorisation procedures and physical counts.

Although **stock records** may vary considerably from client to client, the control objectives of a sound system of internal control over inventories are the same in all cases, namely:

- authorisation and purchase procedures
- control over goods inwards
- inventory records substantiated by physical counts
- control over despatches and goods outwards
- adequate steps taken to identify all stock for which provisions may be required
- stock levels controlled so that materials are available when required but that stock is not unnecessarily large.

Control procedures over inventories

KEY POINT

Stock control procedures focus on **document control**, **accuracy**, **control accounts** and the audit of **assets** against **records**.

Approval and control of documents

- Issues from stocks should be made only on properly authorised requisitions.
- Reviews of damaged, obsolete and slow moving inventories should be carried out. Any write-offs should be authorised.

Arithmetical accuracy

- All receipts and issues should be recorded on stock cards, cross-referenced to the appropriate GRN or requisition document.
- The costing department should allocate direct and overhead costs to the value of work-in-progress according to the stage of completion reached.
- To do this, standard costs are normally used. Such standards must be regularly reviewed to ensure that they relate to actual costs being incurred.
- If the value of work-in-progress is directly comparable with the number of units produced, checks should periodically be made of actual units against work-in-progress records.

Control accounts

- Total stock records may be maintained and integrated with the main accounting system; if so, they should be reconciled to detailed stock records and discrepancies investigated.

Comparison of assets to records

- Stock levels should be periodically checked against the records by a person independent of the stores personnel, and material differences investigated.
- Where continuous stock records are not kept adequately, a full stocktake should be held at least once a year.
- Maximum and minimum stock levels should be pre-determined and regularly reviewed for adequacy.
- Re-order quantities should be pre-determined and regularly reviewed for adequacy.

Access to assets and records

- Separate centres should be identified at which goods are held.
- Deliveries of goods from suppliers should pass through a goods inwards section to the stores. All goods should pass through stores and hence be recorded and checked as received.
- Stocks should be held in their locations so that they are safe from damage or theft.
- All stock lines should be identified and held together, e.g. in bins which are marked with all relevant information as to size, grade, origin, title for identification.
- Access to the stores should be restricted.

KEY POINT

Tests of controls for stock focus on material movement authorisation, and the control of stock against records.

Tests of controls

- Observe physical security of stocks and environment in which they are held.
- Test procedures for recording of stock movements in and out of stock.
- Test authorisation for adjustments to stock records.
- Test authorisation for write-off or scrapping of stocks.
- Test controls over recording of stock movements belonging to third parties.
- Observe physical security of stocks and environment in which they are held.
- Test procedures for recording of stock movements in and out of stock.
- Test authorisation for adjustments to stock records.
- Test authorisation for write-off or scrapping of stocks.
- Test controls over recording of stock movements belonging to third parties.
- Test procedures for authorisation for stock movements, i.e. the use made of authorised goods received and despatch notes.
- Inspect reconciliations of stock counts to stock records (this gives overall comfort on the adequacy of controls over the recording of stock).
- Check sequences of despatch and goods received notes for completeness.
- Assess adequacy of stocktaking procedures and attend count to ensure they are carried out.

ACTIVITY 1

What are the main categories of internal control over stock?

Feedback to this activity is at the end of the chapter.

4 Physical counts

KEY POINT

Stock records substantiated by **physical counts** are the most important.

From the audit point of view, the stock records substantiated by physical counts (stocktakes) are most important. **Physical counts** for the various stock categories may be taken at various intervals:

- at or close to the year end (**periodical**)
- on a continuous basis over the whole year (**continuous**)
- some combination of the above.

4.1 Client's procedures at stocktaking

KEY POINT

The two methods of stocktaking are **continuous** and **periodical**.

The two methods of stocktaking are **continuous** and **periodical**. Note that the periodical stocktake need not be exactly at the year end provided that the client's internal control procedures over stock are satisfactory. In fact it is common practice to take stock some time before the year end, then to update for movements between the stocktaking date and the year end. This procedure is especially useful where the accounts are being produced to a tight deadline.

4.2 Continuous stocktaking

Where a suitable record of stock is maintained, it is often backed up by a programme of continuous stocktaking as part of general stock control procedures. This programme should ensure the following outcomes.

- Each item is physically inspected at least once a year, and more frequently in the case of items liable to loss etc.
- Adequate records are kept up to date.
- The records are amended as a result of physical inspection, and there are appropriate reports and investigation procedures for discrepancies.
- Two persons carry out each check, and there is a rotation of pairing of the checkers.

KEY POINT

Continuous stock checking can cause less disruption, be more accurate and generate increased discipline in storekeepers.

There are several advantages of continuous stock checking:

- no disruption caused by a periodical stocktake
- more accurate and regular stocktaking, earlier identification of errors and slow moving stocks, etc.
- increased discipline over storekeepers caused by the surprise elements of random checks
- providing the above conditions are met, auditors can rely on the continuous stocktaking procedures, rather than a full year end count.

4.3 Periodical stocktaking

This is necessary in most cases, i.e. where continuous stocktaking is not carried out. It can also be undertaken to back up a continuous stocktaking system.

It will usually be undertaken on or around the financial year end. If undertaken around the financial year end, the time gap between the physical count and financial year end should be kept to a minimum, so as to ensure the accuracy of the records which are necessary to adjust the year end figures.

KEY POINT

Auditors must ensure that stock is **counted**, **identified** and **recorded**.

Whether continuous or periodical stocktaking occurs, the audit practice is the same, that is the auditor must ensure that the stock is properly **counted, identified** and **recorded**.

4.4 Organisation of stocktaking

KEY POINT

When organising the stocktake, the client should consider the **permanent organisation** of the stores and issue **comprehensive instructions** or procedures.

Firstly the **permanent organisation** of the stores should be considered, particularly ensuring the following points:

- Goods are kept in bins and on racks, with complete descriptions of each item by bin cards etc.
- Goods are protected against deterioration and misappropriation (restriction of access to stores).
- Goods held for third parties, and slow-moving, obsolete stock, etc. are identified and separated.
- There is an adequate plan of the area to be covered, which should be tidy.

Secondly, **comprehensive written instructions** should be issued for the undertaking of the stocktaking, detailing:

- The procedure to be followed by each centre, dividing each centre into areas for stocktake purposes.
- The appointment of competent supervisors (both technically and managerially) for each area, with teams (pairs) of technically competent counters under them. One person for each team should be responsible for counting, the other for recording and checking the count. The storekeepers should not be responsible for counting

unless their work is independently checked. It is rare in practice to find anyone checking stock other than those responsible for stock on a day-to-day basis. Auditors need to be aware of the possibility of misappropriation of assets combined with falsification of the related records.

- The mark to be applied to stock to indicate that it has been counted, e.g. chalk mark, docket etc.
- A standardised pre-numbered form for recording the stock count, the issue and return of which should be controlled so that all stock counted and areas are accounted for, and that proper accounting records are kept.
- Movement of stock during the stocktake should be halted or closely controlled.
- Comparison as soon as practicable after the stocktake with the continuous stock records so that any discrepancies may be investigated and adjusted.

The stocktaking arrangements and instructions should be discussed with management.

5 The auditor and the stocktake

5.1 Auditor's attendance at stocktaking

KEY POINT

The *overall* purpose of the auditor's attendance is to assess the *effectiveness* of the client's **stocktaking procedures**.

ISA 501 states that, where inventory is material to the financial statements, the auditor should attend the physical inventory counting unless this is impracticable.

The *overall* purpose of the auditor's attendance is to assess the *effectiveness* of the client's **stocktaking procedures**. Attendance at stocktaking is primarily a test of controls, not a substantive procedure. It is not the auditor's responsibility to count stock, but the client's. The auditor will perform test counts but these tiny samples are not intended to be representative of the populations they are drawn from. They are tests of controls by re-performance. There are three aspects of the auditor's duties, covering the times before, during and after the stocktaking.

5.2 Before the stocktaking

In order to ensure that the auditor's attendance at the stocktake is as effective as possible, certain planning procedures should be followed:

- Review prior year's working papers, familiarise themselves with the nature, volume and location of stocks, consider the controlling and recording procedures over stock.
- Identify problem areas in relation to the system of internal control and decide whether reliance can be placed on internal auditors.
- If stock held by third parties is material, or the third party is insufficiently independent or reliable, then arrange a stocktake attendance at the third party's premises; otherwise, arrange third party confirmation.
- If the nature of the stocks is specialised then arrange expert help or review the client's own arrangements (this includes work in progress).
- Examine the client's stocktaking instructions: if found to be inadequate, the matter should be discussed with the client with a view to improving them prior to the stocktake.
- Auditors should perform analytical procedures on stock as part of the planning process; these will consist of consideration of the ageing of stock, stock turnover rates etc.

KEY POINT

Auditors should perform **analytical procedures** on stock as part of the planning process.

5.3 During the stocktaking

The main task is to ensure that the client's staff are carrying out their duties effectively. The auditor should perform the following steps:

- make two-way test counts from factory floor to stock sheets, and from stock sheets to factory floor
- make notes of items counted, damaged stock, instances where the stocktaking procedures are not being followed
- examine and test control over the stock sheets. The client should keep a stock sheet register
- examine cut-off procedures (see below)
- pay particular attention to goods held on behalf of third parties (for example, goods on consignment)
- reach a conclusion as to whether or not the stocktaking was satisfactory, and hence provides reliable evidence supporting the final stock figure.

It is important to remember that attendance at stocktaking is only part of the audit of stock and that there are many other audit procedures that will be used to support the final opinion.

If the auditors in attendance at the stocktake do *not* feel that the procedures are being carried out adequately, they must bring this to management's attention immediately and seek to rectify the position as it may not be possible to obtain the relevant evidence at a later date.

Although the main reason to attend the stocktake is to obtain evidence in respect of stock, it can also enhance the auditor's understanding of the business and provide evidence of the adequacy of the accounting and internal control systems.

5.4 After the stocktaking

KEY POINT

It is vital that the auditor examines **cut-off** procedures to ensure correct accounting.

The auditor should check the **cut-off** details obtained at the stocktake to the ledgers to ensure stock is accounted for in the correct period, review the final **stock sheets** and follow up **test counts** to the final statements of stock. This is not always easy where the **audit trail** is poor. We may have counted 15 red washing-up bowls at the stocktake and there may be 150 in the final statement of stock, but do they include ours? We would obviously be even more concerned if the final statement of stock showed none of the items we counted. The auditor should also ensure that any continuous stock records have been adjusted or reconciled to the physical count and all differences investigated.

5.5 Cut-off

The auditor should examine the link between purchases records and stocks, and between sales records and stocks, to ensure that there is complete accord between stock and the financial records of purchases and sales, debtors and creditors. These are known as **'cut-off' procedures**. Also note that the same term may encompass the recording of cash in the correct accounting period.

Tests the auditor would carry out to ensure correct cut-off include the following:

- during stocktake attendance note the serial numbers of the last sales invoice, despatch note and goods received note generated before the stocktake
- after the stocktake, check the year-end despatch notes to sales invoices and the sales daybook and vice versa to ensure that despatches and the related invoice both fall before the year end
- similarly for purchases, ensure year-end goods receipts notes and related purchase invoices are correctly treated in the current period
- take a sample of goods received and goods despatched just after the year end and ensure that the related stock was *not* included in the count in the case of goods received, and that it was included, in the case of goods despatched.

5.6 Internal audit and stock audits

KEY POINT

Internal auditors also undertake stock audits and external auditors may be able to rely on this work.

The **internal auditor** will also undertake audits of stock and the external auditor may be able to rely on the work undertaken by internal audit. What work is undertaken will be dependent on the organisation and the nature of the risk exposure. The internal auditor will approach a stock audit in the same way as any other auditor as explained in previous chapters. In particular, the internal auditor will perform the following steps:

- Conduct detailed planning, including evaluation of background information, previous audits (whether internal or external), company policy and procedures relating to stock, management information and performance measures and overall objectives.
- Identify risks associated with stock and assess impact and probability of risks for the organisation concerned.
- Review controls in place against those expected. Are the controls appropriate, and are they operating effectively and in a timely manner? Key controls already identified and commented on in detail are the operation of procedures and stocktaking.
- Test key controls:
  - review evidence of stocktakes being undertaken on a regular basis (see above for testing procedures on stocktakes)
  - confirm accuracy of data input to other systems
  - inspect a sample of despatches to confirm evidence of authorisation of transactions, despatches within policy and correct accounting; and a sample of goods receipts to confirm evidence of order authorisation, receipts checked to order and correct accounting
  - check accuracy of management information relied upon for decision making
  - inspect the records of liaison with other departments to confirm awareness of changing needs for stock.
- The internal auditor will be able to formulate a report based on conclusions from the testing including an overall evaluation of the level of risk exposure. Findings are discussed with management and an action plan formulated for any issues identified.

ACTIVITY **2**

You are an internal auditor for Harvey Supplies and have been asked to undertake a stock audit. Stock is a key asset of Harvey Supplies and the last audit was carried out by the external auditors. Outline your approach to the audit.

Feedback to this activity is at the end of the chapter.

6 Stock valuation procedures

As pointed out above, attendance at the stocktake to gain evidence about the **existence** of stock cannot prove that stock is **correctly valued**. Suggested **valuation tests** are set out below.

6.1 Raw materials and consumables

- Ascertain what elements of cost are included, e.g. carriage in, duties etc. and confirm their appropriateness.
- Ascertain the method of valuing stock issues.
- If standard costs are used, enquire into basis of standards, how these compare with actual costs and how variances are treated.

KEY POINT

Stock valuation tests cover consumables, raw materials, work in progress, goods for resale and finished goods.

- Test check cost prices used with purchase invoices received in the month(s) prior to stocktaking.
- Test check quantities with stock records or bin cards with a particular aim of finding items which have been in stock for, say, more than six months. Discuss these items with a responsible official in order to find out when they might be used; if it is unlikely that they will be used, try to ascertain a reasonable net realisable value.
- Follow up valuation of all damaged or obsolete stocks noted during observance of physical stocktaking with a view to establishing a net realisable value.

6.2 Work in progress

- Ascertain what elements of cost are included. If overheads are included, ascertain the basis on which they are included and review this basis with the available costing and financial information.
- Ascertain how the various stages of process are measured and if estimates are made, on what basis they are made.
- Ensure that any materials costs exclude any abnormal wastage factors.
- Ensure that any addition for overheads includes only normal expenses based on normal production capacity and that any costs arising from under-utilisation of production facilities, excessive waste or exceptional circumstances are not carried forward in the stock valuation.
- Enquire into any old, obsolete or damaged items and ensure that these are valued at a reasonable estimated net realisable value. Check this with previous or subsequent sales of similar items.

6.3 Finished goods and goods for resale

- Enquire into what costs are included, and how these have been established. Ensure that the overhead addition is based on normal costs and is reasonable in relation to the information disclosed by the draft accounts.
- Test check prices on stock lists with official sales list, bearing in mind any trade discounts which are normally granted off the list prices. Ensure that stocks are valued at net realisable value if this is less than cost. For any such items, also check back and see if the relevant partly processed stocks and raw materials have also been written down.
- Follow up any items which stock records show are more than, say, six months in stock. Enquire into reasons for this and ascertain possible realisable value of such items.
- Follow up any stocks which at the time of observance of physical stocktaking were noted as being damaged or obsolete.
- Discuss with sales manager any possible policy of selling off certain lines at less than usual selling prices, e.g. 'loss leaders' due to competition, substitute products on the market etc.
- Follow up valuation of all 'seconds' items and ensure that they are valued at a reasonable estimated net realisable value if less than cost.

7 SSAP 9: Problem areas

7.1 Problem areas

Appendix 1 of SSAP 9 contains general guidance on certain practical matters which may cause difficulty in particular businesses. These are explained briefly below.

7.2 Allocation of overheads

Overheads are expenses incurred in the manufacture of goods and include items like factory rates and lighting and heating.

KEY POINT

Overheads included in stock should be based on normal production levels.

Production overheads should normally be added to the cost of goods being produced based on the normal activity level of the company. An estimate of overheads to be incurred at this level of activity will be produced, and allocated to the goods produced based on this activity level. If the company produces less output than expected, then the 'unused' overheads will be written off to the profit and loss account and not included in the stock figure.

Activity levels in excess of budget may require a reapportionment of overheads. This will ensure that too much overhead cost is not included in stock.

The overheads to be included in stock should be only those relating to production (the factory rates etc.). Some companies will try to include all overheads in their stock figures. This happens because their accounting system cannot isolate the production overheads from the non-productive. Where this type of absorption costing is used, an estimate should be made of the non-productive overheads. These will then be excluded from the stock valuation. This estimate is unlikely to be accurate, but as good a 'guess' as possible should be made.

7.3 Choice of costing method

There are many different ways of including overheads into the cost of stock. Each company must make its own decision about which method to use. The method must give a close approximation to the actual cost of overheads incurred in making the stock. It should contain as few matters of judgement as possible.

7.4 Net realisable value (NRV)

Stocks should be valued at the lower of **cost** and **net realisable value**.

DEFINITION

NRV is the selling price less all **costs to completion**, including marketing, selling and distribution.

NRV is the actual or estimated selling price less all further **costs to completion** and all costs to be incurred in marketing, selling and distribution.

It is not always easy to find a figure for NRV. Some estimates must be reached, based on sales of stock after the year end, or from other evidence such as price lists. This estimate should be made for each individual stock line.

Post balance sheet events may influence the net realisable value calculation. Low selling prices after the year end may result in net realisable value being less than cost.

Where NRV is found to be less than cost, the individual stock lines affected should be revalued at the (lower) NRV. The only exception to this rule is for raw materials and components to be used in manufacture. These items may have their NRV being less than cost. No reduction in value is needed if it can be shown that the product made from these items can still be sold at a profit.

Here are some of the circumstances in which NRV may be less than cost:

- increased costs of manufacture
- reduced selling prices of products
- deterioration of stocks (particularly food stuffs)
- obsolescence of products (perhaps due to technological changes)
- deliberate selling at loss (supermarket 'loss leaders')
- buying and production errors.

Conclusion

Stock is a major asset which is relatively easily manipulated and therefore will be audited by both internal and external auditors. In conducting an audit, the auditor will identify the risks to the organisation and the control procedures required and produce an audit programme identifying tests including stock valuations and review of stocktakes. Good stocktaking procedures are required by a client and the auditor should attend the stocktake to assess the effectiveness of the procedures.

SELF-TEST QUESTIONS

The audit of stocks and work in progress

1 What are the CA85 disclosure requirements for stock? (1.3)

Risks associated with stock

2 What are the main risks associated with stock? (2)

Physical counts

3 What are the two methods of the timing of stocktaking? (4)

The auditor and the stocktake

4 What is the purpose of the auditor's attendance at the stocktake? (5.1)

SSAP 9: Problem areas

5 In what situations may NRV be less than cost? (7.4)

EXAM-TYPE QUESTIONS

Question 1: Nero Scrap and Haulage Ltd

You are the auditor of Nero Scrap and Haulage Ltd, carrying out the audit of the accounts for the year ending 30 June 20X7. The company owns 30 lorries and a large yard. Ferrous scrap is collected from numerous metal-working firms in the area, and stored in the yard until it can be compressed with the company's scrap pressing machine. The scrap is then taken by lorry to a steel works, 100 miles away. The lorries are then used to take new steel billets from the steel works to steel stockholders.

Required:

(a) You have been sent the company's instructions to its employees on the assessment of stock quantities. State what you would expect to see in these instructions in respect of unpressed stock in the yard. **(3 marks)**

(b) Scrap prices vary greatly from day to day. State how the stock should be valued. **(2 marks)**

(c) List the steps you could take to verify that correct valuation of the stock of scrap had been made. **(4 marks)**

While engaged on the audit, the new transport manager brings you a plain envelope containing four £10 notes and tells you that it had just been received from the company's lorry tyre suppliers with a message that it was last month's commission to the previous transport manager.

(d) Discuss the audit implications of this discovery. **(4 marks)**

(e) The company carries the billets on behalf of the steel stockholders and charges haulage. Draft an audit programme for the audit of haulage charges made to the steel stockholder customers. Specific tests of control should be included. The company's records are maintained manually. **(7 marks)**

(Total: 20 marks)

(ACCA Jun 85)

Question 2: Camry Products Ltd

In connection with your examination of the financial statements of Camry Products Ltd for the year ended 31 March 20X7, you are reviewing the plans for a physical stock count at the company's warehouse on 31 March 20X7. The company assembles domestic appliances, and stocks of finished appliances, unassembled parts and sundry stocks are stored in the warehouse which is adjacent to the company's assembly plant. The plant will continue to produce goods during the stock count until 5pm on 31 March 20X7.

On 30 March 20X7, the warehouse staff will deliver the estimated quantities of unassembled parts and sundry stocks which will be required for production for 31 March 20X7; however, emergency requisitions by the factory will be filled on 31 March.

During the stock count, the warehouse staff will continue to receive parts and sundry stocks, and to despatch finished appliances. Appliances which are completed on 31 March 20X7 will remain in the assembly plant until after the physical stock count has been completed.

Required:

(a) List the principal procedures which the auditor should carry out when planning attendance at a company's stocktake. **(8 marks)**

(b) Describe the procedures which Camry Products Ltd should establish in order to ensure that all stock items are counted and that no item of stock is counted twice. **(8 marks)**

(c) Describe the audit procedures you would carry out at the time of the stock count in order to ensure that stock cut-off is correct. **(4 marks)**

(Total: 20 marks)

(ACCA Jun 89)

Question 3: Chingford Potteries

Your firm is the external auditor of Chingford Potteries, and you recently attended the year-end stock count at the company's warehouse. The company manufactures high quality tableware (plates, cups and saucers etc.) and it maintains an integrated computerised system that shows the stock held at any given point in time. At the year-end stock count, the various categories of stock (but not the quantities) are printed off the system and the quantities of stock actually counted are inserted manually by the counters, for later comparison with the computerised quantity. This system has proved successful in recent years but unfortunately, your notes show a number of weaknesses in the current year-end count.

The count instructions were received by both you and the counters the day before the count was due to take place. Many areas in which the count took place were untidy and stock was sometimes difficult to find, because it was not in the allocated area. The same categories of stock were sometimes found in several different areas and some stock was incorrectly labelled. The count was conducted in a hurry in order to close the warehouse before a public holiday and there were insufficient counters to conduct the count properly in the time available. The issue and receipt of stock sheets (on which the quantities were recorded by counters) was not properly controlled. It was difficult to reconcile the stock quantities recorded at the count to the computerised records and some significant differences remain outstanding.

Required:

(a) Explain why stock valuation and the year-end stock count are important to the audit of financial statements and describe the alternatives to a year-end count as a basis for the year-end valuation. **(4 marks)**

(b) Draft for inclusion in a report to the management of Chingford Potteries:

- the weaknesses you found
- the potential consequences
- your recommendations for remedying the weaknesses in the current year count, and
- your recommendations for future years. **(6 marks)**

(c) Describe the basis for valuing stock as required by SSAP 9 *Stocks and long-term contracts* and list the types of stock which may be worth less than cost at Chingford Potteries. **(5 marks)**

(d) Describe the work that you would perform to establish which stocks are worth less than cost at Chingford Potteries. **(5 marks)**

(Total: 20 marks)

Note: In part (c) of this question, you are not required to deal with long-term contracts.

For the answers to these questions, see the 'Answers' section at the end of the book.

FEEDBACK TO ACTIVITY 1

The main categories of internal control over stock are as follows:

- authorisation and purchase procedures
- control over goods inwards
- stock records substantiated by physical counts
- control over despatches and goods outwards.

FEEDBACK TO ACTIVITY 2

For Harvey Supplies, stock is clearly a major risk to the company, which would influence the audit approach. Key aspects of the approach are:

- Plan the audit effectively. This would include reviewing the findings from the last audit of stock and understanding the approach undertaken by the external auditors. Also identify any future planned work by the external auditors and any more recent work undertaken. Obtain all necessary background information, including management information and reports available for example on stock trends. Agree objectives and scope of the audit with Management.
- Assess the key risks relating to stock including overstocking, loss of stock, damage to stock, stock not available when required, obsolete stock, high levels of write-offs. The impact and likelihood of such risks will be evaluated.
- Review the controls in place to manage the risks and consider whether they are adequate and whether they are operating effectively. For example stocktaking, system input and output controls, authorisation of stock changes including write-offs.
- Identify findings from the review, including their significance and the level of risk exposure.
- Discuss findings with Management, formulate an action plan and publish a report from the audit.

Chapter 15

THE AUDIT OF LIABILITIES AND CAPITAL

CHAPTER CONTENTS

This is the final chapter on the detailed aspects of the balance sheet audit. The nature of share capital, reserves and long-term liabilities is such that there are few transactions during an accounting period. Internal audit will also be involved in audits of liabilities and capital. These would normally form part of a wider audit for internal audit rather than a specific financial audit. However, they may also work with external audit and rely on their work in this area, particularly if internal auditors do not have the required financial expertise.

As usual, you should recognise the possibility of the possible impact on the audit work of computer based systems. Here, possible applications could be the creditors/purchase ledger and a computer-maintained register of members, relating to share capital.

Objectives

By the time you have finished this chapter you should be able to:

- describe, and tabulate for inclusion in a work programme, the substantive procedures used in obtaining evidence in relation to current and long-term liabilities and accruals, and the related income statement entries
- explain the purpose of substantive procedures in relation to financial statement assertions concerning current and long-term liabilities and accruals
- understand the main legal requirements for share capital and reserves and the consequential audit tests.

1 Liabilities

1.1 Classification

Liabilities can be classified as follows:

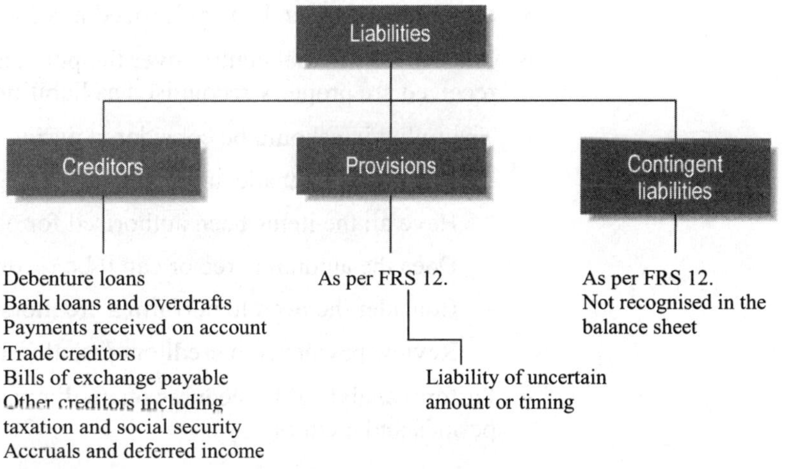

Amounts falling due within one year (current) must be shown separately from amounts falling due after more than one year (long-term) for each item. Therefore the balance sheet will disclose current liabilities, long-term liabilities and provisions, while material contingent liabilities will be disclosed in a note to the accounts.

KEY POINT

The item requiring most work under the general heading of current liabilities will be **trade creditors**.

1.2 Amounts falling due within one year (current liabilities)

Of the various types of creditor in the above listing, the item requiring most work under the general heading of current liabilities will be trade creditors, which will probably be tested by extracting appropriate samples.

The other items are likely to be checked in detail. The relevant items are covered below.

1.3 Internal controls over trade creditors

This is a revision of previous chapters on controls. Internal controls over trade creditors are designed to ensure that:

- purchased goods/services are ordered under proper authorities and procedures
- purchased goods/services are only ordered as necessary for the proper conduct of the business operations and are ordered from suitable suppliers
- goods/services received are effectively inspected for quality, quantity and conditions
- invoices and related documentation are properly checked and approved as being valid before being entered as trade creditors
- all valid transactions relating to trade creditors (suppliers' invoices, credit notes and adjustments), and only those transactions, should be accurately recorded in the accounting records.

1.4 Trade creditors – substantive procedures

The main procedures are as follows:

- Obtain a schedule of the trade creditors with appropriate age analysis and check this with the control account and the creditors' ledger.
- Debit and credit balances should be separated, debit balances being included in debtors (this is known as 'grossing up'). Any debit balances should never be netted off against credit balances.
- Review the individual accounts with the largest throughput of transactions during the period (not necessarily the largest balances at the year end).
- Review the year-end cut-off procedures for purchases.
- Review the internal control over the purchases system which ensures that all goods received are properly recognised as liabilities of the company.
- The following should be considered during the tests of individual balances:
  - Is the balance made up of specific items outstanding within a reasonable period?
  - Have all the items been authorised for payment?
  - Does the amount agree or can it be reconciled with creditors' statements?
  - Consider the need to perform a creditors circularisation.
  - Review payments to creditors just after the year end.
- Perform analytical procedures on creditors, comparing age analysis with previous periods and creditor days.

There are two specific audit procedures that deserve special consideration – supplier statement reconciliations and creditor circularisations.

Supplier statement reconciliations

It is common for suppliers to send monthly statements to their credit customers, listing the movements on the amount owed during the month (e.g. new invoices issued and cash payments received) and the balance still owing at the end of the month. A common internal control in purchases systems is for the creditors ledger clerks to receive these statements and compare them to the balance due to that supplier on the creditors ledger. If the balances are different, a reconciliation statement is drawn up, showing the reconciling items such as invoices in transit and cash in transit.

The auditor can inspect these reconciliations, re-performing the checks where necessary to ensure that the statement is accurate. The auditor will gain valuable audit evidence from the supplier statements since they are generated by a source external to the client being audited.

Credit circularisations

We saw in an earlier chapter that carrying out a debtors circularisation is a typical audit procedure. In theory it would also be possible to carry out a creditors circularisation writing to the client's creditors and asking them to confirm direct to the auditor the balance that the client owes them.

In practice a creditors circularisation is not often carried out. The auditor is able to gather sufficient appropriate audit evidence from the other audit procedures (testing the purchases system, reconciling supplier statements, examining after-date payments to creditors, etc) so that a creditors circularisation is unnecessary. However, if alternative audit procedures are not possible, then such a circularisation could be performed.

1.5 Bank overdraft

KEY POINT

Bank overdrafts are shown as liabilities even though there may be other bank balances shown as an asset.

Bank overdrafts are shown as liabilities even though there may be other bank balances shown as an asset. The only exception is where there is a legal right of set-off; in such cases, the accounts presentation is to net off the two balances against each other.

Verification of bank overdrafts is in other respects identical to the verification of cash balances.

1.6 Accruals

KEY POINT

Accruals are often immaterial and reliance is often placed on analytical procedures. Any errors are likely to be those of understatement.

Accruals, like prepayments, are commonly made for rent, gas, electricity, telephone and other items where the expenditure has been incurred in the current period but where no invoice has yet been recorded. Accruals are often immaterial and reliance is often placed on analytical procedures. Nevertheless, as year-end adjustments, there are rarely any tight controls over accruals and any errors are likely to be those of understatement. If however, accruals are significant the auditor would expect there to be much tighter controls.

Tests for accruals include the following:

- Consider the client's own system (if any) for capturing accruals.
- Obtain a schedule of accruals, ensuring that it is cast correctly, comparing it with prior year accruals and performing other analytical procedures.
- Test check a sample of accruals for correct calculation, referring to supporting invoices received in the next period.
- Include confirmation of the completeness of accruals in the management representation letter. This is dealt with in further detail later.

1.7 Long-term liabilities

KEY POINT

If all or part of a **loan** has a **due date of payment** within one year of the balance sheet date, then it must be disclosed under current liabilities.

The main long-term liabilities will be debenture loans and bank loans. There may be the occasional other amount, such as a creditor who has agreed a specially extended date of payment. If so, the audit procedures are the same as for a similar item under current liabilities. It should also be appreciated that if all or part of the debenture loan has a due date of payment within one year of the balance sheet date, then that loan (or the part requiring payment) must be disclosed under current liabilities.

1.8 Debenture loans

A debenture loan is defined as a written acknowledgement by a company, usually under seal, of a loan made to it, containing provisions as to payment of interest and repayment of capital.

Issue

KEY POINT

The procedure for checking the issue of **debentures** involves referring to the company's constitutional documents and borrowing agreements, as well as any registration documents.

The procedure with regard to the issue of debentures is similar to that in the case of an issue of shares and the work to be performed by the auditor in vouching the issue will be of the same nature. On vouching the issue, the auditor should always refer to the memorandum and articles to ascertain the borrowing powers of the company, since, although a trading company has implied power to borrow up to any amount, it is possible that such power may be restricted by the memorandum or articles. The auditor should inspect the certificate of registration given by the Registrar.

When a new issue of debentures takes place in the year, it is necessary to disclose the class of debentures issued, the amount issued for each class and the consideration received.

Redemption

KEY POINT

Auditors should examine the provisions of the trust deed or the debenture bonds relating to the **redemption**, and ascertain that they are duly complied with.

Debentures may be redeemable according to the terms of the issue, at specified dates, by annual or other drawings, or at the option of the company, after due notice has been given of intention to repay. Auditors should examine the provisions of the trust deed or the debenture bonds relating to the redemption, and ascertain that they are duly complied with.

The auditor's principal duties with regard to the redemption are as follows:

- Examine the trust instrument as to the terms of the redemption, and note that these have been complied with.
- Check the payment of cash to the debenture holders.
- Inspect the cancelled bonds.
- See that the entry in the register of charges has been cancelled, and inspect any 'memorandum of satisfaction' filed with the Registrar.

2 Contingent liabilities

2.1 Definition

KEY POINT

FRS 12 states:

- probable losses should be accrued
- possible losses should be disclosed
- probable gains should be disclosed.

A contingency may be defined as a condition which exists at the balance sheet date where the ultimate outcome (gain or loss) will only be confirmed by the occurrence or non-occurrence of one or more uncertain future events not within the control of the entity. Under the rules of FRS 12, probable losses should be accrued, **possible** losses should be disclosed. **Probable** gains (contingent assets) should be disclosed.

It is, therefore, very important to consider whether a possible liability should actually be **incorporated** into the accounts as an actual liability or merely **disclosed** as a note to the accounts (a contingent liability). Auditors and directors have often fallen out over such issues.

Examples

Typical contingent liabilities include the following:

- bills discounted
- guarantees given to third parties, e.g. to guarantee a subsidiary company's overdraft
- forward contracts
- damages and costs in actions pending
- claims under guarantees, warranties (express or implied) arising out of past transactions.

2.2 Disclosure

The Companies Act 1985 requires that, for any contingent liability not *provided* for in the financial statements, disclosure should be made of:

- the amount or estimated amount of that liability
- its legal nature
- whether any valuable security has been provided by the company in connection with that liability and if so, what.

2.3 Sources of audit evidence

KEY POINT

Sources of audit evidence the auditor should consider in respect of contingent items include:

- standard letter of request to the bank
- investigations about pending legal matters
- directors' minute book
- letters of representation.

Standard letter of request to the bank

This is likely to provide the necessary evidence in respect of bills discounted and guarantees. This letter was considered in an earlier chapter as the primary method of verifying bank balances.

Pending legal matters

Pending lawsuits and other actions against the company often present problems to auditors. They should take the following steps:

- Review the client's system of recording claims including the procedure for bringing them to the attention of management.
- Discuss with the legal department or company secretary the procedures for instructing solicitors.
- Examine board or management minutes for indications of possible claims.
- Examine correspondence with solicitors, including bills rendered.
- Obtain a list of matters referred to solicitors with the company's estimates of possible liabilities.
- Obtain a letter of representation from the relevant director that he is not aware of any other matters referred to solicitors.
- Consider consulting an independent legal expert if any uncertainty exists that the auditor feels should have been addressed.

The auditor may also consider it useful to obtain the client's consent to send a letter requesting confirmation of specific matters to the client's solicitor. An example of such a letter is:

In connection with the presentation and audit of our accounts for the year ended . . . . . . the directors have made estimates of the ultimate liabilities (including costs) which might be incurred, and which are regarded as material, in relation to the following matters on which you have been consulted. We should be obliged if you would confirm that in your opinion these estimates are reasonable.

Matter	*Estimated liability including costs*
Libel action against the company in connection with statements appearing in newspaper.	£25,000

Signed . . . .

Dated . . . .

Directors' minute book

This was referred to above. The directors' minute book may also refer, for example, to guarantees given to third parties relating to financial commitments of employees.

Letter of representation

This will be considered later as a form of audit evidence. It also acts to remind the directors to acknowledge their responsibilities.

The knowledge of contingent liabilities may very well be confined to management and is therefore a suitable matter for inclusion in such a letter. In addition, it will remind the directors of their responsibility to disclose such matters to the auditor.

2.4 The audit of accounting estimates

The use of accounting estimates is relevant in respect of liabilities; this has been considered in detail in the earlier chapter on Audit Evidence.

3 Share capital

3.1 Classes of share

DEFINITION

Capital is most often divided into **preference** and **ordinary shares**.

There are many distinct types of shares of limited companies, but capital is most often divided into **preference** and **ordinary shares**. The rights of the respective shareholders are governed by the terms of the articles. The preference shareholders, as a rule, are entitled to a fixed dividend out of profits. The surplus profits after such payments belong to the ordinary shareholders.

Depending on the terms of the articles, the preference shares may also carry a preferential right as regards capital, that is to say, that they are entitled to the return of their capital before there is any return on the ordinary shares in the event of liquidation, and possibly they may also be entitled to a premium on liquidation.

3.2 The nature and purpose of share capital and reserves

Share capital represents part of the capital invested in the company by its shareholders, but may also represent past reserves of the company which have been 'capitalised' by a bonus issue of shares.

DEFINITION

Net assets is represented by the total of **share capital** plus **reserves** (book value).

Reserves represent the balance of net assets accruing to the shareholders and may include part of past issues of share capital (known as share premium), retained trading profits and revaluation gains on the revaluation of fixed assets.

The total of share capital and reserves represents the book value of the net assets of the company.

3.3 Statutory requirements

DEFINITION

Called up share capital is the amount of nominal share value paid by shareholders plus further amounts agreed to be paid by shareholders on set dates in the future.

Only two items are required to be shown on the face of the balance sheet:

- called up share capital
- called up share capital not paid at the balance sheet date.

Most capital is issued on a fully called basis and this is the only type of share capital which we will have to deal with at this level of examinations.

In the notes to the accounts, the authorised and issued share capital must be disclosed by class of share.

DEFINITION

Authorised share capital is the total amount of shares the company is allowed to issue.

The issued share capital is the total amount of the authorised share capital which has actually been issued. In most cases this will equal the called up share capital.

In addition, full details must be given of any changes in the share capital during the year.

3.4 Audit of share capital

KEY POINT

Any **change in share capital** is likely to be a material transaction subject to special legal requirements, and so all changes should be checked.

As any change in share capital is likely to be a material transaction subject to special legal requirements, all changes should be checked. Sampling would not be appropriate except for an issue of shares for cash involving a substantial number of shareholders.

Audit procedures

- Check authorised capital limit to memorandum and articles.
- Check changes to issued capital in year and agree to board minutes.
- Trace all transactions involving cash to the cash book and bank statement.
- Ensure that appropriate returns have been made to the Registrar of Companies.
- Ensure appropriate disclosure in accordance with FRS 4 and FRS 25.
- Ensure that all transactions are legal and that any share premiums in particular have been accounted for in accordance with the CA 1985 requirements.

4 Reserves

4.1 Definition

KEY POINT

The treatment and presentation of **reserves** can be affected by both the Companies Act 1985 and the company's Articles of Association.

The term **reserves** can cover a wide range of items. It is important to appreciate that the treatment and presentation of reserves can be affected by both:

- the Companies Act 1985
- the company's Articles of Association.

Possible categories of reserves include the following:

- share premium account
- revaluation reserve
- capital redemption reserve
- reserves provided for by the articles of association, e.g. a capital reserve
- other reserves, e.g. plant replacement reserve
- profit and loss account.

4.2 Disclosure

It is necessary to disclose all the information required by the Companies Act. This includes:

- following the standardised formats laid down in Sch 4 CA 1985
- showing the opening and closing balances on reserves and any transfer to or from the reserves during the year
- disclosing the source and application of any amount so transferred.

4.3 Share premium

A share premium account is created on an issue of shares where the consideration received exceeds the nominal value of the shares. The audit of this area has been dealt with in the audit of share capital above.

4.4 Revaluation reserve

KEY POINT

If a company makes use of the alternative accounting rules allowed by CA 1985, then any profit or loss arising from the revaluation must be transferred to the **revaluation reserve**.

If a company makes use of the alternative accounting rules allowed by CA 1985, then any profit or loss arising from the revaluation of an asset must be transferred to the revaluation reserve. This reserve must be shown separately on the balance sheet and will be reduced if the directors of the company are of the opinion that the reserve is no longer necessary for the purpose of the accounting policies adopted by the company.

The most common example of the use of the alternative accounting rules is showing tangible fixed assets in the balance sheet at market value.

You should note the double entry in relation to revalued assets as mistakes are often made in this area.

- Dr Asset Cost Account
  Cr Revaluation Reserve
  with revalued amount less cost
- Dr Asset Accumulated Depreciation Account
  Cr Revaluation Reserve
  with accumulated depreciation up to the date of revaluation

Note that these are all balance sheet transactions. The cost account is increased up to the new revalued amount; the accumulated depreciation is reduced to nil. The revalued asset is from then on depreciated on the higher, revalued amount.

KEY POINT

The audit of the revaluation reserve will involve reviewing:

- the **revaluation** – reason for it, its basis and reasonableness
- the **valuer** – qualifications, experience and independence
- adequacy of **disclosures**.

The audit of the revaluation reserve will involve the following steps:

- Assess the reason for the revaluation, the basis of valuation and its reasonableness in the light of the auditor's knowledge of the business and the position of the property market.
- Evaluate the qualifications and experience of the valuer, which must be disclosed in the year in which the valuation takes place (the year of the valuation is given in subsequent years). Reliance on experts has been dealt with in an earlier chapter.
- Ensure that adequate disclosures are made as above and that any difference between market value and the recorded value is disclosed.

ACTIVITY 1

An asset which originally cost £1,000 and which now has a net book value of £250 is revalued to £1,200.

What is the double entry relating to the revaluation?

Feedback to this activity is at the end of the chapter.

4.5 Capital reserve

The term **capital reserve** does not appear in the Companies Act, nor is it used in any accounting standard. Nevertheless, on occasions, the Articles of Association of a company may require that certain profits of a capital nature (such as profits on sale of property) be transferred to a capital reserve account.

The auditor must ensure, therefore, that the company has complied with the relevant rules contained in its Articles.

4.6 Replacement reserves

During a period of inflation, historical cost accounting generally overstates the profit of a business. Over a period of years, if a business were to distribute as dividends all its available historical cost profits, it might find that it had insufficient funds to finance replacement of stock and fixed assets.

Some businesses, therefore, set aside additional amounts from profit and transfer them to **plant replacement reserve** and **stock replacement reserve**. Within the conventional accounting system, these should be regarded as appropriations of profit. Although these reserves are *legally* distributable, the directors have effectively indicated that they should not be distributed. The auditor should examine the basis of the transfers to reserves and their disclosure in the financial statements.

4.7 Debenture redemption reserve

Debentures are often issued to finance the purchase of fixed assets. Thus, in the balance sheet, the liabilities of the debentures are represented by fixed assets. When the debentures are redeemed, the liability is removed by a payment of cash. In such circumstances, some companies transfer an amount equivalent to the nominal value of the debentures redeemed out of unappropriated profit and into a **debenture redemption reserve** account.

This transfer is not required by law and the reserve is therefore *legally* distributable, although the directors have indicated that it should be regarded as non-distributable.

4.8 Profit and loss account

This represents accumulated retained profits of the business. The balance at the year end consists of the balance brought forward from the previous year plus the retained profit for the current year.

KEY POINT

The audit procedures for reserves mainly comprise verifying that **legal requirements** have been complied with and **correct disclosures** made.

4.9 Audit procedures

The audit procedures for the reserves noted above mainly consist of verifying that legal requirements have been complied with and correct disclosures made. The following is a summary of the procedures.

- Prepare a schedule of reserves showing movements in the year.
- Check material movements, and ensure compliance with legal regulations.
- Ensure all gains and losses have been included in the profit and loss account or other reserves as appropriate.

5 Internal audit and the audit of liabilities and capital

The liabilities, capital and estimates obviously present significant risks to the company, in particular financial loss, and therefore the internal auditor will also be required to do audits in this area. Internal audit will be interested in the same types of controls as the external auditor, albeit less concentrated on the year-end work. Any audit in this area will be approached in the same way as any other audit – planning, review of risks, evaluation of tests, formulation of conclusions, reporting and follow up.

Conclusion

Creditors will be subject to various audit procedures, with trade creditors likely to be tested by the extraction of a sample.

The audit of share capital and reserves mainly consists of checking that the various legal requirements and disclosures have been complied with.

SELF-TEST QUESTIONS

Liabilities

1 Should bank overdrafts be netted off against bank balances? (1.5)

2 What are the main types of long term liabilities? (1.7)

Contingent liabilities

3 Are contingent liabilities accrued in the financial statements? (2.1)

4 Are contingent gains accrued in the financial statements? (2.1)

Share capital

5 What are the two main classes of share? (3.1)

6 What is meant by called up share capital? (3.3)

Reserves

7 What disclosures are required for all types of reserves? (4.2)

8 When is a share premium account created? (4.3)

9 How does a capital reserve arise? (4.5)

10 What does the balance on the profit and loss account represent? (4.8)

EXAM-TYPE QUESTIONS

Question 1: Contingency

(a) What is a contingency?

(b) What audit tests would you carry out in respect of an amount of £50,000 disclosed in the notes as a contingent liability? **(10 marks)**

Question 2: Retail fashion store

List the tests covering purchases and year-end suppliers' balances in respect of a medium sized retail fashion store. **(18 marks)**

For answers to these questions, see the 'Answers' section at the end of the book.

FEEDBACK TO ACTIVITY 1

Dr Asset Cost
Cr Revaluation Reserve
with £200 (£1,200 – £1,000)

Dr Accumulated Depreciation
Cr Revaluation Reserve
with £750 (£1,000 – £250)

We can see that the net effect on the revaluation reserve is plus £950 (£200 + £750) which is the equivalent of the revalued amount (£1,200) less net book value (£250).

Chapter 16

AUDIT SAMPLING AND COMPUTER ASSISTED AUDIT TECHNIQUES

CHAPTER CONTENTS

Audit sampling is a technically difficult area to understand in terms of its detailed application. However, the emphasis in the examination will be on the general principles of why samples are taken in the first place, what conditions are necessary for sampling and what conclusions can be drawn from the sample. In this chapter we will also consider the use of computers by the auditor which can assist the auditor significantly when it comes to sampling, enabling him to use far greater samples in his testing.

Throughout the audit the auditor is likely to use computers to assist him with the audit work, particularly when the client has a computer system which is used to produce all or some of the financial accounting data.

The use of audit sampling and computer assisted audit techniques are equally applicable to the internal auditor. The internal auditor needs to make decisions on the method and approach to sampling and draw conclusions from testing undertaken and these need to be justified in working papers. Computer assisted audit techniques are very important to the internal auditor and can be a powerful tool for a more efficient and effective audit.

Objectives

By the time you have finished this chapter you should be able to:

- describe and illustrate the application of the basic principles of statistical sampling and other selective testing procedures
- describe and illustrate the use of computer assisted techniques in obtaining evidence
- understand why sampling is necessary
- understand sampling risk
- set out the main procedures in sampling
- understand the main uses of a PC by the auditor for audit work
- explain the controls operated by the auditor when using PCs for audit work
- explain the use of computer assisted audit techniques (CAATs).

1 Audit sampling

1.1 Definition of audit sampling

ISA 530 *Audit sampling and other means of testing* defines audit sampling as the application of audit procedures to fewer than 100% of the items within an account balance or class of transactions such that all the individual items in the population have a chance of selection. This will enable the auditor to obtain and evaluate evidence about some characteristic of the items selected to assist in forming a conclusion concerning the population from which the sample is drawn.

1.2 Reasons for sampling

KEY POINT

Sampling is not inevitable for all audit areas, but is normally appropriate for areas in which there are a large number of similar transactions, where it is not cost-effective to test them all.

Sampling is normally appropriate for areas in which there are a high number of similar transactions. In such areas, e.g. credit sales for the period, it is not cost-effective to test all transactions. Even if the costs were of no concern, full testing would not necessarily achieve the specified audit objectives for that area. For example, full testing on sales invoices would not verify that all sales are recorded (i.e. it may not demonstrate completeness), nor would it deal with human error on the part of the auditor.

The use of sampling allied to properly thought out objectives and properly constructed tests allows more valid conclusions to be reached than the (now outdated) traditional system of testing 'as many transactions as possible' in the time available.

Cases where sampling is not appropriate include the following situations:

- The auditor is 'on enquiry' as a result of previous information.
- Populations are too small for valid conclusions to be drawn and, in any event, it is quicker to test all transactions rather than spend time constructing a sample.
- All the transactions in a particular area are material.
- The data may be 'sensitive' items, such as directors' emoluments which require precise disclosure in the financial statements, regardless of their size.
- The audit area does not consist of items of the same kind, i.e. there is a non-homogeneous population.

1.3 Sampling risk and non-sampling risk

DEFINITION

Sampling risk: the risk that the conclusion auditors draw will be different from that which they would have drawn had they examined the entire population.

Because auditors do not examine all the items in the population when applying audit sampling, there is a risk that the conclusion they draw will be different from that which they would have drawn had they examined the entire population. This is **sampling risk**.

Non-sampling risk arises from factors that cause the auditor to reach an erroneous conclusion for any reason not related to the size of the sample. For example, the auditor might misinterpret audit evidence and fail to recognise an error.

Auditors should use a rational basis for planning, selecting and testing the sample and for evaluating the results so that they have adequate assurance that the sample is representative of the population, and that sampling risk and non-sampling risk are reduced to an acceptable level.

1.4 Statistical and non-statistical sampling

DEFINITION

Statistical sampling: the use of mathematical procedures to draw conclusions about the population. **Non-statistical techniques** rely on the individual's use of judgement to draw conclusions.

Statistical sampling involves the use of mathematical procedures, such as probability theory, to draw conclusions about the population. Non-statistical techniques rely on the auditors' judgement to draw conclusions. In practice, firms use a combination of both, but it must be noted that auditors do not eliminate the need for judgement when using statistical techniques, as judgement is still needed, for example, when setting materiality levels.

1.5 Sampling and selective testing distinguished

KEY POINT

Samples must be **representative** of the population.

Sampling is the application of audit procedures to less than 100% of the items in a population in order to extrapolate a conclusion about the population. The object is to select a sample that is expected to be representative of the population, and to examine the sample items.

Selective testing is any examination of less than 100% of the items in a population. For example, applying audit procedures to all items within a population which have a particular characteristic (e.g. all items over a certain amount) would qualify as a selective testing procedure, but is not audit sampling since these items were not selected from the total population on a basis that was expected to be representative.

2 Constructing samples

2.1 Applying sampling techniques

KEY POINT

The three steps involved in sampling are **design**, **selection** and **evaluation** of the sample.

The steps involved in sampling can be summarised as follows:

- sample design
- selection of the sample
- evaluation of the sample.

2.2 Designing the sample

When designing the size and structure of an audit sample, auditors should consider the specific audit objectives, the population from which they wish to sample and the selection methods.

2.3 Audit objectives

Objectives may relate to tests of control or substantive procedures. The auditor may want to be 90% certain that 95% (+/– 3%) of credit notes have been authorised in accordance with company procedures, i.e. that control procedures are being applied. He may want to be 95% certain that debtors are not overstated by more than 5%. Statistical procedures facilitate this degree of accuracy.

DEFINITIONS

The degree of certainty within which auditors wish to work is known as the **confidence level** and the parameters are known as the **precision limits**.

The degree of certainty is known as the **confidence level** and the parameters are known as the **precision limits**. Clearly, the more confident auditors wish to be and the narrower the precision limits they wish to work with, the larger the sample size will be.

Note that there is no linear relationship between sample size, and confidence levels and precision limits. If a sample of 10 items gives me a confidence level of 40%, a sample of 20 items will not necessarily give me a confidence level of 80%.

2.4 Population

DEFINITION

The **population** is any group of items sharing a common characteristic.

The **population** is the entire set of data from which a sample is selected and about which the auditor wish to draw conclusions. Examples are all debtors at a balance sheet date and all the goods and services received in a year. The essential feature of a population is that it must be homogeneous, that it must be composed of similar or uniform parts. Suppose that the population consists of all wage calculations for a year, but the auditor knows that the wages supervisor changed half way through the year. They may judge that the possibility of error is greater after the change than before. Hence, there are really two populations. The sampling plan for each population will be different.

Note that sampling **from** a population does not establish its completeness. This has been considered earlier. To test for understatement (or completeness) the test should go from source documentation (sometimes referred to as the reciprocal population) to the financial statements.

2.5 Stratification

KEY POINT

Stratification is used to reduce the degree of variation between items within a population.

Stratification is used to reduce the degree of variation between items within a population and enables auditors to direct attention to those areas where there is the greatest potential monetary error. It often has the effect of reducing sample sizes.

In cases where auditors are concerned with the discovery of overstatement errors and consider that the largest monetary errors are likely to occur in the largest individual items, they will wish to stratify the population by value. They may then direct the major part of their audit effort to those items with the highest individual value.

For example, the invoices for the year could be stratified into the classes in the table below.

Invoice value	*Number of items in stratum*	*Value of stratum*	*Test size*
Above £1m	10	£36m	10
£250,000 to £1m	150	£95m	50
£50,000 to £250,000	1,000	£93m	50
£10,000 to £50,000	3,000	£60m	35
Less than £10,000	7,000	£15m	15

2.6 Sample size

When determining the sample size, auditors should consider sampling risk, the amount of error that would be acceptable and the extent to which they expect to find errors.

Sampling risk

Sampling risk was defined earlier.

KEY POINT

Auditors are faced with **sampling risk** in both tests of control and substantive procedures.

Auditors are faced with sampling risk in both tests of control and substantive procedures as follows.

In tests of control:

- the risk of placing a higher than necessary assessment on control risk because the error in the sample is greater than the error in the population as a whole
- the risk of placing a lower than required assessment on control risk because the error in the sample is less than the error in the population as a whole.

In substantive procedures:

- the risk of concluding that a recorded account balance or class of transactions is materially misstated when it is not, because the error in the sample is greater than the error in the population as a whole
- the risk of concluding that a recorded account balance or class of transactions is acceptable when it is materially misstated, because the error in the sample is less than the error in the population as a whole.

Impact on sample size

- The greater the reliance on the results of a test of control using audit sampling, the lower the sampling risk the auditors are willing to accept and, consequently, the larger the sample size.
- The lower the assessment of control risk, the more likely the auditors are to place reliance on audit evidence from tests of control.
- A high control risk assessment may result in a decision not to perform tests of control.

Tolerable error

DEFINITION

Tolerable error is the maximum error in the population that the auditors are willing to accept and still conclude that the audit objective has been achieved.

Tolerable error is the maximum error in the population that the auditors are willing to accept and still conclude that the audit objective has been achieved.

This means that auditors will accept a certain number of instances of a failure to apply a control procedure and still conclude that the procedure is operating properly. It means they will accept a certain number of substantive errors in a sample and still conclude that the population it is drawn from is not materially misstated.

Tolerable error is considered during the planning stage and, for substantive procedures, is related to the auditors' judgement about materiality. The smaller the tolerable error, the larger the sample size needs to be.

Expected error

If the auditors expect error to be present in the population, a larger sample than when no error is expected needs to be examined to conclude that the actual error in the population is not greater than the planned tolerable error. Smaller sample sizes are justified when the population is expected to be error free.

In determining the expected error in a population, the auditors consider such matters as error levels identified in previous audits, changes in the entity's procedures and evidence available from other procedures. In the absence of indicators of problems, populations are generally expected to be error free.

2.7 Selection of the sample

The auditor should select sample items in such a way that the sample can be expected to be representative of the population.

For sampling conclusions to be valid, a **representative sample** must be selected i.e. all the items in the population are required to have an equal or known probability of being selected.

2.8 Random selection

KEY POINT

Random selection involves selecting from a source of random numbers, using computer programs or random number tables.

Simple **random sampling** is a method of selection in which every item in a population has the same statistical probability of being selected as every other item. The sample will therefore be representative of the population as a whole. This involves selecting from a source of random numbers, either by the use of computer programs which generate random numbers or of random number tables. An acceptable alternative to random selection is haphazard selection (see below).

This method of selection is also appropriate in non-statistical sampling, but it is often more time-consuming than other sample selection methods.

2.9 Value weighted selection

KEY POINT

Value weighted selection involves using the currency unit value rather than the items as the sampling population.

Value weighted selection involves using the currency unit value, rather than the items as the sampling population. Each individual pound in the population is given an equal chance of selection. For example, one pound is selected out of the first two thousand and thereafter each two thousandth pound is selected. Since an individual currency unit cannot be examined, the item which includes that pound is selected for examination. The advantage of value weighted selection is that high-value items have a greater chance of being selected and audit effort is directed to them. Since each currency unit, and thus each item, has a chance of being selected, this method achieves a representative sample.

This should not be confused with 100% examination of items above a certain value, in which items below that value stand no chance of being selected and thus the result cannot be representative. The chance of each item being selected is proportional to the value of that item and, in effect, a perfectly stratified sample is selected. Formal value weighted selection involves totalling cumulatively the currency value of each item in the account balance, which can be time-consuming unless computer assisted audit techniques are used.

The most common form of value weighted selection used in practice is monetary unit sampling (MUS). Such techniques are useful where the objective of the test is to test for overstatement, but not for understatement. Items materially understated have less chance of being selected using this method.

KEY POINT

In **systematic sample selection** the auditor calculates a uniform sampling interval by dividing the population size by the sample size.

2.10 Systematic selection

In **systematic sample selection**, the auditor calculates a uniform sampling interval by dividing the population size by the sample size. Having determined a starting point, every item corresponding to the sampling interval is selected. For example, if a population to be sampled is 600 items and the sample size is 50, the sampling interval will be 12. One of the first 12 items will be selected as the starting point and thereafter every twelfth item will be selected. In determining the starting point, each of the first 12 items (in this example) should have a chance of being selected. The starting point may be selected haphazardly or randomly.

Systematic selection is particularly useful when sampling from non-monetary populations, for example despatch notes.

One problem with systematic selection is that it may not achieve a representative sample where the population is arranged in a fixed pattern. For example, if every 50th item in a population has a particular characteristic (say it arises from the Bristol branch) then systematic selection may result in a sample containing a greater or smaller proportion of items with that characteristic than exist in the population as a whole.

2.11 Block sampling

KEY POINT

Block selection consists of selecting a number of adjacent transactions or items, e.g. all sales invoices in a particular week or all debtors with a name beginning with particular letters.

Block sampling is not generally an appropriate selection method because populations might be expected to be structured in such a way that items in a sequence have similar characteristics to each other but different characteristics to items elsewhere in the population. **Block selection** consists of selecting a number of adjacent transactions or items – for example, all sales invoices in a particular week or all debtors with a name beginning with particular letters.

There are two main disadvantages of this approach:

- The block selected may not be typical of the characteristics of the population as a whole. Although of course this is an inherent problem in any form of sample selection it is more apparent in block sampling where all testing is concentrated in a small part of the population.
- In order to minimise costs, it is probable that only relatively few blocks of items may be selected. This is particularly the case where the sampling unit is a period of time rather than individual items. For example, if transactions are being selected for vouching, it may seem to be practicable only to select a few days' transactions out of the whole year. A sample with only a few blocks is then unlikely to be adequate to reach a reasonable conclusion.

Despite these disadvantages, block selection can result in significant cost savings in audit time, and there are some occasions where practical considerations may require the use of block selection, for example when visiting a branch.

2.12 Haphazard selection

KEY POINT

In **haphazard selection** the auditor attempts to give all items in a population a chance of being selected by choosing items haphazardly.

This is a selection process in which the auditor attempts to give all items in a population a chance of being selected by choosing items haphazardly rather than following a structured technique. The auditor should avoid conscious bias and predictability in selecting items. For example, a tendency to favour items that appear to be 'easy', i.e. items that do not have crossings out and corrections around them or are simply easily located, should be avoided. Also bias should not be introduced by only examining items from current periods or by selecting items consciously because of their size or because they appear unusual. Haphazard selection is only acceptable as an alternative to random selection providing the tendency to bias is resisted. As a general rule, haphazard selection is not appropriate when using statistical sampling.

2.13 Evaluation of test results

KEY POINT

After testing the sample items, the auditor should:

- **analyse any errors** in the sample
- **consider implications** for the population.

Having carried out, on each sample item, those audit procedures which are appropriate to the particular audit objective, auditors should:

- analyse any errors detected in the sample
- draw inferences for the population as a whole.

2.14 Analysis of errors in the sample

In analysing the errors detected in the sample, the auditors first need to determine that an item in question is, in fact, an error.

In designing the sample, the auditors define those conditions which constitute an error by reference to the audit objectives. For example, in a substantive procedure relating to the recording of debtors, a misposting between customer accounts does not affect the total debtors figure. Therefore, it may be inappropriate to consider this an error in evaluating the sample results of this particular procedure, even though it may have an effect on other areas of the audit such as the assessment of doubtful debts.

2.15 Projection of errors to the population

Errors identified in the tests are projected across the population as a whole.

For example, out of a population of £10,000, errors of £42 are discovered in a sample of £2,500. The following projection could be performed.

$$\text{Total errors in the population} = \frac{£42}{£2,500} \times £10,000 = £168.$$

KEY POINT

If tolerable error is exceeded when the error is projected to the population, the auditor may perform additional procedures.

If this is less than the tolerable error, the auditor will have obtained sufficient assurance. If tolerable error is exceeded, the auditor may perform additional procedures, and perhaps finally suggest adjustments to the financial statements.

3 Statistical and non-statistical sampling procedures compared

- **Statistical sampling** requires the use of random selection and uses probability theory to determine the sample size, evaluate quantitatively the sample results and measure the sampling risk.
- **Non-statistical sampling** may use non-random sample selection methods, does not rely on probability theory and requires more subjectivity in making sampling decisions.

Non-statistical sampling is sometimes referred to as **judgement sampling**.

Statistical sampling is relatively expensive as the procedures need to be developed and staff need to be trained. This is balanced by the fact that the techniques are designed to keep sample sizes small. There is always a danger with non-statistical techniques that sample sizes are larger than necessary.

Some auditors can shy away from using statistical techniques either because they are not sufficiently confident in their use or that they feel more comfortable with using their judgement. The auditor must justify whatever method is selected.

KEY POINT

There is less scope for bias with statistical methods.

As we have seen, statistical methods are not as universally applicable as non-statistical methods. There is less scope for bias and auditors can draw precise conclusions about the nature of a population, whilst being clear about the degree of risk attached to those conclusions. As such, statistical techniques are probably more defensible than judgemental techniques (auditors can explain *exactly* why they chose the items that they did), but they can stifle the use of professional judgement.

ACTIVITY 1

You have just completed an audit of Hart Publications. During the course of the audit, you carried out statistical sampling of debtors and judgemental sampling of the pricing of publications. There have now emerged significant problems with the control over debtors and inconsistencies in the pricing of publications, with the pricing policy frequently ignored. What would be your considerations in understanding why your sampling had not identified the problems arising?

Feedback to this activity is at the end of the chapter.

3.1 Conditions necessary for the use of statistical sampling

KEY POINT

If statistical sampling is to be used:

- the population to be tested must be homogeneous
- the population should be large
- expectation of error must be low
- the items in the population must be easily identifiable.

If statistical sampling is to be used, the following conditions need to be present:

- The population to be tested must be homogeneous – that is to say, it must consist of items of the same kind, subject to the same level of audit risk. This is necessary if the statistical theory is to be valid.
- The population must be fairly large, otherwise the benefits of the technique will not be achieved. Statistical techniques need to be adjusted to work on small populations.
- Expectation of error must be low – in other words control risk must already have been assessed by the auditor as less than high. (High control risk gives impractically large sample sizes.)
- The items in the population must be easily identifiable once selected, so that checking of the items chosen is easily carried out. This means in practice that items such as invoices must be pre-numbered and filed in sequence.

An illustration will clarify the procedure.

Example

An auditor wishes to test a population of 100,000 purchase invoices using statistical sampling.

Confidence level	90%
Precision	±1.5%
Expected error rate	2%

In other words, at the conclusion of the test, the auditor will be able to conclude, if the actual error rate in the sample does not exceed 2% – 'I am 90% confident that the error rate in the whole population lies between ½% and 3.5% (2% plus or minus 1.5%).'

Statistical tables give a sample size in this case of 235.

235 invoices will be selected *at random* and checked. If in fact the error rate encountered does not exceed 2%, the conclusion stated above may be drawn. If the error rate exceeds 2%, it is not possible to apply the same confidence and precision level to the error rate actually discovered. This is because the higher the error rate assumed in the calculation, the larger the sample to be checked becomes. If, for example, a 3% error rate were encountered, the auditor would need to check (per statistical tables) 348 invoices. It would therefore be necessary to select and check a further 113 items (348 minus 235), if the auditor is to be able to conclude with 90% confidence that the error rate in the total population is 3% plus or minus 1.5%.

4 Further aspects of statistical sampling

DEFINITION

Attribute sampling provides results based on two possible values (i.e. correct and not correct).

DEFINITION

Monetary unit sampling (MUS) is an attribute sampling technique used in substantive testing to express a conclusion in monetary terms.

4.1 Attribute sampling for tests of control

Attribute sampling provides results based on two possible attributes (characteristics) of data (i.e. correct and not correct). As a consequence, it is generally used in tests of control where the objective of a test is non-monetary in nature, i.e. does a control operate or not. Each deviation from a prescribed control procedure is therefore given an equal weight in the evaluation of results.

The title of this subsection is therefore correct as far as the origin of this technique is concerned. However, in response to demands from audit firms for a statistical method which could measure monetary deviations, an attribute sampling technique was developed by statisticians which could express a conclusion in monetary terms – monetary unit sampling (MUS).

DEFINITION

Variables sampling is concerned with sampling units which can take a value within a continuous range of possible values.

4.2 Variables sampling for substantive test purposes

Variables sampling is concerned with sampling units (the individual items constituting the population) which can take a value within a continuous range of possible values and is used to provide conclusions as to the monetary value of a population. It can test either whether a certain statement is true or false, or give an estimate of the true value of a population.

For example, the technique can result in a conclusion that the auditor is 95% confident that the true value of the trade debtors lies between £59.6m and £60.4m, and the best estimate is £60m. It is therefore ideally suited to substantive testing which needs to be expressed in monetary terms.

However, the calculations involved are lengthy and can only be performed easily by computer applications. As a consequence the attribute sampling method MUS has been widely adopted instead by auditing firms.

5 Use of computers within the audit

KEY POINT

Auditors can **use PCs** to:

- flowchart client's systems
- evaluate audit risk
- prepare audit programmes
- carry out analytical procedures
- prepare audit working papers.

Auditors use computers extensively to assist them with audit sampling. In addition, they also use computer technology to help them control and manage the audit. In this section, we cover how auditors can use a PC to assist them with their audit work.

Flowcharting client's systems

Specialist flowcharting packages can assist the auditor in the production of clear, well presented flowcharts. Although the package cannot review the system for the auditor, it does produce legible output and can be easily updated when systems change, unlike manually produced flowcharts.

Evaluation of audit risk

The auditor can input into the computer an assessment of audit risk for the various transactions and balances in the client's systems. The computer can record these assessments in a word processing package, and may also provide guidance to the level of testing required via an expert systems shell.

Preparation of audit programmes

Audit programmes can be typed into a word processor, which again will allow for easy updating in the following years. Many firms may also have standard audit tests kept on a database within the word processor. When the test is required, it is simply copied out of the database into the audit programme. This is far quicker than typing the whole test into a computer.

Analytical procedures

A standard template can be set up on a spreadsheet package or specialist software can be used. The auditor inputs key details such as balance sheet totals from the financial statements. The spreadsheet then calculates key accounting ratios to assist the auditor with the analytical procedures.

Preparation of audit working papers

Where a computer is available to audit staff at the client's premises, it can be used to type up audit working papers. Audit documents with a lot of writing, such as memos and summaries of tests, will benefit from being produced more quickly on the computer and to a higher standard of legibility.

5.1 Audit software

Commercially available packages

Most audit firms will purchase at least one word processor package and one spreadsheet package. These programs will then be used as outlined above to assist auditors in their audit work.

Specialist audit software is also available providing audit working papers etc. These can be tailored to the client's needs. The working papers are often linked to minimise duplication and for control purposes.

Specialist programs written in-house

Larger audit firms will employ computer programmers in-house to write specialist software for use only by that audit firm. Examples of this type of software include databases of standard audit tests that can be copied into audit programs, and expert systems that will assist the auditor in determining audit risk and setting testing levels.

5.2 Controls

KEY POINT

Important **controls** when using computers include:

- taking regular backups
- following security procedures
- documenting key issues
- testing to ensure programs are error free.

The controls that must be exercised by auditors when PCs are used in their audit work include the following:

Backup of files

Backup copies of all audit files kept on the computer should be made regularly (at least once per day). These backup copies should be kept in a separate location from the PC. If then the PC is lost or damaged, the copy files can be used to continue work on that client.

When an audit is finished, and the client files are taken off the computer to make room for the next client's files, at least two and preferably three backup copies should be made. This ensures that if one copy becomes corrupted or lost, then the files can be retrieved from the second copy of the files.

Security of files

Audit information on clients can be very sensitive. Adequate procedures must therefore be in force to ensure that only authorised audit staff can gain access to the audit information. All audit computers should be protected by passwords, and disks with client data stored in safe locations, e.g. a fireproof safe.

Care must also be taken to ensure that computers holding client data are not stolen. If a computer is left at a client's premises overnight, then it should either be locked in a safe, or securely chained and padlocked to a table.

Adequacy of documentation

There is a danger with computers that not all the data or reasoning used to reach a particular decision will be documented. Adequate documentation must therefore be kept, including print-outs of all major documents, for future reference, together with the reasons for the decisions made.

Testing of programs

Before any program is used on audits, it should be tested to ensure that it is as far as possible error free. This is particularly true of programs written by the audit firm itself. Auditors could be particularly exposed in court if they made a wrong decision because of faulty or inadequately tested software.

6 Computer assisted audit techniques (CAATs)

6.1 Audit evidence

Audit evidence was considered in detail in an earlier chapter; however, it is worth considering again here as it is relevant to the use of CAATs.

ISA 500 states that 'the auditor should obtain sufficient appropriate audit evidence to be able to draw reasonable conclusions on which to base the audit opinion', and that paragraph is clearly relevant here.

General guidance on how the paragraph may be applied is contained in ISA 500. However, the form of evidence in computer-based accounting systems differs from that encountered in manually based systems. This has led auditors to consider the use of the computer in the course of their audit, and the various uses are described as computer assisted audit techniques (CAATs), the most commonly used being audit software and test data:

KEY POINT

The two most important **computer-assisted audit techniques (CAATs)** are **audit software** and **test data**.

- **audit software** – computer programs used for audit purposes to examine the contents of the enterprise's computer files
- **test data** – data used by the auditor for computer processing to test the operation of the enterprise's computer programs.

There are other more complex techniques. Such techniques will be considered later in this section.

6.2 The advantages of CAATs to the auditor

- In a computer-based system the large volume of transactions is likely to force the auditor to rely upon programmed controls. CAATs are likely to be the only effective way of testing programmed controls.
- The use of CAATs will enable auditors to test a much larger number of items quickly and accurately, and therefore increase the confidence they have in their opinion.
- CAATs enable auditors to test the accounting system and its records (i.e. the tapes and disk files) rather than relying on testing printouts of what they believe to be a copy of those records.
- Once set up, CAATs are likely to be a cost effective way of obtaining audit evidence provided that the enterprise does not regularly change its systems.
- Careful planning by auditors should enable the results of their work using CAATs to be compared with results from the traditional clerical audit work to increase confidence.

KEY POINT

Audit software may be:

- generalised package programs
- purpose-written programs
- utility programs used by the client.

6.3 Audit software

Types of audit software

Audit software comprises computer programs used by the auditor to examine an enterprise's computer files. It may consist of generalised package programs, specially written programs or the client's own programs.

- **Generalised package programs**

These are programs already written either by the auditor or a specialist software company, designed to be used on different types of machine. They need to be tailored to each specific case by defining the format of the files to be interrogated and by specifying the parameters of output data required and the form of that output. In some cases supplementary program coding is required.

- **Specially written programs**

In some cases it is not possible to adapt a package program because of the type of machine, processing or file organisation used. In such cases a purpose-written program is required. It could be written by the auditor, by a software specialist or by the client acting on the instructions of the auditor. In all cases it should be fully tested before being used 'live'.

- **The client's own programs ('enquiry programs')**

These are used by the entity to perform common data processing functions such as sorting and printing files. For example, when using a terminal, it is necessary to use the existing enquiry programs to refer to data held on files, or to obtain a print-out of parts of a file. In many cases, however, the client's own programs will not provide all the facilities needed by the auditor. It is likely that the team responsible for writing the enquiry programs produced the rest of the system and there is therefore a danger that the same defects apply to all such programs in the system.

Use of audit software

KEY POINT

Audit software is particularly relevant during substantive testing of transactions and balances.

Audit software may be used during many audit testing procedures. Its use is particularly appropriate during substantive testing of transactions and balances, as it can scrutinise large volumes of data and extract information, leaving skilled manual resources to concentrate upon the investigation of the results.

Typical uses of such programs include:

- **calculation checks** – e.g. the program adds the value of open items on a file to ensure that they agree with control records which are maintained
- **detecting violation of systems rules** – e.g. the program checks all accounts on the sales ledger to ensure that no customer has a balance above a specified credit limit
- **detecting unreasonable items** – e.g. a check that no customer is allowed trade discount of more than 50%, or that no sales ledger balance is more than total sales made to that customer
- **conducting new calculations and analyses** – e.g. obtaining a statistical analysis of stock movements to identify slow-moving items
- **selecting items for audit testing** – e.g. obtaining a stratified sample of sales ledger balances to be used as a basis for a debtors circularisation.
- **completeness checks** – e.g. checking continuity of sales invoices to ensure they are all accounted for.

Difficulties in using computer audit programs

- **Costs**

There will be substantial set-up costs even in using a generalised package. This is because the client's procedures and files need to be investigated thoroughly prior to identifying audit tests. The use of specially written programs will be even more expensive.

- **Changes to client's systems**

  These can mean costly amendments to the programs and the programs may need to be run during the year to test the system at different dates.

- **Small installations**

  There may be no suitable audit software package for use on mini-computer or PC installations. Software documentation may be incomplete so that it is very difficult to identify all procedures. It may be impossible to justify and hence recover the cost of specially written audit software.

- **Over-elaboration**

  There may be a tendency to produce over-elaborate enquiry programs which are expensive to develop, take up considerable computer running time and extensive reviewing time. Auditors should be able to justify the costs of using the program to the benefit in audit terms of its use.

- **Quantities of output**

  An enquiry program may produce huge quantities of output. This may be because the system is wrong or the enquiry program was badly designed. To avoid this problem, some packages can be set to terminate after a given number of items have been included in the count. Auditors must distinguish between cases where they have merely misjudged the parameters and obtained too large a sample, and cases where the print-out is long because lots of items are wrong. In the latter case, they must follow the audit work through and consider the implications of the problems encountered.

- **Version of files used in the test**

  The audit software only tests the files against which it is run. It is therefore preferable to use the software on the actual files of the client. The permission of the client is needed and the software must be carefully tested prior to its use on 'live' data.

  An alternative approach is to run the programs against copies of the data file. To be valid there must be adequate general controls to ensure that the client uses the same files. Provided this is so, the use of copy files enables the auditor to be more flexible in deciding when to test and to retain the copy files for further testing.

6.4 Test data

Description

DEFINITION

Audit test data is data submitted by the auditor for processing by the client's computer-based accounting system.

Audit test data consists of data submitted by the auditor for processing by the client's computer-based accounting system. It may be processed during a normal production run (running test data 'live') or during a special run at a point in time outside the normal cycle (running the test data 'dead').

Test data could be held in the form of a batch of documents put through the system to test both manual and computer controls. It is more often meant to refer to data used to test programmed controls. Its primary use is in the testing of application controls.

Note that the use of test data is not confined to the external auditor. It is a method used by programmers, analysts and internal auditors as part of systems development and monitoring procedures. There may be scope for co-operation between internal and external auditors in creating such test data.

Use of test data

KEY POINT

The three major approaches to the **use of test data** are:

- using live data
- using dummy data in a normal production run
- using dummy data in a special run.

There are three major approaches to the use of test data.

- **Using live data**

At its simplest level auditors could use real data that has been processed which involves the controls they want to test. They should then predetermine the results which they would expect from the processing of the data. They later check that the actual processing has been carried out in the expected way and investigate any differences.

This method is not usually feasible. Auditors will usually want to use a collection of normal, exceptional and even absurd data to test controls. They are unlikely to find all these conditions in a batch of real data. The vast bulk of day-to-day items will contain few exceptions and no absurd data. It would take auditors a long time to find a suitable range of data items to use.

- **Dummy data in a normal production run**

The auditor constructs a series of dummy transactions which contain the required conditions. These are processed along with normal data. Actual results are then compared with predetermined results.

This method has the advantage of producing a realistic test environment. The client's actual programs and data files are being used in the test.

The dangers of this method are, however, considerable. Computer-generated documentation may have to be intercepted before it is released. There may be a need to reverse the transactions after testing to eliminate the effects of test data. This may be time-consuming and require program amendments. It may distort management information by swelling the number of cancelled orders and credit notes. It would indeed be ironic if a client's accounting records were corrupted by the auditor's own test data. Therefore, great care is needed in planning and controlling the test.

- **Dummy data in a special run**

In this method the auditor creates special data and uses it against copies of the client's computer programs. The dangers associated with 'live' testing are therefore largely eliminated, although the interaction of one file with another must still be carefully considered.

It is still essential to obtain the client's permission, which reduces the independence of the test. It is also necessary to obtain assurance that the programs being used in the test run are identical to those used by the client for production runs and not special programs kept aside for the auditor's use!

Difficulties in using audit test data

KEY POINT

Difficulties in using audit test data are:

- costs
- limited objectives
- dangers of live testing
- dangers of testing during a special run
- need to record, i.e. produce working papers.

- **Costs**

There may be considerable costs involved in ascertaining the relevant controls and in constructing test data from scratch. It may be very difficult to identify all relevant conditions. The need to predetermine the results manually may be both time-consuming and tedious. These costs, however, are normally substantially less than for audit software. The benefits to the audit would have to be weighed against the costs.

- **Objectives of the test**

Test data is likely to be confined to tests of control and may therefore be less valuable in audit terms than using audit software.

- **Dangers of live testing**

Careful planning and control is needed to expurgate the test data from the records.

- **Dangers of testing during a special run**

If special test runs are used, an artificial testing environment is created. Assurance is needed that the normal programs and files have been used.

- **Recording**

The use of test data does not necessarily provide visible evidence of the audit work performed. Working papers should therefore include details of the controls to be tested, an explanation of how they are to be tested, details of the transactions and files used, details of the predicted results, the actual results and evidence of the predicted and actual results having being compared.

6.5 Other techniques

EXAM HINT

An exam question is likely to concentrate on audit software and test data, but more sophisticated techniques could be tested in part of a question.

An examination question would be likely to concentrate on audit software and test data; however, more sophisticated techniques do exist and they could be tested perhaps in part of a question. Try to grasp the main principles and don't spend too much time on this section. In many cases the techniques were first developed for internal purposes, e.g. during program development. They often require considerable DP expertise to be used accurately.

KEY POINT

The **integrated test facilities** (**ITF**) technique is where test data, input as part of a normal run is applied to 'dummy' test records held on master files.

- ***Integrated test facilities (ITF)***

This is an extension of the test data technique. The system is designed at the output stage to handle audit test data without unwanted side effects. The auditor uses test data, input as part of a normal run, and applied to 'dummy' test records held on master files. The weakness of this is that there is a danger of test data being subject to special procedures which are not applied to normal transactions.

ITF allows test data to be left in the system to see what happens, e.g. a dummy sale record eventually creates an overdue sales ledger balance. The auditor can use ITF to carry out regular testing of the system without using a special test run and indeed without being present during processing.

ITF is used largely to test application controls.

DEFINITION

Embedded audit facilities: a module of a computer program written by the auditor and incorporated into the client's computer system, which allows tests to be made at the time the data is being processed.

- ***Embedded audit facilities***

A wide variety of terms is used to describe this technique, including 'integrated audit monitors', 'resident audit software' and 'integrated audit modules'. It consists of a module of a computer program written by the auditor which is incorporated into the client's computer system either temporarily or permanently.

This technique allows tests to be made at the time the data is being processed. It is 'real time auditing'. It is useful where the audit trail is deficient so that historical audit work is difficult, or where files are constantly being updated, e.g. in a real time or database system. The facilities may allow results to be printed immediately or to be saved as a file for later evaluation by the auditor.

This technique may achieve the following objectives:

- to store information as it is processed for subsequent audit review
- to check the integrity of files which are being processed
- to spot and record items which are of some special audit interest, as previously defined by the auditor.

- ***Systems software data analysis***

Most systems software provides facilities for logging information relating to computer activity. For example, details may be kept of invalid passwords used, attempts to gain unauthorised access to data, operator interventions or keying errors.

The data from this software may be analysed to provide evidence during the audit testing of general controls. It may be particularly useful in systems which allow easy access to data through terminals but which have sophisticated software available to provide such data.

- ***Application program examination***

This involves detailed examination of the program instructions within the client's system.

It can be done manually, but there are also some specially written computer programs which can be used to assist in this task.

Auditors may wish to check that a program is operating in the way that it should be. For example, the program code which performs a complex discount calculation may be examined to ensure that the discounts are properly computed. This would be done as part of the audit testing of the application controls.

Alternatively, auditors may examine programs as part of their testing of general controls. For example, in testing the controls that ensure that all program changes are adequately tested and documented, they may use software to compare two versions of the program in the production library before and after the changes and check them against the program change documentation.

- ***Parallel simulation***

This is a technique whereby the auditor writes a program which is intended to perform the same operation as a client's program.

Identical data is submitted to each program and the results are compared. Obviously they should be identical: if they are not then it means that one of the programs is not operating correctly.

- ***Tracing***

Tracing involves following a transaction through its processing from start to finish to determine which program instructions are executed. This is a means of determining what the system is.

6.6 CAATs in database management systems (DBMS)

Unfortunately, generalised audit software may be of limited use in database systems because:

- there are many different DBMS and a lack of standardisation in languages used
- the enquiry programs may be geared to conventional sequential files and it may be difficult to convert the database into this form
- management may be reluctant to allow auditors access to the database without restrictions on their actions which all other users must suffer.

A more effective approach may be to use some sort of embedded facility – either integrated test facilities or embedded audit facilities. The auditor can then maintain a regular check of the controls and operation of the database. This approach requires considerable expertise and the software costs may be extremely high.

ACTIVITY **2**

(a) What do the initials CAAT stand for?

(b) How is the use of CAATs advantageous to the auditor?

(c) Describe two main types of CAAT.

Feedback to this activity is at the end of the chapter.

Conclusion

Sampling is a necessary and valid means of forming conclusions on audit evidence for internal and external auditors. The sampling process involves sample design, selection of the sample and evaluation of the sample.

Sampling may either be by statistical or non-statistical methods and the auditor must justify the method chosen.

Auditors can use PCs to assist in the management and performance of their audit work. They can also use CAATs, which principally consist of audit software and test data to assist them in their audit testing. Such techniques can provide a more efficient and focused audit.

SELF-TEST QUESTIONS

Audit sampling

1 What is the definition of audit sampling? (1.1)

2 What is sampling risk? (1.3)

Constructing samples

3 What are the three steps in audit sampling? (2.1)

4 What is the meaning of population in the context of audit sampling? (2.4)

5 When determining the sample size, the auditors should consider what three factors? (2.6)

6 What is tolerable error? (2.6)

7 What two things should the auditor do in the evaluation of test results? (2.13)

Statistical and non-statistical sampling procedures compared

8 What conditions are necessary for the use of statistical sampling? (3.1)

Computer-assisted audit techniques (CAATs)

9 What are the two main types of CAATs? (6.1)

10 What are the three types of audit software available? (6.3)

EXAM-TYPE QUESTIONS

Question 1: Statistical sampling

(a) Explain the main advantages that can be derived by an auditor from the successful employment of statistical sampling techniques, as opposed to non-statistical sampling. Discuss whether you would conclude that statistical sampling should be preferred. **(8 marks)**

(b) Explain the conditions under which statistical sampling is likely to prove most successful in an audit? **(5 marks)**

(Total: 13 marks)

Question 2: Auditing in a computer environment

The following quotations have been made by a group of auditors discussing auditing in a computer environment.

A 'Computer systems give rise to such possibilities as a lack of visible evidence and systematic errors.'

B 'The nature of computer-based accounting systems is such that the auditor is afforded opportunities to use the enterprise's computer to assist him in the performance of his audit work.'

C 'In choosing the appropriate combination of computer assisted audit techniques and manual procedures, the auditor will need to take a number of factors into account.'

D 'In performing tests on application or general controls, the auditor should obtain evidence which is relevant to the control being tested.'

Required:

(a) Explain each of the phrases 'lack of visible evidence' and 'systematic errors' referred to in **A** above and state in respect of each THREE ways in which the auditor might attempt to overcome the problems arising from these two possibilities. You should illustrate your answer by reference to a stock control system. **(8 marks)**

(b) State briefly TWO computer assisted audit techniques (CAATs) which the auditor can use in the enterprise's audit. (Refer to **B** above.) **(2 marks)**

(c) State and explain FIVE factors which the auditor will need to take into account in choosing the appropriate combination of computer assisted audit techniques and manual procedures. (Refer to **C** above.) **(5 marks)**

(d) Explain the words 'application control' and 'general control' in the computer audit context. Illustrate your answer by outlining one relevant audit test on:

  (i) an application control

  (ii) a general control.

(Refer to **D** above.) **(5 marks)**

(Total: 20 marks)

For answers to these questions, see the 'Answers' section at the end of the book.

FEEDBACK TO ACTIVITY 1

All methods of sampling have an element of sampling risk and therefore there is no guarantee that any sampling method would have identified the problems. The statistical sampling approach is seen as being less biased and more scientific and judgement sampling may have been more flexible but both methods can be valid. In view of the types of items being examined, statistical sampling would be appropriate to debtors and publications pricing may have been a more varied population sample justifying a judgement approach.

Considerations would include:

- How was the sampling method justified and what were the objectives of the sampling?
- Were there any indications of problems from the review of internal controls?
- What sample size was selected?
- Was the population homogenous?
- How were the results concluded and summarised?
- For the statistical sampling, what level of confidence could be obtained?
- For the judgement sampling, was an appropriate and representative sample selected?

FEEDBACK TO ACTIVITY 2

(a) Computer Assisted Audit Technique.

(b) CAATs are of use to auditors in the following ways:

  - In a computer-based system the sheer volume of transactions is likely to force the auditor to rely upon programmed controls. CAATs are likely to be the only effective way of testing programmed controls.

- The use of CAATs will enable auditors to test a much larger number of items quickly and accurately and therefore increase the confidence they have in their opinion.
- CAATs enable auditors to test the accounting system and its records rather than relying upon testing print-outs of what they believe to be a copy of those records.
- Once set up, CAATs are likely to be a cost-effective way of obtaining audit evidence.
- Careful planning by auditors should enable the results of their work using CAATs to be compared with results from the traditional clerical audit work to increase confidence.

(c)

- Audit software comprises computer programs used by the auditor to examine an enterprise's computer files. It may consist of generalised package programs, specially written programs or the client's own programs.

  Audit software may be used during both tests of control and substantive procedures, although it is particularly appropriate for use in the substantive testing of transactions and balances as it may scrutinise large volumes of data and extract information leaving skilled manual resources to concentrate upon investigation of the results.
- Test data consists of data submitted by the auditor for processing by the enterprise's computer-based accounting system. It may be processed during a normal production run ('live' test data) or during a special run at a point in time outside the normal cycle ('dead' test data).

Chapter 17

GOING CONCERN

CHAPTER CONTENTS

Having completed the detailed audit testing, the auditor needs to consider whether or not the going concern basis is appropriate. This is the standard basis on which financial statements are prepared unless there are indicators that this is not appropriate, and these are what the auditor must consider. This process is fundamental in ensuring that the financial statements are prepared on the correct basis, thereby ensuring that the user of the statements obtains a proper understanding of the financial statements.

Whilst it is useful for internal auditors to understand the principles associated with going concern reviews, they are less likely to be involved in this area, unless specifically requested by external audit or management. This is an area of expertise which is generally the concern of the external auditor. If internal auditors are involved, exactly the same principles apply.

Objectives

By the time you have finished this chapter, you should be able to:

- explain the importance of going concern reviews
- describe the procedures to be applied in performing going concern reviews
- describe the disclosure requirements relating to going concern
- describe the reporting implications of the findings of going concern reviews.

1 The auditor and going concern evaluation

1.1 The going concern concept

DEFINITION

The **going concern concept** is defined in FRS 18 as the assumption that the enterprise will continue in operational existence for the foreseeable future.

The preparation of accounts must follow the fundamental accounting principles laid down in FRS 18 and the Companies Act 1985. One of these, the **going concern concept**, is defined in FRS 18 as the assumption that the enterprise will continue in operational existence for the foreseeable future.

Financial statements are usually prepared on the basis that the reporting entity is a going concern because measures based on break-up values tend not to be relevant to users seeking to assess the entity's cash-generation ability and financial adaptability.

FRS 18 states that 'an entity should prepare its financial statements on a going concern basis, unless

- the entity is being liquidated or has ceased trading, or
- the directors have no realistic alternative but to liquidate the entity or to cease trading,

in which circumstances the entity may, if appropriate, prepare its financial statements on a basis other than that of a going concern'.

Any consideration involving the foreseeable future involves making a judgement about future events, which are inherently uncertain. Uncertainty increases with time and the judgement can only be made on the basis of information available at the time. Subsequent events can overturn that judgement.

KEY POINT

Auditors should generally look ahead **at least one year** from the date of the directors' approval of the accounts, in assessing the validity of the going concern basis.

The auditors should generally look ahead at least one year from the date of the directors' approval of the accounts, in assessing the validity of the going concern basis, but there may be circumstances in which it is appropriate to look further ahead. This depends on the nature of the business and the associated risks.

The auditors will need to satisfy themselves that the going concern assumption is reasonable. Auditors should not assume that the going concern concept will continue to apply, but need to conduct a specific examination of the relevant factors to reach a decision. This will involve an overall review of financial factors, preferably before the client's year end, in order to establish whether there are factors which cast doubt on the going concern basis. If there are, further investigation is required.

KEY POINT

It is the **directors' responsibility** to assess the company's ability to continue as a going concern. FRS 18 requires them to disclose any uncertainties in the financial statements.

It is the directors' responsibility to assess the company's ability to continue as a going concern when they are preparing the financial statements.

If they are aware of any material uncertainties which may affect this assessment, then FRS 18 requires them to disclose such uncertainties in the financial statements.

When the directors are performing their assessment they should take into account a number of relevant factors such as:

- current and expected profitability
- debt repayment
- sources (and potential sources) of financing.

The auditor, when performing the going concern review, should determine how well the directors have performed this assessment and whether they have taken all relevant factors into consideration.

1.2 ISA 570 *Going concern*

KEY POINT

ISA 570 requires auditors to consider the entity's ability to continue as a going concern and any relevant disclosures in the financial statements.

EXAM HINT

You must clearly understand WHY the auditor undertakes this review and be able to explain it.

ISA 570 requires auditors to consider the entity's ability to continue as a going concern and any relevant disclosures in the financial statements.

Specifically, it requires auditors to assess the adequacy of the means by which *directors* have satisfied themselves that:

- the going concern basis is appropriate
- the financial statements contain appropriate disclosures, if any.

Auditors should make 'enquiries' of directors and, having regard for how far directors have looked into the future, plan and perform procedures designed to identify matters which could indicate concern about the entity's ability to continue as a going concern.

The auditor should consider that same period of time as that used by the directors in their assessment. FRS 18 indicates that the directors should at least consider the period up to one year after the date of approval of the accounts.

You should note carefully that it is the *directors'* responsibility to gather evidence to indicate that the entity *is* a going concern, and that auditors are required to consider this evidence.

The auditor is NOT responsible for **ensuring** that the company is a going concern.

The volume of work that is required depends on the auditors' knowledge of the business and its size. Many of the matters referred to below will be inappropriate to a small business.

Auditors should consider:

- whether the period the directors have considered is appropriate
- any systems that exist to provide timely warnings of future risks
- budget and forecast information and the procedures for keeping this up to date, and the sensitivity of that information to factors which the directors may not be able to control, such as inflation and exchange rates
- obligations and guarantees to other entities which might precipitate the collapse of the entity under consideration. It is common for all companies in a group to cross guarantee the obligations of all the other companies to the bank. When one badly insolvent company in the middle of such a group goes under, many other profitable companies in the group may be taken with it
- the existence, adequacy and terms of borrowing facilities and the directors' plans to deal with matters giving rise to concern.

Such matters are dealt with below.

KEY POINT

Auditors should consider:

- the appropriateness of the period considered
- systems in place to provide timely warnings of future risks
- budget and forecast information
- obligations and guarantees to other entities
- the entity's borrowing facilities.

1.3 Indicators of problems

KEY POINT

Events or conditions that may cast doubt on the going concern assumption include **financial**, **operational** and **other events** such as major litigation.

Financial

- An excess of liabilities over assets or net current liabilities.
- Necessary borrowing facilities have not been agreed.
- Defaults on loans, breach of loan covenants.
- Significant liquidity or cashflow problems.
- Substantial operating losses.
- Substantial sales of fixed assets which are not to be replaced.
- Major restructuring of debt.
- Denial of trade credit by suppliers.
- Inability to pay debts as they fall due.

Operational

- Changes in the market or technology to which the entity is unable to adapt.
- Reductions in operations through legislation.
- Loss of key management or staff, labour difficulties or excessive dependence on a few product lines where the market is depressed.
- Loss of key suppliers or customers or obsolescence of a product.

Other

- Major litigation which could result in substantial fines/legal costs.

ACTIVITY 1

You are about to undertake the going concern review for a small manufacturing organisation.

(i) What procedures would you follow?

(ii) Comment on whether the denial of trade credit from a new supplier would give you cause for concern.

Feedback to this activity is at the end of the chapter.

1.4 Key audit procedures

KEY POINT

Auditors should request that **cashflow forecasts** be prepared (when none exists and there is doubt about the applicability of the going concern basis).

Cashflow forecasts

Cashflow forecasts should normally be prepared by management as a matter of course. In situations where there is doubt about the applicability of the going concern basis, and such forecasts are not prepared, the auditors should request that they be prepared.

Where a cash forecast is prepared, the auditors will review it critically, and consider whether the cash requirements indicated will in fact be available.

KEY POINT

Auditors should seek assurances about the **availability of financial support**, where necessary.

Availability of financial support

Where the cash forecasts indicate borrowing requirements beyond those currently available, the auditors will need to satisfy themselves that such funds will be available. Assurances that such funds will be available should be in writing and if they are not, because negotiations with the bank are continuing, the implications for the audit report should be considered.

The auditor will also need to consider the following issues:

- the company's ability to maintain the financial viability of both itself and its pension fund
- limits on the company's borrowing powers imposed by trust deeds, Articles of Association, and so on.

KEY POINT

Auditors should consider the need to obtain **written representations** from directors, where necessary.

Evidence from directors

Auditors should consider the need to obtain **written representations** from directors with regard to the appropriateness of the going concern basis and the adequacy of disclosures.

These may be necessary where there is concern over the applicability of the going concern basis and the directors' representations should of course tie in with the auditor's other evidence obtained.

1.5 Reporting

KEY POINT

The auditor needs to consider whether or not there is significant concern about the entity's ability to continue as a going concern, for his report.

The key issue in relation to reporting is whether or not there is significant concern about the entity's ability to continue as a going concern.

Where for example a key member of staff has been lost, where a key product has become obsolete and most commonly, where the company has still not finalised the provision of essential finance with the bank, providing auditors do not disagree with the going concern basis (i.e. providing they do not think that the entity is definitely *not* a going concern), they should consider the adequacy of disclosure of the matter in the notes to the financial statements.

If the disclosures relating to the uncertainty are absent or inadequate, the auditor will disagree with the truth and fairness of the financial statements and will qualify the audit report by issuing an 'except for' or 'adverse' opinion. We will look at details of these in a later chapter.

If the auditor disagrees with the going concern basis as a whole (a very rare situation in practice), then they should issue an 'adverse' opinion.

On completion of the detailed audit testing, the auditor must now consider whether or not the organisation is a going concern. If the auditor assesses that the organisation is not a going concern, or that this is in some doubt, then they need to discuss the issues with the organisation's management and determine how the financial statements have been prepared. If the organisation is assessed as not being a going concern and the auditor agrees with this, then this does not necessarily result in automatic qualification of the financial statements; it depends on the attitude of management and how they have prepared the financial statements.

Conclusion

The post-balance sheet period needs to be considered to decide whether the going concern basis is appropriate and whether there are any events which change the items included in the financial statements or the amount at which items already in the financial statements are stated.

SELF-TEST QUESTIONS

1 What is the definition of the going concern concept? (1.1)

2 Whose responsibility is it to collect the evidence regarding an organisation's going concern status? (1.2)

3 What are the financial indicators of going concern problems in an organisation? (1.3)

4 What are the operational indicators of going concern problems in an organisation? (1.3)

EXAM-TYPE QUESTION

Caffyn plc

ISA 700 contains examples of qualified and unqualified audit reports; any reader of an unqualified audit report can assume that the financial statements are prepared on a going concern basis, i.e. that the company will continue in business for the foreseeable future.

You are a partner of Heaton & Partners in charge of the audit of Caffyn plc. The audit manager has completed her work on the audit for the financial year ended 30 September 20X5 and has given you the draft financial statements and audit file containing all the working papers. You are conducting your final review prior to signing the audit report. However, you have identified that Caffyn plc does not appear to have complied with some aspects of FRS 15 *Tangible Fixed Assets*; this had not been picked up by the audit senior.

You have also identified that Caffyn plc currently has borrowings of £4 million which are due for repayment on 1 November 20X5, but it is currently trying to extend the due date. In addition, it also has an overdraft of £100,000, which is £20,000 over the authorised limit; this was not identified as a cause for concern by the audit manager.

Required:

(a) Identify ten issues that you think the audit manager should have considered when assessing whether or not Caffyn is a going concern. **(10 marks)**

(b) Detail typical types of evidence that you would have expected the Audit Manager to have considered when performing her going concern review. **(7 marks)**

(Total: 17 marks)

For the answer to this question, see the 'Answers' section at the end of the book.

FEEDBACK TO ACTIVITY 1

(i) The going concern procedures that I would use are to consider the following:

- whether the period the directors have considered is appropriate
- any systems that exist to provide timely warnings of future risks
- budget and forecast information and the procedures for keeping this up to date and the sensitivity of that information to factors which the directors may not be able to control, such as inflation and exchange rates
- obligations and guarantees to other entities which might precipitate the collapse of the entity under consideration. It is common for all companies in a group to cross guarantee the obligations of all the other companies to the bank. When one insolvent company in the middle of such a group fails, many other profitable companies in the group may be taken with it
- the existence, adequacy and terms of borrowing facilities and the directors' plans to deal with matters giving rise to concern.

(ii) Denial of trade credit by a new supplier is not in itself an indicator that the organisation is experiencing going concern problems. The organisation is a small one and therefore the supplier may have a policy that credit is refused for organisations until they reach a certain size or it may be that credit is refused until organisations have been a customer for a minimum period and no problems have been experienced with payment. The auditor should review all other financial circumstances before deciding whether or not this is a relevant factor to the organisation's going concern status.

Chapter 18

AUDIT FINALISATION AND THE FINAL REVIEW STAGE

CHAPTER CONTENTS

An overall view needs to be taken of the work performed and the auditor must stand back from the detailed work in order to gain an appreciation of the overall contents of the financial statements and the impression gained as a whole when reading them.

Having considered whether or not the organisation satisfies the necessary criteria for the financial statements to be prepared on a going concern basis, the auditor also needs to assess whether there are any events which change the items included in the financial statements or change the amount at which items already in the financial statements are stated.

The internal auditor is unlikely to be involved in the audit completion work on the financial statements, as reliance will be placed on the expertise of the external auditor in this area. Furthermore, as the external auditors report to the shareholders independently of the organisation, if the internal auditors were relied upon in part for this stage, this could be seen by the shareholders to be conflicting with their organisational status of reporting to management, and perceived as less reliable than the external auditors.

Finally, we will consider the need to obtain statements (representations) from management, on certain items appearing in the financial statements, which provide additional evidence to support the assertions contained in the financial statements.

Objectives

By the time you have finished this chapter you should be able to:

- describe circumstances in which obtaining management representations is necessary and the matters on which representations are commonly obtained
- describe the purpose of the subsequent events review
- describe the procedures to be undertaken in performing a subsequent events review
- describe the importance of the overall review of evidence obtained
- analyse the problems associated with the application of accounting treatments
- explain the significance of unadjusted differences.

1 Financial statement review procedures – timing, scope and nature

1.1 Overall review of financial statements

KEY POINT

Auditors should consider whether the financial statements are prepared in accordance with **statutory requirements** and **accounting standards**.

The **auditor's review**, in conjunction with conclusions drawn from other audit evidence obtained, should give them a **reasonable basis for their opinion** on the financial statements.

Auditors should consider whether the financial statements are prepared in accordance with **statutory requirements** and **accounting standards**. Accounting policies should be properly disclosed, consistently applied and appropriate to the entity. Checklists may be useful to the auditor for these purposes.

Auditors should ensure that the financial statements are consistent with their **knowledge of the business** and other audit procedures and that the manner of disclosure is fair.

1.2 Procedures – accounting policies

KEY POINT

The auditor should review the **accounting policies** adopted by the enterprise to determine their appropriateness.

The auditor should review the accounting policies adopted by the enterprise to determine whether such policies:

- comply with relevant accounting standards or, in the absence thereof, are otherwise acceptable
- are consistent with those of the previous period
- are consistently applied throughout the enterprise
- are disclosed in accordance with the requirements of FRS 18 *Accounting Policies.*

When considering whether the policies adopted by management are acceptable, the auditor should have regard, *inter alia,* to the policies commonly adopted in particular industries and to policies for which there is substantial authoritative support.

Where the policy is not covered by accounting standards, the organisation should adopt accounting policies that enable its financial statements to give a true and fair view. The entity should consider the key concepts of recognition, measurement and presentation, and when considering the appropriateness of accounting policies to the entity the objectives to be taken into account are:

- relevance
- reliability
- comparability
- understandability.

Pronouncements in other countries, or generally accepted practice in the industry, may also be considered. The firm's technical department, or other partners, will obviously be consulted, especially if a qualification of the financial statements is under consideration.

Where an 'acceptable' policy conflicts with specific Companies Act requirements, the true and fair override of Companies Act provisions (S228) would apply. This states that the directors of a company shall depart from the relevant Companies Act requirement to the extent necessary to give a true and fair view.

Particulars of the departure, the reasons for it and its effect should be disclosed in a note to the accounts.

1.3 Procedures – consistency with knowledge of the business

KEY POINT

Auditors should conduct a detailed review of the figures disclosed in the financial statements and consider compatibility, comparability and consistency.

Auditors should conduct a detailed review of the figures disclosed in the financial statements in order to determine whether:

- individual amounts are compatible with each other and with comparative figures
- amounts appearing in the financial statements compare and are consistent with internal data such as management accounts, budget statements and forecasts.

With regard to the first point, the auditor will, for example, check the relationship of cost of sales to turnover to ensure that the figures are reasonable by calculating the gross profit percentage and comparing it:

- with that of previous years
- with those of other companies or businesses in the same field of operations.

Likewise the auditor will compare the figure for trade debtors with turnover, expressing debtors in terms of the number of days' sales outstanding to ensure that it appears reasonable in the light of previous results and his knowledge of the industry in which his client operates. (Local authorities, for example, are notorious for the long credit periods they negotiate with their contractors. If the client carries out a large percentage of local authority work, the number of debtor days will be a lot more than the norm of 30.)

When it comes to comparing amounts appearing in the financial statements with internal data, auditors should obtain the relevant documents, insofar as they are prepared by the management, so that they can compare actual performance with expected performance. The inspection and comparison of monthly levels may highlight areas beyond the management's control – e.g. a particularly cool summer will depress ice-cream sales or an internal dispute with employees will affect production.

1.4 Procedures – presentation and disclosure

KEY POINT

Auditors should ensure that the financial statements reflect the substance of the underlying transactions.

The auditor should not be influenced by management's desire to present facts in a more favourable (or unfavourable) form. The financial statements should reflect the substance of the underlying transactions and not merely their form, so that for instance the nature of each of the various types of liability is disclosed separately, i.e. they are not simply lumped together under one heading. Debtors too should be scrutinised to check for example that those debtors recoverable more than a year after the balance sheet date are disclosed separately.

2 Subsequent events

2.1 ISA 560 *Subsequent events*

DEFINITION

Subsequent events are events occurring and facts discovered between the period end and the laying of financial statements before members.

Subsequent events are events occurring and facts discovered between the period end and the laying of financial statements before members.

There are two types:

- adjusting events
- non-adjusting events.

Adjusting events

DEFINITION

Adjusting events are events providing additional evidence relating to conditions existing at the balance sheet date; they require *adjustments* in the financial statements.

Events providing additional evidence relating to conditions existing at the balance sheet date are known under FRS 21 *Events after the balance sheet date* as **adjusting events**. Such events require **adjustments** in the financial statements.

Examples include:

- provisions for damaged stock and doubtful debts
- amounts received or receivable in respect of insurance claims which were being negotiated at the balance sheet date
- the determination of the purchase or sale price of fixed assets purchased or sold before the year end.

Non-adjusting events

DEFINITION

Non-adjusting events are events concerning conditions which arose after the balance sheet date, but which may be of such materiality that their **disclosure** is required to ensure that the financial statements are not misleading.

Non-adjusting events are events concerning conditions which arose after the balance sheet date, but which may be of such materiality that their **disclosure** is required to ensure that the financial statements are not misleading. Such events, therefore, will not have any effect on items in the balance sheet or profit and loss account for the period. However, in order to prevent the financial statements from presenting a misleading position, some form of additional disclosure is required, by way of note or pro forma balance sheet indicating what effect the events would have had on the year end balance sheet.

Examples of non-adjusting events include:

- the issue of new share or loan capital
- major changes in the composition of the group (for example, mergers, acquisitions or reconstructions)
- financial consequences of losses of fixed assets or inventory as a result of fires or floods
- major changes in the nature of the business
- strikes, government action such as nationalisation, and declines in the value of fixed assets or fixed asset investments.

2.2 Accounting and disclosure

A material post balance sheet event requires *changes* (i.e. adjustments) in the amounts to be included in financial statements where:

– it is an adjusting event, or

– it indicates that application of the going concern concept to the company is not appropriate.

A material post balance sheet event should be *disclosed* where:

– it is a non-adjusting event of such materiality that its non-disclosure would affect the ability of the users of financial statements to reach a proper understanding of the financial position.

For each post balance sheet event which is required to be disclosed, the following information should be stated by way of notes in financial statements:

– the nature of the event

– an estimate of the financial effect, or a statement that it is not practicable to make such an estimate.

2.3 Procedures

Auditors should perform procedures to identify subsequent events that might require adjustment or disclosure, up to the date of their audit report.

Procedures include:

- enquiring into management procedures/systems for the identification of subsequent events
- reading minutes of members' and directors' meetings, and of audit and executive committee meetings, and enquiring about matters not yet minuted
- reviewing accounting records including budgets, forecasts and interim information
- making enquiries of directors to ask if they are aware of any subsequent events, adjusting or non-adjusting, that have not yet been included or disclosed in the financial statements
- normal post balance sheet work performed in order to verify year-end balances
- obtaining a letter of representation – this will be dealt with later in this chapter.

KEY POINT

Auditors do not have a duty to actively search for evidence of events occurring after the date of the audit report but, before the financial statements have been issued or presented to members, but they should not ignore any knowledge which they acquire, from whatever source.

2.4 Procedures after the date of the audit report

Auditors do not have a duty to actively search for evidence of events occurring after the date of the audit report but before the date of the general meeting at which the accounts are presented to members. However, they should not ignore any knowledge which they acquire, from whatever source. If they feel that the information would have altered their audit opinion, had they been aware of it prior to the date of their report, then they should discuss the matter with the directors.

Directors should be encouraged to amend financial statements where required, if they have not yet been sent to members, and auditors should issue a new audit report on the new financial statements.

If financial statements have already been sent to members, directors are permitted in certain circumstances to revise the accounts. In such circumstances, auditors are required to issue a new audit report and also to report on whether the financial statements have been revised correctly in accordance with the legislation.

Whenever a new audit report is issued, auditors should update their subsequent events review up to the date of the new report.

Where directors refuse to amend financial statements where auditors consider this to be necessary, auditors should consider speaking at the relevant Annual General Meeting, taking legal advice and consider the possibility of withdrawing their audit report. The last option is rarely used in practice.

Auditors have *no* duty to enquire specifically into events occurring *after* the general meeting, but they should inform the directors of any event materially affecting the financial statements. They may also wish to consider taking legal advice on their own position.

2.5 Contingent items

DEFINITION

A **contingency** is a condition which exists at the balance sheet date where the outcome will only be confirmed by uncertain subsequent events.

A **contingency** is a condition which exists at the balance sheet date where the outcome will only be confirmed by one or more uncertain future events outside the control of the entity.

The detail of FRS 12 has already been dealt with earlier in this text. It should be appreciated that a post balance sheet event may clarify the treatment of a contingent item. The key points are revised below.

KEY POINT

Probable losses should be accrued, **possible losses** should be disclosed. **Probable gains** should be disclosed.

The ultimate outcome (gain or loss) of contingencies will only be confirmed by the occurrence or non-occurrence of one or more uncertain future events. **Probable losses** should be accrued, **possible losses** should be disclosed. **Probable gains** should be disclosed.

It is, therefore, very important for the auditor to consider whether a possible liability should actually be **incorporated** into the accounts as an actual liability or merely **disclosed** in note to the accounts (as a contingent liability). Auditors and directors have often disagreed about such issues.

ACTIVITY **1**

Hope Engineering

You are auditing the financial statements of Hope Engineering for the year ended 31 March 20X8. The partner in charge of the audit instructs you to carry out a review of the company's activities since the financial year end. Mr Smith, the managing director of Hope Engineering overhears the conversation with the partner and is surprised that you are examining accounting information which relates to the next accounting period.

Mr Smith had been appointed on 1 March 20X8 as a result of which the contract of the previous managing director, Mr Jones, was terminated. Compensation of £50,000 had been paid to Mr Jones on 2 March 20X8.

As a result of your investigations, you find that the company is going to bring an action against Mr Jones for the recovery of the compensation paid to him, as it had come to light that two months prior to his dismissal, he had contractually agreed to join the board of directors of a rival company. The company's lawyer has informed Hope Engineering that Mr Jones' actions constituted a breach of his contract with them, and that an action could be brought against the former managing director for the recovery of the moneys paid to him.

(a) Explain the nature and purpose of a review of subsequent events.

(b) List the audit procedures which would be carried out in order to identify any material post balance sheet events.

(c) Discuss the audit implications of the company's decision to sue Mr Jones for the recovery of the compensation paid to him.

Feedback to this activity is at the end of the chapter.

3 Management representations

3.1 Introduction

Representations by management are one source of audit evidence. They may be an important part of audit evidence in the audit of companies of all sizes.

KEY POINT

ISA 580 *Management representations* requires that auditors obtain written confirmation of appropriate representations before the audit report is issued.

ISA 580 *Management representations* requires that auditors obtain written confirmation of appropriate representations before the audit report is issued.

Representations are required:

- to allow directors to acknowledge their collective responsibility for the preparation of financial statements and to confirm that they have approved them
- to confirm matters material to the financial statements where the representations are *critical* to obtaining sufficient, appropriate audit evidence.

KEY POINT

Critical representations are those where **knowledge of the facts** is confined to management and those where the matter is principally one of **judgement** and **opinion**.

Critical representations will be those where other sufficient appropriate audit evidence cannot reasonably be expected to exist e.g. *knowledge of the facts* is confined to management (e.g. management's intention to dispose of a business segment), and those where the matter is principally one of *judgement and opinion* (e.g. with respect to litigation in progress or on the trading position of a particular customer, or on the appropriateness of a change in accounting policy).

Representations are *not* a substitute for other evidence that should be available, and auditors should ensure that representations are reasonable and consistent with the auditor's knowledge of the business. Any contradiction of other audit evidence should be thoroughly investigated.

Auditors will often seek representations from directors individually as well as collectively, to confirm that all transactions have been disclosed.

3.2 Procedures

Arrangements for signing letter

KEY POINT

A letter of representation should be signed by persons with an appropriate level of authority.

A letter of representation should be signed by persons whose level of authority is appropriate to the significance of the representations made – normally by one or more of the executive directors (for example by the chief executive and the financial director), on behalf of the whole board. The signatories of the letter should be fully conversant with the matters contained in it.

KEY POINT

Auditors should request that the consideration of the letter and its approval by the board for signature be **minuted**.

Auditors should request that consideration of the letter and its approval by the board for signature be minuted. Auditors may request that they be allowed to attend the meeting at which the board is due to approve the letter. Such attendance may also be desirable where the representations are to be formally minuted, rather than included in a letter. The auditor may also wish to check that the minutes have been appropriately completed.

Actions if management refuse to sign letter

KEY POINT

Any disagreements between management and auditors should be discussed and clarified.

Procedures regarding written representations should be agreed at an early stage in order to reduce the possibility of the auditor being faced with a refusal by management to co-operate in providing such representations. The representations can take the form of a letter from management, a letter from the auditors confirmed by directors, or minutes of a meeting of the board of directors.

If management disagrees with the auditor's statement of representations, discussions should be held to clarify the matters in doubt and, if necessary, a revised statement prepared and agreed. Should management fail to reply, the auditor should follow the matter up to try to ensure that the understanding of the position, as set out in the auditor's statement, is correct.

Qualification

KEY POINT

If auditors are unable to obtain the written representations they need, they should consider **qualifying** the audit report.

There may, however, be circumstances where auditors are unable to obtain the written representations they need. This may be because of a refusal by management to cooperate, or because management properly declines to give the representations required on the grounds of its own uncertainty regarding the particular matter. In either case, if auditors are unable to satisfy themselves, they may have to conclude that they have not received all the information and explanations they need, and consequently may need to consider qualifying the audit report.

3.3 Dating

KEY POINT

The formal record of representations by management should be dated on the same day that financial statements are approved.

The formal record of representations by management should be dated on the same day that financial statements are approved. It should never be dated after the audit report since it is part of the evidence on which the auditor's opinion, expressed in the audit report, is based.

3.4 Contents and wording

The precise scope of the formal record of representations should be appropriate to the circumstances of each particular audit. The representations will be necessary where there are matters which are material to the financial statements, in respect of which the auditor cannot obtain independent corroborative evidence and could not reasonably expect it to be available, as indicated above.

3.5 Example of a letter of representation

Set out below is an example of a letter of representation. It is not intended to be a standard letter because representations by management will vary not only from one enterprise to another, but also from one year to another in the case of the same audit client.

However, there are certain matters on which representations are commonly obtained, which you would expect to see in most letters of representation, because the auditor is unable to gain alternative evidence:

- all books and records have been made available to the auditor
- management believe that the financial statements are free of material misstatements and give a true and fair view
- there are no subsequent events that require adjustment to or disclosure in the financial statements.

Example of letter of representation

(Client's letterhead)

(Date)

(To Auditor)

We confirm to the best of our knowledge and belief, and having made appropriate enquiries of other directors and officials of the company, the following representations given to you in connection with your audit of the company's financial statements for the year ended 31 December 20X1.

(a) We acknowledge as directors our responsibility for the financial statements, which you have prepared for the company. All the accounting records have been made available to you for the purpose of your audit and all the transactions undertaken by the company have been properly reflected and recorded in the accounting records. All other records and related information, including minutes of all management and shareholders' meetings, have been made available to you.

(b) We acknowledge our responsibility for the fair presentation of the financial statements and we believe that the financial statements are free of material misstatements, including omissions.

(c) The legal claim by Mr G H . . . . . has been settled out of court by the company paying him £38,000. No further amounts are expected to be paid, and no similar claims by employees or former employees have been received or are expected to be received.

(d) The company has had at no time during the year any arrangement, transaction or agreement to provide credit facilities (including loans, quasi-loans or credit transactions) for directors nor to guarantee or provide security for such matters.

(e) There have been no events since the balance sheet date which necessitate revision of the figures included in the financial statements or inclusion of a note thereto.

As minuted by the board of directors at its meeting on . . . . (date)

. . . . (Chairman) . . . . (Secretary)

4 Unadjusted audit differences

4.1 Identifying errors

During the course of the audit the auditor will have identified errors within the account balances and transactions. For example, a number of debtors may not agree, or perhaps the auditor considers that stock has been mis-counted. Ideally, the auditor should persuade management to adjust the financial statements for the effect of these differences.

4.2 Impact of differences

If management do not agree to adjust the financial statements for these know or actual errors, then the auditor must consider their impact on the view given by the financial statements (ISA 320 *Audit materiality*).

Also, ISA 320 requires the auditor to consider the potential impact of the extrapolated or estimated errors on the view given by the financial statements. As discussed in earlier chapters the auditor requires reasonable assurance that items in the financial statements are not materially mis-stated and that estimated errors fall within tolerable error. (The auditor should, in the first instance, extend audit procedures if the results of audit sampling indicate otherwise.)

The auditor should summarise and assess the actual and extrapolated audit differences before reaching a final audit conclusion and deciding whether or not to issue a qualified audit opinion.

A 'summary of audit differences' which usually includes previous year comparatives is normally included in the firm's planning documentation.

Conclusion

Auditors must form an audit judgement on the detailed work carried out on the audit. They need to take an overall view of the work performed and hence must stand back from the detail, in order to gain an appreciation of the contents of the financial statements.

The post balance sheet period needs to be considered to decide whether the going concern basis is appropriate and whether there are any events which change the items included in the financial statements or the amount at which items already in the financial statements are stated.

Representations from management on certain items appearing in the financial statements may be required which provide additional evidence to support the assertions contained in the financial statements.

SELF-TEST QUESTIONS

Financial statement review procedures – timing, scope and nature

1 What procedures should the auditor follow in a general review of the financial statements to assess whether the selected accounting policies are acceptable? (1.2)

2 What happens when the company uses the true and fair 'override' provisions? (1.2)

Subsequent events

3 What is a non-adjusting event? (2.1)

4 What is an adjusting event? (2.1)

Management representations

5 Representations by management are a source of what? (3.1)

EXAM-TYPE QUESTION

Representation

Management representations are an important source of audit evidence. These representations may be oral or written, and may be obtained either on an informal or formal basis. The auditor will include information obtained in this manner in his audit working papers where it forms part of his total audit evidence.

Required:

(a) Explain the nature and role of the letter of representation. **(6 marks)**

(b) Explain why it is important for the auditor to discuss the contents of the letter of representation at an early stage of the audit. **(4 marks)**

(c) Explain why *standard* letters of representation are becoming less frequently used by the auditing profession. **(4 marks)**

(d) Discuss the implications for the auditor of a small company, if the directors refuse to sign the letter of representation. **(6 marks)**

(Total: 20 marks)

(ACCA Dec 90)

For the answer to this question, see the 'Answers' section at the end of the book.

FEEDBACK TO ACTIVITY **1**

Hope Engineering

(a) Financial statements should be prepared on the basis of conditions existing at the balance sheet date, but consideration must be given to events and transactions which have occurred, or will occur, after the balance sheet date, since these may have a material effect on the financial position or viability at the balance sheet date.

An 'adjusting event' is one which is important enough to require the financial statements at the recent, or previous, year end to be amended. These arise from additional evidence on conditions existing at the balance sheet date which provides a basis for more realistic estimates or provisions including stock valuation, bad debts, insurance claims and changes in taxation law.

Certain events do not concern amounts recognised in the financial statements, but their effect in the future may require some form of additional disclosure by way of note or pro forma balance sheet to prevent a misleading position being shown. Such non-adjusting events include changes in share capital or the composition of the group or company (e.g., from acquisitions or disposals).

The identification of post balance sheet events as defined by FRS 21 requires auditors to perform a review that covers all significant events up to the date of their report and that such events, if material, are accounted for or disclosed in the financial statements. Such a review should encompass all sources of knowledge available to them and should be adequately recorded in the working papers.

(b) Appropriate audit procedures:

- Review interim financial statements for period since year end to detect trends and potential trading difficulties.
- Investigate material differences between values of audited balance sheet figures and latest balance sheet figures.
- Review major entries in nominal ledgers or journal records since year end and agree to supporting evidence.
- Review after date cash from debtors and credit notes issued for sales returns and allowances.
- Check the bank reconciliation to ensure all 'unpresented cheques' and 'outstanding lodgements' have been cleared.
- Check market prices or material prices for impact on stock valuation.
- Review the cash book for evidence of large loans or financing arrangements, significant sales of fixed assets or other unusual transactions.
- Review minutes of the meetings of shareholders and board of directors in the period since the balance sheet date.
- Review contingencies and provisions included in the financial statements in the light of the latest available information to determine whether adjustment is required.
- Obtain details from the company or its legal counsel concerning pending litigation, settlements, claims or contractual charges.
- Consider the need to obtain written representation concerning events which may have occurred.

(c) The compensation paid to Mr Jones will be included in the 'directors' emoluments' note to the financial statements at 31 March 20X8. The potential recovery of the compensation from Mr Jones requires the auditor to consider whether the event will determine the value of 'compensation for loss of director's office' in the financial statements and thus be an 'adjusting event'.

Alternatively, since the outcome of the case is uncertain, it could be disclosed as a 'non-adjusting event', giving the nature of the event and an estimate of the amount to be received (net of legal fees). However, FRS 12 requires that contingent assets should not be recognised in the financial statements unless it is reasonably likely that the gain will be realised. If realisation is only probable then the gain should be disclosed by way of note with a prudent estimate of the financial effect.

In order to assess the potential outcome, the auditor should consult both the client's counsel and independent legal advice, as well as checking the resolution to take action and the opinion of the directors, from the board minutes.

Chapter 19

STATUTORY AUDIT REPORTS AND OTHER EXTERNAL REPORTS

CHAPTER CONTENTS

The audit report is the major channel of communication between the auditor and the user of the financial statements. Some concepts underlying the audit report were covered in an earlier chapter. Here, we consider the detailed wording of the standard audit report, the changes that may be required for modifications to the report for inherent uncertainties and modifications for the various forms of audit qualifications.

This chapter also considers reports other than the standard audit report which the auditor may be required to make by company law in certain circumstances or other engagements such as a review report.

Internal audit reporting is covered in the next chapter.

Objectives

By the time you have finished this chapter you should be able to:

- describe, illustrate and analyse the format and content of unmodified and modified statutory audit reports
- describe and analyse the format and content of an external review report
- set out the main elements in an audit report
- appreciate the circumstances in which a qualified audit report is required
- recognise the need for disclosure of inherent uncertainties
- understand the provisions relating to small companies
- understand the circumstances in which additional reports are required.

1 *ISA 700 The auditor's report on financial statements*

1.1 The unqualified audit report

KEY POINT

ISA 700 sets out the basic elements of an audit report. More detail is contained in Bulletin 2001/2.

In the UK, ISA 700 explains the basic principles of audit reporting and identifies the basic elements of the auditor's report. Example wording of an unqualified report, tailored to the UK environment, is provided in Bulletin 2001/2 *Revisions to the wording of auditor's reports.*

We start by considering the general unqualified report.

Independent auditors' report to the shareholders of XYZ Limited

We have audited the financial statements of (name of entity) for the year ended … which comprise [state the primary financial statements such as the Profit and Loss Account, the Balance Sheet, the Cash Flow Statement, the Statement of total Recognised Gains and Losses] and the related notes.*

These financial statements have been prepared under the historical cost convention [as modified by the revaluation of certain fixed assets] and the accounting policies set out therein.

Respective responsibilities of directors and auditors

The directors' responsibilities for preparing the Annual Report and the financial statements in accordance with applicable law and United Kingdom Accounting Standards are set out in the Statement of Directors' Responsibilities.

Our responsibility is to audit the financial statements in accordance with relevant legal and regulatory requirements and United Kingdom Auditing Standards.

We report to you our opinion as to whether the financial statements give a true and fair view and are properly prepared in accordance with the [Companies Act 1985] [Companies (Northern Ireland) Order 1986]. We also report to you if, in our opinion, the Directors' Report is not consistent with the financial statements, if the company has not kept proper accounting records, if we have not received all the information and explanations we require for our audit, or if information specified by law regarding directors' remuneration and transactions with the company is not disclosed.

We read other information contained in the Annual Report, and consider whether it is consistent with the audited financial statements. This other information comprises only [the Directors' Report, the Chairman's Statement and the Operating and Financial Review].** We consider the implications for our report if we become aware of any apparent misstatements or material inconsistencies with the financial statements. Our responsibilities do not extend to any other information.

Basis of audit opinion

We conducted our audit in accordance with United Kingdom Auditing Standards issued by the Auditing Practices Board. An audit includes examination, on a test basis, of evidence relevant to the amounts and disclosures in the financial statements. It also includes an assessment of the significant estimates and judgements made by the directors in the preparation of the financial statements, and of whether the accounting policies are appropriate to the company's circumstances, consistently applied and adequately disclosed.

We planned and performed our audit so as to obtain all the information and explanations which we considered necessary in order to provide us with sufficient evidence to give reasonable assurance that the financial statements are free from material misstatement, whether caused by fraud or other irregularity or error. In forming our opinion we also evaluated the overall adequacy of the presentation of information in the financial statements.

Opinion

In our opinion the financial statements give a true and fair view of the state of the company's affairs as at … and of its profit [loss] for the year then ended and have been properly prepared in accordance with the [Companies Act 1985] [Companies (Northern Ireland) Order 1986].

Registered auditors

Address

Date

---

* *Auditors' reports of entities that do not publish their financial statements on a web site or publish them using 'pdf' format, may continue to refer to the financial statements by reference to page numbers.*

** *The other information that is 'read' is the content of the printed Annual Report other than the financial statements. The description of the information that has been read is tailored to reflect the terms used in the Annual Report.*

You should note that, in an examination, you would not be required to reproduce a full audit report as set out above. You might, however, be asked to describe the type of report that would be appropriate and to draft sections from the opinion paragraph.

1.2 Preparing a formal audit report

To prepare a formal audit report the following elements need to be considered.

Title

The auditors' report should have an appropriate title. Using the term '**Independent auditors report'** distinguishes the auditor's report from any other report reproduced from employees of the company.

Addressee

KEY POINT

Audit reports should be **addressed** to the **members** of the company.

The auditor's report should have an appropriate title. Using the term '**independent** auditor's report' distinguishes the auditor's report from any other report reproduced from employees of the company.

Audit reports should be addressed to the **members** of the company (on whose behalf the audit is undertaken), in the absence of alternative statutory or contractual arrangements.

Introductory paragraph

KEY POINT

The **introductory paragraph** identifies the financial statements audited, as well as the accounting convention used.

This identifies the financial statements audited by name or by the use of page numbers, to distinguish such information from other documents that have not been subject to audit. The primary financial statements and associated notes that are subject to audit comprise the following:

1 balance sheet

2 profit and loss account

3 cash flow statement

4 statement of total recognised gains and losses.

Items **1** and **2** are required by CA 1985; item **3** is required by FRS 1; and item **4** is required by FRS 3. Note that the opinion paragraph in the example given above only refers to items **1** and **2**. This is because items **3** and **4** are deemed to be necessary in order that the 'financial statements' give a true and fair view. Therefore, if they were omitted or defective, a qualification may arise.

The introductory paragraph also refers to the accounting convention under which the financial statements have been prepared ie historic cost, current cost etc.

Statement of responsibilities of directors and auditors

KEY POINT

The audit report should include a **statement of responsibilities** of directors and auditors.

Auditors should distinguish between their responsibilities and the directors in their audit report. If the financial statements (or usually the directors report) do not contain an adequate description of the directors' responsibilities then the audit report should include a description.

An example wording for this statement is as follows.

'Company law requires the directors to prepare financial statements for each financial year which give a true and fair view of the state of affairs of the company and of the profit or loss of the company for that period. In preparing those financial statements, the directors are required to:

- select suitable accounting policies and then apply them consistently
- make judgements and estimates that are reasonable and prudent
- state whether applicable accounting standards have been followed, subject to any material departures disclosed and explained in the financial statements
- prepare the financial statements on the going concern basis unless it is inappropriate to presume that the company will continue in business.

The directors are responsible for keeping proper accounting records which disclose with reasonable accuracy at any time the financial position of the company and to enable them to ensure that the financial statements comply with the Companies Act 1985. They are also responsible for safeguarding the assets of the company and hence for taking reasonable steps for the prevention and detection of fraud and other irregularities.'

Auditors are required to form an opinion as to whether:

1 proper accounting records have been kept by the company

2 proper returns adequate for their audit have been received from branches not visited by them (where applicable)

3 the company's balance sheet and (if not consolidated) its profit and loss account are in agreement with the accounting records and returns

4 such information and explanations as auditors think necessary for the performance of their duties have been received from the company's officers

5 the directors' report is consistent with the financial statements.

KEY POINT

Auditors must report on various matters only if, in their opinion, these requirements have not been met (reporting **by exception**).

Auditors must report on these matters only if, in their opinion, these requirements have not been met. This is known as reporting **by exception**. The absence of any comment in the report is, therefore, equivalent to a positive statement that they have satisfied themselves on all these matters.

In addition, if the financial statements do not properly disclose the details of directors' remuneration and particulars of transactions with directors and officers required by the CA 1985, auditors have a duty to include a statement in their report giving the required particulars. Auditors would also need to qualify their report as the financial statements would not have met the requirements of the CA 1985.

Note that a report by exception is not in itself a qualification. However it can lead to one. For example where the company has not kept proper accounting records the auditor may not have been able to gather sufficient evidence and this would lead to a limitation of scope uncertainty (see below).

Basis of opinion

The wording here is not dissimilar to the wording covering the same area in ISA 210 *Terms of audit engagement*. Note that if a fraud, however serious, did not lead to a material misstatement it would not give rise to a qualification in the audit report.

If auditors have not conducted their audit in accordance with Auditing Standards, they should explain their departure. Normally this will be as a result of client-imposed restrictions and will give rise to a qualification (see below).

Opinion

This covers the four primary statements and associated notes referred to in the introductory paragraph described above (even though only the first two are referred to explicitly).

The opinion stated is on:

- truth and fairness
- preparation in accordance with CA 1985
- *by exception only* – the matters referred to in the Statement of responsibilities, described above. Items **2** and **3** of these matters are almost unheard of. Items **1** and **4** are more common and invariably give rise to a qualification. Such a statement would be made at the end of the qualified opinion paragraph. Item **5** does not normally give rise to a qualification, as the directors' report is not subject to audit. The statement would be made in this case at the end of an unqualified opinion paragraph, as a separate paragraph.

Auditor's signature

This should include reference to the auditor's status as a Registered Auditor. The report may be signed by the firm, by the auditor individually or both. Normally the firm's signature is given as the firm as a whole assumes responsibility for the audit.

Auditor's address

The audit report should name a specific location, which is normally the city where the auditor maintains the office that has responsibility for the audit.

Date of report

This must be *after* directors have approved the financial statements (as the statements do not legally exist before then) and preferably on the same day. The post balance sheet events review extends to the date on which the auditor signs his report. FRS 21 on post balance sheet events, however, only extends to the date on which the financial statements are approved for issue by the directors.

It is not necessary that the final typewritten copies of financial statements are available for signature – draft copies may be signed provided the draft documents are sufficiently clear to enable a proper overall assessment of presentation to be made.

ACTIVITY **1**

(a) What matters should be disclosed in an unqualified audit report?

(b) What further matters may have to be reported in the audit report to comply with the requirements of the Companies Act 1985?

Feedback to this activity is at the end of the chapter.

2 *The qualified audit report*

2.1 The form of audit qualifications

KEY POINT

Qualified audit opinions arise from either disagreements or limitations of scope.

All qualifications arise from either disagreements or limitations on the scope of the auditor's work.

The qualification 'grid' below is a useful summary of the decisions to be made in drafting a qualified audit report.

Reason for qualification	*Material*	*Pervasive*
Limitation of scope		
The scope of the audit work is limited. The auditor is unable to carry out procedures because of a lack of evidence, e.g. a lack of accounting records that have been lost or destroyed, or a lack of adequate information and explanations from directors.	'Except for' opinion	The auditor is unable to form an opinion and *does not know* whether the financial statements give a true and fair view. 'Disclaimer' of opinion
Disagreement		
The auditor disagrees with the accounting treatment or disclosure of a matter such as the non-provision for a doubtful debt.	'Except for' opinion	The financial statements *do not* give a true and fair view. 'Adverse' opinion

A **pervasive qualification** is one that affects the view given by the financial statements as a whole. In the case of disagreements it is one that renders the financial statements seriously misleading; in the case of limitations of scope it renders the auditor unable to form an opinion.

KEY POINT

Qualifications may be **pervasive** or **material**, the difference between them being a matter of degree and materiality.

The difference between a **material qualification** and a **pervasive qualification** is a matter of degree and materiality. There are no absolute cut-off points, and what is material to one auditor may be pervasive to another. Pervasive qualifications are very rare in practice; adverse opinions are almost unheard of and it would be unusual for a listed company to have any sort of qualified opinion. The issue of a qualified opinion has certain legal effects such as the requirement for additional auditors' reports if the company wishes to pay dividends. We will look at this in greater detail later. It is important to appreciate that if the auditor considers that a qualified opinion is necessary then he should consult with the other partners in the company before a decision is made. The matter(s) should also be discussed in detail with the directors of the company in question – a qualified audit report (especially one with an adverse opinion) is likely to have very serious implications for the company and should only be issued where absolutely necessary.

KEY POINT

When a qualified opinion is issued, the auditor should **describe** and **quantify** the **reason** for the disagreement or limitation of scope.

In all cases where a qualified opinion is issued, the auditor should adequately describe and quantify, if possible, the reason for the disagreement or limitation of scope. In the case of limitations of scope, the report should distinguish between:

- limitations imposed on the auditors (for example, where not all the accounting records are made available to the auditors or where the directors prevent a particular procedure considered necessary by the auditors from being carried out); and
- limitations outside the control of the auditors or the directors (for example, when the timing of the auditors' appointment is such that attendance at the entity's stock-take is not possible and there is no alternative form of evidence regarding the existence of stock).

The position of this description within the audit report is slightly different for disagreements and limitations of scope, as can be seen in the examples below.

2.2 The circumstances in which it is necessary to qualify audit reports

As stated in an earlier paragraph the audit report should only be qualified as a last resort. The auditors would initially attempt to try and resolve the problem with management to avoid the need for a qualification. Management generally want to avoid a qualification and are therefore often willing to change their position or provide more information, if the auditor has given a firm view of the need to qualify.

Examples

(a) An example of an 'except for' opinion relating to a disagreement

In this report, the auditors disagree about whether a particular debt is recoverable. The amount is material, so qualification is necessary, but it is possible for readers of the report to isolate the effect of the disagreement, so the matter is not pervasive to the accounts.

AUDITORS' REPORT TO THE SHAREHOLDERS OF XYZ LTD

Opening paragraphs – as normal.

Qualified opinion arising from disagreement about accounting treatment

Included in the debtors shown on the balance sheet is an amount of £Y due from a company which has ceased trading. XYZ Ltd has no security for this debt. In our opinion the company is unlikely to receive any payment and full provision of £Y should have been made, reducing profit before tax and net assets by that amount.

Except for the absence of this provision, in our opinion the financial statements give a true and fair view of the state of the company's affairs as at 31 December 20 . . and of its profit (loss) for the year then ended and have been properly prepared in accordance with the Companies Act 1985.

Registered auditors *Address*

Date

(b) An example of an 'adverse' opinion

In this report, the auditors disagree about the accounting for certain loss-making long-term contracts. The disagreement and the amounts involved are so serious that the disagreement has been judged to be pervasive, leading to an adverse opinion.

AUDITORS' REPORT TO THE SHAREHOLDERS OF XYZ LTD

Opening paragraphs – as normal.

Adverse opinion

As more fully explained in note . . . no provision has been made for losses expected to arise on certain long-term contracts currently in progress, as the directors consider that such losses should be offset against amounts recoverable on other long-term contracts. In our opinion, provision should be made for foreseeable losses on individual contracts as required by Statement of Standard Accounting Practice 9. If losses had been so recognised, the effect would have been to reduce the profit before and after tax for the year and the contract work in progress at 31 December 20. . by £. .

In view of the effect of the failure to provide for the losses referred to above, in our opinion the financial statements do not give a true and fair view of the state of the company's affairs as at 31 December 20. . and of its profit (loss) for the year then ended. In all other respects, in our opinion the financial statements have been properly prepared in accordance with the Companies Act 1985.

Registered auditors *Address*

Date

(c) An example of an 'except for' opinion relating to a limitation of scope

In this report, the auditors have suffered a material limitation in the scope of their work, but have judged that the matter is not pervasive.

AUDITORS' REPORT TO THE SHAREHOLDERS OF XYZ LTD

Opening paragraphs – as normal.

Basis of opinion

We conducted our audit in accordance with Auditing Standards issued by the Auditing Practices Board, except that the scope of our work was limited as explained below.

Remainder of this paragraph as normal, followed by.

We planned our audit so as to obtain all the information and explanations which we considered necessary in order to provide us with sufficient evidence to give reasonable assurance that the financial statements are free from material misstatement, whether caused by fraud or other irregularity or error. However, the evidence available to us was limited because £ . . . of the company's recorded turnover comprises cash sales, over which there was no system of control on which we could rely for the purpose of our audit. There were no other satisfactory audit procedures that we could adopt to confirm that cash sales were properly recorded.

In forming our opinion we also evaluated the overall adequacy of the presentation of information in the financial statements.

Qualified opinion arising from limitation in audit scope

Except for any adjustments that might have been found to be necessary had we been able to obtain sufficient evidence concerning cash sales, in our opinion the financial statements give a true and fair view of the state of the company's affairs as at 31 December 20 . . and of its profit (loss) for the year then ended and have been properly prepared in accordance with the Companies Act 1985.

In respect alone of the limitation on our work relating to cash sales:

- we have not obtained all the information and explanations that we considered necessary for the purpose of our audit; and
- we were unable to determine whether proper accounting records had been maintained.

Registered auditors *Address*

Date

(d) An example of a 'disclaimer' of opinion

In this report, the auditors were appointed after the stocktake had taken place, so did not attend it. They have judged that the effect of this limitation in scope is pervasive.

AUDITORS' REPORT TO THE SHAREHOLDERS OF XYZ LTD

Opening paragraphs – as normal.

Basis of opinion

First part as normal but with the following added.

We planned our audit so as to obtain all the information and explanations which we considered necessary in order to provide us with sufficient evidence to give reasonable assurance that the financial statements are free from material misstatement, whether caused by fraud or other irregularity or error. However, the evidence available to us was limited because we were appointed auditors on (date) and in consequence we were unable to carry out auditing procedures necessary to obtain adequate assurance regarding the quantities and condition of stock and work in progress, appearing in the balance sheet at £.. . Any adjustment to this figure would have a consequential significant effect on the profit for the year.

In forming our opinion we also evaluated the overall adequacy of the presentation of information in the financial statements.

Opinion: disclaimer on view given by financial statements

Because of the possible effect of the limitation in evidence to us, we are unable to form an opinion as to whether the financial statements give a true and fair view of the state of the company's affairs as at 31 December 20.. or of its profit (loss) for the year then ended. In all other respects, in our opinion the financial statements have been properly prepared in accordance with the Companies Act 1985.

In respect alone of the limitation on our work relating to stock and work-in-progress.

- we have not obtained all the information and explanations that we considered necessary for the purpose of our audit; and
- we were unable to determine whether proper accounting records had been maintained:

Registered auditors *Address*

Date

2.3 Uncertainties and inherent uncertainties

KEY POINT

Auditors may be uncertain about the financial statements either because:

- there are **inherent uncertainties**, or
- some **limitation** has been imposed on the scope of the auditors' work.

Auditors may be uncertain as to whether the financial statements give a true and fair view, etc., for one of two reasons:

- either the matter is **inherently uncertain**, i.e. insufficient evidence is available because the matter can only reasonably be expected to be resolved at some future date, e.g. going concern doubts or major liquidation
- or some **limitation** has been imposed on the scope of the auditors' work and insufficient evidence is therefore available even though it *does* (or could reasonably be expected to) exist. In this situation the audit report is qualified as above, 'except for' or 'disclaimer', if the effect is material.

2.4 Inherent uncertainties

Important points to note are as follows:

- Inherent uncertainties, provided they are **adequately disclosed**, do *not* give rise to qualified opinions. Instead, reference is made by the auditor to the inherent uncertainty via an explanatory paragraph within the 'basis of opinion' section, where inherent uncertainties are **fundamental**.

KEY POINT

The auditor's action(s) and opinion is affected by whether an inherent uncertainty is fundamental or not.

- Where inherent uncertainties are **not fundamental**, no reference is necessary.
- Where inherent uncertainties are **inadequately disclosed**, a **disagreement** qualification will arise.
- If an explanatory paragraph is included in the report, it should be made clear that the report is **unqualified**.

An inherent uncertainty is fundamental when the magnitude of its potential impact is so great that, without clear disclosure of the nature and implications of the uncertainty, the view given by the financial statements would be seriously misleading.

The magnitude of an inherent uncertainty's potential impact is judged by reference to:

- the risk that the estimate included in financial statements may be subject to change
- the range of possible outcomes
- the consequences of those outcomes on the view shown in the financial statements.

Example of unqualified opinion with explanatory paragraph describing a fundamental uncertainty

AUDITORS' REPORT TO THE SHAREHOLDERS OF XYZ LTD

Opening paragraphs as normal.

Basis of opinion

First part as normal but with the following added

Fundamental uncertainty

In forming our opinion, we have considered the adequacy of the disclosures made in the financial statements concerning the possible outcome to litigation against B Limited, a subsidiary undertaking of the company, for an alleged breach of environmental regulations. The future settlement of this litigation could result in additional liabilities and the closure of B Limited's business, whose net assets included in the consolidated balance sheet total £ . . . and whose profit before tax for the year is £ . . . Details of the circumstances relating to this fundamental uncertainty are described in note . . . Our opinion is not qualified in this respect.

Opinion

As normal

The most common types of fundamental inherent uncertainties are those relating to litigation, as above, and those relating to the going concern status of the entity as follows.

AUDITORS' REPORT TO THE SHAREHOLDERS OF XYZ LTD

Opening paragraphs as normal.

Basis of opinion

First part as normal but with the following added

Fundamental uncertainty

In forming our opinion, we have considered the adequacy of the disclosures made in the financial statements concerning the possible outcome of negotiations for additional finance being made available to replace an existing loan of £.. which is repayable on 30 April 20. . The financial statements have been prepared on a going concern basis, the validity of which depends upon future funding being available. The financial statements do not include any adjustments that would result from a failure to obtain funding. Details of the circumstances relating to this fundamental uncertainty are described in note . . . Our opinion is not qualified in this respect.

Opinion

As normal

ACTIVITY 2

Qualifications

(a) What are the four types of audit report other than an unqualified report?

(b) Give an example of when each type of report would be appropriate.

Feedback to this activity is at the end of the chapter.

2.5 Clarification of terminology

KEY POINT

International practice refers to **unmodified** and **modified** audit reports rather than unqualified and qualified.

UK practice tends to refer to 'qualified' or 'unqualified' reports, whereas international practice refers to 'unmodified' and 'modified' audit reports. The terms relate as follows:

- **unmodified** audit report – a standard audit report which has neither a qualification nor an explanatory paragraph
- **modified** audit report – an audit report which has either a qualification or an explanatory paragraph.

You may also come across a 'fundamental uncertainty' being referred to as a 'significant uncertainty', and the additional paragraph that is added to the audit report being called an 'emphasis of matter' paragraph.

3 *Formulating an audit opinion*

3.1 Flowchart

The following flowchart is based on ISA 700 and may be helpful in problem type questions in deciding the action(s) auditors should take in respect of their report:

Decision making process re: audit opinion

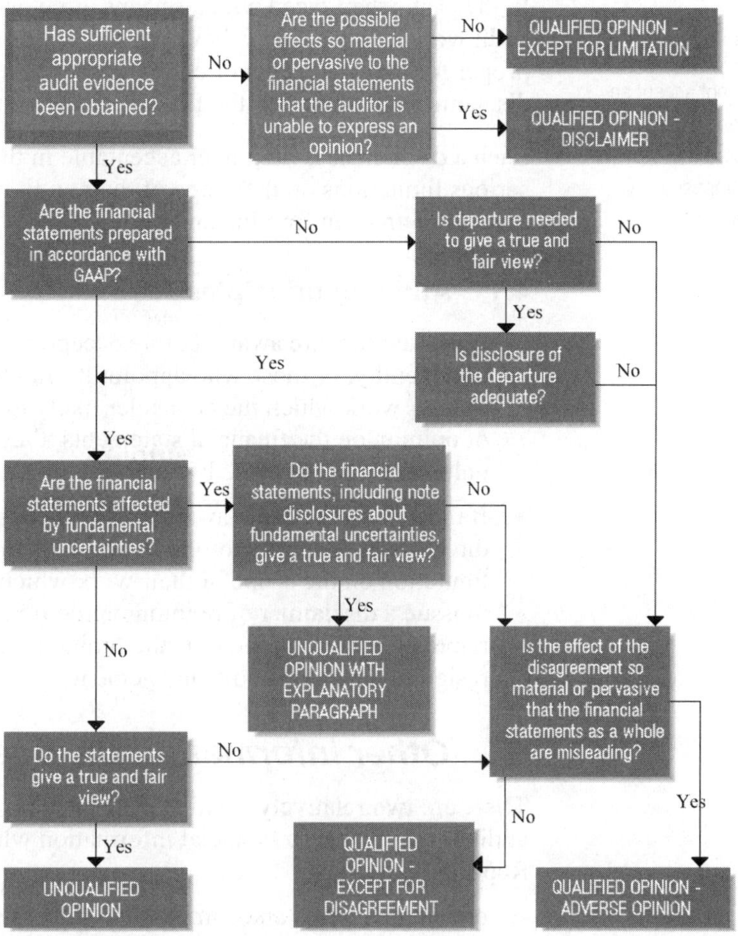

Questions concerning limitation of scope and disagreement are presumed to involve matters considered to be material. GAAP = Generally accepted accounting practice.

3.2 The impact of auditors' reports

KEY POINT

An unqualified report adds **credibility** to the contents of the financial statements.

The unqualified report is a summary of the auditor's work and conclusions. It adds credibility to the contents of the financial statements. This is perhaps easier to understand in the context of situations where audit reports are not required, such as for partnerships and unincorporated traders. In the latter cases, major creditors, e.g. the bank, may require further evidence from the owners of the business before a loan is granted.

Clearly, if the audit report has any impact, the management should be reluctant to get themselves into a position where a qualification is required.

If the subject matter of the qualification is a disagreement, then a large or public company faces the possible/probable investigation of the financial statements by the Financial Reporting Review Panel. This can require a company to reissue its accounts with the ultimate sanction that it can take the company to court if it does not comply with its wishes.

If the subject matter is a limitation of scope, the company may find itself in financial difficulties. Trade creditors may be reluctant to supply goods on credit terms and the bank may call in any overdraft. It should be appreciated that overdrafts are technically repayable on demand.

The severity of these potential effects helps to ensure that the auditor decides very carefully whether a qualification is required and ensures that management take the 'threat' of qualification seriously.

4 *Imposed limitation of audit scope*

KEY POINT

Auditors should not accept an audit engagement, where it is clear from the start that they will have a serious imposed limitation of audit scope.

In the past, when faced with a serious director-imposed limitation on the scope of their audit work, some auditors have not given sufficient consideration to whether it is proper for them to accept or continue such an engagement, but have simply issued a disclaimer of opinion on the financial statements.

Such a disclaimer is no longer acceptable in the situation when auditors encounter serious limitations on the scope of their audit work, that are likely from the start to prevent them from forming an opinion on the financial statements.

4.1 Auditing principles

- If the auditors are aware, before accepting an audit engagement, that the directors of the entity, or those who appoint its auditor, will impose a limitation on the scope of their work which they consider likely to result in the need to issue a disclaimer of opinion on the financial statements, they should not accept that engagement, unless required to do so by statute.
- If the auditors become aware, after accepting an audit engagement, that the directors of the entity, or those who appointed them as its auditors, have imposed a limitation on the scope of their work which they consider likely to result in the need to issue a disclaimer of opinion on the financial statements, they should request the removal of the limitation. If the limitation is not removed, they should consider resigning from the audit engagement.

5 *Other information disclosed in the annual report*

There are two relatively small areas which are particularly relevant near the end of an audit as they relate to financial information which may be disclosed in the Annual Report:

- opening balances and comparative figures
- other information issued with audited financial statements.

5.1 Opening balances and comparatives

KEY POINT

ISA 510 and **ISA 710** require that auditors must pay particular attention to opening balances, accounting policies and comparatives.

ISA 510 *Opening balances* and ISA 710 *Comparatives* require that auditors ensure that:

- **opening balances** have been appropriately brought forward, and do not contain misstatements affecting the current period
- **accounting policies** have been consistently applied and changes adequately disclosed
- **comparatives** (i.e., last year's figures presented alongside the current year figures) agree with the preceding period's financial statements or have been properly adjusted to reflect changes.

Note that the auditor is *not* expressing an opinion on the comparative figures.

Where the prior period was audited by another auditor or unaudited, the auditor will need to perform additional work in order to satisfy themselves regarding the opening position. The auditor's work would include:

- consulting the client's management
- reviewing records and accounting and control procedures in the preceding period
- consulting with the previous auditor and reviewing (with their permission) their working papers and relevant management letters
- substantive testing of any opening balances where the above procedures are unsatisfactory.

Some evidence of the opening position will also usually be gained from the audit work performed in the current period.

KEY POINT

If auditors are unable to satisfy themselves with regard to the **preceding period**, they will have to consider qualifying the audit report.

If auditors are unable to satisfy themselves with regard to the preceding period, they will have to consider qualifying the audit report.

If the auditor themselves issued an unqualified audit report on the preceding financial statements and nothing has arisen in the current audit to suggest any doubt as to the validity of those statements, then the auditor must ensure that:

- amounts have been correctly brought forward
- corresponding amounts have been properly classified and disclosed
- accounting policies have been consistently applied.

Particular attention needs to be paid to opening balances where the company has not previously had an audit on the grounds of size.

Difficulties may arise where the prior period financial statements were qualified and the matter is unresolved, and the matter has a material effect on the current period financial statements. If, for example:

- there was a disagreement over the non-provision for a debt in the prior period that is still at issue in the current period, the auditor will need to ensure that the current period qualified report refers to the fact that the matter arose in the previous period.
- there was a qualification on the grounds of disagreement or limitation of scope over closing stock in the prior period, this will affect the *current* period's profit and loss account. This is because last year's closing stock is this year's opening stock and the auditor will need to qualify the report on that basis. This might also apply where the prior period was unaudited and the auditor was not able to verify opening stock because they were appointed too late during the year.

The auditor should also qualify the report on the grounds of lack of compliance with the CA 1985, where the comparative figures are, or may be, misstated, as the CA 1985 requires that comparatives be shown properly. This might arise, for example, where the prior period financial statements were qualified for disagreement in respect of opening stock. This would cast doubt over the comparative profit and loss account figures.

5.2 Other information in documents containing audited financial statements

KEY POINT

CA 1985 requires that auditors report on any **inconsistencies** between the directors' report and the audited financial statements.

ISA 720 *Other information in documents containing audited financial statements* requires that the auditors should read the other information issued. If they become aware of/identify any material inconsistencies with the audited financial statements they should seek to resolve them. They should consider whether the financial statements or other information needs amendment and discuss the matter with directors.

The annual report and accounts of a company will contain a number of unaudited statements. A distinction is drawn between the directors' report and other unaudited statements, as the CA 1985 requires that auditors report on any inconsistencies between the directors' report and the audited financial statements. This does not apply to other information such as the chairman's report or employee reports.

KEY POINT

Auditors are not required to form an opinion on the **directors' report**, but should be satisfied that it is consistent with the audited financial statements.

The directors' report

Auditors are not required to form an opinion on the directors' report itself. As a result, under normal circumstances, auditors should confine their work to satisfying themselves as to whether or not the directors' report contains any matters which are inconsistent with the audited financial statements to comply with S235 CA 1985.

Such matters may include the following:

- an inconsistency between actual figures or narrative appearing in, respectively, the audited financial statements and the directors' report
- an inconsistency between the bases of preparation of related items appearing in the audited financial statements and the directors' report, where the figures themselves are not directly comparable, and the different bases are not disclosed

  An example of this would be where the fixed assets in the financial statements were depreciated at 25% per annum, but were depreciated at 20% per annum in the directors' report when showing a projected estimate of fixed assets additions, *without* explaining the difference between the two bases. In practice, such information is not likely to be found in the directors' report, as the requirement for a directors' report, and its contents are determined by the CA 1985, which does not require such information.
- an inconsistency between figures contained in the audited financial statements and a narrative interpretation of the effect of those figures in the directors' report.

Such inconsistencies arise very rarely in practice.

KEY POINTS

Auditors should consider the implications of any **inconsistency** and should hold discussions with directors or senior management in order to eliminate any such instances.

Where, after holding such discussions, the auditor is of the opinion that an inconsistency still exists, they should refer in their report to the inconsistency, in order to comply with S235 CA 1985.

The auditor does *not* have a responsibility to search the directors' report for items which, while not inconsistent with the audited financial statements, are **misleading** in some other respect. An example might be a statement by directors to the effect that they intended to use cash generated to invest in fixed assets, where the auditor knows that the cash will be used for directors' bonuses in the subsequent year. The directors' statement is not *inconsistent* with financial statements, but it is *misleading.*

Auditors may consider including an *explanatory* paragraph in their report, but they should take legal advice before doing so. They should also be aware that counsel has advised that it is doubtful that auditors have a right to comment on misleading, as opposed to inconsistent, items in their report on the audited financial statements.

Other financial information

The auditor has no statutory responsibilities in respect of other financial information issued with audited financial statements. Nevertheless, it should be reviewed by the auditor as, where there is a material inconsistency with the audited financial statements or contains an item which is misleading in some other respect, the credibility of the audited financial statements may be undermined. However, where he found any such instances he would always attempt to resolve them before their issue.

The auditor's reporting duties here are the same as they are where the directors' report is misleading, but not inconsistent, as above.

6 Small company audit reports

The CA85 requires auditors to make other reports arising from their normal audit work. Those that relate to small companies are as follows:

- reports on abbreviated accounts for the registrar of companies
- accounts with reduced disclosures for members.

Other examinable reports include those on:

- summary financial statements
- revised accounts
- distributions following an audit qualification.

KEY POINTS

Small and medium-sized companies may submit 'abbreviated' accounts to the Registrar of Companies.

The qualifying limits have been increased for accounting periods post 30/1/2004.

6.1 Abbreviated accounts

Sch 8 of the CA 85 permits companies to prepare 'abbreviated' accounts for submission to the Registrar of Companies if the company concerned is 'small' or 'medium-sized'. The Act defines such companies as those which meet at least two of the following three criteria for the current year and the immediately preceding year.

For accounting periods ending after 30/1/2004, the definition of small and medium sized companies changed as detailed below:

	SMALL		MEDIUM	
	Post 30/1/04	Pre 30/1/04	Post 30/1/04	Pre 30/1/04
Employees	50	50	250	250
Gross Asset Value	£2.8m	£1.4m	£11.4m	£5.6m
Turnover	£5.6m	£2.8m	£22.8m	£11.2m

Small and medium-sized companies must not be:

- a public company; or
- a banking or insurance company; or
- an authorised person under the Financial Services and Markets Act 2000.

KEY POINTS

Abbreviated accounts must include a statement that the company is entitled to file abbreviated accounts and must be accompanied by a special auditors' report.

Where abbreviated accounts are delivered to the Registrar of Companies, the balance sheet must include, above the director's signature, a statement that the company is entitled to file abbreviated accounts.

Where abbreviated accounts are delivered, they must be accompanied by a special auditors' report in which the auditors confirm:

- that the company is entitled to deliver abbreviated accounts
- that the abbreviated accounts have been properly prepared.

If the audit report on the full accounts was qualified in any way, the special report must include the full text of the qualified report. The special report must also include any statements in the audit report referring to inadequate records, accounts not agreeing with records and returns, and failure to obtain all necessary information.

The special report must be signed by the auditor in the same way that an audit report is.

6.2 Accounts with reduced disclosures for members

Companies that qualify as small under the criteria above are also permitted to prepare accounts with reduced disclosures for their members under Sch 8 CA 1985.

We will now consider the *audit* requirements for small companies. Keep clear in your mind the distinction between *accounting* requirements (above) and *auditing* requirements (below).

6.3 Total exemption from audit

Rules were originally issued in 1994 exempting certain small companies from the requirement for annual audit. The exemptions are not available to:

- a public company
- a banking or insurance company
- an authorised company under the Financial Services legislation.

These companies must always have an annual audit.

KEY POINT

The audit threshold increased from £1m to £5.6m on 30/3/2004.

The statutory audit threshold increased from £1m to £5.6m on 30/3/2004. So, companies with a turnover up to £5.6m and a gross assets threshold of £2.8m are no longer required to have an audit. These companies will still have to prepare accounts which comply with accounting standards and the Companies Act. There are some concerns within the profession about increasing the threshold as 'an audit provides a measure of comfort and reassurance for directors, shareholders, the Inland Revenue, lenders and creditors by providing an independent check on the company's accounting function'.

Also, growing businesses in need of external investment may encounter problems if they have not had an audit as investors will require proof of good corporate governance, and an audit can provide this detail.

It is also important to remember though that if at least 10% of the nominal value of the company's issued share capital have deposited a written notice at the company's registered office then the company has to have an audit.

6.4 Dormant companies

Under S220 CA 1985, a dormant company is not required to appoint auditors providing it is small, is not required to prepare group accounts and is not a public, banking, insurance, or financial services company.

6.5 Elective regime

You may remember from earlier chapters that auditors of *private* companies can be appointed indefinitely under the elective regime, by unanimous resolution.

6.6 Other relevant documents

The FRSSE (Financial Reporting Standard for Smaller Entities) simplifies the accounting standards that are applicable to smaller entities and how they should be applied. The FRSSE is optional, and companies can choose not to adopt it but comply with the other accounting standards instead.

There is also an APB Practice Note PN 13 on the audit of small businesses, identifying them as those with a concentration of ownership and management, often a single individual, with few sources of income, simple record keeping, or limited internal controls.

The Practice Note takes each auditing standard in turn and sets out how, and to what extent it should be applied to smaller entities.

The conduct of the audit of small businesses has been dealt with in an earlier chapter on planning.

7 Engagements to review financial statements

KEY POINTS

In **review engagements**, auditors carry out a review of financial statements (not a full audit).

Auditors may be required to carry out a review of financial statements – work falling short of the standard of a full audit but nevertheless providing some assurance as to the financial statements. Reporting is in the form of 'negative assurance'. The nature and extent of procedures carried out in respect of review engagements was discussed in an earlier chapter.

Because as yet there is little established guidance in the UK in respect of review engagements, the vast majority of guidance in this section is based on international practice issued by the IAASB. This can be regarded as accepted best practice.

ISRE 2400 *Engagements to review financial statements* regulates this type of assignment.

KEY POINT

The objective is to provide **negative assurance**, i.e. to state that there is nothing to indicate that the financial statements are not prepared in accordance with an identified reporting framework.

7.1 Objective of a review engagement

International Standard on Review Engagements (ISRE) 2400 defines the objective of a review engagement as follows:

> 'The objective of a review of financial statements is to enable an auditor to state whether, on the basis of procedures which do not provide all the evidence that would be required in an audit, anything has come to the auditor's attention that causes the auditor to believe that the financial statements are not prepared, in all material respects, in accordance with an identified reporting framework (negative assurance).'

7.2 Form of unqualified review report

REVIEW REPORT TO …

We have reviewed the accompanying balance sheet of Goliath plc at 31 December, 20XX, and the related statements of income and cash flows for the year then ended.

These financial statements are the responsibility of the company's management. Our responsibility is to issue a report on these financial statements based on our review.

We conducted our review in accordance with the International Standard on Review Engagements 2400 (or refer to relevant national standards or practices applicable to review engagements). This standard requires that we plan and perform the review to obtain moderate assurance as to whether the financial statements are free of material misstatement. A review is limited primarily to enquiries of company personnel and analytical procedures applied to financial data, and thus provides less assurance than an audit. We have not performed an audit and, accordingly, we do not express an audit opinion.

Based on our review, nothing has come to our attention that causes us to believe that the accompanying financial statements do not give a true and fair view (or 'are not presented fairly, in all material respects,') in accordance with International Accounting Standards (or indicate the relevant national accounting standards).

Date *AUDITOR*

Address

7.3 Misstatements

If the auditor has reason to believe that the information subject to review may be materially misstated, the auditor should carry out additional or more extensive procedures as are necessary to be able to express negative assurance or to confirm that a modified report is required.

7.4 Negative assurance

As mentioned earlier, the form of assurance provided for this type of assignment is referred to as **negative assurance** (i.e. nothing has come to the auditor's attention).

For an audit, the auditor will provide a **positive assurance** about the truth and fairness of the accounts. Although auditors cannot give absolute assurance on audited financial statements, the work carried out and the level of evidence obtained during the audit work should be sufficient to allow them to provide a high level of assurance that the financial statements are free from material misstatements.

In contrast, the negative assurance will provide some comfort to the intended user. In most cases, the auditor will be able to identify any material anomalies/errors or at least highlight risks in particular areas.

7.5 Preliminary announcements

KEY POINT

All listed companies have to issue a 'preliminary announcement' which notifies the Stock Exchange of their preliminary statement of annual results and dividends.

Companies listed on the London Stock Exchange are required to notify the Exchange of their preliminary statement of annual results and dividends as soon as possible after board approval. Such a statement is generally known as a **preliminary announcement**.

The ASB issued a non-mandatory statement of best practice on preliminary announcements in July 1998. The APB then issued a Bulletin 'The auditor's association with preliminary announcements' to give guidance to auditors in discharging their responsibilities in this area. The Stock Exchange Listing Rules require the directors of a listed company to have agreed the preliminary statement with the auditors before it is notified to the Exchange.

Conclusion

The audit report is the major channel of communication between the auditor and the user of the financial statements. The unqualified audit report consists of a number of elements, which must follow ISA 700.

Audit qualifications arise due to either disagreements or limitations in scope. Inherent uncertainties give rise to disclosures by management in the financial statements and do not normally give rise to a qualification.

A different form of reporting will be required for review engagements, where reporting will be more flexible to meet the client's requirements.

SELF-TEST QUESTIONS

ISA 700 *The auditors' reports on financial statements*

1 Who is an audit report addressed to? (1.2)

2 What do the financial statements consist of? (1.2)

3 What is the principle of reporting by exception? (1.2)

4 What should be included in the auditor's signature? (1.2)

The qualified audit report

5 What are examples of disagreements between the auditor and management? (2.1)

6 What is an inherent uncertainty? (2.3, 2.4)

Small company audit reports

7 One of the criteria for defining when a company is small is when its turnover is below what limit? (6.1)

8 One of the criteria for defining when a company is medium-sized is when its number of employees is below what limit? (6.1)

9 Is the full audit report included in the special audit report on the abbreviated accounts? (6.1)

Engagements to review financial statements

10 What is the objective of a review engagement? (7.1)

EXAM-TYPE QUESTIONS

Question 1: Audit report terminology

Explain the meaning of each of the following terms which are used in connection with audit reports:

(a) an adverse opinion

(b) a disclaimer of opinion

(c) circumstances of disagreement

(d) an 'except for' opinion

(e) limitations in the scope of the audit

(f) inherent uncertainties. **(12 marks)**

Question 2: Eastern Engineering

The following table of tangible assets appeared in the draft financial statements of Eastern Engineering, a large manufacturing concern, at 31 March 20X6:

	Land and buildings	*Plant and equipment*	*Assets in course of construction*	*Total*
	£'000	£'000	£'000	£'000
Cost:				
Balances at 1 April 20X5	161	976	13	1,150
Additions	6	124	35	165
Transfers	3	29	(32)	-
Disposals	(1)	(18)	-	(19)
Total cost at 31 March 20X6	169	1,111	16	1,296
Depreciation:				
Balances at 1 April 20X5	30	397	-	427
Charge for year	5	88	-	93
Disposals	-	(18)	-	(18)
Total depreciation at 31 March 20X6	35	467	-	502
Net book value at 31 March 20X6	134	644	16	794
Net book value at 31 March 20X5	131	579	13	723

Notes:

The net book value of land and buildings at 31 March 20X6 comprised:

	£000
Freeholds	116
Long leases (over 50 years unexpired)	8
Short leases	10
	134

The company's statement of accounting policies included the following:

- Tangible fixed assets are stated at historical cost less depreciation. Where assets are constructed by the company's employees, cost includes materials, direct labour and related overheads.
- Depreciation of plant and equipment is charged on a straight line basis from the time assets are brought into use, so as to write off their historical costs over their estimated useful lives.

The company's directors' report included the following.

> 'Following a professional valuation of a proportion of the company's land and buildings, the directors are of the opinion that there was no significant difference between market and book values at 31 March 20X6.'

The company's profit and loss account for the year ended 31 March 20X6 included the following.

Profit and loss account for the year ended 31 March 20X6

Profit before tax	£100,000

During the course of your audit of the fixed assets of Eastern Engineering at 31 March 20X6 two problems have arisen:

- The calculations of the cost of direct labour incurred on assets in course of construction by the company's employees have been accidentally destroyed for the early part of the year. The direct labour cost involved is £10,000.
- The company has received a government grant of £25,000 towards the cost of plant and equipment acquired during the year and expected to last for ten years. The grant has been credited in full to the profit and loss account as exceptional income which is not in accordance with SSAP 4 *Accounting for government grants* which requires that such grants be deferred to the balance sheet and credited to income over the useful life of the related asset.

Required:

(a) List the general forms of qualification available to auditors in drafting their report and state the circumstances in which each is appropriate. **(4 marks)**

(b) State whether you feel that a qualified audit report would be necessary for each of the two circumstances outlined above, giving reasons in each case. **(8 marks)**

(c) On the assumption that you decide that a qualified audit report is necessary with respect to the treatment of the government grant, draft the section of the report describing the matter (the whole report is not required). **(4 marks)**

(d) Outline the auditor's general responsibility with regard to the statement in the directors' report concerning the valuation of land and buildings. **(2 marks)**

(Total: 18 marks)

(ACCA Dec 86)

For the answers to these questions, see the 'Answers' section at the end of the book

FEEDBACK TO ACTIVITY 1

(a) An unqualified audit report should state:

- a title
- the addressee(s) of the report
- an introductory paragraph identifying the financial statements audited
- separate sections, appropriately headed, dealing with:
  - respective responsibilities of directors and auditors
  - the basis of the auditors' opinion
  - the auditors' opinion on the financial statements
- the manuscript or printed signature of the auditors
- the auditors' address
- the date of the auditors' report.

(b) Matters that may have to be reported include:

- if proper accounting records have not been kept or proper returns not received from branches
- if the accounts do not agree with the underlying records
- if the auditor has not received sufficient information or explanations necessary for his audit
- if the information contained in the directors' report is not consistent with information contained in the financial statements.

FEEDBACK TO ACTIVITY 2

(a) The four types are summarised in the grid below:

	Material	*Pervasive*
Limitation in scope	Except for	Disclaimer
Disagreement	Except for	Adverse

(b) **Limitation in scope – material**

No stock count carried out at a branch.

Limitation in scope – pervasive

Destruction of accounting records.

Disagreement – material

Difference of opinion between directors and auditor as to whether to provide for a doubtful debt.

Disagreement – pervasive

Non-compliance with an accounting standard, and the auditor does not agree with the non-compliance.

Chapter 20

INTERNAL AUDIT REPORTS AND INTERNAL REVIEW REPORTS

CHAPTER CONTENTS

KEY POINT

The **audit report** is the end product of an internal audit or internal review and the objectives will vary depending on the nature of the audit/review.

This chapter builds on Chapter 5, which outlined types of internal audit and internal review reports. Reporting is an important part of any review and you need to understand the objectives of reporting as well as the standards required. The chapter will also look at examples of the format and content of reports.

Objectives

By the time you have finished this chapter you should be able to:

- understand the reporting process and different objectives of reports
- describe, illustrate and analyse the format and content of reports.

1 Purpose and objectives of internal audit and review reports

1.1 Why produce an audit report?

The audit report can be seen as the end product of an internal audit or internal review. It is important therefore to understand the reasons for producing the report and its objectives. There are a number of potential objectives for the report. These are set out below and will vary depending on the type of audit or review to be carried out.

- To **recommend and influence change**

  The report can be used as a catalyst for change within the organisation. This can particularly be the case for reviews across structural boundaries, since the review will be seen as independent with no vested interests in any particular solution.

- To provide an **understanding and overview of control issues**

  Management need to understand the control issues within the area under review and be able to form an overall picture. If the objective of the report is to provide an overview, not just a list of evidence and findings, it is important to ensure that the structure and approach lead to this. A clear and concise report will facilitate this understanding.

- To ensure **action is taken** on audit findings and recommendations

  A formal report will identify agreed action and provide a focus for addressing findings and recommendations.

  Management are more likely to implement changes if the decisions and agreed actions have been formally communicated in writing and, in particular, if there are clear timescales and accountabilities.

- To **document the work carried out** on the audit and any limitations of scope (for example because of disputes)

  The report provides a form of documentary evidence of the work carried out including scope, objectives, findings and recommendations.

  A documented report showing scope can also protect the auditor in cases of dispute or subsequent problems by clearly showing any exclusions or omissions from the work carried out.

- To **provide assurance** to management

  The role of internal audit and review should be to provide some form of independent assurance. The report can be used to provide such assurance.

- To **provide information** to management

  Management are looking for information and this can be a further objective of the report: to provide independent advice, guidance and information, particularly on risk or corporate governance.

- As a **marketing tool** for internal audit and review

  The most visible output of the review will be a report and this can be an important marketing tool for internal audit or for those undertaking internal reviews. If reports are effective, they can be the shop window for management to see what auditors have done and what they are capable of.

1.2 Customers of the audit report

KEY POINT

The reports need to be targeted at the **appropriate audience**.

There is likely to be a **prime customer** to whom the report will be addressed.

There are a number of customers of the audit report. For each report it is important to be aware of who the customers are and what their objectives are likely to be. The reports need to be targeted at the appropriate audience. The usual customers of a report would be the following:

- operational management
- audit committees
- board
- organisation as a whole
- risk committees
- finance director
- chief executive
- external auditors
- regulatory bodies.

There will be a prime customer to whom the report will be addressed. This will usually be the director or senior executive of the business or area under review. However, the audit committee will need to see all high-risk reports in detail and a summary of all reports issued to allow an evaluation of the overall controls.

ACTIVITY 1

An audit trainee in your department is keen to understand who the customer is for internal audit and review reports produced. Explain the importance of understanding who the customer of the report is, the different needs that customers may have and how this may influence the content and style of report produced.

Feedback to this activity is at the end of the chapter.

2 Types of report provided in internal audit assignments

2.1 Reports for different purposes

KEY POINT

An **audit report** is the key output of internal audit work undertaken and is often seen as a key measure and marketing tool.

An audit report is the key output of internal audit work undertaken and is often seen as a key measure and marketing tool.

The type of report produced by internal audit will vary according to the nature of work undertaken and the type of organisation involved. A detailed, formal report may be appropriate for traditional audits in a large organisation. However, advice and guidance on change or a project may be more appropriately communicated through discussion papers or memorandum reports.

Whatever the style of report, the internal auditor should take care to ensure that it meets the organisational needs, as well as communicating clearly, concisely and effectively the findings from the audit.

2.2 Report ratings

KEY POINT

In some organisations, internal auditors provide '**ratings**' of the area under review, indicating the extent of concern over control or the level of risk. Ratings may be colours, numbers, letters, phrases or star ratings.

In some organisations, internal auditors provide 'ratings' of the area under review, indicating the extent of concern over control or the level of risk. This can be in various forms.

- colours – red/amber/green
- numbers/letters – A, B, C or 1, 2, 3
- wording such as 'acceptable' or 'satisfactory' and 'unacceptable' or 'unsatisfactory'
- star ratings *, **, ***.

The appropriateness of the rating will depend on the culture and style of the organisation and demands of management. Such ratings can help senior management to form an overall opinion of the organisation and to identify trends, and can also help with high level reporting. However, they can also be seen negatively if they result in management responding defensively to a report on their area that will result in a poor rating.

The most important consideration for rating a report is the basis on which any evaluation or measure will be carried out. This needs to be consistent and clear to ensure credibility of the ratings. The rating may be against a formal control or risk model that drives out the decision or opinion.

2.3 Formal reports

KEY POINT

The **formal report** is the traditional style of report, it usually includes:

- an executive summary
- summary of key findings and recommendations
- detailed findings, recommendations and agreed action
- appendices.

This is the traditional style of report emerging from an internal assignment, setting out a conclusion on the outcome of a review and detailed findings and recommendations.

Reports should contain the following components.

Executive summary

This may include a short overall section on the scope, approach and objectives of the review.

It would include an overall conclusion from the audit and may include an opinion. It may also include a balanced overview of the area including both good and bad findings.

The executive summary should tell any reader the major points arising from the audit so that without reading any further a view on the area and priorities can be formed. It should be sufficient to read as a stand-alone document if necessary.

It should make maximum impact and be short and punchy. Senior management do not want to wade through many pages of executive summary to try and form an opinion.

Summary of key findings and recommendations

Short, clear summaries of the key findings and recommendations from the review.

Detailed findings, recommendations and agreed action

This will set out agreed actions, timescale for action and responsibilities for resolution and will be the meat of the report for line management.

Appendices

This will depend on the type of area under review, but could include additional evidence and analysis, any definitions or explanations or terms of reference.

2.4 Discussion papers and reports

KEY POINT

Discussion papers and **discussion reports** are used in particular for ad hoc work and guidance.

Discussion papers and discussion reports may be used for certain types of audit report but in particular for ad hoc work and guidance. These will be less formal and may be less structured than the reports described above.

One type of discussion report is the project report.

2.5 Project reports

There are a number of different types of project audit reports that could be produced:

- project management review reports
- business case review reports
- review of implementation
- post-implementation reports
- due diligence reporting.

The types of reports produced will depend on the approach to project auditing within the organisation, but as the audit of change becomes more important, so the use of more formalised audit project reporting will increase. To an extent, the type and nature of reporting on projects will be driven by the organisation's approach to reporting.

2.6 Presentations

As internal audit moves towards a consultancy type of audit, then presentations can be an appropriate means of communicating. Presentations can make particularly good impact when there are a large number of customers or the area is very complex. By getting line/senior managers together and presenting findings, there is more scope for using effective communication to agree the best way forward.

2.7 Memorandum reports

KEY POINT

Memorandum reports are appropriate for small reviews.

Memorandum reports are appropriate for small reviews that do not warrant a full report but need to have findings and outcomes communicated.

2.8 Compliance reports

KEY POINT

Results of standard questionnaires or tests may be summarised into **compliance reports**.

Despite the move to a consultancy, risk-based approach, there is still a need to report on compliance activities undertaken. These may be the results of standard questionnaires or tests that need to be summarised into compliance reports at individual and consolidated levels.

2.9 Follow-up reporting

KEY POINT

All findings raised should be followed up to ensure that agreed action has been implemented.

Professional standards require that all findings raised are followed up to ensure that agreed action has been implemented. This follow up can take various forms:

- obtaining management confirmation of resolution of the action
- testing by internal audit to ensure satisfactory clearance
- formal follow-up reviews, where significant findings and level of risk had been found.

2.10 Risk reports

KEY POINT

Risk reports from internal audit analyse risk exposure within an organisation, including risk impact and probability.

These are reports from internal audit analysing risk exposure within an organisation, including risk impact and probability. They may be specific reports produced showing an overall picture of risk and control within the organisation to meet the corporate governance requirements.

2.11 Reports from risk and control workshops

KEY POINT

Where internal auditors facilitate **risk and control workshops**, the results will need to be captured and formally reported.

Where internal auditors facilitate risk and control workshops in which risks are brainstormed with operational management, the results will need to be captured and formally reported. The style of reporting will be different because of the nature of the work undertaken, which is more participative in nature.

Reports should identify key risks identified, the impact and probability of such risks and the controls in place to minimise the risks. Reports should also capture agreed actions, which should be monitored in the same way as any other agreed actions.

2.12 Monthly and annual reporting

KEY POINT

Internal auditors should produce **monthly and annual reporting** to provide organisations with the assurances required.

Internal auditors should produce monthly and annual reporting to provide organisations with the assurance required on the level of risk, overall control environment and compliance with corporate governance requirements. These should consolidate all the individual audit work undertaken to give a more rounded and complete picture to management. Such reporting could also include:

- performance statistics for the department, including productivity and achievement of agreed service standards
- summary of key outstanding recommendations
- key risk issues identified but not reported upon
- future internal audit plans.

ACTIVITY **2**

What different types of internal audit and review reports are there?

Feedback to this activity is at the end of the chapter.

3 Process for producing an internal audit report or review report

3.1 Overview of process

KEY POINT

The report may be produced **in various stages** over the life of the audit project.

Producing a report is not necessarily a single exercise at the end of a review. It may be produced in various stages over the life of the audit project. Each stage of the review will identify information that needs to be incorporated within the report. Key findings together with the associated risks may come to light at an early stage of the review and should be promptly documented.

The following table outlines the key stages and how they feed into the report.

Stages of review	*Feed to the report*
Planning Terms of reference	Objectives – agreed audit objectives documented in the report Report put in context by explaining the scope and approach
Identifying and evaluating risks	Key risks should be highlighted in the report, in particular those with high impact and probability
Control evaluation	As control evaluation is undertaken, there may be findings that arise that do not need testing. These should be documented and discussed with management during the audit.
Testing	Testing will identify any control weaknesses and risk exposures, which should be documented as findings/issues and discussed with management.
Analysing and forming opinions	Once the audit work is complete, an overall picture and opinion can be formed on the area under review. An initial decision on any audit rating and categorisation will need to be made.
Draft report	The draft report will need to consolidate the work carried out by the members of the review team and act as a useful discussion document with management.
Exit/wrap-up meeting	An exit or wrap-up meeting will be extremely useful to finalise the audit, communicating with management, confirming facts and agreeing actions and responsibilities.
Final report	The final report will be issued after the exit/wrap-up meeting and once all the facts and actions have been agreed. This will be the report used for summarising into other types of report and for monitoring purposes.
Follow up	The reporting process continues after the report has been issued. The findings will need to be followed up to ensure that agreed action is implemented within the timescales set out.

Liaison with Management and Ongoing Communication of Findings

3.2 Draft versus final reports

KEY POINT

A report is generally issued **in draft form** to allow management to understand and respond to the points identified in it.

An important aspect of the reporting process is discussing findings and agreeing final reports with management. Initially, a report will be issued as a draft to allow management to understand the points raised in the report before final issue and also to provide an opportunity for them to challenge the facts contained.

An exit meeting is normally held to encourage an open discussion and debate about the content and opinion expressed. During this meeting or any subsequent discussions, the report may be modified to reflect new information or clarify any areas of dispute.

Once the review team are satisfied that the report is complete, clear and accurate the report will be issued in its final form.

3.3 Disagreements between management and the internal auditor

On some occasions, management may still disagree with the report produced. Every effort should be made to communicate the risks effectively and to make clear the facts and reasoning behind the conclusions.

KEY POINT

The audit opinion **cannot be compromised** because of the dissatisfaction of management.

The report should result in proposed action. This can only be made effective if those responsible agree to take the action required. However, if there is disagreement between management and the internal auditor, even after all steps have been taken to explain the basis of the recommendations, the internal auditor still has an obligation to produce a documented audit report and to provide an independent and unbiased view. The audit opinion cannot be compromised because of the dissatisfaction of management.

It is important to include within the report the reasons for any disagreement. Those areas that can be agreed should have clear recommended actions and timescales. Whilst the report should highlight any management comment to reflect areas of disagreement, the most important concern should be how to address any serious risks highlighted.

4 Format of the internal audit report and review report

4.1 Key elements of reports

KEY POINT

Formats and **styles** of reports vary, but all audit reports need to be appropriately structured with a logical flow of information.

Audit reports need to be appropriately structured, with a logical flow of information. The format of reports can vary significantly according to the organisation and the approach of the department. Some internal audit or review teams have moved to a consultancy style approach, with presentations or landscape reports which are easy to read and bullet points setting out key issues. For other departments, a more traditional style of reporting is appropriate. Sometimes the organisation themselves may have an approved way of working that should be followed as far as possible in terms of format and style.

Cover of report
- Subject
- Distribution list
- Date of issue
- Any rating/evaluation

Executive Summary – this could include
- Overall summary of outcome from the review
- Introduction
- Overview of scope
- Key risks
- Opinion

Key findings and recommendations
- The major exposures identified during the review and their significance

Detailed findings and agreed action
- Findings
- Risk exposure
- Agreed action
- Responsibility
- Deadline/timescale

Appendices
- Explanations/further detail
- Appropriate analysis to back up the matters referred to in the main body of the report.

4.2 Cover of the report

The cover of the report gives a first impression and should be clear and attractive. This will include the information illustrated, including the name of the review and the business area examined, a date, reference, name of person the report is addressed to and any evaluation or opinion formed.

Need for clear and consistent use of subject of the audit

Subject: Internal Review of XXXXXXXX

Business Area: XXXXXXXX

Evaluation/Opinion

If a rating system is used, this should be shown on the cover page, with explanations for the rating in the appendix

To: Director; Business Area XXXXXXX

Distribution of the report should have been agreed at the start of the review

Reference: 01/DIV/0

Reference for the audit or review, which should have been agreed at the start of the review

Date: XX.XX.0X

4.3 Executive Summary

KEY POINTS

The **Executive Summary** is the key part that the audit committee and senior executives will read.

The Executive Summary is the most important and the most difficult part of the report. It is the key part that the audit committee and senior executives will read, as they will often have limited time and will want to identify any concerns as quickly as possible.

The report should be succinct and concise. Some audit departments specify that the Executive Summary is required to be no more than 1 to 2 pages long.

The purpose of the Executive Summary is to provide a high level summary of the effectiveness of the control environment and a concise summary of the audit findings.

The Summary should usually give a balanced view and include any positive comment, especially about key controls.

Sometimes, the Executive Summary will include other information, such as introduction to the area and scope. Alternatively, this could appear as a separate section.

The following is an example extract from an Executive Summary:

Executive Summary

Staff turnover of 20%, accompanied by high volumes and a new system being implemented, have affected the ability of the department to operate effectively and there are a number of significant risk exposures.

The new system was implemented at year end, which resulted in additional pressures on processing. Backlogs of up to 1 month (1,000 invoices) caused increased complaints and damage to company reputation.

There is a large reliance on temporary contractors, which is adding additional cost to the unit.

Management have recognised the risk exposures faced and have immediately implemented measures to address these, including:

- switch of an experienced finance manager to support the purchasing process
- review of processes for implementing new systems
- reduction in reliance on temporary contractors
- review of reasons for high turnover of staff.

4.4 Findings and recommendations

KEY POINT

Findings should emphasise significant weaknesses, which can normally be done by assigning some form of rating.

Findings should be categorised as appropriate to the department. In particular, it is important to emphasise significant weaknesses, which can normally be done by assigning some form of rating. This could be done in a number of ways, including indicators to flag up high-risk findings or categories such as A, B and C to show scale of any risks.

Findings should show the risk exposure arising, quantified where possible.

An example finding and risk would be:

1. USE OF AD-HOC SPREADSHEETS

Significance: ***High Risk/A category***

Finding

The department are using four ad-hoc spreadsheets for calculating key financial data, including level of claims, and for producing management information. These have been developed in an uncontrolled manner, outside of the end user computing guidelines published by the company. There is no documentation available to support the compilation of the spreadsheets. The employee who produced them is no longer with the company.

A check of one spreadsheet revealed an error in the calculation embedded in the system, which has resulted in an under claim of £35,000 over the last six months.

Risk

Inaccurate claims submitted for payment, resulting in financial loss and potential damage to reputation. Management relying on data from spreadsheets that may be inaccurate or incomplete, resulting in poor decision-making and failure to achieve objectives.

Recommendation

- The current spreadsheets should be re-checked for accuracy before further use.
- The extent of any further under-claim should be calculated and rectified.
- All spreadsheets should be documented and any further development carried out, following the company's policy and guidelines.
- Management should also investigate the potential for using the existing Financial Control system to calculate the information required, avoiding where possible reliance on these spreadsheets.

Management	Action
• All spreadsheets have been checked and the erroneous calculation corrected.	Complete
• The under claim is currently being addressed.	1 month SC
• Spreadsheets are being documented and revision procedures will be established by xxx	2 months SC
• Any further developments will be carried out using the end-user guidelines.	Immediate SC

In this example, the problem has been identified, including failure to abide by a key control where the end-user guidelines were not being followed. The problem was quantified (one out of four spreadsheets wrong and the value of £35,000 over a six-month period). The risks were identified and a management action plan included.

The findings and agreed action could be produced in a table format or text format, depending on the company style and preference and the level of detail required. Findings and recommendations could be reported to line management using an audit findings sheet, with more summarised details in the main report, as below.

Ref	*Finding*	*Action:*	*Action by:*	*Date*
1	**Purchase invoices** Of 30 invoices reviewed, 10 had no evidence of being checked and had no supporting data to support payment. **Risk** Fraudulent payment. Payment being made for goods or services not received. Damage to reputation.	All invoices will be supported by a corresponding purchase order and evidence of receipt of goods or service, with a check by the manager being evidenced prior to processing.	DCXX	By end of month

Another way of presenting findings and recommendations could be through a presentation type format, which is much more succinct, with bullet points emphasising the concerns raised.

ACTIVITY **3**

What are the advantages and disadvantages of applying risk ratings to audit findings and recommendations?

Feedback to this activity is at the end of the chapter.

5 Enhancement of business performance

5.1 Difference between reports to enhance business performance and standard internal review reports

KEY POINT

Reports aimed specifically at **enhancing business performance** may vary from standard internal review or audit reports.

Reports aimed specifically at enhancing business performance may vary from standard internal review or audit reports in a number of ways. In particular, reports to enhance business performance will:

- be more consultancy, in style and approach
- be less exception-based and more concentrated on the future delivery of performance rather than past errors or risks
- focus less on risk and controls, and more on performance, objectives and processes

- be more analytical of business performance rather than analytical of risks and findings
- include more recommendations on improvements rather than focus on actions to address specific findings raised
- be tailored to the individual demands of the review rather than using a standard reporting format.

5.2 Reporting to enhance business performance

As with any other report, objectives for the review and subsequent reports need to be clearly agreed at the start of review, along with the format and agreed distribution list. This allows the report to be constructed during the course of the review.

The report should have an Executive Summary that makes maximum impact and that is clear and concise.

The report will include analysis of business performance, along with proposals and recommendations for improving performance.

6 What makes a good report?

6.1 Tips for good reporting

KEY POINT

Tips for good reporting:

- discussing issues with management as they arise
- clear, easy to read format
- balanced and constructive reporting
- consistency across reports
- focus on customers and on meeting organisational needs
- concise reporting style.

- Discuss with management as points arise. This will mean less argument over facts or detail when the draft report is issued and will allow management to take steps promptly.
- Clear, easy to read format will mean it is more likely to be read and understood.
- Balanced and constructive reporting will be welcomed by management and the organisation. For example, recognising where controls are good and how they could be used elsewhere within the organisation.
- Ensure consistency across reports, particularly where 'ratings' are used. If management feel unfairly treated or criticised, they will respond negatively to the report.
- The report should be customer focused, meeting organisational needs. The internal auditor should always be conscious of the organisational philosophy, management styles and reporting objectives.
- Use a concise reporting style. If reports are too long, they will not be read and their impact will be lost.

Conclusion

Reporting is the key output for an internal audit or review. There are different types of reporting and formats, depending on the nature of the review and the approach and culture of the organisation.

Reports should follow the standard rules of any report and be clear, concise, consistent, timely and meet the objectives and standards of the review.

Reports to recommend improvements in business performance will follow the standard reporting requirements, but will be more flexible and consultative in style.

SELF-TEST QUESTIONS

Purpose and objectives of internal audit and review reports

1 Provide five objectives of reporting. (1.1)

2 Who are the key customers of the internal audit report? (1.2)

Process for producing an internal audit or review report

3 At what stage in the audit is the report produced? (3.1)

4 What is the difference between the draft and final report? (3.2)

Format of the internal audit and review report

5 What are the major elements that make up an executive summary? (4.3)

Enhancement of business performance

6 How does a report to enhance business performance vary from a standard internal audit report? (5.1)

EXAM-TYPE QUESTION

Reporter

Your organisational review department has a very poor reputation for reporting within the organisation. In particular, reports are issued late, with frequent lack of agreed action or timescales on findings raised and generally negative reaction from management experienced by the department. In the last six months, an average delay of 2 to 3 months has occurred between completion of field work and issue of final report. Moreover, reports have included findings without any agreed action. You have been asked to look at how you could improve the reporting process within the team and address the concerns raised.

Required:

Prepare a report for the Chief Executive including key recommendations.

Identify any additional information you require to further analyse the problems with reporting. **(20 marks)**

For the answer to this question, see the 'Answers' section at the end of the book.

FEEDBACK TO ACTIVITY 1

Importance of understanding who the customers of the report are:

- For any type of report produced, it is important to understand who the customer is and what the customer requires. In this way, the auditor can focus the report on delivering to the objectives, requirements and expectations of the customer.
- There are multiple customers of audit, although there will usually be a prime customer. This does not mean that other customer needs are ignored, rather that focus will be on tailoring the report as much as possible to ensure that the appropriate parts of the report are instantly accessible.

Different customer needs:

- Different customers will have different needs and priorities, which will affect the content, style and format of the report. It may be that different sections of the report will be sent to different customers.
- The Chief Executive, Board and other Senior Management may only be interested in receiving executive summaries, so that they can understand quickly the risks and then receive more detailed reports as required.
- The audit committee will need to see high risk reports and a summary of all reports issued, to help them evaluate the effectiveness of the corporate governance framework.
- Operational management or the manager of the area will be interested in reading and understanding the detailed work undertaken, both to ensure that the correct facts have been established but also to help address concerns raised.
- Regulators will be interested in regulatory risks identified and the robustness of the processes in place to comply with requirements.

FEEDBACK TO ACTIVITY **2**

Different reports are appropriate for different purposes. The key types of reports are as follows:

- formal, detailed level reports
- presentations
- discussion reports
- compliance reports
- project reports
- monthly and annual reports
- follow-up reports
- risk reports
- reports from risk and control workshops.

FEEDBACK TO ACTIVITY **3**

Advantages:

- Highlights significant findings to management, providing an indication of those that should be addressed as high priority and therefore helps management to prioritise their actions.
- Provides useful management information on levels and significance of outstanding actions and may support corporate governance work.
- May provide a mechanism for identifying common and systemic weaknesses across the organisation.
- Provides a risk focus to audit work and to reports.

Disadvantages:

- Can mean management do not take seriously lower risk rated recommendations.
- More time spent negotiating with management about the level of risk rating than on the merits of the recommendations.
- Difficult decisions on assessing ratings – can be subjective and may be particularly difficult when looking across diverse businesses.
- Inconsistency in applying risk ratings can undermine the whole process.

Chapter 21

NOT-FOR-PROFIT ORGANISATIONS

CHAPTER CONTENTS

This chapter examines the challenges of auditing small not-for-profit organisations, where the risks and types of controls in place may be quite different from an organisation with profitability as a key objective.

The internal auditor also needs to understand the challenges of auditing small, not-for-profit organisations, although such organisations may often not be in a position to support the employment of a full-time internal audit unit.

Objectives

By the time you have finished this chapter you should be able to:

- apply audit and review techniques to small not-for-profit organisations
- explain how the audit and review of small not-for-profit organisations differs from the audit and review of profit-oriented organisations.

1 Charities

KEY POINT

Charities may be trusts, incorporated under the *Companies Acts*, or friendly or provident societies.

Charities may be constituted in a variety of ways. Some are trusts; some are corporate bodies usually incorporated under the *Companies Acts*; some are friendly or provident societies. In all cases, the objectives of the charity will be set out in its constitution and its activities should accord with its objectives. A copy of the constitution should be kept on the auditors' permanent file.

EXAM HINT

If a question on charities arises, apply *basic auditing principles* and use your imagination!

The scope of the audit will depend upon the status of the charity, but auditors must always apply the same professional standards. If they are to give an expression on truth and fairness, they should work in accordance with auditing standards. This applies even if the fee charged is nil or negligible. There is substantial legislation governing the requirement for accounts and audit of charities. You are not required to know these for the purposes of this exam. Apply *basic auditing principles* and use your common sense if such a question arises.

1.1 Some audit problems

KEY POINT

Many charities will employ few, if any, full-time professional advisers and the level of internal control may well be low.

It is unlikely that a charity will employ many, if any, full-time professional advisers. The level of internal control may well be low and it may be difficult for the auditor to require many detailed checks on the actions of unpaid volunteers. Nevertheless, auditors should do all they can to communicate the importance of key controls. They should encourage the charity to employ professional personnel at least on a part-time basis.

The charity may wish to present a reasonably favourable picture in its annual report to encourage further donations. Auditors must, however, guard against the possible window-dressing of the financial statements.

1.2 Audit procedures

- Auditors should properly plan and control their work in the light of the accounting and auditing requirements of the charity under review.
- Collections from the public should be checked for validity and completeness.
  - There should be strict numerical control over collection tins and boxes, which should be sealed to prevent unauthorised opening.

  - The boxes should be regularly collected and dual counting and recording of the contents should be made.
  - There should be dual control if possible over the opening of mail, and all postal receipts should be immediately recorded and later reconciled to cash books.
  - Acknowledgements sent to all donors should be considered.
  - Deeds of covenant should be safely filed and a regular check made to follow up outstanding receipts.
  - Tax on covenants should be recovered on a regular basis.
- Legacies should be related to detailed correspondence files and outstanding legacies receivable should be followed up.
- Central and local government grants should be checked. Auditors should familiarise themselves with the grants receivable and ensure that such grants are used in accordance with the terms. The accounting treatment should be in line with SSAP 4.
- Branches should make regular reports to the charity. Auditors should check that all reports due have been received and then carry out detailed testing on a rotational basis. Auditors should check that such branches are included within the financial statements of the charity where appropriate.
- Auditors should consider the requirement of the charity or donors to set up separate funds. Separate records controlling the revenue and assets of such funds may be necessary.
- Grants to beneficiaries should be checked against correspondence and should be authorised by the management committee. They should be in line with the objectives of the charity.
- Auditors should check that:
  - bankings are made promptly upon receipt
  - bankings are checked to receipt records
  - regular bank reconciliations are made
  - returned cheques are examined for date, signature, payee, endorsements, etc.

1.3 Auditors' report

This should be in line with the auditing standard on the form of the audit report.

KEY POINT

With smaller charities, it may be hard to obtain suitable evidence with regard to income, but an unqualified opinion may still be issued, if accounting systems and controls in operation are reasonable.

For smaller charities, there is likely to be difficulty in applying proper controls over voluntary donations prior to entry in the accounting records. The audit problem is similar to that experienced in auditing a small company, i.e. the difficulty of obtaining suitable evidence with regard to income. Provided that auditors satisfy themselves on the reasonableness of the accounting systems and controls in operation, and there is no reason to suspect that income has been omitted, they may be able to issue an unqualified report.

ACTIVITY 1

What problems will the auditor face when auditing a small not-for-profit organisation or charity?

Feedback to this activity is at the end of the chapter.

2 Other not-for-profit organisations

2.1 Auditing other not-for-profit organisations

In an exam you may be faced with the audit of a not-for-profit organisation that is not a charity, such as a sports club, political or religious organisation or a pension fund (you are unlikely to be presented with a bank or insurance company, as these are too complex at this level). There is much legislation surrounding some such organisations but you are not required to know this. The approach to such audits is as follows:

- Is an audit required? If so, auditing standards will apply.
- Is the organisation large or small? It is likely to be small, and all the problems of small companies will apply: lack of complete records, lack of controls, lack of qualified accounting staff and the need to take a substantive approach.
- What are the risks associated with the organisation and what are the likely controls?
- What accounting records will the organisation maintain? Most will maintain membership lists and the members will pay in subscriptions, a principal source of income for such organisations. There will be membership fees in advance and arrears, i.e. accruals and prepayments to audit.
- What are the main outgoings of the organisation? Does it have any fixed assets such as buildings, computers, office furniture?
- How is the organisation constituted, e.g. is there a trust deed which limits the activities of the organisation? If so, the auditor will have to ensure that the organisation has acted within its powers (e.g. only paying amounts due to genuine pensioners in a pension fund).
- What are the principal accounting policies? Are they appropriate?
- Are the financial statements arithmetically accurate?

KEY POINT

When auditing a not-for-profit organisation that is not a charity, you should consider:

- whether an audit is needed
- size of the organisation
- risks and controls
- accounting records
- main outgoings
- constitution
- principal accounting policies
- accuracy of the financial statements.

3 Internal audit and small not-for-profit organisations

3.1 Potential role of internal audit

As already explained, small not-for-profit organisations rarely have professional advisors and this means that they often cannot afford the provision of an internal audit service either. However, in some arenas a number of similar organisations work together and have a small internal audit service either on a short-term consultancy basis or as a shared resource. Internal auditors face exactly the same dilemmas as external auditors, including the same audit problems over lack of risk awareness, lack of funding, difficulty in applying standard controls, etc. As for external audit, it is necessary to take a commonsense perspective: what is appropriate to the organisation to manage the risks?

KEY POINT

Internal auditors face the same dilemmas as external auditors when auditing small not-for-profit organisations, e.g. lack of risk awareness, lack of funding, difficulty in applying standard controls.

There may be a further role for internal auditors in larger organisations who may be required to audit small not-for-profit organisations, for example sports clubs or pension funds. They will need to follow the same steps as for any other audit, including:

- understand the area under review including purpose, objectives, constitution, legal obligations, funding sources
- identify and assess risks which could relate to financial areas, operational areas, provision of services etc.
- establish and evaluate the controls in operation, confirm whether they are appropriate to manage the risks and for the type of operation
- test key controls
- make recommendations for improvement and draw conclusions
- report.

ACTIVITY 2

A small professional institution, operating as a not for profit organisation, has decided to employ an internal audit service on a part time basis for a pilot period. They have agreed to undertake this on the advice of a newly appointed director but are not clear on the service that can be provided. You have been approached to offer this service but the board have asked a number of questions:

- What is the purpose of the internal audit of the institution and what value can you provide?
- How can the auditor overcome practical difficulties faced in auditing such an organisation?
- What approach will you follow in undertaking an internal audit assignment?

Feedback to this activity is at the end of the chapter.

4 Differences between auditing profit versus non-profit organisations

4.1 Key differences

It is clear from a review of the role of audit in charities and small not-for-profit organisations that there are some differences between small, not-for-profit organisations and organisations with a profit motive. These key differences tend to present audit problems and have to an extent been covered already. However, it is worth revisiting the potential areas of difference and their impact as follows:

KEY POINT

Differences between small, not-for-profit organisations and organisations with a profit motive include differences in:

- the constitution
- controls operated
- risk profile and materiality levels
- number and type of people and motivation for the work undertaken
- funding basis.

- The constitution of the organisation and objectives will be different from those in a profit-orientated organisation. In particular, an overriding objective for many larger organisations is to maximise profitability. For not-for-profit organisations, there will be different objectives. The auditor will need to review and understand the constitution and objectives and the risks arising.
- The small size of the organisation means that the same controls cannot operate as for a larger profit-orientated organisation and also may not be required or appropriate. Procedures will be simpler and less formalised, and there will be less opportunity to demonstrate segregation of duties. The auditor will therefore need to consider the most appropriate controls for the purpose and avoid the accusation of being over-bureaucratic in recommendations.
- The risk profile and materiality will be different – again a commonsense approach by the auditor is required.
- The people may be different, including number and type of individuals, and motivation for the work undertaken. In particular, not-for-profit organisations may rely heavily on volunteers. Volunteers tend to be less easy to control and may be less structured in approach. There may also be other heavy demands on their time and, as mentioned earlier, they may be difficult for the auditor to check up on. Even the small number of permanent staff may be driven by different attitudes and style from those prevailing in a larger, profit-centred organisation.
- The auditor needs to understand the different motivations and sensitivities of their work and help the organisation have a greater understanding of risks and controls.
- Not-for-profit organisations will be dependent on income received through different means including fund raising and subscription income rather than income generated to make profit. Therefore the funding basis is different and issues facing the auditor in reviewing funding may be different.

4.2 Similarities

Whilst there are special features of small not-for-profit organisations, auditors need to take the same type of approach to audits: reviewing background information, regulatory environment, constitution and objectives, identifying and evaluating risks, reviewing controls, carrying out tests and reporting.

Conclusion

Not-for-profit organisations can still present significant risk, where they are dealing with substantial income. There have been cases of significant levels of fraud occurring in such organisations because they are seen as relatively low risk and therefore audits have not been very detailed or perhaps have not taken place at all.

Not-for-profit organisations have certain special features and challenges but most work is similar to any other audit work. The internal or external auditor needs to consider the legal structure and objectives of the organisation in undertaking the work and in making recommendations needs to consider the practicalities of providing the necessary controls.

SELF-TEST QUESTIONS

Charities

1 Where will the objectives of a charity be set out? (1)

2 What key audit checks should be undertaken on the audit of a charity? (1.2)

Other not-for-profit organisations

3 What approach will be followed for auditing other not-for-profit organisations? (2.1)

Internal audit and small not-for-profit organisations

4 What steps will be followed for an internal audit review of a not-for-profit organisation? (3.1)

Differences between auditing profit versus non-profit organisations

5 What are the key differences between auditing a 'not-for-profit' organisation compared to a 'for profit' organisation? (4.1)

EXAM-TYPE QUESTION

ESCAPE

ESCAPE is a small 'not-for-profit' leisure facility providing an 'escape' route for people in deprived areas. They provide a number of key facilities including:

- drop in centre with IT facilities and specialist help for those in need to acquire valuable skills
- gymnasium and sports facilities, to encourage fitness and well-being
- specialist working holidays to allow development of confidence, interpersonal and other skills and help people to a better future.

Their overall aim is to help people escape from their circumstances and to maximise their opportunities for the future. The prime users of ESCAPE are in the age bracket 16 to 30, although there are some users outside this age level.

There are five permanent staff and up to 20 volunteers employed by ESCAPE.

ESCAPE was originally started with funds from an individual (SM) who had lived in deprived areas but who is now a self made millionaire and wanted to help others facing the same challenges in life. This is now run as a not-for-profit organisation, that relies on a combination of funding through fund raising income as well as local and central government grants, which tend to be erratic. Last year, a lottery award was made to help establish the IT facilities.

The founder, SM, has agreed to fund an audit consultancy review of ESCAPE, to provide assurance of the effective use of the funds and to establish that the organisation is operating efficiently and effectively. However, the employees have never experienced any type of audit review before and are unsure of what is involved or expected.

Required:

(a) Outline the potential difficulties of such a review and how you would overcome them. **(4 marks)**

(b) Explain how you would address the concerns of staff and volunteers who had never been audited before. **(3 marks)**

(c) Outline the approach you would take in undertaking the review, including the key steps and key information required. **(3 marks)**

(d) Describe the key risks and controls that you would anticipate finding for ESCAPE. **(10 marks)**

(Total: 20 marks)

For the answer to this question, see the 'Answers' section at the end of the book.

FEEDBACK TO ACTIVITY 1

The following problems will need to be managed:

- A small, not-for-profit organisation may not have a good understanding of the concepts of risk and control. Therefore, the auditor will need to spend some time explaining the impact of risk and the importance of control.
- Risks associated with such organisations may be quite different. There will still be a financial risk arising from expenditure within organisations and clearly there will be a risk to reputation where a small not-for-profit organisation fails to deliver their mandated role.
- The organisation is unlikely to employ many, if any, professional advisors, which may make the audit role difficult. The auditor should encourage use of professional advisors where appropriate.
- There may be difficulties in obtaining sufficient evidence of controls and in operating the standard controls that would be expected in a larger organisation.

FEEDBACK TO ACTIVITY 2

Purpose and value of the internal audit service

- Internal audit provides an independent and objective review of the organisation. This includes examining and evaluating the organisation's risk management processes and systems of control, and makes recommendations for the achievement of organisational objectives.
- The independence of internal audit adds value because within such an organisation it is not always easy to find time to be able to stand back and look at how the organisation operates. There is no vested interest from the auditors because they are not part of the processes being reviewed.
- The value of the internal audit service also lies in the link to organisational objectives. By focusing on what the organisation wants to achieve, constructive and effective advice and guidance can be provided.
- Internal auditors understand risks and the requirements for controls, which is particularly valuable for a small organisation that does not necessarily have the awareness of the consequent risks of decisions made. Therefore providing an internal audit service can help the overall institution's management of risks and generate greater risk and control awareness within individuals.

The **challenges facing internal audit** in such an environment can be overcome in a number of ways including:

- Understanding the objectives, environment and framework of the organisation, to ensure that recommendations are practical and realistic. Particularly important is understanding the scale of the organisation.
- Investing time in explaining the purpose and method of reviews to ensure a clear understanding of what is being done and why.
- Understanding and explaining risks facing the organisation and encouraging management to gain a greater understanding.
- Measuring performance and providing a cost effective, value for money service. Such organisations can ill-afford an internal audit service and therefore demonstrating what is being provided through a cost benefit analysis will aid greater understanding. In the case of this organisation, the proposal is for a pilot, part time service and therefore the challenges may be greater because there will be up-front time spent in getting to know the organisation.

Approach to auditing

- Effectively research and understand the area under review including purpose, objectives, constitution, legal obligations, funding sources.
- Identify and assess risks facing the organisation, for example financial loss, loss of income, poor service to members, loss of members, difficulty in recruiting the right skills.
- Evaluate and test the controls in operation and confirm whether they are appropriate to manage the risks for the type of organisation.
- Make constructive recommendations for improvement, highlighting the level of risk the organisation faces and advising on the best way of managing the risks in view of the nature and scale of the organisation.
- Provide conclusions and reports.

Answers to exam-type questions

Question 1: New client

ABC & Co
Certified Accountants
20 New Rd
London W2

Dear Mr Lee

Thank you for your recent enquiry. I have set out below brief details of the services we can offer your company.

Accountancy

It is your responsibility as directors to ensure that the financial statements are prepared on a timely basis and in compliance with accepted accounting principles. However, we can provide assistance if required with the following:

- Writing up the books of account such as the cash book, sales, purchase and nominal ledgers.
- Extracting a trial balance
- Preparing the financial statements in compliance with legal and professional requirements.

We would not check the underlying information in the course of our work except for ensuring that the financial statements and trial balance are in agreement with the accounting records.

Consequently any report we attach to the financial statements would make it clear that an audit was not performed and simply state that we had prepared the accounts from the records of the company and from information and explanations supplied.

Audit

The main purpose of the financial statements is to provide information to the shareholders on your stewardship of the company. It is a legal requirement in the UK that companies with an annual turnover greater than £5.6m must be subject to an annual audit.

The audit is usually performed in two stages.

- The interim audit – the emphasis at this stage is on recording, evaluating and testing your system of internal control. It is our normal practice to report any weaknesses found to the directors in a management letter.
- The final audit – is concerned with verifying the balances in the final accounts and would include attendance at the stock-take and direct confirmation of balances with third parties such as your bank. The extent of such work may be reduced if reliance can be placed on internal control. We would also review the final accounts to ensure they meet with legal and professional requirements.

At the conclusion of the audit a report will be included in the financial statements that are sent to the shareholders in which we will express an opinion on the 'truth and fairness' of the financial statements.

This is designed to provide the shareholders with a relatively high level of assurance and increase the reliability of the financial statements. However, it is not feasible to guarantee that the accounts are accurate in every respect of free or all fraud and error.

Review engagements

Instead of an audit an independent accountant may perform a review of financial statements.

The work will involve analysing the accounts and making enquiries of the directors where anomalies appear to warrant explanation. Detailed testing of internal control and account balances will not be performed.

Consequently the level of assurance provided falls short of an audit and is often referred to as 'negative assurance' as the review report will state that nothing has come to our attention to indicate that the financial statements are not prepared in accordance with the relevant regulatory requirements.

This letter provides only a general outline of the above services and if you require further clarification or if I can be of any further assistance please contact me.

Yours sincerely

P Smith ACCA

Question 2: Introduction to audit

An audit is the independent examination of evidence from which the financial statements of an enterprise are derived in order to give the reader of those statements confidence as to the '*truth and fairness*' of the state of affairs which they disclose. The Auditing Practices Board describes the objective of an audit as being '. . to enable auditors to express an opinion whether the financial statements give a true and fair view . . . and have been properly prepared in accordance with the applicable reporting framework':

- **Independent** – Auditors should be, and be seen to be, independent of the enterprise on which they are expressing an audit opinion.
- **Examination** – There is a separation of audit and accountancy functions, with audit being the examination of the financial statements.
- **Opinion** – Auditors do not certify that the financial statements are correct; they merely express an opinion on whether a true and fair view is given.
- **Financial statements** – This term includes the balance sheet, profit and loss account, statement of total recognised gains and losses and any supporting notes, and cash flow statement required for public limited companies and large private companies. The term does not include the directors' report.
- **Applicable reporting framework** – The audit is carried out in accordance with CA85 for a limited company, the Building Societies Act 1986 for a building society, and so on.

Question 3: Concept of materiality

(***Tutorial note:*** It is normal to give a definition and discussion in this sort of question to make some relevant points about the term being queried.)

It is the auditor's chief duty to express an opinion as to whether or not the accounts being audited show a true and fair view. The true and fair concept is a general one and the auditor is often faced with deciding if a particular error or omission is so fundamental that the accounts do not show a true and fair view.

ISA 320 *Audit materiality* attempts to give guidance in this area. It points out that a matter is material if its omission or misstatement would reasonably influence the decisions of users of the financial statements.

Before auditors qualify the accounts under scrutiny, they must, therefore, consider whether or not the points on which they are unsatisfied are material or not. To do this, the following points must be considered:

- Is the item so fundamental that the accounts can no longer be said to show a true and fair view?
- Materiality is a relative factor and the item must be considered in relation to the accounts as a whole, the total of which it would form part, and the corresponding amount in the previous years
- Some items are capable of exact calculation; others, such as depreciation, are merely estimated and, provided the estimate is reasonable, should be acceptable.

Under the CA85, the disclosure of certain items depends upon whether or not they are material, e.g. amount of contingent liabilities, capital commitments and transfer to reserves. Other items, however, are specifically required to be shown, e.g. directors' emoluments and the audit fee. If these are incorrect, the items must be material since the accounts will not then comply with the Companies Act.

In conclusion, therefore, an auditor must take into account the degree of approximation necessary in calculating a particular item, the size of the company and the level of its profits and its significance in relation to the company as a whole. Then the basic question to be answered is: 'Does the misstatement or omission of this item impair the true and fair view principle?'

CHAPTER 2 EXAM-TYPE QUESTION

Growfast plc

(***Tutorial note:*** This is a question where it is easy to pick up marks if the basic facts are known. Remember that some questions in the exam are factual and that you will score highly if you have learnt the basic facts before the exam.)

(a) ***Need for an audit***

The need for an audit arises from the division in many companies between ownership of the company, and the day-to-day running of the company.

In many companies, particularly plcs, the owners of the company (i.e. the shareholders) will not normally be involved in the actual running of the company. The company will be run by the directors, who are elected by the shareholders at the annual general meeting (AGM) of the company. The owners of the company thus buy shares in the company, and expect a return on their investment in the company in the form of dividends, whilst the directors run the company and are paid a salary for doing this.

At the end of each year, the directors will produce the financial statements to show the results of the company. The shareholders need confidence that these financial statements are accurate, i.e. that the directors have actually told the truth regarding the company's results. To ensure that the financial statements are accurate, the shareholders employ an auditor. The job of the auditor is to 'audit' or check the financial statements, and then report back to the shareholders whether these financial statements are accurate, or show a 'true and fair view'. By having this independent check, the shareholders gain confidence that the accounts are accurate and therefore that their investment in terms of money, is being handled properly.

(b) ***Appointment of an auditor***

The auditor of a plc is appointed in different ways, depending on the situation, as noted below.

Initial appointment – new company

In a company that has just commenced trading, the directors have the power to appoint the auditors, who will remain in office until the end of the first AGM. The appointment of auditors can be made at a general meeting by the shareholders, if they wish to do this. If the directors or the shareholders do not appoint auditors, then the Secretary of State will, although this is rare in practice.

Ongoing appointment

All public companies, in their AGM, appoint auditors to serve from the end of that meeting until the end of the next AGM. The auditor's term of office therefore allows them to report back to the meeting that initially appointed them. The appointment of auditors is a statutory requirement of the AGM of a plc. If the meeting does not appoint auditors, then the Secretary of State must be informed within seven days, and the Secretary of State will then appoint auditors. If the company does not inform the Secretary of State, then both the company and the directors are liable to fines.

Appointment to fill a casual vacancy

At certain times the office of auditor may fall vacant, e.g. a sole practitioner may die, or the current auditor resigns, perhaps owing to a conflict of interest that has been brought to light. In this situation, the directors may appoint a new auditor whose term of office will cease at the end of the next AGM of the company. Alternatively, the members in general meeting may appoint a new auditor, or failing both of these the Secretary of State will appoint.

Note that where the new auditor is being appointed at an AGM where the directors previously made the appointment, special notice is required of the resolution. This is to try and ensure that the members always have the final choice in who audits the financial statements.

(c) ***Rights of an auditor***

The rights of an auditor under the CA85 are as follows:

- to receive information and explanations from the directors and officers of the company – it is a criminal offence to provide the auditor with false information
- to have access to the company's books and records at all times
- to receive notice of all general meetings of the company as if the auditor were a member of the company
- to attend and to be heard at any general meeting of the company concerning matters affecting them as auditor or former auditor
- where the company is attempting to remove the auditor, to make written representations to the members, and to attend and speak at the meeting where the auditor is being removed and the meeting where their term of office would otherwise have expired if they were previously removed
- where the auditor resigns, to make written representations to the members of the company, and to require the directors to convene an extraordinary general meeting to consider the circumstances of the resignation
- to give notice to the company in writing that a general meeting should be held to lay the accounts and auditor's report before the members of the company.

(d) ***Directors' responsibilities***

The responsibilities of the directors in relation to the accounting function of the company are as follows:

- To safeguard the company's assets and to prevent fraud and errors in the company.
- To ensure that the company keeps proper accounting records as defined in S221 CA85.
- To prepare annual financial statements to show the results of the company for the year and the state of affairs of the company at the balance sheet date – these accounts must show a true and fair view (S228 CA85).
- To deliver to the Registrar of Companies a copy of the company's audited financial statements within (for a plc) seven months of the end of the accounting year.
- To set up an internal control system in the company to ensure that all of the above are carried out. The directors cannot run the company by themselves; they must employ staff to carry out many of the accounting and other duties in the company. The system of internal control tries to ensure that the directors' other responsibilities above are met.

CHAPTER **3** EXAM-TYPE QUESTIONS

Question 1: Regulation of independence

(***Tutorial note***: Part (a) is a knowledge question – if you are unsure of these rules, then revision is needed. Part (b) – some positive ideas will gain marks here; peer reviews and stronger audit committees are always good examples to mention in this type of question.)

(a) ***Independence***

(i) An established practice should ensure that the recurring fees from one client (or group of clients) do not exceed 15% of the gross income of the practice.

(ii) Auditors should ensure that personal relationships do not affect their objectivity.

(iii) A partner in a practice or a spouse or minor child or any member of staff employed on the audit should not hold shares in the client company except in special cases (see (vii) below).

(iv) A practice should not make a loan to a client nor guarantee a client's borrowings. Neither should it accept a loan from a client or have its borrowings guaranteed by a client. This also applies to a partner in a practice or spouse or minor child.

(v) A partner or his spouse or minor child or any employee of the firm should not accept goods or services from a client unless the value is modest. Acceptance of undue hospitality can also threaten independence.

(vi) Auditors should take care where involved in litigation with their clients. A minor dispute over fees may not cause a problem; a writ for negligence almost certainly will.

(vii) Where any shares are held in an audit client company due to special cases, they should not be voted at any general meeting in any matters concerning the role of the auditor. These special cases are:

- where shares are acquired involuntarily (for example, a bequest) – these should be disposed of at the earliest opportunity

- where an Act of Parliament or company's Articles require an auditor to hold shares – the auditor should hold the minimum necessary.

(b) ***Strengthening and improving the independence of the auditor***

The independence of the auditor might be strengthened and improved in several ways and there has been much recent discussion among the accountancy bodies on this subject. One area for discussion is whether the provision of other services detracts from an objective approach to an audit. These other services could include accountancy, consultancy, taxation advice, etc. Such services should be charged separately from audit work and the auditor's involvement must be advisory only. The auditor must not perform executive functions or take executive decisions. The prohibition of other services would clearly affect the small company particularly in a detrimental way as it often relies on its auditors for this type of support.

A further suggestion has been the compulsory setting-up (for all companies subject to an audit) of audit committees which are becoming increasingly common in the UK. These audit committees consist of non-executive directors who are able to view a company's affairs in a detached and independent way, and can liaise effectively between the main board of directors and the external auditors. An audit committee can increase public confidence in the credibility and objectivity of published financial information. The Combined Code of the London Stock Exchange requires all listed companies to have an audit committee, or to explain why not. The overwhelming majority of large companies in the UK now have an efficient functioning audit committee.

Other changes proposed include the rotation of auditors on, say, a three-year cycle. However, this would prove costly as additional time would be required at the start of each new cycle for each firm to familiarise itself with the client and its systems, staff, etc.

Question 2: Billington Travel

(a) ***Independence***

- It is important for external auditors to be independent of their audit clients because external auditors act on behalf of the owners of the business (normally the shareholders) and report on the financial statements prepared by management for the benefit of shareholders.
- If external auditors are not independent of their clients, for example if they hold shares in the companies that they audit, their ability to form an objective opinion on the financial statements is impaired.
- External auditors must also be seen to be independent because, if they are not, the owners of the business will not have confidence in the audit reports that the auditors issue.
- The ACCA's Rules of Professional Conduct require that auditors are independent, and that they are seen to be independent. The Rules cover a number of areas in which the auditor's independence may be, or be seen to be, impaired.
- Legislation also requires external auditors to be independent.

(b) ***Ethical matters***

(i) **The statutory audit**

- The Rules of Professional Conduct state that it is important that the firm is competent to undertake the audit; it must have adequate resources in terms of staff with sufficient experience in this sector. The fact that the services to be provided would constitute a substantial amount of fee income in a new area of business indicates that the firm might not, at present, have those resources.

- It may be appropriate to consider whether experience in this sector can be bought in, by the recruitment of additional staff.
- The firm should consider whether staff are available at the right time of year and whether the work fits in with the firm's existing obligations.
- The Rules of Professional Conduct also state that the firm must be independent of its clients; in particular, this means that it must not take too much of its fee income from one client (or group of clients).
- Generally, for non-public interest clients, the fee income (including income from additional services) should not exceed 15% of the gross practice income. If that figure is exceeded, it may be possible to consider providing some, but not all, of the services requested.

(ii) **The provision of other services**

- Preparation of financial statements: it is generally acceptable under the Rules of Professional Conduct for auditors to provide assistance with the preparation of financial statements for private company clients, provided that the client takes full responsibility for the accounting records and financial statements.
- It is important to know why the company needs assistance in this area and it would be preferable in the long run for the company to be able to prepare its own financial statements.
- It is important that those preparing the financial statements are independent of those performing the audit as far as possible, in order that the firm is seen to remain independent.
- Systems review: the external auditor is often well placed to provide assistance with such reviews as the firm obtains a working knowledge of systems during the course of the audit.
- However, there is always the danger that the firm finds itself in the position of having to report on a system that it has helped to improve, and it may be difficult in such circumstances to be critical of the system. This detracts from the firm's ability to remain independent, and in this case, given that it is the first year of audit and that assistance is also needed with the preparation of financial statements, it seems preferable not to tender for the systems review, this year.

(c) ***Actions to be taken***

- It may be appropriate to discuss the matter, discreetly, with other staff members to establish whether or not it is of concern to them, as well as to you. It would be preferable to discuss the matter with persons who are known to be reliable.
- If the concerns are shared, or if the other staff have no knowledge of the matter, or if you are still concerned about the matter, it may be appropriate to discuss the matter with the chief internal auditor to try and establish why the matter has not been reported, as there may be a good reason. If other staff support you in your view, it may be appropriate to take another member of staff along to the discussion.
- If the chief internal auditor is able to reassure you (either that it is not necessary to report the matter, or that the matter will be reported), no further action will be necessary, although it may be useful to make a brief note of the discussion.
- If you are not satisfied, or if the chief internal auditor undertakes to report the matter but does not do so within a reasonable time, the situation may be more serious and it is more important in such circumstances to make notes of

any discussions. It may be appropriate to have further discussions with the chief internal auditor.

- If you are still not satisfied, and you consider that the matter is sufficiently serious, it may be appropriate to approach a more senior member of management to voice your concerns. You may wish to avoid this situation, but it may be necessary in order to protect yourself.
- On the assumption that the matter is one of internal concern to the company and there is no question of illegality, the question of reporting the matters to third parties outside the organisation does not arise.

(d) ***Doing nothing***

- The principal danger in doing nothing lies in the possibility that you may be accused of not bringing attention to the matter or even of being actively involved in a 'cover-up'.
- Professional ethics do not permit Chartered Certified accountants to take no action at all where serious matters are concerned, and to do nothing might, in extreme circumstances, involve you in disciplinary proceedings by the ACCA, even as a student.
- To do nothing might also mean that the business of the company you work for is damaged, and therefore your own employment prospects.

CHAPTER 4 EXAM-TYPE QUESTION

Internal vs external auditors

(a) ***Fraud and error***

(i) The duties of internal auditors are generally determined by the organisation that has set up the internal audit department and employs the internal auditors. Internal auditors normally have a general responsibility to perform their work and their reviews of systems with the possibility of fraud and error in mind. This means that when they review the structure and operation of systems they have regard to strengths in the system that will prevent or detect fraud and error and weaknesses that will facilitate fraud and error.

(ii) When internal auditors discover structural or operational weaknesses that facilitate or fail to prevent or detect fraud and error, they generally have a duty to report such matters internally. The precise method of reporting varies from organisation to organisation. If internal auditors discover actual instances of fraud or error, they also have a duty to report it.

(iii) It can be difficult in practice for internal auditors to deal with actual or suspected management fraud. The 'Rules of Professional Conduct' do not permit auditors to remain silent on the subject. There is no general duty to report fraud or error outside the organisation and internal auditors, like other employees, have a duty of confidentiality to the organisation they work for. In extreme circumstances however, it may be necessary for internal auditors to report matters to persons outside the organisation (where money laundering is discovered, for example).

(iv) External auditors plan and perform their work with an attitude of professional scepticism. The audit must be designed to detect material errors, which may be due to fraud or error, but this does not mean that the audit can be guaranteed to detect material fraud or error. Fraud or error should only be reported in the financial statements to shareholders if they are material. Like internal auditors, external auditors are bound by a duty of confidentiality to their clients. External auditors do have a number of legal rights and duties to report certain types of suspected fraud to certain bodies (such as the National Criminal Intelligence Service). Confidential advice is available to external auditors from their professional bodies.

(b) ***Internal audit's role***

(i) Corporate governance

(1) The objectives of good corporate governance include: the proper constitution of the board, proper arrangements for the remuneration of directors, proper mechanisms for shareholder relations, and proper accountability and audit.

(2) Accountability and audit includes the maintenance of a proper system of internal control. A proper system of internal control includes appropriate risk management systems and overall organisational control.

(3) Internal audit's role in the context of these objectives includes assisting management by suggesting ways in which these objectives can be achieved, and by monitoring progress.

Example for manufacturing company

The internal auditors can recommend to the board those areas in which structural changes need to be made in order to comply with codes of corporate governance, such as the 'Combined Code' on corporate governance. They can recommend processes for setting objectives and targets, and for measuring their achievement.

(ii) Risk management

Internal audit has a particular interest in investigating and evaluating the company's risk management structures. Internal audit can manage the provision of the basic data which management can use in order to identify, prioritise and manage the risks facing the company. Internal audit can also help by developing models and techniques for identifying, prioritising and managing risk.

Examples for manufacturing company

(1) In a manufacturing company, risk management issues to be addressed include operational, financial, health and safety and other regulatory issues. Internal audit can help in identifying the issues, evaluating their importance and suggesting mechanisms for managing or transferring the risk.

(2) The management of risk depends on the business objectives, short and long term, strategic and operational, and conflicts between objectives. These objectives include, for example, the need to provide a return to investors, the need for long-term investment, and the need to produce a quality product. Internal audit can help classify those risks.

(iii) Organisational control

The simple existence of an internal audit function is an example of organisational control. Internal audit can investigate and document existing control systems, and recommend improvements.

Example for manufacturing company

Areas of control to be addressed include the overall control environment, operational control and other areas designed to manage the risks as identified above. Internal audit can help in providing cost-benefit analyses in respect of the implementation of control procedures, as well as making recommendations on structural control.

(c) Out-sourced internal audit issues

The issues to be considered include:

(i) The costs of out-sourcing the function, including the internal administrative costs and the costs of managing the function. These may be more or less than internal costs, and a cost-benefit analysis will help establish the likely financial implications.

(ii) An out-sourced internal audit function will be more independent than an internal function, but this has to be set off against the (probably) superior knowledge of the business of the existing function.

(iii) Out-sourcing the internal audit function probably means a loss of control, whilst the responsibility for the function will remain with the company.

(iv) Change management issues have to be addressed which can be time consuming and expensive. Existing staff have to be re-deployed (perhaps to the company to which the function is out-sourced) and there may be resentment of the new internal auditors and deliberate attempts to frustrate them.

(v) The choice of the out-sourcing company is important – it must have sufficient resources and experience and there is always a risk associated with this: the contract with the out-sourcing company will have to be carefully worded and the initial contract should only be for a limited period of time.

CHAPTER 5

EXAM-TYPE QUESTION

Roxy Hotels (Part 1)

(a) ***Checking transactions and balances***

- The internal audit department might trace representative samples of room bookings and the booking of conference facilities from source documentation through the system, to ensure that the correct amounts are billed, that the facilities are paid for within the time limits agreed and that the correct amounts have been recorded in the correct accounting period.
- The department might trace representative samples of orders for food and other consumables through the system to ensure that authorised suppliers are used where necessary, that the correct prices have been billed by suppliers, that payment has been made on the agreed terms, and that the correct amounts have been recorded in the correct accounting period.
- The department might trace representative samples of additions to and disposals of assets through the system from the physical assets themselves, through the daybooks and ledgers to the original authorisation for purchase, to ensure that all assets acquired are properly authorised.
- The department might trace representative samples of additions to and disposals of assets in the opposite direction, i.e. from authorisations to assets to ensure they are in good condition and still in the hotels.
- The department might select representative samples of debtors and creditors for direct confirmation.
- The department might check on the existence of certain employees and on the accuracy of the payroll calculations with reference to records of hours worked kept at the hotels.

(b) ***Reviews of systems***

- The internal audit department might review the documentation of the centralised booking systems and evaluate it. They might then review the actual operation of the system in practice and make recommendations for improvements or change.
- The department might review the integrity of the systems by the use of computer assisted audit and other techniques to ensure that access to the system is restricted to those who should have access and to ensure that the system produces exception reports as it should. Dummy data and false passwords might be used in such an assessment.
- Analytical procedures could be performed to evaluate the relative financial and operational performance of individual hotels, hotels in certain regions and the performance of the various classes of business (tourist and business accommodations, conference and leisure facilities, restaurants and bars, etc.) Performance could also be evaluated against budgets, on a seasonal basis and by comparison with prior years and periods.
- Analytical procedures could be performed on relationships such as those between drinks and meals consumed, and those between occupancy rates and other facilities used.

CHAPTER 6 EXAM-TYPE QUESTIONS

Question 1: Koala Limited

OVERALL AUDIT PLAN

To: Mr X (Partner in charge)

From: Ms Y

Date: X-X-20XX

Subject: Koala Limited

Audit planning – year end 30 September 20X7

(a) ***Knowledge of the business***

(i) **Background**

The main point arising in 20X6 was the continuing weakness in internal control over expenses. This led to our spending considerable time on detailed substantive testing in this area.

No particular problems were discovered during the testing, however, and there are no other specific matters of continuing importance.

(ii) **Changes during the year to 30-9-X7**

The most significant change this year was the appointment of Helen Jones in late 20X6 as Chief Accountant.

Helen has considerably strengthened the systems for payment and recording of expenses with new systems being fully operational from 1 January.

There are no changes in legislation or best accounting practice which affect Koala Limited.

(b) ***Risk and materiality***

(i) **Systems evaluation and tests of control**

Obviously, this is most critical for the systems which have changed, but we will need to confirm that other systems may still be relied on.

(ii) **Salesmen's expenses**

As always, this is a critical expense in the profit and loss account.

(c) ***Nature, timing and extent of procedures***

In all areas except purchases, wages and salesmen's expenses, the approach adopted will be exactly as in 20X6. We will place reliance on the effective operation of internal controls to reduce the level of substantive testing.

In relation to purchases, wages and salesmen's expenses, we will carry out our testing in three sections.

In testing transactions up to 31 December, we will adopt the purely substantive approach used in 20X6.

For the nine-month period from 1 January to 30 September, however, we will perform tests of controls, evaluating and testing the systems, then aiming to place reliance on the controls to reduce our substantive testing.

We will carry out some additional work on the changeover period where there is the greatest chance of errors occurring.

We will carry out a debtors' circularisation as at 30 September 20X7.

We will attend the annual stocktake on 20 September 20X7.

(d) ***Co-ordination, direction and review (with example dates)***

July	18	Interim visit – systems work and detailed testing of transactions.
July	22	Systems work completed: End of interim visit.
August	5	Management letter sent.
September	19	Audit confirmation letters sent.
September	20	Inventory count.
October	20	Final audit visit.

The client would like the accounts signed by Christmas.

Helen Jones is under pressure in this new job, but we must seek her assistance in preparing balance sheet schedules, stock summaries, aged stock and debtors' analyses, etc. With this co-operation I propose the following budget for audit hours:

Partner	5	hours
Manager	10	hours

Senior	100	hours	*includes 35 extra each in relation to*
Junior	70	hours	*extra systems evaluation work this year.*

I shall be in the office all next week if you wish to discuss any of the points raised in this memorandum.

Question 2: EWheels.com

(a) ***Audit risk***

- Audit risk is the product of inherent risk, control risk and detection risk. Audit risk is often 'set' by the audit firm at a certain level (say 3% to 5%), and the nature and extent of testing in a particular audit are determined by an assessment of the other elements of risk.
- Inherent risk is the risk that material errors will occur both at the entity level, and at the level of individual transactions and balances. Certain account balances and certain entities are more inherently risky than others. For example, stock is more inherently risky than cash, volatile businesses are more inherently risky than stable businesses.
- Control risk is the risk that internal controls will not prevent or detect material errors, both at the entity level, and at the level of individual transactions and balances.
- Detection risk is the risk that auditors will fail to detect material errors (due to human error or sampling risk, for example).

(b) ***Risks associated with the audit***

- In the case of EWheels, the levels of inherent risk and control risk appear to be higher than normal.
- EWheels is in a volatile sector of the economy. It has grown rapidly and is planning further expansion, which will require additional resources. There is a real risk of 'over-trading', i.e. that the business will exhaust its cash resources too soon as a result of rapid growth. In such circumstances, there is a risk that creditors will go unpaid and that the business will be forced into liquidation. This is risky for both the directors and for the auditors.
- In a highly competitive sector, there is a possibility that the company itself will be vulnerable to take-over, particularly if it is in a weak financial position which it appears to be with net liabilities. The dispute between the ex-director and the current directors possibly means that the current directors do not have overall control of the company. It is particularly important in take-over situations for auditors to be cautious in the audit opinion they give.
- The overall control environment at EWheels is weak. There has been no proper control of the accounting function for six months and errors are appearing as a result. This may mean that the accounting records are unreliable and the financial statements may be materially misstated.
- The attitude of the directors (which is relevant to the overall control environment) is suspect, as they appear to be overly ambitious in their expansion plans.
- EWheels is suffering from financial pressures. It wishes to expand, but additional resources are needed and they are becoming scarcer; loan finance may become more expensive. The ex-director is claiming a substantial amount of money from the company. It may be preferable for the company to seek further equity finance or to delay the expansion plans.
- The audit is also risky for the firm because this is the first year of audit (and mistakes are therefore more likely to be made). It will be important for the firm to ensure that adequate time and resources are allocated to

what is likely to be a difficult audit. Any pressure by the directors to complete the audit quickly should be resisted.

Question 3: Role of small company auditors

(***Tutorial note:*** Remember to plan your answer and use headings to assist presentation.)

Now that the statutory requirement for an audit of the financial statements of small companies has been removed, the auditor still has a very useful role to play. The needs of the various users of financial statements must be considered and in doing so, the usefulness of the auditor is revealed.

Needs of the users

Third parties may require financial statements to be considered by an independent expert and so the company can choose to have a voluntary audit. This might be the situation if the company decides to continue with an annual or less frequent audit at the request of a bank, the Inland Revenue or some other interested third party.

It is likely to be the case that most companies would continue to feel that they gain some positive benefit from an audit either for themselves directly or indirectly because their financial statements are considered to be more reliable. Suppliers to the company are in a better position to assess credit risk if the accounts have been audited, provided that the audit does not create undue delay in their publication.

An audit may be performed on behalf of minority shareholders. If there is no audit, the minority shareholders within a company may have little confidence in the financial statements. The auditor could be appointed by them to consider the financial statements either as before, to express an audit opinion, or in some modified role to give them some credibility.

Advisory role

The auditor can adopt a professional advisory role. Many small companies still need the advice of a qualified accountant in matters such as taxation, computers and other systems work and compliance with legislation. The auditor can be of considerable use to the company and its directors in matters such as corporation taxation, VAT and personal taxation.

It is hoped that they will retain a professional firm to give them this advice, rather than turn to non-qualified accountants or other institutions such as banks. Also the former auditors who had detailed knowledge of the company could give valuable advice on the choice of accounting policies and the effect of changing an accounting policy. The auditor would be free to prepare the accounting records for the company. He could also extend the service of preparation of the financial statements to cover monthly management accounts, budgets, forecasts and cash flow projections.

The auditor can assess the adequacy of internal controls and offer useful advice to the company on the cost effectiveness of different types of controls.

Management involvement

A former auditor who is no longer governed by the need to remain objective could become much more involved in doing management consultancy work for the company. This could bring a degree of skill to the management of the company that it could not previously afford. The auditor could offer the company valuable advice on various sources of finance and government grants. The auditor could also assist the directors in the recruitment of financial staff and other management employees.

Review work

The auditor could be engaged to perform a review rather than an audit, for any of the above reasons. This would probably be cheaper for the company without necessarily being much less useful. Currently the value of an audit to small companies is being challenged because its cost is said to outweigh its benefits and because the auditor may have to rely on management assurances to a significant degree. A review might remove both of these criticisms.

Conclusion

There will always be a role for the qualified accountant in assisting small companies but the precise nature of that role will depend on the circumstances of the company and the needs of the users of its financial statements.

Question 4: BLD Risk Model

(a) ***Advantages and limitations of risk modelling***

How a model could operate for BLD

BLD have a range of divisions, operating at different levels and with very different risks. The risks within the main support areas (IT, Finance and Sales/Marketing) are quite different from those in the operational areas. Therefore, any risk model needs to be able to accommodate these differences. However, the risk model would be particularly useful for focusing on the different risks of the customer facing areas.

Advantages of use of risk model

- Using risk models can help the auditors direct their attention towards greatest areas of risk both in the overall planning stage and for individual assignments. The model can help to prioritise the audit work, both at the high-level planning stage and at assignment level.
- Risk models can demonstrate professionalism and support decision-making, with a clear reasoning to support plans put in place.
- They can be used to support judgement on a more scientific basis and therefore provide more credibility to plans and decisions.
- They can aid understanding of the nature and extent of risk within an organisation and help contribute to their achievement of corporate governance.
- BLD could use a risk workshop approach to identify and assess risks within the organisation, which would aid understanding of risks both by the auditor and by the senior managers within the organisation. Output from the workshop could help to build the picture required by the risk model and supplement information gained purely from a risk model.

Potential limitations

- Models can be too complex or mathematical – this could affect understanding of what the data is providing.
- They may be too focused on financial risk and not consider the broader understanding of risk.
- Models could be inaccurate or inappropriate.
- They could form an incorrect basis for planning and decision-making.
- The company could fail to get buy-in to the model.
- Models do not replace the need to make professional judgements and decisions.

(b) ***Attributes of a good risk model***

- Simple, easy both to understand and use.
- Easy to maintain, without a high cost of time and money to keep the data up-to-date.

- Defensible, with clearly justifiable outputs and limited subjectivity.
- Considers laws, standards and regulations in helping to derive decisions.
- Uses familiar terms.
- Uses historical data and is therefore factual.
- Considers controls and residual risk and prioritises against risk.
- Considers change and is responsive and flexible.
- Cost-effective and efficient.

(c) ***Types of risk factors that could be considered by BLD***

Risk can be viewed in relation to impact and probability. By reviewing and rating a mix of factors, then an overall score can be produced for any given audit area and used for comparison against other areas. For example, if the potential financial impact of any risk is £100,000 and the probability is 0.8, then the comparative risk could be assessed as £80,000.

The type of business operated in each area will affect both the impact and probability of risk. For example:

Level/impact of risk

- Size of revenue for example income in each area and profitability. It is clear that there is a wide variety of turnover and profitability in each area. An evaluation of international contracts reveals that a loss of £1.5m is being made on an income of £8m. The biggest income-generating area is major commercial contracts. For each operating division, level of expenditure and staffing is a factor as well as the assets over which they have control.
- Liquidity of assets could be a factor, although there is limited information on assets for BLD.
- Political exposure or adverse publicity will result in a reputational and potential financial impact. The fast-track division is vulnerable to fines for failure to deliver contracts on time, which could be an impact type risk that should be considered.

Factors affecting control of risk and therefore probability of risk occurring

- Competence and integrity of management, which will influence the next two factors in this list – If BLD management culture in any of these areas is poor, this will significantly impact on how well risks are being managed. Often, the attitude of management at the top will permeate the organisation and can be an important risk indicator.
- Quality of internal control system – This will affect how well the risk is being managed.
- Recent changes, including changes in personnel – These could result in a higher probability of risk. BLD is a fast-growing company, which could present significant risks. The international division is relatively new and poorly performing and therefore also presents risks.
- Deteriorating economic conditions – For example, if the international division is primarily in a country that is entering a major recession, this will impact on the assessment of risk.
- Extent of computerisation will impact on how reliable and effective controls are.
- Extent of external regulation.

- Geographical barriers – For example, the international division will present different risks to that of the UK areas and remoteness of international projects will make controls more difficult to operate.
- Complexity of operations and staffing – Major projects and fast track rely significantly on contractors, which present their own level of risks.

In generating the audit plan, the chief internal auditor should analyse all of the factors listed and apply sound judgement to the decision on what to look at and priorities in each area. Discussions with senior management and use of audit workshops would help to refine the analysis of risks and firm up decisions.

Question 5: Roxy Hotels (Part 2)

(a) ***Role of internal audit***

- Internal audit is part of the organisational control of a business; it is one of the methods used by management to ensure the orderly and efficient running of the business as a whole and is part of the overall control environment.
- A properly functioning internal audit department is part of good corporate governance, as recognised by national and international codes on corporate governance.
- One of the objects of good corporate governance is to ensure that the needs of all stakeholders are met as far as possible and that internal audit procedures meet the needs of the owners of the business, its employees, and the business community at large, as well as the needs of management.
- The main way in which internal audit exercises its functions is by enabling management to perform proper risk assessments in relation to corporate objectives by means of properly understanding the strengths and weaknesses in all of the control systems in the business.
- The role of internal audit has expanded considerably in recent years and the scope of internal audit is no longer routine or low level; internal audit is involved at all levels of management and includes non-routine matters such as assisting in setting corporate objectives and assessing performance against them.

(b) ***Types of activities***

- The review of management, organisational, operational, accounting, internal control and other business systems.
- Making recommendations in relation to the improvement of systems and monitoring the performance of systems against targets.
- Performing value for money (economy, efficiency and effectiveness), best value and similar audits.
- Compliance work involving the review of compliance with legislation, regulations and codes of practice.
- The detailed examination of financial and operating data.
- Special investigations, such as fraud investigations.

Question 6: Hardy Stores

(a) ***Challenges facing a modern internal audit department***

The challenges facing a modern internal audit department ('IAD') arise primarily from the nature of the 'modern business organisation' by which the auditors are employed. Hardy Stores is a company of a significant size (it operates through 100 outlets nation-wide) and is likely to show many of the characteristics of a modern business organisation.

In this context, it is likely that the challenges facing the IAD will include the following:

- The large scale of business activity. This will make it difficult to audit a significant proportion of transactions on a regular basis. As Hardy are retailers there is likely to be a very high number of transactions each year and they are likely to carry a relatively large volume and wide range of stock items.
- The wide geographical spread of many modern businesses – this applies to Hardy (to an extent) which operates through 100 outlets.
- The difficulties of controlling organisations with more complex, often de-centralised structures. Hardy presumably has a head office as well as the 100 outlets. There will need to be sound communication systems and appropriate controls in place in order to manage the business effectively. In the case of Hardy there may also be transactions between the outlets, and the company is likely to need a sophisticated logistics and stock management system to ensure that each of the 100 outlets are stocked to an appropriate level.
- The increasing use of information technology and e-commerce. Hardy Stores is likely to use computer based accounting systems. They may well have point of sales systems in their outlets. They may operate their supply chain logistics via computer links with suppliers. These systems will produce additional problems for the IAD in any organisation.
- The pressure to improve efficiency as a result of an increasingly competitive business environment. This may lead to organisations looking to reduce operating costs, which may, in turn, prompt them to take short cuts in control systems. One specific aspect of this may be the tendency of management to rely more heavily on the services of the IAD in areas, such as consultancy studies of various types, which were previously contracted out. This will tend to widen the scope of the role of the IAD into less 'traditional' areas, such as efficiency or value for money audits. The staff of the IAD will need to be fully trained and aware of modern business practices if they are expected to handle a wider scope of work assignments.

(b) ***Benefits and impact of a risk-based approach to internal auditing for Hardy Stores***

A risk based approach to auditing involves the auditor identifying high risk areas (areas where there is the greatest chance of significant errors, omissions or misstatements arising) and then focusing audit attention and resources on those areas. Risk can be thought of in this context under two main headings:

- **Inherent risk** – resulting from the nature of the transactions subject to audit and the nature of the entity being audited.
- **Control risk** – the risk that the control systems in place may fail to prevent or detect errors, omissions or misstatements.

(A third category of risk, detection risk, is referred to below.)

The benefits from such an approach may include:

- A more efficient audit, with audit time and resources devoted primarily to the more 'important' areas. In the case of Hardy Stores, this may involve such areas as control and management of cash and stocks, store security procedures to minimise losses from shoplifting or pilferage, effective checking of credit sales (credit cards and store accounts if relevant).
- A more effective audit, with a lower chance of major errors or omissions being overlooked.

- By carrying out a detailed risk assessment (or reviewing a risk assessment exercise performed by the directors or management) the auditor will develop a better knowledge of the organisation which will benefit all aspects of the IAD's work. This might involve here an assessment of the petty crime rates in the areas where stores are located, an assessment of the strength of the competition, a review of the background of outlet managers and staff members etc.

However, a risk based approach will typically mean that areas assessed as 'low risk' will receive less audit attention. It may be that, on occasions these areas include undetected errors – 'detection risk' could be higher in certain areas as a consequence of the IAD switching to a risk based approach.

The introduction of a risk based approach (it appears not to be in use in Hardy Stores at present) will involve a major change in the philosophy and working practices of the IAD. There will need to be commitment throughout the IAD to the adoption of such an approach. Audit staff will need to be fully trained in the use of risk based auditing techniques. In addition, it will be of vital importance that the IAD carries out a full risk assessment and keeps this up to date. Such an assessment may be performed by the IAD itself or the company may appoint a risk manager to perform the assessment, which should then be reviewed by members of the IAD.

(c) ***Importance of corporate objectives and control culture in making decisions on the new role of internal audit***

The IAD should operate in such a way that will assist the organisation to achieve its objectives. In general terms, the objective of all profit-oriented organisations is assumed to be that of maximising profit for the shareholders. It will therefore be valid for the company to introduce the new (risk based) role of the IAD if, in the longer term, it will improve the profit performance of the company. Hardy Stores should be encouraged to undertake a cost benefit analysis of the decision to introduce a risk based audit approach in order to evaluate its impact on the ability of the company to achieve its objectives.

Control culture is a term used to refer to an organisation's general approach and attitude to control procedures and systems. It may also be referred to as the 'control environment'. The existence of an IAD could be seen to indicate that the company is committed to promoting a strong and effective control culture within Hardy Stores. The operating methods of the IAD should be changed to focus on a risk-based approach if this would make the department more effective and efficient – in other words, if it would further strengthen the control culture of the company.

CHAPTER 7 EXAM-TYPE QUESTION

Peters & Co

(a) ***Working paper***

Client Name:	Peters & Co
Working Paper Ref:	E1/1
Prepared by:	RRT
Financial Year End:	20X2/X3
Date:	30/9/X3
Reviewed by:	
Subject:	Reliance on internal audit
Date:	

The factors to be considered when deciding whether or not to use the work of the internal audit department of Peters & Co are as follows.

Organisational status

The department currently report to the finance director who cannot be said to be independent of operational responsibilities. The director clearly has a vested interest in the success of the accounting systems and would not want them to appear to be in error or have any faults. As the reports are being addressed to the director in whose department the work is filed, the risk of such files being 'mislaid' or work being amended is high. In this situation the audit department does not appear to have a satisfactory level of status within the organisation to assure their total independence.

Scope of the internal audit function

Up until the appointment of the audit manager the department did not have an audit plan and performed audits as directed by the Finance Department. This is clearly unsatisfactory as the internal audit department should have the freedom to select what areas of the company they wish to audit and should ensure that they cover all areas of the company over a period which they deem appropriate; this is one of the reasons why an audit plan is a necessary form of control.

Technical competence of the internal auditors

All of the audit staff have some form of accountancy qualification and the two senior staff have a number of years post qualification experience. However, my concern with these staff is that they have only ever worked for Peters & Co so their experience is clearly somewhat limited. In addition, the audit manager who is ACCA qualified, having only recently passed the final exams has limited experience as a manager of the department, and therefore this is also a weakness.

Internal audit standards

There are no audit standards currently in the department, and the work is manually prepared. These factors are not conducive to easy retrieval or reference of information, nor does it ensure that the work is prepared on a consistent or complete basis. This major weakness in the department increases the risk involved in relying on the work of the department as part of the audit evidence.

Due professional care

There does not appear to be a proper system of planning the work of each audit, although the audit manager wishes to introduce a methodology. Up until now there does not appear to have been any reasons why any particular areas have been selected for audit.

Audit conclusion

In conclusion I would therefore recommend that in this instance the work performed in the 20X2/20X3 financial year by internal audit should not be relied upon. However, as the new audit manager is clearly seeking to improve controls this situation may change for future audits.

(b) ***Recommendations***

Tarranty & Partners
New Street
London
SE1 2EQ

4 November 20X3

Dear Mr Smith,

Further to our meeting please find details below of our recommendations as to how controls could be improved in the internal audit department and how the overall position of the department could be enhanced.

Reporting line/organisational status

Ideally, the internal audit department should have an independent reporting line within the organisation and report into the board of directors rather than the finance director. Internal audit should not report to those on whom they are required to comment, which is currently the case with Peters & Co as the reporting line is to the finance director. The department should be able to plan and carry out the work that they determine is necessary, and also ensure that all the organisation's controls are reviewed on a cyclical basis (e.g. at least every three years with key areas being reviewed more frequently). The department currently appears to be free of any operating responsibility, and this situation should remain because it is important that the department is truly independent.

Scope

The internal audit department should be able to perform audits within the organisation as they determine necessary. The plan of work should also be overseen by the Board of Directors, who may provide some useful input to the process, and could highlight areas which they are aware of which would benefit from a review. It can also be useful to consult with the external auditors on the forthcoming programme of work as this could ensure in advance that they would be able to rely on the work performed if in line with external audit requirements. We would be happy to assist you with this.

Authority

The internal audit department should be granted sufficient authority to enable them to perform the required work such that they have access to all records and information that is necessary for the purposes of the audit.

Due professional care

The work of internal audit should be properly controlled; this requires a proper system for planning, recording, supervising and reviewing the work performed. We are aware that you are currently preparing an audit plan for the forthcoming year which will assist with this process; it is also important that a proper methodology for recording and controlling the work is implemented as soon as possible and the current staff given training in its use.

Technical competence

The staff within internal audit all currently have accountancy qualifications at different levels. However, there is some concern at the depth of their experience outside of Peters & Co which would help to broaden their knowledge. Clearly an advantage of this length of service is the depth of their knowledge of the company. However, we feel that one useful way to expand their knowledge would be to introduce a system of secondments (e.g. for a one year period), within Peters & Co to and from the finance department.

If you have any further queries, or would like to discuss the points in more detail please do not hesitate to contact me.

Yours sincerely,

A S Auditor

Audit senior

CHAPTER 8 EXAM-TYPE QUESTIONS

Question 1: Internal controls

(a) ***Internal control system objectives***

A system of internal control should have the following objectives:

- ensure that the business of the enterprise is carried on in an orderly and efficient manner
- ensure adherence to internal policies
- prevent and detect fraud and error
- safeguard the assets
- secure, as far as possible, the completeness and accuracy of the records
- secure the timely preparation of reliable financial information.

(b) ***Categories of internal control***

The main categories of internal control are as follows:

- approval and control of documents
- controls over computerised applications and the IT environment
- checking the arithmetical accuracy of the records
- maintaining and reviewing control accounts and trial balances
- comparing the results of cash, security and stock counts with the accounting records
- comparing internal data with external sources of information
- limiting direct physical access to assets and records.

Question 2: Rothwell Ltd

(***Tutorial note:*** The first part is asking about the systems change, so any information about system changeover (e.g. parallel running) and the evaluation of new systems for audit trail can be incorporated into an answer.

The second part requires some thought, although 'standard' items like back-up, staffing and service contracts can be used effectively.

The third part requires detail not only on whether the situation can be remedied, but also the final effect of this – a potential qualification.)

(a) ***Audit implications of the PC-based system***

The introduction of the new IT system will require the auditor to evaluate and test the internal controls relating to the new system, in order to assess the level of additional testing and procedures required to ensure the accuracy of the accounting records in the period between the interim audit and the year end.

The auditor will have to assess whether the installation procedures adopted were satisfactory and whether adequate audit trail is available from the system. The auditor will check the systems controls using tests of control, having regard to the previous assessment of controls, the length of the interim period, the volume of transactions in that period and the fact that the system has suffered a breakdown since the year end.

(b) ***Protection against corruption***

The controls necessary to protect against corruption of data files are those relating to data file and program security. The controls which would have been required are as follows:

- Procedures to ensure the quality of documentation, including manuals laying down the content of program files and hard copies of important documents at various stages of the processing cycle.
- Back-up procedures in the event of disaster including the use of alternative hardware.
- Maintenance of back-up copies of all the data files and the software program files to replace the originals in the event of corruption. All back-up files should be clearly marked as to content, date and time, and must be stored securely and in fire-proof storage facilities. Additional copies should be kept at a location outside the company's premises.
- The company should have a service agreement with the manufacturer or the supplier of the system covering the effect of major corruption and the assistance offered in such circumstances.
- The accounting staff should have been given proper training in the use of the hardware and software including procedures in the case of emergencies and other 'helpline' facilities.
- The introduction of the system should be properly planned over a realistic timescale including a period of parallel running during which both systems will be operated and the results from both compared for accuracy and completeness. This period should continue until all operational and systems problems have been overcome.

(c) ***Audit implications of data file corruption***

The audit implications of data file corruption depend upon the extent to which the missing data and transactions can be reconstructed. Partial reconstruction may be assisted by supplementary manual records or controls, batch totals, control totals etc.

The client should be informed of the audit implications of lack of evidence and audit trail, since considerable extra work and expense may be involved in the reconstruction. Qualification of the audit report may be required with a partial reconstruction and will certainly result if records cannot be reconstructed, on the grounds of limitation in the scope of the audit.

The form of qualification will depend on the materiality of the missing records. The auditor should ensure that the cause of the corruption is ascertained. System failures may require a partial or full rewrite of the software. Hardware failure or user error can be corrected quickly though additional or improved training may be required.

CHAPTER 9 EXAM-TYPE QUESTIONS

Question 1: Sticky Bar Chocolates Limited

(***Tutorial note:*** This is a relatively short question that could give time pressure problems due to the many sub-parts. State the definitions quickly, and then list the other information required to speed up the writing of the answer (i.e. don't write long paragraphs when point form answers are sufficient and clearer too).

(a) ***Shortcomings and improvements***

Shortcomings

- There is no check that the expenses claimed by the salespeople were actually expended.
- There is no check that the expenses were properly incurred by the salespeople in carrying out their duties.
- The deputy chief accountant could easily perpetrate a fraud either alone or in collusion with a salesperson.

Improvements

- Each salesperson should complete a weekly log showing calls made and mileage covered. The logs and the expense claims should be submitted to the sales manager who should check and sign the log before passing it to the deputy chief accountant.
- At intervals a member of the accounts staff should verify that claimed mileage is consistent with the mileage shown on the cars' recorders.
- The directors should verify that complete and signed documentation is attached to and is consistent with the cheques presented to them. They should cancel the presented documents to prevent a second presentation.

(b) ***Tests of control***

Tests of control are those tests which seek to provide audit evidence that internal control procedures are being properly applied throughout the period under review.

The tests of control that could be performed are as follows:

- Select a sample of the payments and obtain the documentation. Verify that each claim is fully supported by vouchers and that the additions are correct.
- Examine the returned cheques for the sample chosen and verify that the cheques are made out to the salesperson concerned and are properly signed. This may form part of the audit of the bank transactions.

(c) ***Substantive procedures***

Substantive procedures are those procedures which seek to provide audit evidence as to the financial statement assertions of completeness, existence, measurement, valuation etc.

The substantive procedures that could be performed are:

- Completeness – examine expense claims paid after the balance sheet date to ensure that all outstanding claims are included.
- Measurement and valuation – review mileage claims with mileage records obtained from inspection of cars or repair invoices. Verify that salespeople who have made claims are legitimate employees of the company. Select a sample of hotel and entertaining expenses and verify that they are prima facie valid, e.g. that the salesperson operates in the area and the customers

entertained are customers of the company. Test the analysis of bank payments to ensure that all expense payments and no other payments are correctly charged to the account. Review previous years' accounts, directors' minutes and budgets, if any, to seek evidence of the validity of the total.

(d) ***Auditor's actions on discovering the false claim***

- Inform the management verbally immediately and in writing in the management letter.
- Consider whether the discovery casts doubt on the effectiveness of the system, hence whether further tests may be necessary.
- Consider whether the discovery casts doubt on the company's records in general and hence whether further work may be necessary in other areas.

Question 2: Howden plc

(a) ***Division of duties***

The following duties should be performed by different people:

- initiation of a transaction
- custody or handling of the related asset
- recording the transaction.

If these duties are segregated, then no one person is in a position to execute a complete transaction and therefore collusion would be required for a fraud to be perpetrated.

(b) ***Internal control features***

Buying

- Requisition notes for purchases should be authorised.
- Re-order levels and quantities should be pre-set and preferably recorded in advance on the requisition note.
- All orders should be recorded on official documents showing the suppliers' names, quantities ordered and price.
- All orders should be authorised by a responsible official whose authority limits should be predefined.
- Major items, e.g. capital expenditure, should be authorised by the board.
- Copies of orders should be retained as a method of following up late deliveries by suppliers.

Receipt of goods

- Goods inwards centres should be identified to deal with the receipt of all goods.
- All goods should be checked for quantity and quality. Goods received notes should be raised for all goods accepted. The GRN should be signed by a responsible official.
- Goods received notes should be checked against purchase orders and procedures should exist to notify the supplier of under- or over-deliveries.
- A record of goods returned should be kept and checked to the credit notes received from suppliers.

Accounting for purchases

- Purchase invoices received should be stamped with an approval grid and given a unique serial number to ensure purchase invoices do not go astray.
- The invoices should be checked against the order and the GRN, and casts and extensions should also be checked.
- The invoices should be signed as approved for payment by a responsible official independent of the ordering and receipt of goods functions.
- Invoices should be properly allocated to the nominal accounts, perhaps by allocating expenditure codes. A portion of such coding should be checked independently.
- Input VAT should be separated from the expense.
- Purchase ledger records should be kept by persons independent of the receiving of goods, invoice authorisation and payment routines.
- Invoice sequential numbers should be checked against purchase day book details.
- A purchase ledger control account should be maintained and regularly checked against balances in the ledger by an independent official.
- Statements from suppliers should be checked against the purchase ledger account.

Payment of outstanding balances

- Unused cheques should be held in a secure place.
- The person who prepares cheques should have no responsibility over purchase ledger or sales ledger.
- Cheques should be signed only when evidence of a properly approved transaction is available. Such evidence may take the form of invoices, payroll, petty cash book, etc.
- This check should be evidenced by signing the supporting documentation.
- In a large concern those approving the original document should be independent of those signing cheques.
- Cheque signatories should be restricted to the minimum practical number.
- Two signatories should be required except perhaps for cheques of small amounts.
- The signing of blank cheques and cheques in favour of the signatory should be prohibited.
- Cheques should be crossed before being signed.
- Supporting documents should be cancelled as paid to prevent their use to support further cheque payments. This cancellation could be done by the cashier before the cheque is signed (providing the cancellation identifies the cheque number) or by the cheque signatory at the time of signing the cheque.
- Cheques should preferably be despatched immediately. If not, they should be held in a safe place.
- Returned cheques may be obtained from the bank and a sample checked against cash book entries and supporting documentation.

(***Tutorial note*:** Part (a) should have been straightforward. Part (b) was more difficult, and so try and think of any general principles that you know that could be of assistance. Note that controls over cash and bank will be dealt with in the next chapter.)

CHAPTER **10** EXAM-TYPE QUESTIONS

Question 1: Quicksand Ltd

(***Tutorial note:*** This is a straightforward question requiring the candidate simply to list the expected internal controls, which could be done from memory. As long as sufficient controls are listed (at one mark per control a minimum of seven each for cheque payments and petty cash would be expected), then a pass should be obtained. Finally, note the letter format: marks would be awarded for good style here.)

(a) ***Letter***

KIRK & CO
Certified Accountants
1701 Enterprise Road
Leicester

A Black Esq
Managing Director
Quicksand Ltd
Freeman Industrial Estate
Leicester

14 February 20X7

Dear Sir,

Internal control procedures for cheque payments and petty cash

Following our discussions of last week, I have set out below my recommendations for internal control procedures for the cheque payments and petty cash systems in your company.

The overriding requirement of these systems is that money expended is in respect of valid transactions of the company. Cheques should only be written or petty cash given out when valid authorised vouchers are presented to the appropriate official. Detailed internal controls are as follows.

Cheque payments

- Unissued cheques should be kept in a secure place, e.g. the company safe.
- The person who prepares the cheque should have no responsibility for the sales or purchase ledgers to ensure that this person is not tempted to make out cheques to incorrect payees who may or may not be on these ledgers.
- Cheques should only be signed when evidence of a properly approved transaction is available, e.g. invoice, payroll for wages cheque or petty cash book to reimburse the petty cash balance.
- The supporting documentation should be signed at the same time as the cheque to ensure that the documentation is not used twice.
- The person approving the original documentation should not be the person signing the cheque. This ensures that there is a check over the validity of the purchase before payment is made.
- All cheques should require two signatories, who can be made up from the other four directors of the company.
- Blank cheques should not be signed as these could be filled in later to incorrect payees. Similarly, if cheques have to be made out to a cheque signatory, then other signatories to whom the cheque is not made out should sign it.

- Cheques should be returned to the cashier when signed and despatched as soon as practicable, in order to prevent accidental loss on the premises.
- Cheques should be obtained from the bank (either all cheques or a sample through the year as agreed with the bank) and these cheques agreed back to the cash book.
- Any spoilt cheques should be cancelled but not destroyed; they should be retained as audit evidence.
- Cheques should be crossed 'Account payee only' to ensure that only the payee can cash the cheque.

Petty cash payments

- Petty cash should be kept on an imprest system with the level of the cash float and its location being formally agreed. As the level of petty cash expenditure is around £300 per month, a float of £350 should be maintained to meet this; £600 appears to be excessive here.
- Only authorised persons should have access to the cash. In this case, only the cashier and one director should have the petty cash tin key.
- The cash should be held in a secure location, e.g. the company safe.
- Before cash is given out, the cashier should receive an authorised expense voucher signed by a responsible official. This official should not be the cashier.
- With the use of the imprest system, the cash in the petty cash tin together with the expense vouchers should always equal the amount of the float. Spot checks by a director not involved with petty cash payments could be carried out to ensure that this is the case.
- When the petty cash float is to be reimbursed at the end of the month, the amount of the cheque required should be supported by the vouchers received during the month.
- The expense vouchers should be cancelled after the reimbursement is made to ensure that they are not used twice. Similarly, the petty cash book will be signed to confirm the amount of the reimbursement.

- The cashing of IOUs and cheques for individuals within the company should be prohibited except on express permission of the directors. Similarly, a limit can be placed on the amount of any one petty cash payment which can only be amended by the directors.
- The petty cash book should be reviewed regularly by a director not involved with the petty cash system, the castings should be checked along with the analysis of payments and the postings into the nominal ledger.

I hope that these procedures will be of use to you. Should you require any further advice or assistance please do not hesitate to contact me.

Yours faithfully

L McCoy

(b) ***Director's unwillingness***

The managing directors of many companies may decide not to become involved in the day-to-day running of the company and therefore leave this function to other staff and directors who have more skill in this area. Mr Black has apparently decided to follow this route. There is, though, some value in being involved to some degree in the cash payments of the company, because by signing cheques, the director gains knowledge of what the company is paying for, and can exercise some control over the cash payments of the company. It is, therefore, unusual that Mr Black does not want to involve himself in this respect.

A satisfactory compromise is for Mr Black not to be involved in the smaller cheque payments, and not to be involved at all with the petty cash payments. Larger payments over a pre-determined amount could require his signature so that Mr Black can be familiar with the company's payments and maintain some control over these payments.

Question 2: Management reports

(***Tutorial note:*** Although this could be called an 'essay-type' discussion question, note the use of headings to structure the answer. This improves presentation, makes the answer much easier to mark, and hence increases the mark earning potential.)

There has been much talk recently of improving the image of audit so that it appears more worthwhile. Constructive advice on systems has long been considered an obvious spin-off benefit to be publicised. However, the advice itself has always been given confidentially to management of the business and careful consideration must be given to the implications of making the advice public.

Confidentiality

Clearly this must be the biggest concern. The matters likely to be dealt with in the report (i.e. weaknesses in systems and failures in operation of the systems) are not matters which it is in the interests of the company (and hence the shareholders) to publish to competitors or the bulk of employees. These third parties may be able to use the information to their benefit at the expense of the company. Yet if the report is made available to shareholders, it is effectively (in all but the smallest owner-managed companies) made available to anybody who wants it.

Usefulness to shareholders

One could question in any case the possible benefits to the shareholders. The shareholders do not in general have the technical or commercial awareness to understand properly the report to management. They may be confused as to the purpose of the report and also the limitations, i.e. that the report does not include all weaknesses only those which came to light during the audit.

They may also be unaware (as the auditor may be unaware) of commercial reasons why it is not cost-effective to remove certain weaknesses or implement the auditor's suggestions.

Confusion of responsibilities

Not only the shareholders but also the directors may become confused as to the actual responsibility for systems. If the report is published and hence comes to be regarded as part of the auditor's duties (where in fact it is additional to those duties), the directors may feel that systems are no longer their primary responsibility. They may start to assume that any weaknesses will be reported by the auditor and therefore failure to report will imply that there are no weaknesses. This is clearly not a desirable position for the auditor.

Spur to action on report

On the other hand, as the question implies, the major benefit of showing the report to management and to shareholders is that there will be stronger pressure brought to bear on the management to implement suggestions. This is certainly true but is even this a good thing? It is certainly not necessarily good for the management advice to become effectively a directive to management. It may, for example, prejudice the independence of the auditor when considering systems which he himself suggested.

There is also the problem of the auditor giving advice which then turns out to be incorrect or inappropriate.

Effect on the nature of the report

This leads to the final point, which is that wider publication of the report would make the auditor very cautious about the contents of the report. Comments would have to be carefully reviewed to ensure there was no risk of a defamation action. Advice/solutions would not be provided in case it was incorrect. Overall, the report would become defensive rather than constructive, and again the benefits of the current situation would be lost.

Conclusion

As can be seen from the above, the drawbacks of reports to management being shown to shareholders far outweigh any benefits. However another solution which avoids most of the problems yet still retains the benefit would be to report direct to an audit committee of non-executive directors.

CHAPTER 11 EXAM-TYPE QUESTION

Rolfe Enterprises

(a) ***Draft e-mail***

To: audit.junior@offruler.com

Subject: Review of Board Minutes

Following your query regarding the purpose of examination of board minutes, the reasons why the auditor performs this task is to obtain details of directors' decisions that have been made, and these can often be about very significant matters. Future plans for the company should also be contained in board minutes as these are clearly matters that need to be discussed at board level.

Also the minutes will contain evidence of authorisations for particular transactions – these might be transactions of high value or for specific matters such as dividend declaration and approval of directors' emoluments.

Other matters that may be contained within the minutes are details of reviews of period accounts (e.g. month end, quarter end, interim and final), approval of the financial statements and action on points raised by external auditors in previous years. Details of contingent liabilities may also be found in the minutes.

From the above you will see that the board minutes are a useful source of audit evidence for a number of factors, and although they are not 'independent' clearly if we have always found the information contained within them to be correct and we have no reasons to doubt the integrity of the directors then we can decide to place reliance on them. You should also bear in mind that when conducting our final review we always consider consistency of evidence, and if any inconsistencies were found then clearly we would investigate these.

(b) ***Letter to the Company Secretary***

Diggers & Partners
Glenbrook Way
Heathland
SE1 2WD

Company Secretary
Rolfe Enterprises
Wetor Way
Notlrach
SE5 4RT

X/X/20X0

Dear Company Secretary,

Further to your telephone call, in which you informed me that I would not be permitted access to the board minutes for reasons of confidentiality, I can assure you that all information obtained during the course of the audit is totally secure and disclosure is not permitted to anyone (with exceptions in criminal cases).

As auditors we have a duty of confidentiality and our firm has rules in place to ensure that this duty is complied with.

I am sure that you can understand that the board minutes contain information which is very relevant for the purposes of the audit, and as auditors we need to obtain sufficient, relevant and reliable evidence (in accordance with ISA 500) on which to base our opinion. Clearly, if this was not possible then we may have to qualify our opinion on the financial statements as the scope of our audit will have been restricted.

I would be more than happy to discuss this matter with you in further detail to try and obtain a satisfactory conclusion for both parties. Please do not hesitate to contact me.

Yours sincerely,

A Senior

Diggers & Partners

(c) ***Action in view of apparent lack of transaction authority***

As auditor, if I could not find details of approval by the board of the asset in question in the minutes then I would try to find this authorisation elsewhere. For example, there may have been a purchase order raised prior to the asset's purchase which would contain the authorisation. I would also look at the invoice for the asset to see if there was any reference to any document which may contain the authorisation. I would contact the Company Secretary to see if there are any authorisation details in the files, and I would also contact the Purchasing Manager to identify on whose authority the asset was purchased and whether there was any supporting documentation raised prior to the purchase.

This appears to be a weakness in internal control that I would include details of in the management letter. As it is such a significant purchase I would also include it within the letter of representation.

CHAPTER 12

EXAM-TYPE QUESTIONS

Question 1: Engineering company

(***Tutorial note***: In reaching a decision on each of these points in your answer, remember to give reasons why you decide on a certain answer. For example, simply stating that a company should depreciate assets would be insufficient for the final part. Reasons for the proposed treatment must also be considered, for example giving rise to obsolescence problems. Note should also be made that assets not in use also fall in value; non-depreciation is therefore not appropriate except in a few isolated circumstances.)

(a) ***Authorisation for asset purchase***

The purchase of fixed assets should normally be authorised at two separate stages in the accounting cycle. Firstly, the company should prepare capital budgets. In the capital budget all expected future expenditure on fixed assets should be detailed as to type of asset, estimated cost and expected date of purchase. This budget should be approved by the directors. The auditors should ensure that they have a copy of the budget and proof that the directors have approved the anticipated expenditure (normally through a copy of the minutes of the board meeting). The purchase of all fixed assets should be checked to the budget.

The second stage of authorisation comes when the asset is actually ordered. The directors will establish levels of authority for managers to authorise the purchase of assets. Major items should require the signature of a director. The auditors should ensure that the purchase requisition requesting purchase of the plant is duly authorised by the responsible official. They should ensure that the invoice has been matched to the appropriate goods inward note, purchase order and purchase requisition and approval for payment made by the appropriate official. They should also ensure that the asset has been received in good condition and is being used in the business of the company.

By checking the budget approval and by ensuring that the necessary purchase approvals have been adhered to, the auditor has checked that all major fixed asset expenditure has been authorised.

(b) ***Fixed asset register***

A fixed asset register is a list of all the fixed assets owned by a company. It may be in the form of a hand-written ledger, machine card system or maintained on a computer. The company requires a fixed asset register in order to control and identify all the fixed assets which it owns. The register should show the following information:

- the plant number allocated to the asset (ideally, each asset should have its own unique identity number)
- details of the type and specification
- name of the supplier and date of purchase
- cost
- rate of depreciation and total depreciation charged to date
- location
- expenditure incurred by way of maintenance and repair charges.

Every year the auditor should select some items from the fixed asset register and physically check their existence and condition. This ensures that items shown in the balance sheet are still in existence and are in good condition and have not been scrapped without a record being made in the accounting records. The company should also require that individual assets are checked against the fixed asset register on a regular basis and that periodically the register is reconciled to the nominal ledger, as part of its internal control system.

(c) ***Procedures for scrapping plant***

The procedures for scrapping plant and machinery should be detailed in writing and approved by the directors. All scrapping of plant should be on a systematic basis and should be included in the capital budget in order that replacement assets can be ordered (if necessary). Any major item of plant should be examined prior to scrapping by an engineer to ensure that it is not worth repairing the machine and keeping it for a longer period of time. All major items which are scrapped should be approved by the directors, but they may delegate the authority to scrap small items of plant to the works manager or equivalent. If the plant is still in good working order, the directors should ensure that they sell it for its current market value. These prices may be obtainable in the trade press. If the machine is sold as scrap metal, the directors should ensure that the value received is in line with current scrap metal prices.

(d) ***Depreciation rate authorisation***

All rates of depreciation should be approved by the directors. It is not necessary to allocate rates by individual machine, but generally by type of machine based on its estimated useful life. The auditor should review the rates and check whether the machines are fully depreciated at the end of their useful lives.

The auditor should review profits and losses on disposal of assets. If these show high losses, then it would indicate that the rate of depreciation is too low. If losses are minimal, then the rates would appear to be reasonable.

If the company measures profitability by individual machines, it may be possible that methods of depreciation other than straight line may be applicable; if this is so, then the auditor should review these alternative methods of depreciation to ascertain their validity.

(e) ***Depreciation on unused assets***

If the asset has been purchased recently and the machine is still in the process of installation prior to commencement of use, then it can be reasonably argued that as no revenue is accruing to the company, no expense should be charged. In these circumstances it can be acceptable not to charge depreciation on assets not in use.

However, if the asset is not in use due to bad trading conditions and if there is no indication that these conditions will necessarily improve, then it is less valid to argue that as no revenue accrues, no charges should be made. In these circumstances the machine will be losing value merely due to the passage of time. It may well become obsolete.

The auditor should examine all the circumstances surrounding the non-use of the asset and recommend that, if the valuation is likely to deteriorate merely through the passage of time, then appropriate depreciation should be charged. If it is known that the asset is likely to become obsolete and scrapped, then the auditor should recommend that the machine be written down to its expected realisable value immediately.

Question 2: Stocks and shares

(***Tutorial note***: Note the two part sub-question in part (b) – for the risky areas always think about valuation and fraud.)

(a) ***Five audit objectives in the examination of stocks and shares***

- To ensure that shares are correctly *valued* at the end of the year – particularly for any fall in value.
- To check that the shares *exist* by reference to share certificates, which are kept in a safe location.
- To vouch all dividends received to the profit and loss account for *completeness.*
- To ensure that the company actually *owns* the shares, again by reference to the share certificates.
- To check the financial statements for correct presentation and *disclosure.*

(b) ***Inherent audit risk***

Inherent risk is the risk of material error arising from the nature of the client and its business. This risk will vary according to the client and even the area being audited within one client.

Inherent risk is only part of total audit risk, the other parts being control risk and detection risk. Control risk relates to the effectiveness of the client's internal control system, and detection risk to the effectiveness of the auditor's tests.

When the auditors are planning the audit, they will review the client's business, history, products, assets etc. and try and identify items that by their nature alone could result in a material error in the financial statements. The auditors will then ensure that either there are controls to cover these risks, or perform audit tests to ensure that the risks do not result in material error in the financial statements.

Stocks and shares have a high inherent risk due to the following factors:

Valuation

Shares are normally valued in the financial statements at cost of purchase. At the end of the year, any impairment in value must be accounted for. Assessing whether an impairment has occurred can be difficult due to the fact that future cash flows are uncertain.

Income

Checking completeness of income can be difficult. Dividends are not paid on set days each year, and can be for varying amounts. There is a need to ensure that the company has received all dividends due to it by reviewing dividend records from companies that the client has invested in and agreeing these to the client's bank accounts.

Fraud and theft

Share certificates can be forged and sold by employees for cash. As share certificates are easy to sell, good internal control systems are needed to ensure safe custody of share certificates so they are not misappropriated by employees.

(c) ***Audit procedures***

Audit procedures to confirm the existence and ownership of stocks and shares would include the following:

Checking share certificates

The share certificate will be evidence of both existence of the shares, and ownership, because the client company name will be stated on the share certificate to confirm who holds the shares.

Where the certificates are kept at a third party such as in a bank, for safekeeping, then either a confirmation letter should be sent to agree the shares held, or the auditor should attend the third party premises and inspect the certificates there to confirm existence and ownership.

Any shares that do not have the client's name on, should be agreed to a trust or other document to confirm beneficial ownership in the client's name.

Where shares are held by nominees, the auditor should examine correspondence with the nominee and consider circularising the nominee to confirm investments held.

Contract note examination

If the shares were purchased during the year, then sight of the contract note will also confirm ownership; this will show the shares being sold to the client, with the client name appearing on the contract note.

Contract note review

A review of contract notes during the year will also identify shares sold. These sales should be agreed to the record of sales in the ledgers to ensure that they have been correctly recorded. Certificates for shares that the client no longer owns will therefore be no longer held.

(d) ***Auditing recorded income***

Audit work to ensure that all income had been recorded in the accounts from stocks and shares would include the following:

- Agree an independent summary of dividends due (e.g. Extel cards) to the actual dividends received in the cash book.
- Check the calculation of the dividend by multiplying the number of shares held by the amount of the dividend, and ensuring this matches the cash receipt figure. Care will be needed here to ensure that any shares sold ex-div still have the dividend received by the client.
- For any fixed interest securities, agreeing the calculation of the interest due based on the nominal value and the interest rate, to the actual amount received in the cash book.
- Analytical review of dividends received this year to the last few years to ensure completeness of dividends (taking into account all sales and purchases during this time).

Question 3: Springfield Nurseries

(a) ***Main risks***

All assets in practice are liable to be overstated rather than understated; where assets are overstated it is likely that profits are overstated.

There is a risk that the fixed assets do not exist, or that they are overvalued either because they are impaired in some way or have been under-depreciated.

There is also a risk that fixed assets are overstated because of the inclusion of items (such as small tools) that should be expensed through the profit and loss account rather than capitalised in the balance sheet.

As with all financial statement assertions, there is a risk that the values are misstated because of errors in the accounting and internal control systems.

(b) ***Ownership and cost***

Land and buildings

- Ownership will be evidenced by purchase documents or other documents of title.
- The ownership of land will normally be shown in the Land Registry.
- Ownership may also be evidenced indirectly by the payment of insurance premiums and other costs associated with the ownership of land and buildings.
- The cost of land and buildings may be shown in the purchase documentation, and also in documentation relating to the Stamp Duty that is payable when land and buildings are transferred.
- Payments should be traced through the cash records.

Computers and motor vehicles

- Both ownership and cost of computers and motor vehicles will be shown in the purchase documentation and in the cash records. Motor vehicles also normally have associated documentation that show the road tax payable and the history of ownership (the log book).
- It is common to mark both computers and vehicles with security codes designed to prevent and detect theft, these codes may be invisible to the eye, but visible by using special lights; the knowledge of and a proper record of these codes provide some evidence of ownership.
- Computers and motor vehicles may be held on leases, in which case the leasing documentation should be inspected.
- The physical existence and use by the company of the computers, motor vehicles (and land and buildings) also provide some evidence of ownership.

(c) ***Depreciation rates***

- The depreciation rates on the buildings may be too high (buildings are commonly depreciated over 50 years). The depreciation rates on the computers, motor vehicles and equipment might be too low (computer equipment is often depreciated over three years and motor vehicles over four years, on a straight line basis).
- Enquire of management as to the reasons for the depreciation rates (and why they are different to the rates suggested above, bearing in mind the fact that there may be special considerations to be taken into account), any recent changes in rates, and the reason for the choice of the straight line/reducing balance methods.
- Review the actual life of all of the assets by inspecting assets that are fully depreciated to see if they are still in use; if they are, the depreciation rate may be too high. Where assets that are not yet fully depreciated are no longer in use, the depreciation rates may be too low.
- Review the profit or loss on disposals of assets; profits may indicate that depreciation rates are too high, losses may indicate that rates are too low.
- Inspect a sample of new assets, assets that have been depreciated to half their original value and assets that have been written off, and review the physical condition of the assets.

(d) ***Disagreement with rates***

Assess whether the total error in the depreciation is material to the financial statements; if it is not, it will have no direct effect on the audit report, although the error should be added to the summary of unadjusted differences (and if these are material cumulatively, an adjustment to the financial statements may be necessary).

If the amounts involved are material to the financial statements, it will be necessary to request management to make an adjustment to the financial statements. If management agrees, it will be possible to issue an unqualified audit opinion. If management refuses, it will be necessary to issue an 'except for' opinion (explaining the disagreement), or even an 'adverse' opinion (stating that the financial statements do not give a true and fair view) if the amounts involved affect the view given by the financial statements as a whole. Qualified audit opinions relating to disagreements over depreciation policies are relatively rare (often because the amounts involved are immaterial), adverse opinions are very rare.

If there is a serious disagreement, it may be necessary to review other areas in which management estimates form the basis of the accounting treatment.

CHAPTER **13**

EXAM-TYPE QUESTIONS

Question 1: Askwith Limited

(***Tutorial note**:* A relatively straightforward question on debtors. The answer should state clearly the information required, and also use the question information where possible to make the answer relevant to the question asked.)

(a) ***Steps to be taken if no reply received***

If no reply is received to the initial circularisation letter, a second request should be sent. In addition, the debtors could be contacted by telephone and asked to confirm the balances (provided the client grants permission).

If direct confirmation still proves impossible, the following alternative procedures might be used:

- review cash received after the year-end to see if the balances have been cleared
- agree individual outstanding invoices to independent evidence such as delivery notes signed by the customer
- review credit notes issued after the year-end to ensure debtors should not be reduced
- review make-up of debtors balance and ensure that it consists of recent invoices
- check authorisation for unusual entries (journals, contras) in the accounts.

(b) ***Significance of cut-off tests***

Cut-off tests are intended to provide evidence that transactions have been recorded in the correct period. Companies may wish to manipulate their records to treat transactions as having occurred in an earlier period, so as to improve the appearance of the financial statements.

The following tests would be appropriate to ensure cut-off was correct:

- agree a sample of despatch notes, from either side of the year-end to invoices to ensure that the dates agree (details of the last despatch notes would usually be recorded at the stock-take).
- review credit notes issued after the year-end and check that they do not relate to stock returned before the year-end etc.
- check that cash received has been allocated to the correct period.

Question 2: Defaulters Limited

(***Tutorial note***: This question required the re-drafting of a bank reconciliation to show a potential cash theft. If you could not do this, then it would be advisable to revise the preparation of bank reconciliations. Audit tests related to the bank reconciliation were required in part (a); look down the reconciliation and try and give a test for each item appearing there. By doing this you will ensure that the audit tests given are relevant to the question and that all items on the reconciliation are audited.)

(a) ***Audit schedule***

Audit schedule showing amount of cash missing from Defaulters Ltd cash book at 31 May 20X1

		£	£
Balance per statement			31,100
Less: Unpresented cheques	134	232	
	183	300	
	284	506	
	861	380	
	862	412	
	863	290	
			(2,120)
			28,980
Less: Lodgement on bank statement not yet in cash book			(200)
			28,780
Add: Lodgement to enter into cash book			7,588
Expected cash book balance			36,368
Less: Actual cash book balance			(37,802)
Cash difference			1,434

Audit tests on cash difference statement above

- Agree bank balance to bank statement.
- Agree unpresented cheques recorded in cash book before 31 May, and to bank statements dated after this date.
- Investigate why cheques 134, 183 and 284 have not been presented to the bank. Discuss with client whether the bank balance requires adjustment if these cheques will not be presented.
- Agree lodgement of £200 to bank statement before 31 May and cash book after this date.
- Ensure that the undeposited receipts are banked in early June. Agree entries for these items in the cash book and bank statements.
- Agree cash book balance to the cash book.
- Agree a number of cash book entries to the bank statement during the year.
- Check casting of the cash book and the bank reconciliation above.
- Request the working papers of the internal auditor on the bank balance to confirm amount of work done in this area.

(b) ***Cashier's attempt to conceal the possible theft of cash***

The cashier attempted to conceal the possible theft of cash in three ways:

- Not all the unpresented cheques were included in the bank reconciliation. This understated the deduction from the bank balance making it possible to show a higher cash book balance than actually existed.
- The petty cash float was included in the bank reconciliation. The float is reimbursed on an impress basis, the cheques for which will have already been entered in the cash book; the float does not need including in the bank reconciliation.
- The unrecorded credit was treated incorrectly. It should have been deducted from the cash book figure in the client's reconciliation not deducted from the bank statement figure as in the cashier's reconciliation.

(c) ***Internal control weaknesses***

Internal control weaknesses that could have assisted the theft of cash by the cashier are:

- The cash is banked by the cashier without apparent checking by any other member of staff. If the cashier is to bank the cash then the paying-in slip stamped by the bank should be agreed by an independent official to the listing of cash received on that day. Any differences should be investigated. The cash should also be banked on a daily basis rather than being left for a few days as appears to be the case at the moment.
- The cashier is responsible for the custody of the cash, and also for the preparation of the bank reconciliation. Although this does indicate some lack of internal control, this can be rectified by the bank reconciliation being audited in depth by the internal audit department. Again, any differences should be immediately investigated.

(d) ***Action an auditor should take***

The actions that the auditor should take on the discovery of potential improprieties are as follows:

- Extend audit testing in that area to try and ascertain whether any impropriety has actually occurred.
- Quantify the effect of the potential impropriety discovered as a result of the extended testing above.
- Discuss the matter with management. The discussion should include the findings of the auditor and agree actions to be taken by management.
- Confirm the discussions, and agreed actions, if any, in a management letter either during or at the end of the audit.
- Ascertain at a later date what action has been taken by management. If appropriate action has not been taken remind management again that action is necessary. If no action is forthcoming the auditor may wish to obtain legal advice on whether the matter should be disclosed further (i.e. to third parties).

Question 3: Debtors internal control systems

(a) ***Error, omission and misappropriation***

- Where internal controls are weak, the errors that occur may include the issue of invoices and credit notes for the wrong amounts, the issue of invoices and credit notes to the wrong customers, the incorrect recording of invoices, credit notes, cash and contras in the ledgers and daybooks, and the incorrect setting of credit limits.

- Where internal controls are weak, invoices, credit notes, cash and contras may simply go unrecorded.
- The effect of this will be that debtors may be under- or over-stated in the records and that the company will not receive the money that is due to it, or that goodwill with customers is damaged.
- The assets that may be misappropriated include cash and stock. If records are poor, it will be easy to hide the misappropriation of cash that is received from customers. It will also be possible for stock to be misappropriated and hidden by the issue of false or incorrect invoices, credit notes or contras.

(b) ***Inherent weaknesses***

- No internal control system is perfect and all internal control systems are subject to inherent weaknesses. This means that auditors can never rely on the proper operation of the internal control systems alone. Even if their tests show that the system appears to be working perfectly, it will be necessary to perform some substantive testing.
- Inherent weaknesses include human error. People operate the control systems and people make mistakes.
- Other inherent weaknesses include the abuse of authority. For example, false invoices may be issued towards the year-end to improve the sales figure and false credit notes to cancel them out may be issued just after the year-end. This is sometimes known as 'window-dressing'.
- Fraudulent collusion can happen both within the company and outside the company. Those who have the right to authorise the issue of credit notes may authorise false credit notes for customers who are their friends. Those who have access to cash and the debtors records may collude to misappropriate cash, and make entries in the accounting records to hide the misappropriation. This is sometimes known as 'teeming and lading'.

(c) ***Main internal controls***

- Segregation of duties between those who control the accounting records, those who receive the cash, those who authorise the issue of invoices and credit notes and those who issue the goods to customers.
- Two people should be involved wherever cash or stocks are being handled in order to prevent both the misappropriation of assets and to prevent false accusations of misappropriation.
- The maintenance of a separate debtors ledger showing the individual balances owing from customers. This ledger should be reconciled at least monthly to the total figure in the nominal ledger.
- The issue of statements to customers at the end of each month (from the ledger) showing how much is owed by the customer.
- Arithmetical and accounting controls over the issue of invoices and credit notes, some of which may be computerised, in order to ensure that they are calculated correctly in accordance with authorised prices.
- The use of batch and hash totals, document counts and sequence checks in the input of transactions into the computer system to ensure completeness and accuracy.
- The appointment of a credit controller who limits the credit available to customers, together with restricted access to those sections of the system that contain credit limits.
- The use of exception reporting to highlight overdue accounts and accounts where the credit limits have been exceeded, together with a system for investigating and dealing with such accounts.

- The regular review by the financial controller of debtors amounts and the independent authorisation of the write-off of bad debts.

(d) ***Proper operation of internal controls***

- Auditors seek to rely on the proper operation of internal controls wherever possible because where internal controls are operating properly, reliance on internal controls is the most efficient method of auditing.
- If the auditor's tests show that internal controls are operating properly, the volume of substantive testing on transactions and balances can be reduced.
- It is always possible (in theory) to perform an audit on the basis of substantive testing alone, but given the volume of transactions (in all but the smallest of businesses), such an approach would be prohibitively expensive for the audited entity.

CHAPTER 14 EXAM-TYPE QUESTIONS

Question 1: Nero Scrap and Haulage Ltd

(a) ***Instructions regarding unpressed scrap***

- All movements of scrap should, if possible, cease during the stocktaking. Any scrap entering the yard during the day of stocktaking should be stored separately.
- The yard should be divided into areas during the stocktake.
- Once stock has been assessed in an area, a marker should be placed to show that the area has been counted. Stock movements between areas should be prohibited during the stocktake.
- The assessment should be carried out by two persons. One should be familiar with quantities and types of ferrous scrap. The other should be from an independent department.
- The last numbers of input and output documents should be noted to ensure adequate cut-off procedures are applied.
- Stock sheets should be pre-numbered and their issue and return should be recorded and controlled.
- All stocktaking results should be noted and signed.

(b) ***Valuation of stock of scrap***

- Stock should be valued at the lower of cost and net realisable value.
- Cost might be calculated on an actual basis related to invoices where stock is separately identifiable. A FIFO or average cost basis might be simpler to apply.
- Net realisable value could be estimated from actual prices received in the post-balance sheet period. The cost of transport to the steelworks would need to be deducted from the selling price.

(c) ***Verification of value***

- Ascertain the policies used to estimate cost and net realisable value. Ensure that these policies are consistent with the principles of SSAP 9.
- Test a sample of stock prices with purchase invoices or other input documents.
- Test that the prices used are consistent with the accounting policies.
- Review prices received from the steel mill for goods in stock at the balance sheet date. Ensure provision is made when NRV is below cost.

- Examine stocktaking records for evidence of slow-moving or unsaleable stocks. Test that provision is made for losses.
- Test the arithmetical accuracy of calculations, additions and summaries.

(d) ***Transport manager's commission***

This matter appears *prima facie* to be a corrupt practice but should be investigated carefully by the auditor to see if the matter is material. The auditor should examine the invoices and delivery notes from the tyre suppliers and ensure that prices are reasonable and deliveries and payments are matched.

The auditor should draw the matter to the attention of the management.

The auditor may need to consider if any evidence appears of other doubtful practices which may have implications for the financial statements.

(e) ***Audit programme covering haulage charges***

- Ascertain and record the system for logging journeys and invoicing the customers.
- Evaluate the strengths and weaknesses in the system.
- Design and carry out tests of control which could include the following:
  - inspect loading documents related to vehicle journey log books and delivery notes
  - relate delivery notes to specific invoices made to the steel stockholder customers. This would include a check against agreed prices and arithmetical checks of invoices.
- Ascertain correct cut-off between delivery costs and charges to customers.
- Check invoice totals to day book and to the recording of sales and debtors.

Question 2: Camry Products Ltd

(***Tutorial note***: Part (a) simply concerned normal planning activities with which candidates should be familiar. Parts (b) and (c), however, required detailed use of the information in the question due to the difficult system in use at the company. Candidates who ignored this information, but gave general comments about procedures and cut-off, will have found it difficult to gain sufficient marks to attain a pass.)

(a) ***Principal procedures in planning attendance at a stocktake***

The procedures that will normally be followed by the auditor during the planning stage of an attendance at stocktake are:

- Review the prior year's working papers to gain knowledge of the client and the type and location of stock, and also to identify any problem areas encountered last year to direct additional attention to those areas this year.
- Contact the client to arrange the following points:
  - Obtain a copy of stocktake instructions to be issued to client's staff. These should be reviewed and any potential problem areas brought to the client's attention immediately.
  - Agree the stocktake date.
  - Confirm the location of stock including any new locations and location of material quantities.
  - Discuss the internal control over stocktake.
  - Obtain management accounts to identify large stock types if possible, e.g. large orders in progress.
- Book the required staff to attend the stocktake.

- Consider whether the internal audit department at the company can be relied upon by the external auditors. Reviewing last year's file will give some information on this.
- Brief the staff due to attend the stocktake on material areas to investigate.
- Assess the need for specialist advice if stocks are of a difficult nature, either to count or to value.
- Ensure that if there are any stocks held at third parties, an appropriate confirmation letter is sent and that staff are booked to visit the location if the stock there is material.

(b) ***Procedures to be adopted by client to ensure that all stocks are counted once and once only***

These procedures are important for Camry Products Ltd because production will continue throughout the stocktake, increasing the risk of double-counting or of excluding items from stock.

Procedures to adopt include the following:

- One individual should be given authority over the whole stocktake. Ensure that all employees know who this is and that all queries are referred back to this individual.
- Divide the stock into a definite number of areas and assign teams of two counters to each area. These teams should be impressed that they must count all stock in their area, and no stock from any other area.
- Issue lists to each team of the stock that they can expect to count in each area. In some cases, such as raw material stores, pre-printed sheets showing all stock lines can be issued, although in production and finished goods that is unlikely to be possible. In these cases pre-numbered sheets will be issued and the sequence agreed for completeness both before and after the count has taken place.
- As each stock item is counted it should be identified as being counted by some unique mark. The attaching of an appropriately coloured tag is one method of doing this, with different coloured tags for each location. Thus if stock does move between locations, the colour of the tag will readily identify this.
- Movement of stock should be kept to a minimum. Certainly movement between production and finished goods should not be allowed, while the number of emergency requisition notes should be kept to a small number if possible. Each emergency requisition note issued should be listed by the storeman. The official responsible for the stocktake may then ensure that the stock items are not included on the store sheets as they will be included in work in progress.
- The work in progress area could be counted at the end of work for that day. This will assist the count as items in production will not be continually moving around the shop floor. If both stores and finished goods are counted by this time, then staff will be available to count work in progress in a reasonable time. Care will be needed, however, to assess correctly the state of completion of each stock line, and guidance must be given to counters on this matter. Production staff could assist by being available for, say, one hour after normal work finishes in return for some bonus payment.
- Goods received during the day must be kept in a separate location and counted there so as not to be double-counted within stores.
- Goods despatched should be sent out with the normal documentation from the finished goods store. If the good is tagged to indicate that it has already been counted, this should be recorded on a separate sheet. The official in charge of the stocktake must ensure at the end of the count that the finished goods sheets are reviewed and these items eliminated from stock.

(c) ***Audit procedures on the accuracy of cut-off at stocktake***

Normal audit procedures to ensure the accuracy of cut-off will include the following:

- Review the client's system in operation:
  - ensure that goods entering the client's premises are separated from stock already present and counted separately
  - ensure that as goods are despatched a note is made of any tag attached to them, that this is recorded on the appropriate sheet and that these items are eliminated from stock later by the responsible official
  - check that any emergency requisitions are recorded in the stores and that these goods are eliminated from stock later by the responsible official.
- Ensure that no transfers of goods take place from the production area to the finished goods store.
- List the last goods inwards note, the last goods outwards note along with any numbers noted as unused in numeric sequence before these. After the stocktake, normally at the final audit, the auditor will then:
  - ensure that goods despatched numbers prior to the last number are excluded from stock and that those after this last number are included in stock, and
  - ensure that goods received numbers prior to the last number noted are included in stock and that those after this last number are excluded from stock.
- Discuss with management any exceptions or problems found with any of the above and ensure that appropriate adjustments are made to the stock quantities.

Question 3: Chingford Potteries

(a) ***Stock valuation***

Stock valuation is important to the audit of financial statements because stock is often material to the financial statements. If stock is overvalued, profits will be overstated and if stock is undervalued, profits will be understated. The manipulation of stock valuation is a common method of manipulating profits.

The year-end stock count is often used as a basis for stock valuation, particularly where there are few other controls over stock. Where this is the case it is important that the count is performed correctly at the year-end, and that the auditor attends the count.

If it is not convenient to perform the stock count at the year-end, it may be possible to perform the count shortly before or after the year-end and to 'roll-forward' or 'roll-back' the count to arrive at the year-end figure, taking account of movements in stock in the intervening period.

Where stock is well controlled, and records are kept such that they accurately represent the stock figure at any given point in time, it may be possible to rely on the records, provided that the auditor has performed tests during the period that confirm that the stock records are accurate.

(b) ***Report to management***

Weakness

The stock count was poorly planned. Count instructions were received late, the areas to be counted were untidy, it was difficult to find certain stocks as they were not in their proper places and certain stocks were incorrectly labelled. There was insufficient time to conduct the count properly.

Potential consequence

There is a possibility that certain stocks were not counted at all, and that others may have been counted twice. There is also a possibility that certain stocks may be incorrectly classified. This may ultimately mean that stock is materially misstated both in the financial statements, and in the internal stock records.

Recommendation

The accuracy of the stock quantities and valuation in the current year may be confirmed by means of analytical procedures which focus on unusual movements in stock quantities, or in gross margins, for example. The company should also consider the possibility of recounting certain areas of stock where significant errors or omissions are suspected, and performing a 'roll-back' to the year-end. In future years, it is important to ensure that the count is better planned; that instructions are received on time, that stocks are properly labelled, that they are in their proper places before the count starts and that there are sufficient resources in terms of both time and manpower to conduct the count properly.

Weakness

The issue and receipt of stock sheets was not properly controlled and there are significant differences outstanding between the computerised records and the quantities actually recorded.

Potential consequence

If stock sheets are missing, it is possible that certain areas of stock were not counted at all, resulting in the under-valuation of stocks. The fact that there are significant differences outstanding reinforce this view.

Recommendation for future years

The stock sheets that were issued should be reconciled to a schedule of stock sheets that should have been issued. If certain sheets have been duplicated or omitted, and the amounts involved are potentially material, it will be necessary to re-perform a count in those areas, as noted above. Analytical procedures should also be performed to confirm the accuracy of quantities, as suggested above. In future years, it is essential that all stock sheets are properly recorded before they are issued (by means of pre-numbering, for example), and are properly accounted for when they have been completed.

(c) ***SSAP 9***

SSAP 9 requires that stocks are valued at the lower of cost and net realisable value. The cost of purchased goods includes import duties, transport and handling costs and other directly attributable costs. Trade discounts and rebates are deducted from cost.

For work-in-progress and finished goods, cost includes the direct cost of production, including direct labour costs and production overheads based on a normal level of activity.

Net realisable value is the estimated selling price net of trade discounts, less selling, distribution and marketing costs.

For work-in progress and raw materials, all costs of completing the stock are also deducted from selling price.

The types of stock that may be worth less than cost include imperfectly manufactured pottery ('seconds'), damaged pottery, old and slow-moving pottery and pottery which is intended to be sold below cost.

(d) ***Less than cost***

It is the responsibility of management to identify and account for stock that is worth less than cost. It will therefore be necessary to enquire of management as to how they account for and identify such stocks, and what assumptions they make about the relationship between the age, condition and value of stocks.

It will be useful to inspect sales, marketing and other reports, and to review the extent to which stocks which are worth less than cost have been reduced to net realisable value in prior years. Analytical procedures may be performed to evaluate the appropriateness of the write-down in the current year.

An analysis of the computerised records should enable the identification of goods that are old or slow-moving. The records may also show seconds and damaged goods. The system may automatically produce such information for management purposes, or the information may be specifically extracted at the year-end. Computer assisted audit techniques may be used for these purposes.

What is old or slow-moving will be determined by the business; in this case it is high quality pottery and as such stocks may be held for a considerable period of time before they are considered to be slow-moving.

At the stock count, a note should have been made of any items that appeared to be old, slow-moving or damaged and the count records should be inspected to see if they do show such goods.

CHAPTER 15 EXAM-TYPE QUESTIONS

Question 1: Contingency

(***Tutorial note***: Disclosure is important for contingencies, and checking disclosure is part of audit work, therefore bring this into your answer.)

(a) ***Contingency***

A contingency can be defined as a situation which exists at the balance sheet date where:

- the ultimate outcome will only be confirmed by the occurrence or non-occurrence of one or more substantially uncertain future events; and
- the gain or loss is not reflected in the financial statements in accordance with the concepts of FRS 18 and CA85.

FRS 12 states the appropriate accounting for contingencies. Contingent assets are disclosed where the inflow of economic benefits is possible. Contingent liabilities are disclosed unless the possibility of an outflow of economic benefits is remote.

(b) ***Audit tests***

- Ascertain, confirm, evaluate and test the client's system of recording claims/litigations.
- Obtain a schedule of contingent liabilities and agree the value of individual items to available evidence: solicitors' letters; notice of claims; agree calculations and reasonableness.
- Review board minutes, solicitors' letters, post balance sheet events, bank letter.
- Provision for losses will be accrued as per FRS 18 where it is probable that future events will confirm a loss which could be estimated with reasonable accuracy at the date on which the financial statements are approved by the

directors. Tests should ensure that any item satisfying the above has been accrued.

- Ensure disclosure is adequate.

Sch 5 CA85 requires the following to be stated:

- the amount or estimated amount of the contingent liability
- its legal nature
- details of any valuable security that has been provided by the company in connection with that liability

The disclosure required under FRS 12 is as follows:

- nature of the condition or situation existing at the balance sheet date
- the uncertainties which affect the future outcome
- an estimate of the financial effect at the date on which the financial statements are approved by the directors, or a statement that such an estimate cannot be made; the date should be given.

Question 2: Retail fashion store

(***Tutorial note:*** Apply the basic audit tests for purchases and supplier balances to the particular situation in the question. Consider the need for any additional tests required specific to the type of business concerned.

It is important to get a complete answer here; therefore think of what happens in a normal purchases and creditors audit, and list these tests. If you can then make any relevant comments concerning the fashion store, then do so, but the question does not have any specific factual information, and so specific examples are difficult to bring into your answer.)

Audit programme for purchases and year-end suppliers' balances for a medium-sized retail fashion store

Purchases

- Select a sample of entries in the purchases account in the nominal ledger, after first having checked the cast of this account.
- Agree each item selected with the purchase day book summary totals.
- For each summary total checked, check the cast of the list of invoices making up the total.
- Select a sample of entries in the purchase day book.
- Agree the amounts with the relevant purchase invoices.
- Check that each purchase invoice shows evidence of having been passed for payment.
- Check that the level of authority passing the invoices for payment accords with the client's regulations.
- Check the cast, extension and coding of each invoice.
- Check the details on the invoice with the goods received note.
- Check the details on the invoice with the purchase order.
- Examine the invoice for evidence that the above two procedures were carried out by the client.
- Check that the purchase order carries the correct level of authority according to the client's regulations.

Suppliers' balances

- Agree or reconcile the balance on the control account with the total of the list of balances, and agree with total to the draft financial statements.
- Check the cast of the list of balances.
- Select a sample of balances from the list, and check these to balances on ledger cards.
- Select a sample of major suppliers from a list of opening balances, where these suppliers do not have a closing balance.
- If there are any suppliers with whom the client has done a significant amount of business during the year and who do not have a closing balance, select a sample from these.
- Circularise these suppliers requesting that they confirm directly to the auditors' address the balances shown in the client's records. The firm's standard creditors circularisation letters should be used for this. Insert on each letter the name and address of the supplier, the balance to be confirmed and the date at which the balance exists. Ensure that the client gives permission for this and that each request letter is signed by the client.
- Send the letters independently of the client.
- If the balances are disputed, the reasons for this should be ascertained and balances reconciled.
- If a reply is not received, a second request should be sent.
- Summarise the results. The summary should show the total number of creditors and the total balance, the number and amount of creditors' balances circularised, the number and amount replying, the number and amount agreeing, the number and amount reconciling, and the number and amount disagreeing and being incapable of reconciliation. Each summary should express number and amount as a percentage of the total amount.
- Select a sample of creditors and reconcile the account with the suppliers' statement. Summarise the results in a way similar to that described above.
- Select a sample of goods received notes and ensure that for every item selected, the correct entry is ultimately made in the supplier's account.
- Select a sample of goods received notes dated shortly before the year end, and check that, unless the items shown thereon had been paid for prior to the year end, they were shown as a liability in the supplier's account or had been separately accrued.
- Select a sample of goods returned shortly before the balance sheet date and ensure that the related amounts were deducted from suppliers' balances at the year end or otherwise correctly treated.
- Select a sample of goods received notes dated shortly after the year end and check that these did not result in items being included in creditors at the year end.
- Select a sample of goods returned shortly after the balance sheet date and ensure that no amounts in respect of these were deducted from suppliers' balances before the year end.
- Check invoices received after the year end for items received before the year end. Check that the amounts relating to these were included in creditors.
- Check payments made to suppliers either side of the year end to ensure that these were dealt with in the correct accounting period as far as the creditors' balances were concerned.
- For payments made before the year end, check when these appeared on the client's bank statement. If any significant delay has arisen, request that the client obtains the cheque from the bank. Examine the cheque and check its date and the payee.
- Compare the total balance with last year and also compare the ratio of the total to the total purchases for the year.

- Obtain representations from management that all known amounts owing to suppliers have been provided for in the financial statements.

CHAPTER **16** EXAM-TYPE QUESTIONS

Question 1: Statistical sampling

(***Tutorial note**:* A detailed knowledge of the mathematics underlying statistical sampling is not expected, but you must understand the basic techniques involved.)

(a) ***Advantages of statistical sampling***

The main advantages gained by successfully using statistical sampling are listed below:

- It is possible to state, with a stipulated degree of confidence, that the sample result is not further away from the true condition of the population than some specified amount.
- The result obtained by the sample is not subject to the complaint of bias, e.g. that the auditor has looked at the worst items.
- The method provides a means of knowing in advance the size of the maximum sample needed. If auditors have decided on the degree of risk they are prepared to accept, then they are relieved of the onus of determining sample sizes arbitrarily. Justification is provided for the size of the sample used and thus for the time spent on the audit work.
- Statistical sampling can be more accurate than an examination of every item in a large population. Examining a high volume of data involves tedious detailed work, causing carelessness and different interpretations, and errors may arise.
- The evaluation of results is simplified, but great care is necessary, first, to ensure that each characteristic being tested is evaluated separately and, second, that in fixing a 'tolerable error rate'. For example, a low error rate may be serious if the errors represent irregularities or serious evasions of internal control but, on the other hand, a relatively high error rate may not give concern if the errors are of a random nature, showing no particular trend and indicating no specific control weakness.

It is clear that statistical sampling has many advantages. It is difficult, however, to say that statistical sampling is to be preferred to non-statistical sampling. Auditors must still use their judgement to decide what confidence level and precision limits are acceptable. Furthermore, there are many tests which the auditor will wish to perform where the sample will require selection by judgement. Examples would include a debtors circularisation.

Finally, statistical techniques often take longer to apply than tests using non-statistical sampling. The auditor must be careful that the benefits are not outweighed by the additional costs.

(b) ***Conditions when statistical sampling is likely to prove most successful***

- Where every potential sampling unit has the appropriate chance of selection and where systematic bias is avoided. This is most likely to apply to source documents which are subjected to standard internal control procedures.
- Where the sample size is large enough so that any chance departure from the typical is not significant.

- Where the set-up time and selection time are reasonable in relation to the time needed to verify the items and follow up discrepancies, i.e. large material populations.
- Where records of the entire population are reasonably accessible, e.g. sales/purchase invoices.
- Where the attribute to be sampled is easily identified.
- Where the selection of the statistical sample is facilitated by computerised records.

Question 2: Auditing in a computer environment

(***Tutorial note**:* This is a good question to show more specialised knowledge if you have it – otherwise a good question to avoid if you are unsure on this area. Remember though to explain why comments are being made, and not just repeat problems about computer auditing.)

(a) ***Lack of visible evidence and systematic errors***

'Lack of visible evidence' refers to the fact that in a computerised system the intermediate stages between input and output are not evidenced by hard copies.

In a stock control system, there may be no detailed breakdown of individual transactions, thus causing problems with cut-off at period ends.

The problems may be overcome by:

- arranging with the client for special purpose audit print-outs to be provided
- clerical re-creation of the data
- performance of alternative audit tests.

'Systematic errors' are programmed, and therefore recur consistently.

In a stock control system, a systematic error may be the failure to restrict access to authorised personnel (by means of passwords), thus enabling the data to be tampered with.

The auditor can attempt to detect systematic errors by:

- checking that systems development and testing procedures are fully documented
- testing the general controls which operate within the computer department
- using CAATs to test the processing of data.

(b) ***Types of CAAT***

The two most common types of CAAT are:

- audit software – programs used to examine the enterprise's computer files
- test data – data submitted by the auditor for processing by the enterprise's computer-based accounting system.

(c) ***Combination of CAATs and manual procedures***

In choosing the appropriate combination of CAATs and manual procedures, the auditor will need to take the following into account:

- the question of whether the computer program performs functions for which no visible evidence is available – if so, then it may not be practicable for the auditor to perform tests manually
- the efficiency of the alternatives, taking into account the extent of testing achieved, the pattern of costs, and the ability to use the CAAT for a number of different audit tests

- the reporting time scale (CAATs tend to be quicker to apply)
- availability of computer time, files and programs
- CAATs performed by internal audit staff may be relied upon, depending upon the auditor's assessment of that department's effectiveness.

(d) ***Application controls and general controls***

(i) Application controls relate to the transactions and standing data of each application: they ensure the completeness and accuracy of the accounting records. An audit test appropriate to an application control would be the use of test data with documents missing to ensure a sequence check control was operating correctly.

(ii) The purpose of general controls is to establish a framework of overall control over the computerised activities and to provide a reasonable level of assurance that the overall objectives of internal controls are achieved. An audit test would be to examine the physical security of the computer department.

CHAPTER 17 EXAM-TYPE QUESTION

Caffyn plc

(a) ***Issues to consider (only ten were required)***

Issues that the Audit Manager should have considered when assessing whether or not Caffyn plc is a going concern are as follows:

- Has the company been relying heavily on short-term finance?
- Does the company's market share seem to be declining?
- Does the company have sufficient funds to meet loan and capital repayments due in the next 12 months?
- Is the company collecting its debts without problems?
- Are there any contingent events or post balance sheet events which affect the company's going concern status?
- Does the company rely heavily on one or two major suppliers who are experiencing difficulties?
- Has the company any unauthorised overdrafts?
- Has the company been denied credit by any suppliers?
- Has the company tried to restructure its debts?
- Has the company been experiencing significant staffing problems, with loss of key staff?
- Has the company lost any key suppliers/customers which has significantly affected its business?

(b) ***Types of evidence***

Types of evidence that the audit manager should have considered during her going concern review are as follows:

- Budget, forecast and actual information for the period in question and whether or not the budgeting/forecasting details were accurate. Clearly, if the information provided was very inaccurate, then future information produced by the same system is unlikely to be reliable. The auditor would also review the systems to assess how well these are kept up to date.

- The systems that exist to provide the directors with warnings of future risk areas and potential problems and whether these are satisfactory.
- The directors' plans to address the current borrowing problems.
- Discussions with the company's lawyers to assess whether there are any legal issues surrounding the company's viability/ability to continue.
- Discussions with the company's bank to determine whether the directors' plans for addressing the financial problems are viable and realistic.
- The existence of obligations and guarantees to any other organisations which could result in Caffyn's bankruptcy.

CHAPTER **18** EXAM-TYPE QUESTION

Representation

(***Tutorial note:*** Do not mix up this letter with an engagement letter; the two letters may appear to have similar points being made in them, but their purposes are different.

Part (c) may seem unusual; to get relevant points consider why standard documentation is a problem anywhere. Items such as not allowing for change, and the documentation being ignored may then be thought of.)

(a) ***Nature and role of the letter of representation***

A letter of representation is written by the directors of a company to the auditors of that company, normally towards the end of an audit, before the auditor signs their audit report. The letter confirms verbal representations made by the directors during the audit, as well as providing audit evidence on areas where other audit evidence is not available. An example of this could be where a company settles a legal claim out of court; the directors would then provide representations to the auditor that they know of no other claims on the company in this area. 'Normal' audit evidence on this matter could be difficult to obtain.

The letter of representation will also have the following functions:

- It reminds the directors of their duties concerning the financial statements. In the letter the directors acknowledge their responsibility for the preparation of the financial statements, even though the auditor may have assisted in this area.
- It provides the auditor with a further source of audit evidence. The auditor can normally rely on the letter because the Companies Act S389 makes it an offence to give the auditor false information. This does not in any way relieve auditors of their responsibilities; they must still ensure that they have sufficient appropriate audit evidence to form their opinion on the financial statements.

(b) ***Discussing the contents of the letter of representation***

It is important for auditors to discuss the contents of letters of representation with the directors at an early stage in the audit for a number of reasons:

- It provides time for the directors to consider what representations are going to be required of them, and therefore to raise queries on these areas in good time.
- It facilitates the ending of the audit. The directors will already be aware of the contents of the representation letter, and the signing of the audit report will therefore not be delayed by last minute queries or refusal to sign the letter on the part of the directors.

- It will assist auditors in the planning and control of the audit. Auditors can identify at an early stage in the audit the sources of audit evidence available to them and plan their work accordingly.
- When the directors become aware of the representations requested of them, they may decide to provide auditors with other audit evidence rather than the representation letter in certain areas.
- Keeping the directors informed of the auditors' work will hopefully promote good relations between the auditor and the directors.

(c) ***Standard letters of representation***

Standard representation letters are being used less frequently by the auditing profession for the following reasons:

- Audits are becoming more individually tailored to specific clients; the use of a standard letter is therefore not appropriate.
- A standard letter will lose its impact after a number of years, and the directors may therefore not fully appreciate what they are signing.
- Auditors would find the use of a standard letter for a number of years difficult to justify in court if they had not kept pace with changes at their audit client.
- Changes in audit methods and client circumstances each year will necessitate the rewriting of the representation letter.

(d) ***Implications of directors' refusal to sign the letter of representation***

A representation letter is of particular importance in a small company due to the influence that the directors can have over the running of the company. It is very important to obtain confirmations regarding the completeness of the company's transactions in the books and records, and other representations, such as the directors being responsible for the financial statements, even when the auditor acting as accountant has completely prepared the accounts.

The lack of representations may also put the auditor on enquiry regarding the quality of the other audit evidence received, especially if the company is dominated by the directors.

If the directors refuse to sign the representation letter, then the auditor has a number of options available:

- The auditor could discuss the matter with the directors and try to resolve their problems with the letter.
- The auditor could write a representation letter for the directors, then send this to the directors and ask them to sign it.
- If the auditor considers that they have not received all the information and explanations required for the audit, then the auditor's report should be qualified. The auditor will need to state the reason for the qualification, which will be due to the uncertainty of amounts and balances in the financial statements following a limitation in the scope of their work, and state their qualification accordingly. An 'except for' qualification for the material uncertainty is the most likely form of qualification, although a disclaimer may be necessary if the lack of representations means that the financial statements are potentially meaningless.

  Before taking these actions, the auditor should explain to the directors the consequences of not signing the representation letter to try and avoid a confrontation.

Even if the letter is subsequently signed, then the auditor will still have to evaluate the reliability of this evidence. If, in the auditor's opinion, the letter does not provide sufficient appropriate evidence in those areas required, then a qualification will still be required.

CHAPTER **19** EXAM-TYPE QUESTIONS

Question 1: Audit report terminology

(***Tutorial note:*** This question tests facts about audit reports. Any uncertain areas should be revised and the question attempted again to ensure that these important areas can be quickly explained in an exam.)

(a) ***An adverse opinion***

This arises where the effect of a disagreement is so material and pervasive that the auditor concludes that a simple 'except for' qualification is not adequate to disclose the misleading or incomplete nature of the financial statements. The auditor believes that, as currently presented, the financial statements do not give a true and fair view.

(b) ***A disclaimer of opinion***

This arises where there is a material and pervasive limitation on the scope of the audit, and the auditor is unable to form an opinion on whether a true and fair view is given by the financial statements. For a matter to be pervasive, it should have an impact so great as to render the financial statements as a whole, meaningless. It is, therefore, only used as a last resort.

(c) ***Circumstances of disagreement***

The circumstances giving rise to a disagreement will include the following.

- departures from acceptable accounting practices:
  - failure to follow a SSAP or FRS
  - an unacceptable policy not covered by a SSAP or FRS
  - compliance with a SSAP or FRS where this does not in the circumstances give a true and fair view
- disagreement as to facts or amounts included in financial statements
- disagreement as to the manner or extent of disclosure of facts or amounts
- failure to comply with legislation

and may result in an 'except for' or an adverse opinion.

(d) ***An 'except for' opinion***

This arises on a particular matter which, while being material to the true and fair view given by the financial statements, is not so pervasive as to render them totally misleading. The 'except for' opinion, therefore, indicates that, with the exception of the particular matter, the financial statements do give a true and fair view.

(e) ***Limitations in the scope of the audit***

'Scope' refers to the auditor's ability to carry out audit procedures deemed by him necessary in the circumstances. A limitation in the scope of the audit therefore means that the auditor has been unable to carry out all the procedures deemed necessary. This may result in an 'except for' or a disclaimer of opinion.

(f) ***Inherent uncertainties***

These arise where the circumstances giving rise to an uncertainty relate to an uncertain situation, not being an inability to carry out audit procedures to obtain audit evidence. An example would be the assessment of the likely outcome of major litigation where the outcome is contingent and the probability of its occurrence is not capable of reasonable estimation, even given the opportunity to examine the evidence.

Question 2: Eastern Engineering plc

(***Tutorial note****:* Ensure that all sub-parts of the question are answered fully, giving reference to relevant guidance where necessary, e.g. the Auditing Standards. Also ensure that all parts of the question are read carefully; part (b) actually has two parts to it, although they are not stated on two separate lines.)

(a) ***Forms of qualification available to auditors***

- 'Except for' – material but not pervasive disagreement or limitation of scope.
- Disclaimer – pervasive limitation in scope of the audit.
- Adverse – pervasive disagreement.

(b) ***Need for qualifications***

- **Records destroyed**

  If there is no other evidence available to support the direct labour calculations, then auditors will be uncertain as to the accuracy of figures included in the financial statements. They are therefore limited in the scope of their audit.

  The question of the materiality of the £10,000 then arises. The labour cost represents approximately 30% of the cost of assets constructed during the year, 6% of total fixed asset additions, and only 1% of the year-end net book value. An item is considered to be material when knowledge of it would be likely to influence the user of financial statements. Any error in the calculation of the £10,000 is unlikely to be considered material in relation to the profit figure of £100,000. In such circumstances, a qualification may not be necessary.

- **Government grant**

  SSAP 4 states that grants received in respect of fixed assets should be credited to profits over the expected useful life of the fixed asset. The auditor will, therefore, disagree with the accounting treatment adopted by the company.

  The amount of £22,500 (£25,000 less the £2,500 to be written off each year) does appear to be material. A material disagreement becomes pervasive when the amount is such as to render the financial statements misleading; this is not the case in this example. An 'except for' opinion is therefore appropriate.

(c) ***Auditors' report to the shareholders of Eastern Engineering (extract)***

Qualified opinion arising from disagreement about accounting treatment

A government grant received during the year in respect of the purchase of fixed assets has been credited in full to the profit and loss account instead of being apportioned over the life of the assets as required by SSAP 4. As a result, profits for the year, together with retained earnings, have been increased by £22,500.

Except for . . .

(d) ***Auditor's general responsibility***

The CA85 extends the statutory responsibilities of auditors to require them to consider whether the directors' report is consistent with the financial statements. If not consistent, the auditor should state that fact in the audit report.

CHAPTER **20** EXAM-TYPE QUESTION

Reporter

(***Tutorial note:*** Remember, you have been asked to provide a report to the chief executive, so bear in mind your audience, when compiling the report. The report should be structured logically and effectively, in the same way that any other internal audit or review report would be completed. You should explain why you have recommended certain courses of action.)

REPORT TO CHIEF EXECUTIVE

Subject: Department of Organisational Review (DoOR)

Date: X-X-XX

(a) ***Executive summary***

The DoOR has seen a poor response to their review reports from management and there have been weaknesses in the reporting process. A negative reaction by management may be symptomatic of wider problems in DoOR operating practices and management perceptions. Therefore, it is important that action taken considers the complete reporting process from the start of the review to completion. There are a number of key areas of improvement going forward:

- Terms of reference agreed at the start of the review, confirming scope, approach and timescales. In particular, clear objectives to be agreed and communicated for reporting.
- More professional and timely reporting process, with agreed service levels for production and clearance of reports.
- All reports to include agreed action plans, timescales and nominated person accountable for resolution.
- A report follow up mechanism to be implemented.
- Clear quality standards and service levels published by DoOR and monitored on a monthly basis.
- Feedback from management should include satisfaction with the quality and timeliness of reports agreed, through formal questionnaires and regular interviews with management.

(b) ***Recommendations***

1 Objectives for DoOR reporting

DoOR needs to review the objectives for reporting in line with the objectives of the department and organisation and ensure that these are clearly agreed and communicated.

Terms of reference agreed at the start of the review will build on these objectives and clearly set out the scope, objectives, approach and timescales for the review. This will aim to decrease any potential for misunderstanding between management and the reviewers over how and when the review will be conducted.

2 Reporting process

Reports are continually late, which suggests that the process for producing reports is not as professional as it could be. The new reporting process will cover the following critical areas:

- agreement on timescales and approach to reporting at the planning stage of the review when terms of reference are being agreed with management
- format and standards for reporting agreed up-front by DoOR and management
- reports constructed during the course of the review and findings discussed by management as they arise, with agreed action being documented
- documented evidence for findings raised to minimise the risk of disagreement with facts set out in the report
- formal exit/closeout meetings to agree findings and recommendations and open discussion of any concerns
- quality checking of all reports to ensure that standards set for reports are met.

3 Format of reports

Reports to be completed to a standard internal review format, with all findings containing the following:

- specific and clearly identified agreed action that addresses the points raised
- risk associated with the findings (this will help in obtaining management buy-in and agreement)
- nominated person responsible for implementing the action (this will lead to increased accountability and ensure that action is taken)
- clear timescales and deadlines for resolving all points raised.

4 Follow-up action

All agreed actions should be monitored by DoOR and information circulated to management on the timeliness of resolution of actions and highlighting the scale of outstanding actions. This will help identify any ongoing concerns over management taking the required action to address concerns raised.

5 Quality standards

Quality standards, procedures and service levels should be in place for DoOR and monitored on a regular basis. Standards should include timescales for issue of draft report (e.g. five working days after completion of fieldwork) and for final report (ten working days after publication of draft report or holding exit meetings with management). Monthly reports should be produced showing achievement of service standards and any shortfalls identified, including reasons, and addressed.

6 Customer feedback

Customer feedback should be sought on the quality and timeliness of reporting both through formal satisfaction questionnaires in a standard format and through informal feedback through DoOR management.

(c) ***Further information required***

1 Reporting statistics

A more detailed trend analysis is required of the current level of reports issued:

- delays occurring in issuing reports
- evidence of feedback (positive and negative) from management
- number of findings dropped because of lack of management agreement
- number of findings that do not have agreed action, timescales and responsibilities
- findings past any agreed completion date.

2 Current outstanding actions from reports

A review is required of all outstanding actions from reports, to identify the level of risk exposure associated with the actions.

(d) ***Conclusion***

The reports of DoOR to management are a key deliverable of the department and performance can be assessed through the quality and timeliness of reporting. By looking at all stages of the process to deliver reports, more robust reporting mechanisms can be implemented. Reporting needs to be accompanied by clear service levels and objectives agreed with management, reporting procedures and quality checking.

CHAPTER **21** EXAM-TYPE QUESTION

ESCAPE

(***Tutorial note**:* Candidates should demonstrate awareness of the problems of auditing a not-for-profit organisation, and should apply practically the standard audit principles outlined in this chapter and elsewhere in the text. The marks are weighted towards the last section of the question. This is where the practical and common-sense application of knowledge is required.)

(a) ***The potential difficulties of the review and resolution***

Potential difficulties include the following:

- Understanding who the **customer** is for the audit, as SM has agreed to fund the review, and knowing what is to be delivered as an output to the report.

  SM has asked for an audit consultancy review – the auditor needs to understand the mandate that this provides.

  It is therefore important to agree and document the terms of reference of the audit, including key customers and distribution of the report.
- Understanding the **constitution** and **objectives** of the organisation.

  Since ESCAPE was originally set up by SM but now looks for wider funding, the constitution needs to be clearly understood before the review is undertaken. The organisation seems to be providing a wide-ranging service including holidays, training, keep fit and IT services to a broad age range of customers. Therefore, time needs to be spent understanding what the objectives are and whether they are being implemented appropriately. Have the objectives been thought through?
- Reliance on the role of **volunteers** who may be less accessible and feel less accountable for their actions if carried out on an unpaid basis.

It may also be difficult to do many detailed checks on the work of the volunteers.

- Types of **risks** and **controls**.

  These may be quite different for this organisation than for a standard for-profit organisation and they will face the same dilemma as other smaller organisations in demonstrating the controls that might be expected. There is obviously already a concern at lack of awareness of risks and control, which also might make the role of the auditor difficult.

(b) ***Addressing the concerns of staff***

The concerns of staff who have not been audited before are to be expected. They may not be sure what the audit involves and may feel threatened. Therefore, it is important to spend time explaining:

- the role of the auditor
- how the audit will be conducted
- the role that the staff will have to play
- what risks are, helping the staff understand more clearly the types of things that could go wrong and potential impact
- what controls are and therefore the types of controls that could operate
- the terms of reference, including timing and objectives.

(c) ***Key steps and information required***

The audit will involve the standard key steps of any audit:

- planning of the audit, including
  - researching the constitution and background of the organisation
  - reviewing legal obligations and policies
  - establishing any management/performance information statistics (e.g. number of users of each activity, potential market, income and expenditure)
  - the basis on which funding has been undertaken (e.g. any special conditions attached that must be complied with)
- issuing terms of reference and agreeing them with the key customers (engagement letter)
- identifying and assessing levels and types of risks, including impact and probability of risks
- evaluating controls in place, how they operate, who operates them and what documentation is held
- assessing and testing controls, in particular covering key transactions and processes, such as booking holidays, purchasing and installing IT equipment
- documenting findings, making recommendations, discussing with staff and customers
- issuing a report documenting the outcome of the review.

(d) ***Key risks and controls***

The key risks and controls that might be expected with ESCAPE are as follows:

- **Failure to have clearly defined objectives** or to achieve objectives established.

  This may be a particular risk with ESCAPE because, whilst the overall aim of providing an 'escape' avenue is clear, what the deliverables of the organisation are is less clear, as shown by the diverse nature of the activities. There is also a risk that the objectives of ESCAPE may overlap or compete with other organisations providing similar types of services, for example schemes to get young people into employment.

- The expected controls would include documentation of aims and objectives. Performance measurement should demonstrate how these objectives are being achieved in practice.
- An analysis of similar types of organisations should also be undertaken to establish that there would be no conflict in the aims, objectives and operating of the facilities. Liaison with other types of providers would be expected on a regular basis.

- **Financial loss** or **fraudulent activity**, in particular holidays being provided to people who do not fulfil the criteria of 'deprived', facilities being used by those not entitled, misappropriation of funds for example from fund-raising and grants.
  - Controls over fund-raising activity should be in place, including monitoring and sealing collection tins, checks or dual opening of mail received in relation to fund raising activity.
  - Funds are properly controlled including:
    - bankings are made promptly upon receipt
    - bankings are checked to receipt records
    - regular bank reconciliations are made.
  - Central and local government grants should be checked. Auditors should familiarise themselves with the grants receivable and ensure that such grants are used in accordance with the terms and required accounting treatment.
  - Records should be made of holidays booked, purpose of holidays and documentation of the recipients including reason for selection.
  - Records should be kept of recipients of all services, including members of the facilities, and checks made to ensure that users fulfil the criteria of ESCAPE.
- **Loss of assets**, for example computer equipment or gym equipment arising from theft, vandalism, etc.
  - Asset register should be held, with regular inventory checks to ensure that the assets still exist.
  - There needs to be security over assets, e.g. to ensure that they are kept securely in locked and alarmed premises, and that there is someone on the premises when facilities are being used.
- **Breach of regulatory requirements**, including health and safety requirements for sports and leisure facilities being provided. Controls include:
  - health and safety obligations assessed and managed
  - training of users in the correct operation of gym equipment
  - first aid facilities held
  - other regulatory requirements understood, with assessment of impact and requirements and documentation of how these are being managed and delivered.
  - appropriate insurance cover held.

Index

ftc

FTC Foulks Lynch
A **Kaplan Professional** Company

STUDY TEXT REVIEW FORM
ACCA Paper 2.6 UK

Thank you for choosing this text for your ACCA professional qualification. As we are constantly striving to improve our products, we would be grateful if you could provide us with feedback about how useful you found this publication.

Name: ....

Address: ....

....

Email: ....

Why did you decide to purchase this Study Text?

Have used them in the past ☐
Recommended by lecturer ☐
Recommended by friend ☐
Saw advertising ☐
Other (please specify)..

How do you study?

At a college ☐
On a distance learning course ☐
Home study ☐
Other (please specify)..

Within our ACCA range we also offer Exam Kits and Pocket Notes. Is there any other type of service/publication that you would like to see as part of the range?

CD Rom with additional questions and answers ☐
A booklet that would help you master exam skills and techniques ☐
Space on our website that would answer your technical questions and queries ☐
Other (please specify)..

During the past six month do you recall seeing/receiving any of the following?

Our advertisement in *Student Accountant* magazine? ☐
Our advertisement in any other magazine? (please specify) ☐

....

Our leaflet/brochure or a letter through the post? ☐
Other (please specify)..

Overall opinion of this Study Text

	Excellent	*Adequate*	*Poor*
Introductory pages	☐	☐	☐
Syllabus coverage	☐	☐	☐
Clarity of explanations	☐	☐	☐
Clarity of definitions and key terms	☐	☐	☐
Diagrams	☐	☐	☐
Activities	☐	☐	☐
Self-test questions	☐	☐	☐
Practice questions	☐	☐	☐
Answers to practice questions	☐	☐	☐
Layout	☐	☐	☐
Index	☐	☐	☐

If you have further comments/suggestions or have spotted any errors, please write them on the next page.

Please return this form to: The Publisher, FTC Foulks Lynch, FREEPOST NAT 17540, Wokingham RG40 1BR

Other comments/suggestions and errors

FTC Foulks Lynch
A **Kaplan Professional** Company

ACCA Order Form

Swift House, Market Place, Wokingham, Berkshire RG40 1AP, UK
Tel: +44 (0) 118 989 0629 Fax: +44 (0) 118 979 7455
Order online: www.financial-training.com
Email: publishing@financial-training.com

Examination Date: Dec 05 ☐ **Jun 06** ☐ (please tick the exam you intend to take)		**Study Text £26.00**	**Exam Kit Dec 05 £13.00**	**Exam Kit Jun 06 £14.00**	**Pocket Notes £10.00**	**Drill & Practice £10.00**
Part 1						
1.1	Preparing Financial Statements (UK)	☐	☐	☐	☐	☐
1.1	Preparing Financial Statements (International)	☐	☐	☐	☐	☐
1.2	Financial Information for Management	☐	☐	☐	☐	☐
1.3	Managing People	☐	☐	☐	☐	N/A
Part 2						
2.1	Information Systems	☐	☐	☐	☐	N/A
2.2	Corporate & Business Law (English)	☐	☐	☐	☐	N/A
2.2	Corporate & Business Law (Scottish)	☐	N/A	N/A	N/A	N/A
2.3	Business Taxation – FA 2004	☐	☐	N/A	☐	N/A
2.3	Business Taxation – FA 2005	☐	N/A	☐	☐	N/A
2.4	Financial Management & Control	☐	☐	☐	☐	N/A
2.5	Financial Reporting (UK)	☐	☐	☐	☐	N/A
2.5	Financial Reporting (International)	☐	☐	☐	☐	N/A
2.6	Audit & Internal Review (UK)	☐	☐	☐	☐	N/A
2.6	Audit & Internal Review (International)	☐	☐	☐	☐	N/A
Part 3						
3.1	Audit & Assurance Services (UK)	☐	☐	☐	☐	N/A
3.1	Audit & Assurance Services (International)	☐	☐	☐	☐	N/A
3.2	Advanced Taxation – FA 2004	☐	☐	N/A	☐	N/A
3.2	Advanced Taxation – FA 2005	☐	N/A	☐	☐	N/A
3.3	Performance Management	☐	☐	☐	☐	N/A
3.4	Business Information Management	☐	☐	☐	☐	N/A
3.5	Strategic Business Planning & Development	☐	☐	☐	☐	N/A
3.6	Advanced Corporate Reporting (UK)	☐	☐	☐	☐	N/A
3.6	Advanced Corporate Reporting (International)	☐	☐	☐	☐	N/A
3.7	Strategic Financial Management	☐	☐	☐	☐	N/A
Research and Analysis Project Guide (supporting Oxford Brookes University BSc (Hons) in Applied Accounting)		☐				
Postage, Packaging and Delivery (per item):	**Note**: Maximum postage charged for UK orders is £15				**TOTAL**	

Study Texts and Exam Kits	*First*	*Each Extra*
UK	£5.00	£2.00
Europe (incl Republic of Ireland and Channel Isles)	£7.00	£4.00
Rest of World	£22.00	£8.00

Pocket Notes and Drill & Practice	*First*	*Each Extra*
UK	£2.00	£1.00
Europe (incl Republic of Ireland and Channel Isles)	£3.00	£2.00
Rest of World	£8.00	£5.00

Product Sub Total £.................. Postage & Packaging £................. Order Total £.................... (Payments in UK £ Sterling)

Customer Details

☐ Mr ☐ Mrs ☐ Ms ☐ Miss Other ....

Initials:.................................. Surname: ....

Address: ....

....

....

Postcode: ....

Delivery Address – if different from above

Address: ....

....

Postcode: ....

Telephone: ....

Email: ....

Fax: ....

Delivery please allow: United Kingdom – 5 working days
Europe – 8 working days
Rest of World – 10 working days

Payment

1 I enclose Cheque/Postal Order/Bankers Draft for £....................................

Please make cheques payable to '**The Financial Training Company Ltd**'.

2 Charge MasterCard/Visa/Switch/Delta no:

Valid from: Expiry date:

Issue no:

(Switch only) Verification No.

Signature: .... Date: ....

Declaration

I agree to pay as indicated on this form and understand that The Financial Training Company's Terms and Conditions apply (available on request).

Signature: .... Date: ....

Notes: All orders over 1kg will be fully tracked & insured. Signature required on receipt of order. Delivery times subject to stock availability. A telephone number or email address is required for orders that are to be delivered to a PO Box number.

ACCA Approved Publisher

FTC Foulks Lynch
A **Kaplan Professional** Company

SPECIAL OFFER - Our Distance Learning Students consistently achieve pass rates above the ACCA global average. Increase your chances of success and upgrade your Official ACCA Study Text to a Distance Learning Course for only £88 per paper and gain

- **Personal Tutor Support by telephone and email (local rate 0845 number for UK callers)**
- **The whole range of Official ACCA Publications including Exam Kits and Pocket Notes**
- **Work Programme**
- **Unique 5-Star-Guide written by a Specialist Tutor**
- **Two Progress Tests which you can send to us for marking and feedback**
- **Hints and Tips Audio CD on study skills and exam technique**
- **Student Handbook packed with practical information about your course**
- **10% discount on any FTC revision course.**

This offer is only available if you already own the Official FTC Foulks Lynch ACCA Study Text for the December 2005 or June 2006 Examinations.

ACCA Distance Learning Enrolment Form

Surname ______ First Name ______ Mr / Miss / Mrs / Ms

Home Address ______

______

Post Code ______ Country ______

Home Tel ______ Office Tel ______

Mobile ______ E-mail ______

Date of Birth ______ ACCA Registration Number ______

Exam sitting: ☐ CBE ☐ December 2005 ☐ June 2006

EMPLOYER DETAILS (Sponsor must be UK based company)

Company Name ______

Manager's Name ______

Address ______

Post Code ______ Country ______

Telephone ______ Email ______

SPONSORED STUDENTS: EMPLOYER'S AUTHORISATION

If the above employer is responsible for the payment of fees, please complete the following:

As employer of the student for whom this form is completed, we are responsible for payment of fees due on receipt of the invoice in respect of the student named above and undertake to inform you in writing of any change to this arrangement. We understand that we are fully responsible for the payment of fees due in all circumstances including termination of employment or cancellation of course.

Purchase Order Number ______

Manager's Name ______

Manager's Signature ______ Date ______

DATA PROTECTION ACT:

Your sponsor can be informed of your test results unless we are otherwise notified.

HOW TO ENROL:

By phone: If you are paying by credit card, please telephone +44 (0)113 200 6363

By post: Complete this enrolment form and return to:
FTC Foulks Lynch Distance Learning, 49 St Paul's Street, LEEDS LS1 2TE

By fax: Fax both sides of your completed enrolment form to +44 (0)113 243 0133

Distance Learning Courses include VAT and all materials. Add postage & packing – applicable to both Distance Learning options (for rates see below).		Distance Learning		Distance Learning (excluding Official ACCA Study Text applicable for the December 2005 and June 2006 examinations sittings only)	
		£	✓	£	✓
Part 1					
1.1	Preparing Financial Statements (UK)	114		88	
1.1	Preparing Financial Statements (International)	114		88	
1.2	Financial Information for Management	114		88	
1.3	Managing People	114		88	
Part 2					
2.1	Information Systems	114		88	
2.2	Corporate & Business Law	114		88	
2.3	Business Taxation	114		88	
2.4	Financial Management and Control	114		88	
2.5	Financial Reporting (UK)	114		88	
2.5	Financial Reporting (International)	114		88	
2.6	Audit & Internal Review (UK)	114		88	
2.6	Audit & Internal Review (International)	114		88	
Part 3 Options					
3.1	Audit & Assurance Services (UK)	114		88	
3.1	Audit & Assurance Services (International)	114		88	
3.2	Advanced Taxation	114		88	
3.3	Performance Management	114		88	
3.4	Business Information Management	114		88	
Part 3 Core					
3.5	Strategic Business Planning & Development	114		88	
3.6	Advanced Corporate Reporting (UK)	114		88	
3.6	Advanced Corporate Reporting (International)	114		88	
3.7	Strategic Financial Management	114		88	

FEES	£
Postage & Packing	£
Total	£

POSTAGE & PACKING
Distance Learning (per paper):
UK & NI £6, Europe & Channel Islands £15, Rest of World £40

DISTANCE LEARNING TERMS AND CONDITIONS OF ENROLMENT:

1. A completed enrolment form must be accompanied by the full fee or employer's authorisation.
2. Where an employer's authorisation is received, the full fees are payable within 30 days of the invoice date. The employer is responsible for the payment of fees due in all circumstances including termination of employment or cancellation of course. FTC reserves the right to charge interest on overdue accounts.
3. A deferral can be processed to the following exam sitting subject to a deferral fee of £25 if notified in writing. If new study materials are required due to syllabus changes or changes in Finance Acts, they will have to be paid for in addition to the deferral fee.
4. Refunds are only available on study materials returned within 14 days in a saleable condition.
5. Courses are not transferable between students.
6. Distance Learning fees include VAT and all materials but exclude any taxes or duties imposed by countries outside the UK.

METHODS OF PAYMENT:

☐ Please invoice my employer (details completed overleaf).
☐ I enclose a cheque made payable to The Financial Training Company Ltd. for £ ____________
Payments will only be accepted in UK Sterling.
☐ Please charge my Credit/Debit Card Number for the fees indicated above.

Valid from ☐☐☐☐ Expiry ☐☐☐☐ Solo/Switch Issue No ☐☐ Security Code ☐☐☐

I agree to the terms and conditions of enrolment which I have read.

Student Signature ______________________________ Date ____________________